Women in the Middle East and North Africa

This book examines the position of women in the contemporary Middle East and North Africa (MENA) region. Although it is culturally diverse, this region shares many strong, deep, and pervasive commonalities with relation to women: a space-based patriarchy, a culturally strong sense of religion, a smooth co-existence of tradition and modernity, a transitional stage in development, and multilingualism/multiculturalism.

Experts from within the region and from outside provide both theoretical angles and case studies, drawing on fieldwork from Egypt, Oman, Palestine, Israel, Turkey, Iran, Tunisia, Algeria, Morocco, and Spain. Addressing the historical, socio-cultural, political, economic, and legal issues in the region, the chapters cover five major aspects of women's agency:

- political agency;
- civil society activism;
- legal reform;
- cultural and social agencies;
- religious and symbolic agencies.

Bringing to light often marginalized topics and issues, the book underlines the importance of respecting specificities when judging societies and hints at possible ways of promoting the MENA region. As such, it is a valuable addition to existing literature in the field of political science, sociology, and women's studies.

Fatima Sadiqi is Professor of Linguistics and Gender Studies at the University of Fez, Morocco. A former Fulbright Scholar and recipient of a Harvard Fellowship, she has written a number of books and is a UN Gender Expert.

Moha Ennaji is Professor at the University of Fez and a Visiting Professor at Rutgers University. He is the author and/or editor of numerous books and articles on culture and gender studies in North Africa.

UCLA Center for Middle East Development (CMED)

Series Editors
Steven Spiegel, UCLA
Elizabeth Matthews, California State University, San Marcos

The UCLA Center for Middle East Development (CMED) series on Middle East security and cooperation is designed to present a variety of perspectives on a specific topic, such as democracy in the Middle East, dynamics of Israeli–Palestinian relations, Gulf security, and the gender factor in the Middle East. The uniqueness of the series is that the authors write from the viewpoint of a variety of countries so that no matter what the issue, articles appear from many different states, both within and beyond the region. No existing series provides a comparable, multinational collection of authors in each volume. Thus, the series presents a combination of writers from countries who, for political reasons, do not always publish in the same volume. The series features a number of sub-themes under a single heading, covering security, social, political, and economic factors affecting the Middle East.

1. **The Struggle over Democracy in the Middle East**
   Regional politics and external policies
   Edited by Nathan J. Brown and Emad El-Din Shahin

2. **Women in the Middle East and North Africa**
   Agents of change
   Edited by Fatima Sadiqi and Moha Ennaji

Women in the Middle East and North Africa

Agents of change

**Edited by Fatima Sadiqi
and Moha Ennaji**

Routledge
Taylor & Francis Group

LONDON AND NEW YORK

First published 2011
by Routledge
2 Park Square, Milton Park, Abingdon, Oxon, OX14 4RN

Simultaneously published in the USA and Canada
by Routledge
711 Third Avenue, New York, NY 10017

*Routledge is an imprint of the Taylor & Francis Group, an Informa
business*

© 2011 UCLA

Typeset in Times New Roman by Value Chain International Ltd

British Library Cataloguing in Publication Data
A catalogue record for this book is available from the British Library

Library of Congress Cataloging in Publication Data
Women in the Middle East and North Africa : agents of change / edited by
Fatima Sadiqi and Moha Ennaji.
p. cm.
Includes bibliographical references and index.
1. Women--Middle East--History. 2. Women--Africa, North--History. I.
Sadiqi, Fatima. II. Ennaji, Moha.
HQ1115.W59 2010
305.420956--dc22
2009046222

ISBN: 978-0-415-57320-7 (hbk)
ISBN: 978-0-415-57321-4 (pbk)
ISBN: 978-0-203-85157-9 (ebk)

To our mothers, Fadma Bourhim and Hadda N'Ayt Hsain, with love and gratitude.

Contents

Contributors

Thuwayba Al Barwani is Associate Professor at the Sultan Qaboos University, and a member of the Council for Higher Education in Oman. She has researched and published in areas of Empowerment, Family Cohesion, Teaching English as a Foreign Language, and Quality in Higher Education.

Hoda Ragheb Awad obtained her Ph.D. in 1990 from the Faculty of Economics and Political Science in Cairo University. She was a Fulbright Senior Scholar in Residence at Goucher Collage (1992-1993). With Tawfik Hasanen, she co-authored *The Political Role of the Muslim Brotherhood Movement in Light of Controlled Political Pluralism in Egypt: A Study in Political Discourse, 1984-1990* (in Arabic) and has published a number of articles.

Fatma Umut Bespinar holds a Ph.D. in Sociology from the University of Texas at Austin. She has been involved in numerous national and international research projects on migration in Azerbaijan and women's labor force participation in Mexico and Turkey.

Mounira M. Charrad is Associate Professor of Sociology at the University of Texas in Austin. Her book, *States and Women's Rights: The Making of Postcolonial Tunisia, Algeria and Morocco* (2001), has won several awards. She co-edited *Femmes, Culture et Société au Maghreb* and is currently co-editing a volume on *The Power of Kinship: Patrimonial States in Global Perspective*.

Abdelkader Cheref is Lecturer in Comparative Literature in the Faculty of Arts, Humanities and Social Sciences at the University of Limerick, Ireland, and holds a Ph.D. in comparative literature from the University of Exeter. His research interests include Comparative Literature, Postcolonial Studies, Arabophone and Francophone Maghrebi Literatures, Film, and Human Rights. His publications are mostly concerned with cultural traditions and politics.

Moha Ennaji is Senior Professor of Linguistics and Cultural Studies. He was head of the English Department at the University of Fez, Morocco, and director of Arab Studies at Rutgers University. He has published extensively on language, gender, and cultural studies with a focus on North Africa. His most recent publications include *Women Writing North Africa* (co-authored with Fatima

Sadiqi et al., 2009); *Migration and Gender in Morocco* (co-authored with Fatima Sadiqi, 2008); *Multilingualism, Cultural Identity, and Education in Morocco* (2005); *A Grammar of Moroccan Arabic* (2004). He is the editor of *Language and Gender in the Mediterranean Region* (2008). Dr. Ennaji has also published numerous articles in international journals. He is the President of the South North Center for Intercultural Dialogue and Migration Studies and has been Director of the international journal *Languages and Linguistics* since 1998. Website: www.mohaennaji.on.ma, Email: mennaji2002@yahoo.fr

Nazli Fathi-Rizk has been a teacher of French and Social Studies at Cairo American College for the past 29 years, and has taught a variety of History courses including Modern History of Egypt, Arab Culture, Contemporary Middle East, IB Islamic History, International Relations, and Modern World History. She is a member of the Egyptian Council of Foreign Affairs.

Galia Golan founded the first Women's Studies program at the Hebrew University of Jerusalem. She co-founded the Israel Women's Network, and is head of the Program in Conflict Resolution at the Interdisciplinary Center, Herzliya. She has written on women and politics in Israel as well as on women and peace.

Islah Jad is Director of the Women's Studies Institute and Assistant Professor of Gender and Development at Bir Zeit University. She co-founded WATC (Women's Affairs Technical Committee), a national coalition for women, and has published widely on Palestinian and Arab women's political participation.

Raoudha Kammoun received her Ph.D. from Paris VII University in 1989 and currently teaches in the Department of English at the University of Manouba, Tunis. Her research interests include gender and language, bilingualism, multiculturalism and language planning, humorous studies, translation, gender and humor. She has written several articles about bilingualism, humor, and lexical semantics.

Touria Khannous is Assistant Professor at Louisiana State University. She taught courses on postcolonial literature and theory, Moroccan cinema, African literature, and Women Studies. She has published articles on women's writing from Africa and the African diaspora, North African women's literature and film, and Cultural Studies.

Valentine M. Moghadam is Professor of Sociology and Women's Studies and Director of the Women's Studies Program at Purdue University. She is author of *Modernizing Women: Gender and Social Change in the Middle East* (1993), the award-winning *Globalizing Women: Transnational Feminist Networks* (2005), and the *Globalization and Social Movements: Islamism, Feminism, and the Global Justice Movement* (2009).

Aurora G. Morcillo is Associate Professor of History and Women's Studies at Florida International University in Miami. She is author of *True Catholic Womanhood: Gender Ideology in Franco's Spain* (2000). Her second book *The*

Seduction of Modern Spain: The Female Body and the Francoist Body Politic is forthcoming.

Margaret J. Rausch is Assistant Professor in Religious Studies at the University of Kansas. Her publications include *Bodies, Boundaries and Spirit Possession: Moroccan Women and the Revision of Tradition* (2000).

Fatima Sadiqi is Senior Professor of Linguistics and Gender Studies at the University of Fez, Morocco, and director of the Isis Centre for Women and Development. A former Fulbright Scholar and recipient of a Harvard Fellowship, she is also a UN Gender Expert and an active member of numerous international bodies and projects that deal with language and gender issues. From 2007 to 2009, she served as Director General of the Fez Festival of Sacred Music. Fatima Sadiqi has written extensively on Moroccan languages and Moroccan women's issues. She is the author of *Women, Gender, and Language in Morocco* (2003), *Grammaire du Berbère* (1997), *Images of Women in Abdullah Bashrahil's Poetry* (2004). She has edited and co-edited a number of volumes, including *Migration and Gender in Morocco* (with Moha Ennaji, 2008). Website: www.fatimasadiqi.on.ma, Email: sadiqi_fatima@yahoo.fr

Zahia Smail Salhi is Senior Lecturer in Arabic Literature and Gender in the Department of Arabic and Middle Eastern Studies, University of Leeds. Her recent publications include *The Arab Diaspora: Voices of an Anguished Scream*, (2006), "Between the Languages of Silence and the Woman's Word: Gender and Language in the Work of Assia Djebar," *International Journal of the Sociology of Language* (vol. 190, 2008).

Series editors' preface

The Center for Middle East Development of the International Institute at UCLA (CMED) is pleased to present the second installment in our book series on Middle East security and cooperation. The series is designed to offer discussions on the current problems in the Middle East with volumes that are unique because the participating authors are from a variety of countries and provide a range of perspectives on a specific topic. We envision that this diversity will contribute directly to the global discourse on the ongoing developments in the region.

The Editors want to extend our deepest gratitude to James Whiting, Acquisitions Editor for Middle Eastern and Islamic Studies, Routledge, Taylor & Francis Group, who has served as such a critical asset to us in the complex preparation of these exciting, but complicated to prepare, volumes. We greatly appreciate the patience and dedication of Suzanne Richardson, Editorial Assistant for Middle East and Asian Studies, Routledge, Taylor & Francis Group, who assisted us so admirably in preparing this manuscript. We also want to extend our thanks to Professor David Newman, who first conceived of the exercise and placed us in contact with Routledge. And we deeply appreciate the work and gargantuan efforts that are being pursued by the editors and authors responsible for each volume, and of course our International Advisory Board. We also wish to recognize the support to this project provided by CMED's Faculty Advisory Committee and the Institute on Global Conflict and Cooperation (IGCC) of the University of California based at UC San Diego.

UCLA's Center for Middle East Development (CMED) conducts research and provides educational programs on political, economic, and diplomatic development in the Middle East. CMED programs approach these issues through a multi-tiered regional security program. Through reports and monographs, CMED explores key subjects on the region, including but by no means limited to democratic culture, regional business and economics, gender issues, media, technological cooperation across borders, and a full range of security and political issues including strategic challenges in cooperative and conflictual contexts, Mediterranean and Gulf security, threats of Weapons of Mass Destruction, and specific dynamics of regional problems such as the Arab–Israeli dispute, Iraq, and Iran. This series is a product of these studies and the promotion of intellectual interchange to which CMED is committed.

This series was four years in the making and we were proud to present our first book, *The Struggle over Democracy in the Middle East: Regional Politics and External Policies*, in late 2009. This second book in the series, *Women in the Middle East and North Africa: Agents of Change*, continues our goal of offering the highest possible quality to our readers and providing unique and stimulating discussions as the series expands.

The role of women in promoting change in the MENA region is a subject of great interest among the public, media, and policymakers. As the editors of this volume, Fatima Sadiqi and Moha Ennaji, point out that women's agency in the region is a balance between tradition and modernity at the historical, socio-cultural, political, economic, legal, and symbolic levels. While women have made significant strides in certain areas, there are still numerous obstacles to overcome. As the editors conclude, " What is important from the perspective of this volume is that in spite of overwhelming challenges, progress is being achieved through women's determination and will to change themselves and their societies."

To paint the picture of this struggle for change, this volume includes studies from eleven countries (ten from the MENA region, plus a comparative study of Spain) across several major areas: political agency, civil society activism, legal reform, cultural, social, religious, and symbolic agencies. Through these studies, this book aims to "highlight women's agency in the region and demonstrate their various contributions to the advancement of their countries, as well as their self-assertion in male-dominated contexts." What we present in this volume is a glimpse of the struggle women are undertaking throughout the region to improve the quality of their lives and to advance the societies in which they live.

Steven L. Spiegel, UCLA
Elizabeth G. Matthews, CSUSM

Introduction

Contextualizing women's agency in the MENA region

Fatima Sadiqi and Moha Ennaji

The key conceptual issue of this volume is that of women as active agents of change in the Middle East and North Africa (MENA) region. In much of contemporary social and political theory, the concept of agency is commonly defined as either the capacity to create a difference or the freedom to act otherwise. However, men and women do not self-elect circumstances; they make their own history, not as they please but according to the norms regulating their culture, society, and general historical, economic, and socio-political context. From this perspective, understanding women's agency cannot be achieved without understanding the sources of power and power-negotiation in the region.

MENA is not a homogeneous region; specific historical, political, and economic factors resulted in a number of sub-regional entities such as the Maghreb, Egypt, Iraq and Syria, the Gulf, Turkey and Iran, Israel, etc. (Abun-Nasr 1975; Laroui 1977). From the perspective of this volume, however, the countries of the MENA region share women-linked commonalities that are strong, deep, and pervasive: a space-based patriarchy, a culturally strong sense of religion, a smooth co-existence of tradition and modernity, a transitional stage in development, and multilingualism/multiculturalism—hence the importance of understanding the historical, socio-cultural, political, economic, and legal issues in the region.

Historical context

The Middle East and North Africa are two diverse regions that are often grouped together because of the many important things they share, such as the fact that Islam is the dominant religion and Arabic the dominant language. MENA is not all desert, and many populations do not speak Arabic. However, there are many exceptions to these two facts. For example, most Iranians are Muslim, but speak Farsi and are not Arabs; the Turks, who originally came from the land northwest of India, are also Muslim but speak Turkish rather than Arabic, and the people of Lebanon primarily speak Arabic, but more than one-third of them are Christian. Also, about twenty-five million Kurds live in the mountains between Iran, Iraq, Syria, and Turkey. Most Arabic-speaking countries were Arabized in the seventh or eighth centuries and had previously different civilizations, languages, and religions. In Syria, for example, Aramaic was spoken before the Arab conquest, and in the Maghreb, Berber was spoken before the arrival of Islam. Some of these pre-Islamic languages, such as Berber, have survived while others, such as Aramaic, died. Most of the countries of the MENA region have been colonized by European powers, and today the region is multilingual, including French, English, and Italian (Ennaji 2005).

Although absent from official records, women have significantly contributed to the construction of the history of the MENA region as stated in the preface to the Women Writing North Africa anthology:

> Rich, poor, well connected, orphaned, free, and slave women in North Africa participated in the greatest cultural transformations of written history. The poets, scholars, and religious teachers among them recorded the emotions and conflicts of their times. Illiterate singers of songs and tellers of tales who were respected, and even feared, in communities where the written word was rarely invoked, have preserved an oral tradition of intergenerational transfer that assured the continuity of women's memories. Together they have left a body of literature about the momentous events in women's lives from marriage songs, laments and celebrations of valor to women's religious rites.
>
> (Sadiqi et al. 2009)

Women's versatile contributions to the making of the MENA region are attested in the various oral and written texts that record women's deeds, as well as their experiences and visions of the world, power, and the self. With the advent of social history and memory-honoring, highlighting women's multi-faceted agency in the making of the history of the MENA region has recently become part of many projects in the region. It is a vibrant and promising field of research (Sadiqi et al. 2009).

Women did not only lead the first ascetic movement in Egypt as part of the early Christian search for Grace, they also celebrated Isis and constituted part of deity in Carthage. Women were also among the first to acknowledge Islam as a reaction to tribalism and poverty which deprived them of owning property. Women fought seclusion and polygamy throughout centuries. When the MENA region was colonized, a combination of nationalism and self-empowerment allowed women to indulge in individual achievements and collective action and, thus, forge for themselves new identities and a new self-consciousness that turned them into members of organized resistance. These roles contributed to the transformation of mentalities and the empowerment of freedom fighters. After independence, women used education to secure new roles in the public sphere. In the post-independence era, women contributed to the construction of their countries, struggled to change the social order, and fought for their legal rights. Women's contributions to the making of the history of the MENA region is widely acknowledged in the new twenty-first century (Sadiqi et al. 2009).

Socio-cultural context

The overall socio-cultural context of the MENA region is generally characterized by a space-based patriarchy whereby men are associated with the public space and women with the private space.[1] Various studies (Schaffer-Davis 1979; Becker 2006) have demonstrated that women in fact invest both spaces, especially in semi-urban and rural areas, but the cultural nature of the Arab-Muslim patriarchy, as opposed to mainstream Western patriarchy, is deeply spatial[2] (Mernissi 1975; Saadawi 1982; Sadiqi and Ennaji 2006). The dichotomy public space/private space has been recently investigated within a gender-based dichotomy in which the social hierarchy of men and women is at the center: the public space is the street and the market place where men evolve, and the private space is the home where women live. This view defines the public space as the locus of power and the production of social constraints and the private space as the locus of power-implementation. It is true that women can be in some public spaces – for example, on the street, but they cannot stay there as men are encouraged to. Rather, they must do their business and move on. Also, men do not generally spend any time in the kitchen, for example, so the taboo works for them, too, though with very different consequences. It is within this conception of space that gender identities are constructed and power negotiated in the MENA region. Private space is culturally associated with powerless people (women and children) and is subordinated to the public space, where men dictate the law, lead business, manage the state, and control the economy, both national and domestic. Thus, although women have power in the private space (older women, for example, often decide on the economy of the household and on who marries whom), they lack authority (that is, power sanctioned by society) (Sadiqi et al. 2009).

In the recent decades, and according to the particular historical circumstances of particular countries of the MENA region, the strict public/private space dichotomy has been seriously disrupted since women started to take jobs outside home. Women's salaried work resulted in a space reorganization whereby the tribal mode of production was gradually replaced by a structure of dependence brought about by colonialism and later modernism. The extended family structure (which included grandparents, uncles, aunts, cousins, and other members of kin) shrank to a nucleus of parents and children, especially in urban areas.

The reorganization of space which followed women's salaried work has been greatly enhanced by continuous changes in the economic and educational levels of families in the MENA region (Moghadam 2005). In urban areas, women have had more and more access to authority-related public spaces, which resulted in adopting special types of dress for public and private spaces. Rural and urban women differ as to the degree of access to the powerful public space. If rural women are relatively absent from the mosque, administration, etc., they are present in the fields and the market place. Urban women, on the other hand, have been "individualized" by their jobs in the sense that these gave them an opportunity to be called by their own names, and not be constantly associated with their fathers, husbands, or sons. Women with salaried jobs accommodate two types of work: domestic and production work. The former is learnt in childhood and the latter acquired through education and training. This accommodation imposes new habits and a new time management on women. Not only do they have to be at their jobs at specific times of the day, they also have to mix with male colleagues. These changes engender new social representations of women in society, as well as new behaviors and attitudes. Outside the home, women fulfill themselves as individuals, as citizens with rights and responsibilities; inside the home, they fulfill themselves as homemakers and rearers of children. As a result, a type of dialectical relationship is created between women's public and private spaces.

Although still gendered, the reorganized space renders the dichotomy men/ public and women/private more complex. Both men and women now occupy both spaces with different roles. Men are "inserted" in the private space to satisfy their needs (food, rest, procreation) and some of men's most important life experiences, such as circumcision and marriage, take place in the private space. As for women, they use education and job-taking to gain some power in the public space. The road is, however, long before women can really have genuine authority in the public realm.

Political context

The overall political context in the MENA region is not favorable to women's empowerment. The various social illnesses that characterize this region have a direct impact on women's lives: women are the ones who bear the brunt of extremist religious trends, economic hardships, legal injustices, social insecurity, and political stagnation. Despite their impressive gains in education and health, women in the MENA region still face gender discrimination that prevents them from reaching their potential (Sadiqi et al. 2009). With very few exceptions, such as Tunisia and Morocco, women in this region are legally defined as dependants in the family laws pertaining to divorce, child custody, and inheritance. According the International Development Research Centre's 2007 statistics, women's life expectancy in the MENA indicates a rate of 79.7 percent in Kuwait and 58 percent in Sudan; the maternal mortality ratio (per 100,000 live births) in Bahrain is 46 compared to 370 in Yemen (Human Development Report 2004). The maternal mortality rate in the region as a whole is 396 per 100,000 live births, which is double the rate in Latin America and the Caribbean, and four times the rate in East Asia (Doraid 2000). In 1997, women were found to be illiterate in six of the fifteen Arab countries for which data on female literacy was available, and in the region as a whole 65 million people were illiterate (Doraid 2000). This indicates high levels of inequality between women as the risk of maternal mortality is not equally high for the literate, professional women. While regional estimates of the incidence of income poverty vary considerably, the World Bank found that in 1994, 11 million people in the MENA region lived in poverty or on less than $1 a day. The proportion of women representatives in Arab parliaments remains the lowest in the world at under 10 percent (Arab Human Development Report 2006).

Women's rights in the MENA as well as the wider social and development issues can be understood only within the complex political context of the region. Economic, social, and political development of the region has been constantly hindered by serious ongoing insecurity and conflict: war, stagnating economies, disillusionment with the Arabist project and increasing international pressure to conform to Western-based political and social models. As a result, the region has witnessed an increasing level of social marginalization and widespread poverty, a concentration of power and wealth in the hands of ruling political and financial elites; a general disillusionment with formal politics and absence of the rule of law; and a dramatic resurgence of religious extremism (Sadiqi et al. 2009).

Economic context

From the 1950s onwards, the evolution of social policy in the MENA region has had a heavily gendered history (Moghadam 2005). A combination of neopatriarchal state- and nation-building imperatives in the region and the gender dynamics of these processes and policies greatly impacted development and social policy.

Like most developing regions, MENA has been hit by recurrent severe economic crises since the late 1970s. From that period onward, the countries of the region have adopted "structural adjustments" to restore their economic and financial balance. These policies have been imposed by the International Monetary Fund and the World Bank. As champions of liberalism, these two institutions have hardly been concerned with the fate of the poorest. The most under-privileged classes are paying a high price for the adjustments, the first victims in this process being poor women who are the victims of the decrease in employment prospects and the drastic cuts in social budgets. In the MENA region, the social sectors of health and education are the hardest hit by budget cuts. In Morocco, for example, education expenditure per capita decreased at a rate of 11 percent from 1983 to 1989, resulting in a general decline of 8.7 percent in school enrollment rates between 1985 and 1990 (Ennaji 2006).

Likewise, female job opportunities are more directly hit by economic crises than male opportunities. In times of crises, women are excluded from stable and high-paying jobs and, instead, are encouraged to take up precarious and low-paying jobs in the informal sector. Starting from the mid-1990s onward, poverty has become more and more female (Ennaji 2005). The loosening of family ties and accelerated urban expansion have seriously broken traditional solidarity. This tendency is reinforced by an increase in divorce and has resulted in an increase in the number of female heads of households. In cities, it is in the lower classes that one finds the largest number of female heads of households (Ennaji and Sadiqi 2008). Consequently, poverty typically affects the families supported by a woman's salary. Likewise, women benefit less than men from economic and social progress in periods of growth. They constitute the most vulnerable social group and the least protected one. This situation is due neither to fate nor chance; it is the result of a systematic depreciation of women's work and status in all fields. This is in accordance with the prevalent view that women are not treated on an equal basis with men in the public sphere of work; women have to fight for many considerations that are taken for granted by men.

Thus, in spite of the great benefits that salaried women derive from their jobs, the reorganization of space in the MENA region did not bring about equality of sexes (Ennaji 2008). Colonialism and modernism in the region established the "work-money-modernity" order, and brought about new techniques of exploitation, such as the division of society into traditional (rural) and modern (urban) areas. As cities created anonymity, urban women are confronted with a psycho-sociological conflict inside their society: a clash between an essentially tribal superstructure and a production system whose economic logic is alien to the traditional communal mode. Modernization benefits upper and middle class women to the detriment of rural women who, up to present times, suffer from illiteracy. For example, according to the Department of Statistics (2004), 68 percent of Moroccan rural women are illiterate.

Another modernity-related problem is that in the domain of work, the law does not mirror social inequalities. Women face the same problems as men in jobs: an increase in the cost of living, a decrease in job opportunities, and health and housing problems. In addition, women face problems that are specific to them, some of which are common to all women, and others differ according to social class, legislation, etc. Furthermore, in spite of the fact that the legal texts which regulate social legislation do not discriminate between men and women with respect to individual relations in jobs and protective safety measurements, as well as in salaries, work hours, and health, women suffer from handicaps related to their jobs: huge gaps in their professional training, a very high illiteracy rate, unsatisfactory socialization, weak representation in the unions, and the failure of statisticians and other analysts to treat domestic work as employment. Even in trade unions that are supposed to defend workers' rights, managers do not encourage female employment, especially in periods of economic crises. Women do not generally participate in union/social activist causes because of domestic chores. In addition, husbands and fathers do not generally favor women's attendance at union meetings, which are usually held in the evenings. In all-female professions, some women join unions but they have little chance of reaching positions of high responsibility that would give them the power to decide. Research is scarce in this area.

As pressure for democracy in the MENA region continues to grow, the issue of women's rights is gaining prominence in policy debates. The region's progress depends on a larger role of women in the economy (Moghadam and Roudi-Fahimi 2005). In some parts of the region "the issue of women's rights" has been gaining prominence in policy debates for several generations. In fact, in Egypt, the topic was *more* prominent in the day of Qasem Amin than it is today!

Today, coalitions between feminist groups in MENA countries are gathering momentum. By linking social and economic development to women's rights, these coalitions present women's demands as "society's demands." In doing so, they are attracting the attention not only of human rights organizations but also of decision-makers.

Legal context

The region's family laws codify discrimination against women and girls, placing them in a subordinate position to men within the family—a position that is then replicated in the economy and society. The first family laws show the extent to which the MENA countries have, to a varying degree, built discrimination against women into the culture, government policies, and legal frameworks. Family laws in the MENA govern marriage, divorce, inheritance and other family-related issues; they are drawn from mostly secular sources only in Turkey and Tunisia. In the overwhelming majority of cases, the sources of these laws are mainly (sometimes solely) drawn from the Shari'a (Islamic law). So far as rights and responsibilities are concerned, the Shari'a defines women as dependent and minor in its traditional interpretations. Implemented in heavily patriarchal environments where women and their privileges belong to their male kin, women's mobility is very restricted and their authority and power of decision neutralized. According to Moghadam (2005):

> Women's interactions with the state and society are thus often determined and mediated through their husbands, fathers, brothers, or other male relatives. A woman's position as a dependant of her male guardian is used to justify her second-class citizenship.

For example, according to the traditional interpretation of the Shari'a, a woman needs a permission from her father, husband, or other male guardian not only to marry, but also to seek employment, start a business, travel, or open a bank account for a child. In Iran and Jordan, a husband has the legal right to forbid his wife or unmarried daughter to seek employment or stay in a job.

Women's efforts to push for reforms of the family laws in the MENA region are gradually bearing fruit. Nowadays, women's rights are more and more prominent in policy debates across the region as pressure for democracy continues to grow. Experts see in a larger role for women in the economy and society a vital ingredient in the region's progress. For example in Morocco, the recently adopted family law is based on equal rights for both men and women, while remaining consistent with the spirit of Islam. The fact that a feminist campaign succeeded in helping alter family law in a MENA country such as Morocco shows the force of linking social and economic development to women's rights in countries where laws are based on the Shari'a.

Generally speaking, the family in the MENA region is managed according to the Shari'a; however, as the MENA Islamic societies are heavily heterogeneous, the conception and adaptation of the family laws are country-specific.

Women's overall agency

The locus of women's agency in the MENA region resides in their balance of the vibrant intersecting dynamics of tradition and modernity at the historical, socio-cultural, political, economic, legal, and symbolic levels. Their oral agency has escaped state-building and colonization, and women's poems are still used as a means to spirituality and social cohesion. Tradition, as the sum of ancestral socio-cultural values that make communities distinct from each other, has been evolving in the last decades in the region. Modernity, as continuously new ways of looking at things, is also dynamic and detracts from tradition. In the case of women, the dynamics of tradition and modernity involve attire, behavior in private and public spaces, job, faith, etc. On the politico-economic level, despite the hurdles mentioned above, women in the MENA region have achieved significant advancement in recent years. There are female CEOs, female government officials, female professors, female engineers; women who run e-businesses and financial institutions. Presently, most MENA countries have at least one female government minister, if not more. In Tunisia, 40 percent of doctors and 70 percent of pharmacists are women. Laws and decrees that grant women equal rights to participate in local communes, in consultative and municipality councils have been passed into law in many MENA countries. Women in the Gulf have an estimated $40 billion of personal wealth at their disposal. In Egypt, women form 31 percent of the workforce in the government sector. Most tellingly, in the MENA region overall, 70 percent of university graduates in 2007 are female. At the symbolic level, MENA women have inspired research beyond the region, particularly in Europe and North America.

The limitations on women's agency often lie outside their will. The utilization of their capabilities through economic and political participation remains low in quantitative terms, as evidenced by the low overall share of women in government —6.5 percent compared to a world average of 15.7 percent. The female workforce in civil service (as secretaries in most cases) represents approximately 30 percent, compared to a global average of 45 percent. Although conscious of the economic, social, and political role of women, governments are slow to react. They need to increase cooperation and strengthen links between organizations and nations. It is often said that when women have access to education, capital, and health care, they not only improve the well-being of their own families but the stability of their communities.

Mentalities are also slow to change: the social order in the MENA is still controlled by a space-based patriarchy and gender hierarchy. Despite the commitment made by the MENA countries to gender equality at numerous UN events such as the Millennium Summit in September 2000, gender disparity remains prevalent throughout the region, and gender gaps persist in access to education and quality health care, employment and business opportunities, political participation and decision-making. Further, despite women's impressive gains in education and health, academic and policy-oriented studies across the region have identified chronic gender inequalities in the MENA region as major obstacles to progress in economic and human development. Gender inequality —the differential access to opportunity and security for women and girls—has become an important and visible issue for the MENA economies. Gender equality issues in the region are usually approached from a social, anthropological, or political angle. But the costs of inequality are often borne at the economic level. Women in the region still face gender discrimination that is built into the culture, government policies, and legal institutions.

In spite of discrimination, women in the MENA region have over the past three decades started to play an avant-garde role in the socio-cultural, economic and political development of their countries. Recent trends in women's activism and family law reform are very significant and attest to their vibrant agency. Women's action is in some countries like Morocco and Tunisia part of the official agenda. Often represented as passive in mainstream Western literature and mass media, women of the MENA region have gradually become genuine agents of change over the past three decades. Their agency is multi-faceted, polyvocal, and pervasive. They use education to raise their living standards and those of their families, they help improve the economies of their countries, they change attitudes to gender perception, they feminize the political and civil society spaces, they push for reform of the legal systems of their countries, and they democratize academia by pioneering feminist and gender studies. As such, the women of the MENA region are not only broadening but complicating our understanding of the East– West, Muslim–non-Muslim, and modern–traditional dichotomies.

In sum, on the one hand, significant challenges and prejudices impede the progress of MENA women as agents, but on the other hand, the list of their accomplishments is remarkable and impressive. What is important from the perspective of this volume is that in spite of overwhelming challenges, progress is being achieved through women's determination and will to change themselves and their societies. The resources that women have are not uniform as women are heterogeneous, but each uses whatever is available to her to achieve her goals.

The 16 chapters in this volume range over 10 countries from the MENA region and Spain (where the Orient remains a strong symbol): Egypt, Oman, Palestine, Israel, Turkey, Iran, Tunisia, Algeria, Morocco, and Spain. Five major aspects of women's agency are discussed in the chapters: political agency, civil society activism, legal reform, cultural, social, religious, and symbolic agencies.

At the level of politics, women in the MENA region participated in the political use of Islam, as well as in the debates over the veil. Four chapters in Part I illustrate this agency: in the first chapter, "The veil: religious and historical foundations and the modern political discourse," Nazli Fathi-Rizk traces the history and development of women's position in Islam, analyzing progress and challenges and closing with a call to imitate the Prophet's *Ijtihad* by engaging in "an honest and reasoned re-evaluation of the founding discourse subjugating [women]." While it covers theological ground, the historical approach to the Egyptian case in this chapter provides contextualization. In Chapter 2, "Women, Islam, and political agency in Morocco," Fatima Sadiqi discusses ways in which Moroccan women engaged politically with the notion of Islamization and managed to democratize the debates while highlighting their legal rights. Chapter 3, "Assia Djebar and Malika Mokeddem: neocolonial agents or postcolonial subjects?" by Abdelkader Cheref introduces a different approach and locus from which to consider the issues of women's potential and actual political agency in their representation, and therefore the inquiry into, if not the shaping of, women's images in the MENA region. The chapter underlines the tremendous impact that the work of Djebar and Mokeddem has had on the understanding of Algerian women and their cultural agency in the postcolonial Maghreb throughout the French-speaking world (and beyond that, through translations). In Chapter 4, "Women and political reform in Israel," Galia Golan provides an analytical study of the position of women in Israel. The chapter is focused on institutional and legislative analysis and highlights the idea of women's agency within the political institutional framework.

In Part II, MENA women's agency in the domain of civil society is underlined in two chapters. In Chapter 5, "Women's NGOs and social change in Morocco," Moha Ennaji analyzes the role played by NGOs in the emancipation of Moroccan women and their civic and public participation. It includes an account of the Mudawana (Family Law) and its history and situates the topic in the general field of women's agency, develops a typology of women's NGOs, and assesses the background to and impact of the Mudawana reform. In Chapter 6, "Palestinian women's movements and activism," Islah Jad evaluates the impact of the proliferation of NGOs, assesses the impact of the changing conditions on grass-roots organizations, the subtle distinctions between women's national militant activism, and their effective inclusion in higher ranks of power and the significance of all this in the changing gender ideology.

Part III, at the legal level, includes three chapters. Mounira M. Charrad's Chapter 7, "Tunisia at the forefront of the Arab world," focuses on Tunisian women's use of the legislation front to assert their rights and set an example for the other Arab nations. Chapter 8, "Feminism and family law in Iran," by Valentine M. Moghadam offers information on the implementation of family law in Iran. It underlines the implications of this legal code in terms of women's citizenship and, ultimately, their independence and the definition of selfhood. Hoda Ragheb Awad's "The legal status of women in Egypt," Chapter 9, depicts the legal status of women in Egypt.

At the social, cultural, religious, and symbolic levels, Part IV presents eight chapters. Zahia Smail Salhi's chapter (10) on "Algerian women as agents of change and social cohesion," is an account of the role of women in the Algerian struggle for independence and their resistance in the face of the oppressive patriarchal hegemony that dominated the postcolonial scene and that culminated in the violations of human rights in the 1990s. In Chapter 11 on "Women in Turkey," Fatma Umut Bespinar gives an account of the issues surrounding women's plight in Turkey in terms of the conflicts and challenges of secular/traditional mutual interferences. The chapter includes information and illustration on the politics of head cover in Turkey, as well as women's agency in this regard. Chapter 12, "Women and language in Tunisia" by Raoudha Kammoun, reports on the findings of a study based in Tunis. This chapter highlights how language patterns shape gender perceptions, and how certain idioms and standard addresses or language protocol affect the way we understand and give status and value to gendered entities and to members of each sex. Chapter 13, "Women, education, and the redefinition of empowerment and change in a traditional society" by Thuwayba Al Barwani, underscores the crucial role of education for women's empowerment and describes women's status and agency in Oman, providing some statistics to this effect.

At the cultural level, Chapter 14 on "Perpetuating authority" by Margaret J. Rausch develops an argument about the phenomenon of cultural preservation and transformation via ritual and oral tradition among the Berber women of southwest Morocco. It develops a perspective, historical and cultural, in which the case of Berber women's agency is placed and provides examples to explain this. Chapter 15, by Touria Khannous, "Moroccan women contrabandists," is an inquiry about the current social and cultural transformation of Moroccan society. The chapter also discusses the global cultural productions that have infiltrated Moroccan culture with the laptop and the ways in which the "everyday" has changed.

At the symbolic level, Aurora G. Morcillo's chapter (16) on "The Orient within" discusses the "otherness" of Spain, the gender ideology and reality of its culture, and the very "feminization" of its identity as the borderland between Western/ European and Eastern/African realities is rich with potential for scholarly inquiry. The chapter addresses three focuses: a historical account, a review of Western literature on Spain, and a discussion of sex and gender issues in Spanish culture whose ingredients include Eastern and African roots.

Overall, the primary aim of this book is to highlight women's agency in the MENA region and underline their various contributions to the advancement of their countries, as well as their self-assertion in male-dominated contexts. The volume is inter-disciplinary as the authors of the chapters come from various academic horizons. This book may serve as a course of study on women and contemporary politics in the MENA region. The targeted audience is students/ researchers of the region and others who are interested in women's agency in developing countries, generally. The sample cases are well chosen to support the thesis, as well as intriguing in and of themselves.

Notes

1 The dichotomy public space/private space has received considerable attention from feminist scholars working in various disciplines. Thompson (1994) retraces the roots of this dichotomy to a Greek legend in which human actions take place in a space that is divided into two: public space, the visible male world called "Hermean" (after the Greek God of communication), and private space, the invisible feminine world called

"Hestian" (the Greek Goddess of home). Hermean space is inherently concrete; it is the space where the philosopher exercises his thinking, the citizen practices his politics, and the researcher explores the complexities of the human intellect. As for the Hestian space, it is the space of everyday life which is essentially characterized by domestic chores and the satisfaction of survival needs.

2   Mainstream Western patriarchy is more based on the image. Western women in general gained most of the rights when they became consumers. The increasingly influential impact of capital on daily lives of people, pushed multinationals and media industry to "guess" the needs of women beforehand and create images of women that the latter were forced to adopt.

Part I

Reconsidering the foundations of women, Islam, and political agency

1 The veil

Religious and historical foundations and the modern political discourse

Nazli Fathi-Rizk

Introduction

For an observer of the Muslim social scene during the past thirty years, it is notable that the *hijab* [1] in its different forms—from the headscarf to the *niqab* (full covering of face and body)—became a revealing mark of Muslim women, not only in the Muslim world, but also within Muslim communities all over the world. [2] Confined in the beginning to some few states in the Arabian Peninsula, the veil has systematically propagated, as to acquire the attributes of a symbol. In Egypt, the tendency sporadically sprouted in the 1970s, first on a small scale, and then it gradually and exponentially spread, to include all classes of society. Now, it would not be preposterous to venture that a majority of Egyptian women are donning the veil in one of its forms. What religious, social, economic, and political forces converged to create and sustain such a phenomenon? And from the women's point of view, what considerations, urgencies dictated their adoption of the veil? Are women becoming more pious, more religious, and more aware of their duties as Muslim than their grandmothers who had cast off their veils, last century?

Is the veil a sign of the revival of a pristine age—the age of the Prophet and his Companions, as propounded by the *salafeya* thinking?

Is the veil a religious duty for women to be placed in the order of priorities, just after the five pillars of Islam?

Is the veil a choice now, after having been during past centuries an imposition?

Is the veil an empowerment or an abdication of women's rights?

Is the veil a statement of cultural identity, of allegiance to a community, of enrollment in the ranks of a revived *umma* (community of believers)?

Is the veil a declaration of difference, a statement of protest, and a defense against what is perceived as an encroachment of an alien and pervasive Western culture?

Is the veil, wittingly or unwittingly a reassertion of male supremacy, after the gains of women, in the course of the twentieth century?

Is the veil one of the manifestations of a political discourse, presenting itself as an alternative to the power of the modern secular nation-state?

Is the veil a response to economic deprivation and political alienation?

Is the revival of the veil part of a political program to instate a social, ethical order, in which women are at the vanguard of the Islamic transformation of society?

Is the veil the symbol and the banner of Islamism, the last line of defense against Western imperialism?

Is the veil a protective shield against sexual harassment and the pervasive laxity of social mores?

So many questions raised, that point the finger to an array of complex issues below the surface of the layered *hijab!*[3] In order to understand the *hijab*'s propensity, this study uses a variety of approaches—historical, sociological, and semiotic—and is organized in an attempt to reflect the dynamics of the veil's discourse. Thus, it looks first at the "orthodox"—or what has become a normative—view of veiling as presented by the religious establishment on the basis of their readings of the Qur'anic texts related to the dress code of women, and the *hadith* (saying or reported action) of the Prophet addressing the issue. Second, it considers the political and socio-economic factors contributing to the resurgence of the veil in Egypt: how it first emerged tentatively in the 1970s then gained full vigor in the ensuing decades, to the point that the veil seems now institutionalized. Last, it turns to the "revitalization" of the religious texts and reports on the alternative interpretations of the veil, as expounded by a new trend of Islamic scholarship, which could be perceived as a riposte to the seemingly prevalent consensus that a Muslim woman's duty is to cover her hair.

The orthodox view

Part set of laws and part code of conduct permeating all the aspects of the human experience, the Shari'a stands as a comprehensive way of life. It governs and colors all aspects of the Muslim human experience, allowing the believer to tread a straight path, in accordance with the decrees of God and for the good of the community. Nourished by the main tributaries of the Holy Qur'an and the *Sunna* (example) of the Prophet, it also reflects the *ijmaa* (consensus) of the *umma* (community of Muslims), as well as the *ijtihad* (personal effort of reasoning and interpretation) of the *ulama* (religious scholars) of the eighth to tenth centuries. In the course of its formation, during the heyday of the Islamic civilization, the Shari'a was the axial institution, bonding the various Muslim communities under the rule and guidance of the Caliphate.

The orthodox view of the veil, stated as the obligatory dress code for women, derives from some verses of the Qur'an, especially the one in *surat el nour* (24:31), urging women to pull their veils on their bodies, and not to display their *zeena* (adornments), except to close members of their families. In another verse, God advises the Prophet's female warden and the believing women to *"lengthen their skirts,"* (33:59). A third one urges the believers, both men and women, to hide their private parts and to *"lower their gazes."* A fourth one admonishes the believers not to address the wives of the Prophet, except behind a "curtain" (33:53).[4] A fifth *aya* (24:60) tackles with the status of "prostrated" women (either post-menopausal or sick, depending on the interpretation of the word *moutakaedat*), easing the restrictions put on them. The inference from these *ayas*, following the traditional view, is the necessity for a good Muslim woman to cover her head.[5] To confirm and to ratify that view, a saying of the Prophet is put forward: "All in a woman is *awra* (Pudenda? Private? Immodest?), except her face and hands." And it is presented as a final proof of the absolute necessity of the veil. Therefore, it is incumbent for a believing woman to be veiled.

The demise and resurrection of the veil in Egypt

The veil was not an issue in the course of the history of Islamic civilization. Women became veiled, and then segregated from the view of men, as of the outset of the Islamic conquests and the establishment of the Islamic empires; and it was a fact of life that the private and public spheres were to be scrupulously separated, following a tacit consensus of the times.[6]

The debate on the veiling of women was only raised in times of crisis, when the Muslim world came violently into contact with Western colonialism. Thus, during the brief French occupation of Egypt (1798–1801), the Egyptian chronicler of the time, Al Jabarti, expressed his shock and horror at the sight of French soldiers publicly consorting with women, in the Ezbekkia gardens (Vatikiotis 1991: 45).

In the first decades of the British occupation (1882–1954) the issue of the veil generated passionate debates between modernists and traditionalists, raising the issues of class and culture and reaching deep into the nature of Egyptian identity. Two events happened almost simultaneously in the1920s, which from their outset reveal an antithetical significance. On the one hand, the dramatic and defiant removal of the veil in public by the aristocratic Hoda Shaarawi and her protégée Seza Nabarawi; on the other hand, the "resistant" display of Muslim "traditional garb" by the Muslim Sisters, an affiliate of the surging *haraka* (movement) of the Muslim Brotherhood; two stands which could not be more different in their antecedents, their social basis, and their implications![7]

The first stand was occasioned by the British rule in Egypt, and the domination of Western interests and customs. It epitomized the Westernization of the society mostly in its upper echelons, through its contacts, interplay, and aligned interests with the foreign power in place. It also affiliated itself with the *nahda* (renaissance) movement of the 1850s, which interacting with Western culture had been touching on many aspects of Egyptian life. Moreover, it seemed as a validation of the attack on the veil as expounded in the controversial writings of Kassem Amin, the champion of Egyptian women's "liberation" (Ayubi 1991: 130–132).

The second one was an integral part of the movement of the Muslim Brotherhood formed initially in Ismailia, in 1928, by a secondary school teacher, Hassan El Banna. This movement catered to the afflicted and alienated rural masses that had rushed to the cities in search of employment after World War I.

By offering counsel, services, and a secure sense of belonging to a "purified" Muslim community through the expansion of a network of preaching and support, the *haraka* spread to embrace new adepts from the urban lower class to the lower middle class (Zuhur 1992: 47).

Under the autocratic rule of its Supreme Guide, the Muslim Brotherhood insisted on proper Islamic behavior and conduct, and women were required to cling to their head covers, ostensibly white.[8] The "Islamic" dress was the outer sign and banner of resistance against the Westernizing colonialist project for women. With the same logic, detractors of Kassem Amin perceived "his assault on the veil not as the result of reasoned reflection and analysis, but rather as the internalization and replication of the colonialist perception" (Ahmed 1992: 161). Similar stands vituperated the aristocratic mimicry of the occupier's customs, and denounced the bad faith of the West. Don't they use the feminist discourse which they fight at home; to show that the Muslim world in their seclusion of women is backward, therefore deserves its colonization by the West? Concerning that rapport between Western and Islamist views, Leila Ahmed notes:

> the peculiar resemblance to be found between the colonial and still commonplace Western view that an innate connection exists between the issues of culture and women in Muslim societies and the similar presumptions underlying the Islamist resistance position, that such a fundamental connection does indeed exist. The resemblance between the two positions is not coincidental: they are mirror images of each other. The resistance narrative contested the colonialist thesis by inverting—thereby also, ironically, grounding itself in the premises of the colonial thesis.
>
> (Ahmed 1992: 166)

In the ensuing period up to the 1970s, the modernist view was gaining ground, first, under the liberal experiment of semi-independent Egypt, then during the modernizing socialist rule of Nasser. Women were making huge strides in education, employment, careers, and rights, and their visibility and engagement in the public sphere went unchallenged. The veil, as the symbol of the segregation of women had receded, almost to the point of invisibility, except in the countryside, where the peasant woman costume and head cover had always been more of a national dress than a religious standard.

On the other hand, during the inter-war period, the Muslim Brotherhood was engaged into a political competition with other political parties—parliamentary and extra-parliamentary—for the mind and soul of the people; especially the students of the secondary schools and universities. With active support from their propagandists, they became more militant, more strident in their denunciation of the corruption and inefficiency of the monarchical rule. They launched daring attacks against the British bases in the Canal Zone during World War II; they volunteered en masse in the 1948 war, in defense of the Palestinians' rights against the colonialist Jewish implantation in Muslim land. Moreover, they entered into bloody confrontations with the Egyptian state, assassinating Prime Minister

Nokrashy Pasha, and seeing their Supreme Guide executed in the ensuing police retaliation (Ibrahim 1987: 122–124).

However, as a whole, their call for a return to pure Islam was one among other voices on the Egyptian political stage, and it was also subsumed by the common nationalist cause against British colonial rule and the mounting disaffection with King Farouk's regime. Socially, they were still eager to promote their program of Islamization, but either because of police vigilance, the competition of other parties, or in view of their violent methods, the movement seemed less appealing to a seemingly secularized population.

In the aftermath of the 1952 Free Officers' coup d'état, the power game following the fall of the monarchy set Nasser and his group of Free Officers a formidable task: how to consolidate their rule and acquire legitimacy. A gradual, systematic purge was put in place: the banning of the old parliamentary parties, the cleansing of their influence in the bureaucracy, the house arrest of Muhammad Naguib, the first President of Egypt, the Liberation Rally, etc. Nasser now was emerging as the mastermind of the revolution and he had astutely played his card in doing away with most of his rivals of the Old Regime and in the close circle of the Free Officers. He became president in 1954, with absolute power, and was carried by a huge wave of popular support. However, he still had to deal with a more formidable rival: the Muslim Brothers. Whether the Brotherhood was challenging his dictatorship or was claiming a share in power is not clear; however an attempt on his life, attributed to a Muslim Brother during a public speech in Alexandria, gave Nasser the opportunity to unleash a relentless hounding and brutal repression of the Brothers. The movement was dismantled, its members scattered, killed, or thrown in jail. From then on, during the whole Nasser era, the religious discourse took a backseat in the ideology of the country. Now, it was nationalism, the struggle against imperialism, the liberation from colonialism, populism, the fight against reactionary Arab regimes, defiance of Israel, the call for Arab unity and Arab socialism. Even Al-Azhar, bastion of Sunni Islam, was "nationalized" and operated under the hegemony of the State: its *fatwas* (formal religious opinions) conferred justification and legitimacy to Nasser's policies and decrees (Hopwood 1993: 96).

What about the veil during that period? Simply put, it seemed a remote and archaic idea of the past, not worth even recalling. The Nasserite socialist program of industrialization, free education, full employment, and social mobility had served women well.[9] Thus, they competed with men in jobs and professions, in the media, in the theater, in the cinema; they enjoyed equal opportunities and equity of salaries. Egypt was the center of the Arab world and its songs, films, and stars confirmed its preeminence on the Arab cultural scene. And women were at the forefront of stardom and modernity.

Then the *nakbah* (catastrophe) struck like lightning on the country. Everybody agrees that the Six Day War and the Arab armies' defeat at the hands of Israel had a traumatic effect on the nation. Psychologically speaking, it was a shake-up of assumptions and delusions. The regime was uncovered: its other face of repression, of secret prisons, of torture and human rights violation, of corruption and unaccountability, of economic and political failure was revealed and exposed. Nasser, the embodiment of Egypt, of Arab nationalism, the hero of the masses, the champion of Arab awakening, was broken. The whole edifice of the military dictatorship that he had built and consolidated with an iron fist for 25 years was pitifully crumbling. No matter that crying and desperate masses flocked in a huge demonstration calling him to revoke his resignation, no matter the trials of the officers responsible for the defeat, no matter the sit-ins of leftist students at the universities clamoring for transparency and accountability. The whole ideological fabric supporting the regime was cracking and the prostrated nation exposed its wounds. All the political "isms" of the past—liberalism, communism, socialism, fascism—had revealed their inadequacies and failure to deliver promises of prosperity and social justice.

Religion became a solace, the only haven of certitude in a world shaken in its foundations. (A significant sign: in the aftermath of the defeat, a rumor spread that the Virgin Mary had appeared in tears in a small church of Cairo, causing Copts and Muslims to flock in, in a spontaneous outpouring of religious fervor (Al-Sayyid Marsot 1990: 126).) However, the regime survived, showing its resilience.

Enter Sadat, heralding a new era, based on the same military regime, but outfitted with different strategies and a new vision. "Signal left" as to calm the population's fear that the socialist legacy of Nasser would be lost, and "turn right" to dismantle the past construct ... and woo the Americans![10] The Muslim Brothers are released from jail, or invited back from Saudi Arabia where they were self-exiled. Now, they are allowed to issue their newspapers and encouraged to propagate their message under the protective shield of the state. In accordance with the right-wing program of the government, fundamentalist youth penetrated the universities, monopolized the political discourse, using the double-edged weapon of persuasion and intimidation to dictate their views, and silence the leftist and Nasserite voices. With an eye on the university female body, they initiated "Islamic services" to beleaguered women in the overcrowded university amphitheaters and busses. They protected them from harassment and patronized them.

Quid pro quo? Wear the veil! Rediscover your Muslim identity! Abide by the laws of your faith! Perform the rituals of your religion, among which the endorsement of the veil is a religious duty![11] The *da'wa* (call) was gaining momentum: not only the "petit-bourgeoisie," stronghold of Nasser's support, rallied to the new ideology, but members of the Old and New regimes' elite, willingly or reluctantly followed course. Many families looked in dismay as their daughters converted to this new creed, and turned against their mothers' and grandmothers' Western outlook. In response to that example of righteousness, it was compelling to tread that way and adopt the veil.[12]

The program of Islamization of society did not stop at the spreading of the veil or the growing of beards for men, or even the conspicuous religiosity of the new converts. Emboldened by their success at filling the ideological vacuum left by the discredited Nasserite regime, the Muslim Brothers were politically raising their voices. Clamors from the *minbars* (mosque pulpits) and in their organs of propaganda demanded a change of the constitution in favor of the Shari'a, as the sole source of Egyptian legislation. Their slogan "Islam is the solution" was brandished; any contestation or protest was branded as anathema. Sadat who had adopted the sanctimonious nickname of the "believing president" was embarrassed (Ibrahim 1987: 126). Accommodations were attempted, but the propagation of the call did not abate. On the contrary, it rose more vehemently against Sadat's trip to Jerusalem: it denounced his offer of peace in the Israeli Knesset, and it condemned in no vague terms the peace treaty between Egypt and Israel. Sadat, who had opened a Pandora's box of political Islam, thinking that he could manipulate it to his own ends, fell under the bullets of a radical jihadist group, the *Jamaa Islamiyah*, who had wittingly or unwittingly grown from under the mantle of the Muslim Brotherhood.

The Mubarak regime, inheriting Sadat's legacy, cautiously trod in minefields where it faced increased inter-confessional strife and violence. It relentlessly pursued, harassed, arrested militant Islamists through a vast repressive operation, while tolerating *bon gré mal gré*, the continuing Islamization of the society at the hands of the "good" (pacifist) Islamists. As if by a tacit agreement on a division of powers—render unto Caesar the things that belong to Caesar and render unto God the things that belong to God—political decisions were to remain the exclusive domain of the State. As for matters of religion and morality, the Islamists could continue the education of the masses ... with some media support from the government.

The rising star of the Islamists on the societal level, shone in many directions. On the positive side, they performed the rescue services that the State failed to provide, as in the aftermath of the earthquake which shook Egypt in 1992. In fact, they willingly provided the social protection that the State was gradually dropping in its pursuit of rentier capitalist gains; and they came to be seen as the helpers of the poor through their charitable organizations and medical facilities. On the other hand, "teleshari'asts," using the successful PR and marketing methods of the American televangelists, stole the show from the old television and cinema icons, some of whom had turned ostensibly religious and veiled. Islamic investment banks, and shady financial companies, cloaked in religious self-righteousness, proliferated, playing on the gullibility of devout investors. Religious tourism with multiple *umrah* and *hajj* became common rituals. The veil tendency was making huge strides, from an existential choice in its beginnings to a peer and social pressure now.[13] As an actual example, during Ramadan young and "modern preachers" attract throngs of affluent women, who after *iftar* bring in to the "show" their daughters, sisters, and cousins to listen to the sermons.[14] The unveiled ones come out of these meetings, convinced that they should put on the *hijab*, that they are making the right choice, that they are invested with the sacred duty of carrying the banner of Islam.

Another cause for the fever of the veil can be detected in the moving of the center of the Arab world from Egypt to Saudi Arabia, as of the 1967 war. Footing the bill for refurbishing the Egyptian and Syrian armies, fabulously enriched by its petrodollars, host to an impressive Egyptian and Muslim workforce in quest of jobs and opportunities, it had acquired the prestige and the means to promote Islam as an ideology. The *Wahabi* movement which had brought the House of Saud to power in the 1920s and ensured its legitimacy had imposed its own rigorist vision on the Kingdom. Spurred by the ambitions of its rulers to lead the Islamic world —a revival of the defunct caliphate?—and by the missionary zeal of its *ulamas*, it worked to mould the *umma* along its conservative lines. Money poured in to build mosques and Islamic centers, within and beyond the Islamic world. Through these organs of diffusion, the *Wahabi* creed projected itself as the pure Islam, cleansed of foreign accretions, the true *salafiyah*, the only Islam.

Moreover, the success of the Iranian revolution and the intent of Ayatollah Khomeni to export his Islamic revolution to the Arab world pushed Saudi Arabia to counteract, by assuming the leadership of the Sunni world against the Shia-led Islamization project. A tightening of the Sunni ranks was necessary: one view of the world, one version of Islam—the *salafi/wahabi* one—to transcend and contain the plurality of Islam, to re-anchor the religion in its primeval milieu. Nothing was spared to ensure that forms are respected. Let literal interpretation of the Scriptures prevail. Let rites be scrupulously followed. Let uniformity be enforced, so that Islam presents an impregnable monolithic front. The *hijab* is de rigueur to distinguish the believer from the non-believer, the righteous from the sinner, the conforming from the strayed, the devout one from the vile secularist.

Naturally, the Egyptian workers and professionals who worked in Saudi Arabia and the Gulf States would absorb these views and import them to their mother country, when they returned. Among a population, impoverished by an ill-planned "Open Door Policy," threatened by the new capitalist trends, and distracted by a fever of consumerism, they came in, armed with the power of their monies, flanked by their wrapped-up and bejeweled wives, brandishing their beads and their respectable title of *haj*.[15] There was a symbol of successful piety and an example to emulate! The veil became a prerequisite, a status symbol, an exclusivity (as for the wives of the Prophet?), an outer sign of righteousness for women (as in Saudi Arabia?). At the same time, an intensified promotion of the veil was taking place, addressing all classes of the society. In the poor slums of Egypt, the veil turned into a convenient and cheap garb to mask economic inequalities. In the circles of the middle and upper classes, it followed fads and fashions, sometimes copying the Christian nun's outfit and at other times, almost defeating its purpose of modesty (a tight pair of jeans enhancing curves, an elaborate *maquillage*, and a coquettish draping of the veil!). From a choice assumed by young women in quest of a spiritual meaning in their lives, animated by idealism, or cowed by a male supremacist discourse, the veil had turned into the conspicuous sign of a successful Islamist discourse, flaunting its achievement. The Mubarak regime, in its grip on all the avenues of the polity, in its repression or marginalization of alternative political parties and ideologies, in its muzzling of all forms of criticism and opposition, had left little room for contestation. And in this vacuum, having worked on the Islamization of society in the course of three decades, the Islamists achieved their quiet and "quietist" (!) revolution. "Islam is the solution" became the panacea for all society's ills, and the only available political opposition to an authoritarian state.

Revitalization of Islam in the modernists' veil discourse

The veil as a symbol of Islam seems now to be institutionalized. However, is the veil a duty incumbent on Muslim women? In spite of the prevailing orthodox view, the issue is not resolved. Away from the consensus of preachers and the Islamic establishment, Arab scholars in academia and Islamic reformers probe the question of the veil, relying on modern, scientific methods used in anthropology, history, linguistics, semiotics, and literary criticism. In light of this approach, they return to the text of the Holy Qur'an, and undertake a fresh and close re-reading of the sacred scriptures as well as a reappraisal of the *Sunna*. In the same reformist path, some scholars study the historical context and the "occasions of revelation" of the *ayas* and come out with interesting results.[16]

Modern analysis of the ayas of the Qur'an concerning the women's dress code[17]

This part of the study intends to scrutinize the above-mentioned *ayas* used by the orthodox view to justify the *hijab*, to revise their meaning and significance following the modernist view, and to highlight some counter-arguments to the veil, as inferred from the re-reading of these texts.

The word *hijab* that Muslim women use nowadays to designate their head cover can be translated as the veil. Etymologically, other meanings include screen, cover, mantle, curtain, partition, or divider. In fact, the term *hijab* appears in the Qur'an seven times, five of them as *hijab* and two times as *hijaban*; these are in the following *ayas*: 7:46, 33:53, 38:32, 41:5, 42:51, 17:45, and 19:17. However, none of these *hijab* words are used in the Qur'an in reference to what the traditional Muslims call today *hijab*, as a dress code or head cover for the Muslim woman.

As for the crucial word *khimar* which is used in *surat al nour*, and which supports the orthodox interpretation of the veil, it means cover, any cover. Thus, a curtain is a *khimar*, a dress is a *khimar*, a table cloth that covers the top of a table is a *khimar*, a blanket can be used as a *khimar*, etc.

Now, if one probes in this subject tackled by the Holy Book, it appears that the first Qur'anic rule of the dress code is "righteousness," applied equally to men and women, with the use of "garment" first in its literal meaning, then in a metaphorical sense. The message clearly urges modesty for both men and women, as part of the program of "righteousness:"

> O children of Adam, we have provided you with garments to cover your bodies, as well as for luxury. But the best garment is the garment of righteousness. These are some of God's signs, that they may take heed.

(7:26)

As for the second rule, which is *"Cover your bosoms,"* it can be found in *aya* 24:31, and is specific to women.

> And tell the believing women to subdue their eyes, and maintain their chastity. They shall not reveal any parts of their bodies, except that which is necessary. They shall cover their chests, (with their *khimar*) and shall not relax this code in the presence of other than their husbands, their fathers, the fathers of their husbands, their sons, the sons of their husbands, their brothers, the sons of their brothers, the sons of their sisters, other women, the male servants or employees whose sexual drive has been nullified, or the children who have not reached puberty. They shall not strike their feet when they walk in order to shake and reveal certain details of their bodies. All of you shall repent to God, O you believers, that you may succeed.

According to Okla, the *aya* clearly says that women should cover their bosoms; however, contrary to what is presented as the normative view, there is no mention of heads to be covered, as *gayb* is the Arabic word for chest, and not for hair (*shaar*) or head (*raas*). The specifically mentioned "bosom" alludes to the pre-Islamic provocative "décolleté" that women displayed. For Shahrour, *gayb* etymologically means "pocket," which refer to all the woman's body parts resembling pockets, of which the inside is hidden—like the underarm, under and between the breasts, the vagina and the anus; the exposure of which would represent a sin. However, the mouth, the ears, the nostrils are not pockets, in the sense that they are features of the face—not hidden ornaments—the visible signature of human identity. Following his definition of God's *huddud* (limits, boundaries) a minimum acceptable is to cover the aforementioned pockets, and the maximum limit would be the injunction of the Prophet to leave visible only the face and hands. What is below and what is above these limits are sins—like the *niqab* that overpasses the limit, or the revealing of the "pockets" that trespasses the borderline. The in-between depends on local customs and traditions. Thus, the Qur'an's limits are part of the dynamic of the text, receptive to the social and historical context in which it operates. Moreover, this is confirmed by the ambiguous *"except that which is necessary"* (Shahrour 1997: 606–607).

In a similar vein to Shahrour, Okla thinks the expression in 24:31, *"They shall not reveal any parts of their bodies except that which is necessary"* is intentionally vague, as to leave the human freedom to decide the definition of *"which is necessary"* according to its time and space. As for Gamal El Banna, he ridicules the interpretation of *"what is necessary"* as meaning the face and the hands, and considers it as so far-fetched as to be open to attack. For him, like for the two other scholars, it is up to women, moved "by ... righteousness" to freely opt for what is suitable to wear. Thus, the last part of the *aya* is a call for modesty, a reaffirmation of the previous *aya*. Do not be provocative by striking your feet so as to expose or suggest certain parts of your body!

The third *aya* regulating women's dress code is in 33:59:

> O prophet, tell your wives, your daughters, and the wives of the believers that they shall *lengthen* their garments.
> Thus, they will be recognised and avoid being insulted. God is Forgiver, Most Merciful.

(emphasis added)

Although it is addressed to the Prophet and means that this regulation applies specifically to the time of the Prophet, the description is in accordance with the spirit of Islam. In this verse, God used the word *lengthen* deliberately. There is no qualification on how long the garment should be, to the ankle, below the knee or above. In his mercy, God left it to the customs, to the perspectives of the different communities to dictate the length of the dress. In last resort, it is righteousness and modesty that distinguishes between what is appropriate and what is not.

In the same spirit, the Qur'an puts no hardship on women in the family setting. It permits them to relax their dress code, as one can see in verses 33:35 and 24:60:

> The women may relax [their dress code] around their fathers, their sons, their brothers, the sons of their brothers, the sons of their sisters, the other women, and their [female] servants. They shall reverence *God. God* witnesses all things.

(33:35; emphasis added)

> The elderly women who do not expect to get married commit nothing wrong by relaxing their dress code, provided they do not reveal too much of their bodies. To maintain modesty is better for them. *God* is Hearer, Knower.

(24:60; emphasis added)

Also there, God in His wisdom did not give details on what this relaxation entails. It is again up to the thinking, reasoning woman to decide, following her discernment and her time. Another point which calls for scrutiny is the *aya* of the *hijab* in *surat al ahzab* (33:53), in which it is enjoined on the believers to address the wives of the Prophet from behind a curtain—a partition, a screen.

> Believers, do not enter the houses of the Prophet for a meal without waiting for the proper time, unless you are given leave. But if you are invited enter, and when you have eaten disperse. Do not engage in familiar talk, for this would annoy the Prophet, and he would be ashamed to bid you go, but of the truth God is not ashamed. If you ask his wives for anything, speak to them from behind a curtain. This is more chaste for your hearts and their hearts.

This *aya* which would appear as a confirmation of the veil for Muslim women, from the orthodox point of view—as enshrined in the fatwa of Sheikh Mohammed Tantawi, Grand Mufti of Egypt at the time—is however put under another light by the modernist interpretation (Al Ashmawy 2002: 7-8; Foda 1990: 18-23). First, the *aya* refers specifically to the wives of the Prophet, and not to the general Muslim female population. Second, it is the Prophet—not his wives—who is set as an example to emulate in the Qur'an. Third, it is clearly stated in the Holy Text that the Prophet's wives are not like the other women. If the women were to imitate them, they should, in that case, never remarry after the death of their husbands:

> You must not speak ill of God's apostle, nor shall you ever wed his wives after him; this would be a grave offence in the sight of God.
>
> (33:54)

Fourth, the circumstances which surround the revelation of this *aya* are specific to the time of the Prophet, to his special status as Prophet and head of the community, and in reference to special events alluded to in the *aya*. In fact following Fatima Mernissi's exegesis, the *hijab* in the Qur'an was "drawn between two men—the Prophet and Anes Ibn Malek—and not between a man and a woman" (Baraka 2002: 112).

From these modernist interpretations of women's dress code in Islam, it appears that the veil, understood nowadays, does not have a solid Qur'anic foundation. Women can choose to cover their heads, if they wish to, but saying that it is in the Qur'an, is overbidding on the word of God, which amounts, as Okla says to "an attempt to correct God or improve on His merciful design. We have no obligation to follow but God's rules."

Counter-arguments to the hadiths *related to women's dress code in Islam*

To stress the necessity of the veil for women, the orthodox view puts forward an argument of authority, the saying of the Prophet that "All in a woman is *awra* (Private? Immodest? Pudenda?), except her hands and face." In retort, two responses are developed and advanced by reformist Islam. First, this saying is a unique (*ahadi*) *hadith*, mentioned only once by *hadith* collections; therefore, it cannot be retained as compulsive in matters of beliefs, as ordained by the rigorous method of *isnad*. In order for a *hadith* to be deemed authentic, it has to be ratified by the proper chain of testimonies, going up to the time of the Prophet and His Companions, and its veracity has to be supported by similar *hadiths*. Second, this *hadith* was not included in the authoritative collections of *hadiths* of al Bukhari, Abu Muslim, and Ibn Hanbal (Baraka 2002: 55). Third, this *hadith* was attributed to Aicha, wife of the Prophet, by a reporter who was not a contemporary of hers, a condition which weakens its legitimacy. As a general rule in the *ilm al hadith* (science of *hadiths*), a saying of the Prophet which is unique, is relegated to matters of *akhlak* (good behavior). This is unlike the *mutawatera* (unbroken chain of reporters' testimonies) *hadiths*, or the *mashhoura* (renowned) ones, which deal with matters of belief. Fourth, this *hadith* is contradicted by two other variations, attributed to the Prophet, in which not only the face and hands are permissible but also half of the arm. To underline another contradiction, a fourth hadith states that "the prayers of a girl reaching puberty" (*al haed*) are not accepted without a *khimar* (covering). Does it not imply that out of prayers, women are not required to cover themselves (Al Ashmawi 2002: 116–117)?

Reflecting on these data, one wonders why this unique *hadith* came to the forefront of the Muslim orthodox discourse to the detriment of many injunctions of the Qur'an, calling for the empowerment of women. From another point of view, it is said that the Companions of the Prophet abstained from collecting his sayings, under his urging or for fear that they would distract the believers from the Qur'an. This can also be explained by the general understanding of his contemporaries that some of his prescriptions were transient (Shahrour 1997: 552).

What remains certain is, "that the Prophet's *Sunna* should not overstretch the meaning of the Qur'an, nor add, nor contradict its words, and only what concords with its words and spirit should be retained" (Okla 2007). With that, Gamal El Banna totally agrees. As for Shahrour, he calls for the revision of the meanings of the *hadiths* in the light of the Qur'an, in contrast with the traditional methodology, which used the *hadiths* to understand and interpret the Qur'an (Shahrour 1997: 554).

The historical and cultural foundations of the veil

Did Islam impose the veil or is it the veil which imposed itself on Islam? When looking at the ancient civilizations of the Middle East with which the Arabs interacted during and after their conquest of the Sassanid (Persian) empire and parts of the Byzantine Empire, one discovers that the custom of the veil was already embedded in the mores of the times. For socio-economic and religious reasons—agricultural and urban institutions, market economy, spread of monotheism, establishment of the family-oriented model—patriarchy had asserted itself as the dominant feature of social organization. Naturally, this dominance had negative and far-reaching effects on women's roles and status. In this context, the veil—literal or symbolic—appears in its various manifestations throughout times, as the convenient device by which male authority consolidated its grip. In the ancient Egyptian culture, hair was considered a sign of strength and power (see the allusion in the biblical story of Samson and Delilah). Therefore, the priests shaved their heads as a sign of their submission to their gods. The custom spread to the lay people: men and women adorned themselves with wigs (Baraka 2002: 32).

The Jews, remembering their stay in Egypt, took the custom with them in the Exodus. Up to now, men cover their heads in the synagogue in deference to God and orthodox married women shave their heads and wear a wig, in deference to God and ... men. Presumably, it is the Assyrians in Mesopotamia who are first credited to have covered their women with veils, as to distinguish free respectable women from slaves or prostitutes (Ahmed 1992: 14–15).

During the Babylonian captivity, the Jews adopted many of the Mesopotamian customs, among which the subordination of women to an oppressive patriarchy. As for the Greeks who glorified the human being—in its male dimension!—they also segregated their women, confining them to their homes and excluding them with the slaves from the privileges of democracy. At the same time, the Persians reduced women even more, by creating the architecturally devised harem in which they secluded behind walls free women, as well as captives and slaves. When Alexander conquered Persia, he seemed to have enthusiastically embraced the practice and he made it a point that his freshly acquired harem of 365 concubines would scrupulously reproduce Darius's in the number of females and eunuchs held (Ahmed 1992: 17)!

Continuing in the same patriarchal vein, the Roman *pater familias,* had the power of life and death on his women and children. In the Byzantine Empire, although Christianity had highlighted the spiritual dimension of the human experience, the misogynist bias of the Church dictated the debasement of women, disparaged as impure, depraved, and deceitful. On the social level, the veil marked the divide between aristocratic women and the masses, becoming a symbol of distinction, wealth, and class status. In fact, "[v]eiling and the confinement of women [was widespread] throughout the region, and became the ordinary social practice, as did the attitudes to women and to the human body (such as a sense of shamefulness of the body and sexuality) that accompanied such practices" (Ahmed 1992: 17).

In the sixth century, on the eve of Islam, Arabia was a world apart, polytheistic, nomadic, and primitive (as opposed to the surrounding high civilizations). Bedouin tribalism was the ideology sustaining its loose institutions and in this harsh desert environment, the "patrilineal, patriarchal marriage had not yet been instituted as the sole legitimate form of marriage" (Ahmed 1992: 17).

However, at the rise of Islam, it was gaining favor, especially in commercialized Mecca, where individual fortunes, and the need to pass them to legitimate children, were eroding the tribal ethos of communal property. Still, it was competing with a variety of marriage customs about the time of the rise of Islam, reminiscent of matriarchy, by which "women were enjoying great sexual autonomy and were active participants, even leaders, in a wide range of community activities, including warfare and religion" (Ahmed 1992: 41–42). They were not veiled in the Islamic sense of the term, but like men wore headgear to protect themselves from the harsh climatic conditions of the desert.

Concerning marriage, Islam, in alignment with the other monotheistic religions and in accordance with the socio-cultural systems already established throughout the Middle East, put a ban on the coexisting loose sexual unions, which derived from residual matrilineal and matriarchal patterns of gender relations. It retains the patrilineal, patriarchal marriage as solely legitimate, thus unleashing the social transformation that will ensue. Regulation of family relations in their aspects of polygamy, divorce prerogative of the male, men's superiority to women, will be increasingly governed by a hierarchization within the family: men become the jealous guardians of women and the masters of their emotional and sexual lives.

However, on the other side, Islam will grant women rights that no other scriptures touched upon: rights in inheritance, economic autonomy, equal spiritual responsibilities and rewards, the honor of being *addressees* of the divine discourse in the Qur'an. This in agreement with the egalitarian concept of gender, inherent in the ethical vision of Islam, as epitomized in s*ura* 33:35:

> For Muslim men and women—
> For believing men and women…
> For devout men and women,
> For true [truthful] men and women,
> For men and women who are
> Patient and constant, for men
> And women who humble themselves,
> For men and women who give
> In charity, for men and women
> Who fast (and deny themselves),
> For men and women who
> Guard their chastity, and
> For men and women who
> Engage much in God's praise—
> For them has God prepared
> Forgiveness and a great reward.
>
> (Yusuf Ali's translation)

Therefore, "two distinct voices within Islam [have appeared], one expressed in the pragmatic regulations for society, the other in the articulation of an ethical vision which stresses the equality of all individuals" (Ahmed 1992: 66).

In a seminal study of the role of patriarchy during the life of the Prophet, Fatima Mernissi argues, proofs in hand, that the male entourage of the Prophet diverted, distorted, or hijacked the economic and social reforms favoring women: for instance, its pressure on the Prophet not to grant women the old right to participate in military expeditions and to share in the captured booty (Baraka 2002: 115).

In the same trend, it is reported that the Qur'anic injunction to the wives of the Prophet to be veiled and secluded, followed the outraged remarks of Umar Ibn Al Khatab, the close Companion of the Prophet and would-be second Wisely-Guided Caliph of Islam, as to the ongoing mingling between the wives and the visitors of the Prophet. Also, it is said that after the military reverse of the battle of Uhud, some "hypocrites" harassed Muslim women, who had gone out at night to relieve themselves, and who later complained to the Prophet. When the men were reprimanded, they justified their action by pretending that they could not in the dark make the difference between a free woman and a slave. It is also said that Umar, coming upon a "veiled" slave, hit her harshly because by donning a veil, she was acting like a free woman![18]

However, as a whole, veiling was not the general rule at the time of the Prophet. It is not prescribed in the Qur'an—except for the Prophet's wives. The only verses dealing with women's clothing are the ones analyzed above, and they instruct women to guard their private parts and throw a covering upon their bosoms. The deterioration of the status of women, their marginalization, the muzzling of their voices followed a gradual but determined course, exacerbating the male-oriented tendencies of Islamic practices which reached their full realization in the Abbassid period.

One can venture that it all started with the Arab conquests which carried Islam to lands fundamentally different from Arabia, to urbanized societies with already established scriptural and legal traditions, and which were much more restrictive towards women than the Arabian surrounding. Islam interacted with the mores of these conquered lands, adopting what was consonant with the male centered perspective, and burying what had survived of *jahiliyah* (time of ignorance as referring to pre-Islamic times in Arabia) women's free will. With the integration of variegated ethnicities and religious communities within Dar El Islam, and the subtle intrusion of regional local customs and perspectives within Islamic beliefs, enormous social changes occurred, encompassing all aspects of life, and affecting relationships between men and women.

Also, the Arab conquests brought in fabulous wealth and an unimaginable amount of slaves, the majority of them women and children. This had far-reaching consequences for the moral fabric of Islam and the situation of women during the late Ummayad and Abbassid periods. In imitation of the Persians—that they had conquered, but who in return exercised a tremendous influence on the shaping of tastes, customs, and manners of conduct later on—the Arab elite installed their own harems, made mostly of concubines acquired as booty or purchased in the thriving slave markets of the big cities. As a consequence, the fateful "trio of polygamy, concubinage and seclusion of women" took the power of institution, eradicating any active role that women played at the rise of Islam or in the transitional period which followed (Ahmed 1992:79). It was over, the free mingling of women and men in the councils of the Prophet, their interventions and contributions in the decision-making of the *umma*, their participation in warfare (like in the battle of Qadyssia in which Hind Bint Otba and her daughter took part as cheerleaders and nurses, or in the Battle of the Camel where Aicha, the beloved wife of the Prophet led the military operations against Ali's army) and religious matters (as attested by the authoritative verbal reports of Aicha, and the other wives of the Prophet, in the *hadiths*). The institutionalization of the harem affected the freeborn Arab, if not more than it did her captive or slave-born sister. She was no more able to negotiate the terms of her marriage or divorce and she had to forgo rights given to her by Islam, in face of the fierce competition of the slave—prettier, younger, and more expendable. Through a seemingly unobtrusive process of crossbreeding, the notions of "woman," "slave," and "sexual object" became interchangeable, thus precipitating the degradation of the idea of woman in the ideology of the time. Invisibility and muted voices became the sad lot of the Muslim woman.

But, the third most devastating impact on the status of women was the Islamic law, which took shape and developed over three centuries, until its final formulation in four Sunni legal schools of interpretation, by the tenth century. "The body of law and legal thought embodied in those four schools was recognized as absolutely authoritative, in part by the application of a juridical principle that had gained general acceptance, *ijma,* or consensus, according to which the unanimous agreement of qualified jurists, on a given point had a binding and absolute authority. Once reached, such an agreement was deemed infallible. To contradict it became heresy" (Ahmed 1992: 90).

However, looking at the Qur'an, which is the primary source of the law, one cannot help but note that it consists more of ethical precepts, and broad recommendations "rather than legalistic formulations." In order to create the legal body by which the community functions, the classical scholars of the late Ummayad and Abbassid period brought in their own understanding of the Qur'anic text and exerted a personal reasoning when they faced its rich complexity and ambiguity. To distinguish it from the scholarly *ijma,* a mental process of selectiveness and omission, of emphasis and occultation dictated by the expectations, biases, and the mindset of their society occurred unconsciously which gathered as a "social" consensus. Women had been subjected to a gradual but systematic degradation during the Ummayad and Abbassid period, and when the laws reached their final codification in the tenth century, their inferior position was once and for all ratified. The veil was nothing but its symbol. The male-centered perspective permeating the laws had "veiled" Islam's emphasis on equality and the equal justice to which women were entitled. Moreover, by declaring that "the gates of interpretation are closed," that all had been said and decreed by the Abbassid *ulamas* in terms of Islamic legislation; that the code of law that they developed and elaborated is the way (Shari'a) of God, eternal, immutable, and infallible, the Islamic religious and political elite consecrated the ideology of a time and place, and inscribed in stone the notion of women's inferiority and dependence.

Conclusion

In this chapter, I attempted to track down the components of the discourse of the veil in its religious and cultural foundations, the reasons for its resurgence and success nowadays; and also to raise the veil put on the dissenting modernist interpretation as to its obligation. Considering the religious discourse, it appears that nothing in the Qur'an recommends the covering of the head or the seclusion of women—with the exception of the Prophet's wives. On the other hand, the *hadith,* which is brandished as the cementing proof of the veil's necessity in the Muslim woman's attire, is considered of doubtful credibility following the rigorous classical method of *isnad.* On the cultural level, the veil—or its more extensive significance in women's exclusion and seclusion—seemed to have been a social fixture of the ancient civilizations preceding and contemporary to Islam. Inspired by a sense of class or religious consideration, it was a mark of distinction and exclusivity, which degenerated into exclusion. The prevailing social model of patriarchy of the times, by supporting it, had reasserted its rights. In Arabia, at the rise of Islam, the male elite, already in the ascent to the detriment of women's autonomy, counteracted the Qur'anic reforms favorable to women, by various devices of control. The conditions of the Arab conquests, putting Islam in contact and interaction with different customs and more sophisticated institutions, submerged the essential Islamic ethical precepts of egalitarianism and social justice. On the other hand, the influx of slaves on the market and the subsequent institution of the harems emphasized the deterioration of women's status. More dramatic, the interpretation of the Law confirmed the male supremacy, by a skewed definition of *ijmaa*. The veil became the eponym of women's invisibility and dehumanization.

As for the present, the case is more complex. Looking at it closely, most of the questions, which are raised in the introduction, could all be answered by a *yes* or a *no*—more or less qualified depending on the ideological position of the responder. An array of circumstances and politico-social motivations in Egypt underscore the discourse of the veil: the disastrous effects of the 1967 war; the release of the Muslim Brotherhood from Nasser's jails and their calculated empowerment by Sadat; the appearance and militancy of the *Jamaat Islamiyah*, inflamed by radical writings; the program of Islamization of the society, targeting the young and the women; the invasion of media space by religious programs; the import of customs, attitudes, and religious rites from *wahabi* Saudi Arabia; the financing of religious organs of propaganda; the failure of the Egyptian state to address urgent social and economic problems; the silencing of alternative political discourses which threaten the monopoly of the state; the division of powers between the political regime and the religious establishment. As for women who in fact are the concerned party in the discourse of the veil, there are also many motivations for their adoption of the *hijab*. Belief that they are submitting to the call of their religion, word of mouth knowledge of their Scriptures, reliance on popularized interpretations of the Qur'an and the *sunna*, a general upsurge of religiosity in the society in response to disillusionment, clinging to the outer forms of the religion, emphasis on the imitation of the popularized *sunna*, peer pressure, patriarchal control, upholding of obedience and "moral" regimentation, financial considerations, projection of an image of respectability, and also the desire to get married. All these reasons, taken separately or as a whole, support the wearing of the *hijab*.

The trend will follow its natural course of rise, culmination, and decline. But maybe there are ways to hasten the process: not the calculating and self-serving agenda of the Bush administration "war on terror" and "democratization" of the Muslim world. This "democratization" which is perceived by the beleaguered Muslims of today as a new colonialism, hypocritical calculations, and pontificating self-righteousness—if not a new crusading onslaught—would entrench more the Muslim world in religious self-defense, thus fueling the poisonous "Clash of Civilizations." Yes! I believe, as a concerned Egyptian Muslim, that we need plenty of reforms, but they have to come from within us, from our rich, polyvocal Islamic heritage, rekindled by the modernist and liberal trends of Muslim scholarship (Murphy 2002: 189–232) and now diffused by informal means of communication (e-mail, blogs, independent press and Internet). We should reactivate the pursuit of knowledge and thinking, this forgotten principle of Islamic philosophy which following Professor Hassan Hanafi, is the nucleus of the Muslim Declaration of Faith (Murphy 2002: 190). We should not accept indiscriminately what the preachers of today dictate (*"You shall not accept any information, unless you verify it for yourself. I have given you the hearing, the eyesight, and the brain, and you are responsible for using them,"* Qur'an, 17:36); and more to the point for the veil, we should work for women's voices to be heard in an honest and reasoned re-evaluation of the founding discourses subjugating them.

To reopen the gates of interpretation is to imitate the Prophet's *ijtihad,* who as the first active interpreter of the Word of Allah, built the "ideal" community of believers, within the understanding of his time. It does not deflate his special place in our heart and reverence as Muslims to scrutinize and reappraise his sayings and actions in the light of our times. Also, we should respect the reasoning effort of the famous doctors of the shari'a, less for bequeathing us their edifice of laws, than for their example of scholarship and dedication. And lastly, we should consciously revise the whole principle of "consensus" to reflect the reality of modern times, a new inclusive *ijmaa* of just and learned believers, excluding the archaic remnants of patriarchy, and rejecting its different forms of totalitarianism. We would then revive the profound ethos of egalitarianism and social justice of Islam, and uphold the eternal Word of God—the Holy Qur'an, guidance for men and women, for all space and time.

Notes

1 Here *hijab* is taken in its present meaning of "cultural symbol" as expressed in the head cover of Muslim women. For the other meanings of *hijab,* beyond the woman's attire, see "hidjab" (Encyclopaedia of Islam 1993: 359–361).

2 As an example, see the controversy surrounding the *hijab* in Canada (Shakeri 2000: 129–143).

3 These questions recall most of the reasons given to Yvonne Haddad by respondents in "Egypt, Jordan, Oman, Kuwait, and the United States for wearing the veil" organized in categories (Zuhur 1992: 104).

4 Following the Indian Muslim Abu al-A'la al-Mawdudi, whose writings have been of a great inspiration to conservatives and fundamentalists all over the world, "the Qur'anic injunctions of sura 33:33 and 53, even though addressed to the Prophet's wives, were and are binding on all Muslim females" (Stowasser 1994: 127).

5 Thus, asserts Al Mawdudi, "[t]hough the veil has not been specified in the Qur'an, it is Qur'anic in spirit" (Stowasser 1994: 128).

6 "At present we know very little about the precise stages of the process by which the hijab in its multiple meanings was made obligatory for Muslim women at large, except to say that these occurred during the first centuries after the expansion of Islam beyond the borders of Arabia.... Classical legal compendia, medieval hadith collections and Qur'anic exegesis are here mainly formulations of the system 'as established' and not of its developmental stages" (Stowasser 1994: 93).

7 See the two stories about the shedding of the veil in *A Short History of Modern Egypt* (al-Sayyid Marsot 1990: 93–94).

8 To their credit, the Muslim Brotherhood did not bar women from education, but deemed it second to women's primordial mission, as mothers and wives (Ahmed 1992: 160 and Stowasser 1994: 127).

9 Some 1,300,000 girls were admitted in primary schools in 1966, showing the stand that the Nasser regime took concerning increased opportunity for women to compete in the public sphere (Ibrahim 1987: 124).

10 This was the joke that the Cairenes invented to characterize Sadat's style of ruling (reported by al-Sayyid Marsot 1990: 132).

11 Reporting on the most popular preacher of the 1980s, Stowasser notes that "in al-Sha'rawi primer for the Islamic woman, the material on the veil is more voluminous than that on any other topic." Thus for the Sheikh, wearing the veil equals belief in God and piousness (Stowasser 1987: 270).

12 Fear-mongering is not far from Sheikh Shahrawi's sermons when he urges all women, young and old to stick to the veil. "The veil is God's gift to the woman in that it ensures for her respect and veneration in her old age, neither of which she will enjoy if she fails to wear it when young. Her worldly punishment will be even worse than that, in actual fact, as in her old age a young woman will appear and entice her husband and her son away from her" (reported by Stowasser 1987: 274).

13 Zuhur judiciously notes the conflation between *hijab* and religiousness, where "the *hijab* is felt to be a sign of religious identity and sincere belief by veiled women and by 40 per cent of unveiled women." Thus to the question, "Do you consider yourself a religious person, and why?" less than thirty responded with the following: "Since I veil, I am religious" or "Because I don't veil yet I am not religious enough" (Zuhur 1992: 74).

14 Nowadays, the most famous of them, Amr Khaled, who had been exiled by the government in 2002 for a few years, still reaches out through uncontrollable satellite channels.

15 Zuhur disagrees with Haddad's economic reason for veiling—"sign of affluence, of being a lady of leisure" that she finds problematic when it comes to the Egyptian samples of veiled and unveiled women she studied in her book (Zuhur 1992: 104). However, this economic category appears valid when it applies to the returning expatriate women from the rich Arab countries, whose exhibiting signs are veil plus money, easily perceived as interchangeable.

16 Especially Fatima Mernissi's approach in *The Veil and the Male Elite* (1991), as well as in her previous book *Beyond the Veil* (1975). In the chapter "Modern Muslim Interpretations," Stowasser's comments on Mernissi's methodology as follows: "At Mernissi's hands, the Qur'anic verses are related so closely to the historical events surrounding their revelation that a [causal] relationship between the two would logically follow; the *asbab al-nuzul*, [occasions of revelation] have (tacitly) become [occasions for revelation] and the verses themselves a record of early *umma* history, while the question of their enduring relevance is (also tacitly) omitted" (Stowasser 1994: 134). However, Mernissi's feminist observations remain among the most insightful and valid modernist commentaries.

17 For this part, I relied first on Okla's online article, accessed on December 4, 2001 on women's dress code in Islam. This article was condensed under his name with the titles "Three Rules for Dress Code in Islam for Women" and "Regulations in Dress Code" in 2007. The same article but without author's name is published online in www. submission.org, under the titles "Dress Code for Women according to the Qur'an" and "Women Dress Code in Islam," I referred also in my analysis to Shahrour 1997: 604–619. For the same purpose, I used the support of Gamal El Banna's interview in the newspaper *Al Masri al-Yom* of December 20, 2008. The *ayas* that I quote in all this part are from the Khalifa translation of the Qur'an that Okla uses. In fact there are six translations of the Qur'an that one can access for every *aya* and *sura* in the submission.org website. I found that the Khalifa translation

was the closest to the Arabic Qur'an. However, for 33:35, I quoted Yusuf Ali's translation, as it is the most poetic and striking.

18 In El Qortoby's interpretation (Baraka 2002: 48).

2 Women, Islam, and political agency in Morocco[1]

Fatima Sadiqi

One of the most important domains where Moroccan women's agency is attested is that of their strategic political use of Islamization in various phases of their country's modern history. This use is unique in at least two ways: not only is it linked to the success of multilingualism and multiculturalism in a country where only one religion dominates: Islam, but it also explains the paradoxical situation where a very high level of female illiteracy co-exists with a spectacular achievement of the Moroccan feminist movement: a very progressive Family Law.[2]

Moroccan women's engagement with Islamization in the last five decades resulted in interesting changes of Moroccan women's political consciousness and power negotiation. Three interrelated factors impacted these changes: (i) feminist political consciousness that came with post-independence urbanity and education, (ii) global synergy consciousness which stemmed from local feminist consciousness, and (iii) democratization consciousness and awareness of the intriguing role of religion in the political power game.

These three types of consciousness kept a strong, albeit "invisible," link not only between legal demands of literate feminists and illiterate women's aspirations, but also between feminists and the state rulers, more specifically monarchy.[3] Women, especially the illiterate ones, have also used orality to express religion and spirituality. As a result, women's issues and their marginalized mother-tongues (Berber and Moroccan Arabic) have gradually become state issues (a means to fight Islamists) while retaining their "feminist" edge allowing women to problematize the centuries-old Islamic practices on which the state itself is based. The clever use of "ethical," "cultural," and "symbolic" Islam by Moroccan feminists blocks the road for the radical Islamists, rallies illiterate women's aspirations to women's issues, and forces the state to satisfy women's legal demands, which also serve current state purposes.[4] Women's multi-faced and fluid involvement with Islamization and the transmission of their self, including their faith, through orality is a good example of political agency that turned out to be a central element in Morocco's postcolonial overall policy where ideologies of modernity, Islamism, democratization, feminism, and global synergy constitute an interesting blend.

Women's political use of Islam

Islam was introduced in Morocco during the Arab conquest of North Africa in the seventh century. The comprehensive[5] social order that Islam brought has never ceased to be appealing to the various royal dynasties that have ruled Morocco thereafter. Throughout the long history of Morocco in which both Arab and Berber kings took power, Islam has remained the official religion and written Arabic the official language of the country. This state of affairs was carried over after Morocco's independence from France in 1956.

As Islam was implemented in a profoundly traditional and patriarchal society, it was used to keep the status quo and build gender hierarchy in and outside home. Female feminist politicians, activists, and writers became aware of this political instrumentalization of Islam from the mid-1940s onward.[6] It is important to note that feminist consciousness has never been the prerogative of literate feminists only; alongside the rich feminist literature in French (Mernissi) and Arabic (Abouzeid, Bennouna) that characterized the 1960s and 1970s, an older, often anonymous, female oral literature continued to be transmitted from generation to generation in defiance of colonization and the supremacy of the written word (Curtin 1969; Ong 1982; Sadiqi, Nowaira, El Kholy, and Ennaji 2009). The women who used writing to express feminist ideas focused on the family law, and thus, had as part of a social movement, much more impact on decision-makers than the ones who used the oral medium.

The pioneer literate feminists may be termed "liberal" insofar as they chose to articulate their legal demands in terms of "liberalizing" society and did not concentrate on religious texts. They used literate languages and addressed issues of legal rights and modernity (Mernissi 1987; Daoud 1996). These women often belonged to upper urban classes and had enlightened male family members (Sadiqi 2003; Ennaji 2005). In spite of the fact that the 1960s and the 1970s were characterized by a strong leftist ideology that highlighted class struggle rather than religion, liberal feminists never targeted Islam as a religion; on the contrary, attacks on patriarchy were supported by Islam's ethical ideals where men and women enjoyed the same rights. Faced with modernity issues, liberal feminists sought to play down the narrow religious aspect, and vis-à-vis international feminisms, they sought in Islam a characterizing identity and a strategy of liberation that standard Western explanatory frameworks, often based on egalitarian and individualistic assumptions, do not include.

In their approach, liberal feminists were conscious of the use of Islam by patriarchy and the state's deliberate confusion between the religious and political discourses. They challenged the separation and opposition between the private and public spheres which constitute the pillar of patriarchal Islam and sought to politicize the private sphere. As Mernissi (1987) states:

One of the functions of theological discourse on women is to slide the debate on real economic, political, and social problems into religious debates. Thus, instead of debating the obstacles to rural girls' schooling, the causes of women's absence in the food industry, the theological discourse moves the debate into "Is such a law or measure authentic?" "Does such a law or measure conform to tradition ... or is it an innovation?" This movement of real problems towards problems relating to Fiqh or religious debate, during the rare meetings about women ..., may be considered one of the hemorrhages which have aborted the skilled potential of public administrators, political parties, associations, and intellectuals who have tried to reflect on women's condition in these societies.[7]

Liberal feminist scholars also realized that women played a central role in the discourse on Islamization and they, consequently, endeavored to react by using this very discourse. This manipulation of the Islamic discourse is in accordance with Islam's capacity to provide Muslims with powerful tools of social analysis (se Dale Eickleman and James Piscatori 1996). As such, Islamization for liberal feminists is a continuous rethinking process where their voices needed to be "well positioned" in order to be heard. These feminists knew that they had to continuously negotiate their position in the Moroccan Islamic discourse and "package" their demands with the right dose of "Islamic intensity."

The voice of the pioneer liberal feminists resonated very well with the then very popular leftist ideology of the political opposition. Pioneer political practitioners such as Nouzha Skalli, Rabea Naciri, and Amina Mrini easily espoused the ideas of the liberal feminist scholars and endeavored to support them. For these politicians, the state, very authoritarian in the 1960s and 1970s, constituted the anti-thesis of their demands, as cultural ideas were harnessed and often exaggerated in the service of political ideologies and practices. For example, women and their sexual purity were often linked to the honor of men and families, and this linkage was "legitimated" through connecting it with Islam. Such linkages were considered by liberal feminists as a way of controlling women's sexuality.

Women and the global context

From the end of the 1970s onward, a mixture of dramatic international events created a context for religious and gender identities to arise and develop in relation to one another. The success of the Iranian Revolution in 1979, the downfall of the Soviet Union in 1981, and the subsequent emergence of the United States as the sole superpower gave way to the emergence of political Islam and the return of conservatism everywhere. In parallel to these events, globalization helped polarize ideas and create token religious symbols and ideals for youth across the globe. Researchers in the field highlighted two things: (i) an increasing role of tradition and religion, as dynamic concepts, in the overall global context and (ii) a re-questioning of the modernity vs. tradition dichotomy. Generally speaking, and contrary to the prevailing theories of modernity and modernization of the mid-twentieth century, religion is said to play an increasingly important role in politics and public life (Casanova 1994; Eickleman and Piscatori 1996). This is very different from the 1950s to the 1970s where academic and social modernization approaches to the Third World attributed the Muslim world's lack of modernization to the pervasive influence of tradition and religion (Halpern 1963; Almond and Powell 1966). The latter theories were reinforced by the Marxist-Leninist views that religion would disappear with the socio-economic structures which fostered it in the first place.

In sum, the unfolding of events and facts from the end of the 1970s onward have shown that tradition and religion interact in deep but complex ways with economic progress and modernity (Hudson 1980; Bill and Leiden 1974; Binder 1986; Weiner and Huntington 1987; Higgot 1983; Wong 1988; So 1990; Eickleman and Pasha 1991; Findley 1992). Consequently, women have become more and more aware that religious beliefs and values play an increasing role not only in thinking about self, but also about society and politics at the local and world levels.

Coupled with Islamization, globalization started to make sense for the younger generations of Moroccan women. Just as the leftist ideology was the means by which the Moroccan youth of the 1960s and 1970s expressed their resistance to oppression within a political context marked by tyranny, religion became a means of expressing resistance to global hegemony and marginalization by today's youth.[8] But these transformations are not the result of globalization only; they are also part of the local post-independence transformations.

The post-independence mass education of boys and girls in urban areas enhanced political awareness among men and women and opened new venues of contestation. One of the 'new' tokens used in this respect was the wearing of the veil which facilitated the investment of the public sphere and the appropriation of religious discourse. The veil allowed women access to the increasingly hostile public space at a time when unemployment, social and political crises made this access difficult. In parallel to this, advancing levels of education, a greater permeability of political borders, and the rise of new communications media facilitated consciousness-raising campaigns through grassroots associations, thus broadening women's horizons. More and more women acquired public-speaking and leadership skills. Liberal feminists gradually came into direct contact with illiterate and rural women's needs and started to link legal rights with women's health and dignity, a linkage that greatly appealed to both the younger generation and the older illiterate women. Liberal feminists packaged their ideas in a moderate Islamic discourse and used Moroccan Arabic and sometimes Berber to pass on their messages and explain the importance of securing legal rights through education and awareness. This adroit use of "public Islam" (Eickleman and Piscatori 1996), whereby thinking about Islam is not limited to self-ascribed religious authorities, scored significant gains for the feminist movement in Morocco.

Gradually, more and more women started to participate in public debates over issues of the Family Law (*Mudawana*), as well as about their role in society. Ideas and practices that had long been taken for granted and understood as Islamic were confronted and challenged by these women. The new generation of "veiled feminists" (Sadiqi 2006) was conscious of the burden of patriarchy. Although the majority of them were affiliated to Islamic associations and/or Islamic political parties, they did not voice themselves as "anti-liberal feminists;" some of them even used liberal feminists as role-models. The relationship between these new veiled feminists and the liberal feminists has never been confrontational as the latter have never attacked Islam and have consistently been fighting Islamic patriarchy.

The emergence of veiled feminists from the 1980s onward may be explained within a broader theoretical framework where tradition and religion are not seen as fixed and "regressive" concepts that are fundamentally incompatible with economic development. Globalization has yet another impact on Moroccan society: the beginning of democratization.

Women, democratization, and political agency

From the mid-1990s onward, Morocco started to witness more political opening and more democratization: the first ever socialist government in 1998, a new and more open king in 1999, a quota system in the 2001 elections, 35 women in the Parliament in 2002, a new Family Law in 2003, and more women in the highest religious offices in 2004. The twin fact of the veil gradually losing its political edge (the veil has become multi-functional and fashion-based) and of the liberal feminists having never jeopardized Islam as a religion reconciled the views of liberal feminists and the new "veiled feminists" in Islamic associations and political parties. Many liberal feminists are veiled and many younger "religious" feminists espouse liberal views. Morocco is unique in the sense that one cannot really posit "Islamic" and "secular" feminisms as categories in complementary distribution. All Moroccan feminists, whether liberal or religious, confront patriarchy and do not put Islam as a religion into question. In the Parliament, women, Islamists and non-Islamists, veiled and non-veiled, managed to form a unified coalition front that sought the promotion of women's rights across party lines. The Family Law was followed by the Nationality Law which allowed women married to non-Muslims to pass on their nationality to their children.

Today's feminists, liberal or conservative, veiled or non-veiled, are genuinely interested in re-visiting the sacred texts with the aim of gaining more public power and voice. Feminist reinterpretation of the classic texts is a new development which constitutes a sweeping challenge to the central assumptions and presuppositions of academic political theory. Women are more and more conscious that they have been deliberately excluded from the sacred not because Islam prescribed so but because Islam was revealed in a heavily patriarchal society which deeply engraved a specific picture of women in the Muslim Unconscious.

Moroccan women started to "discover" and appreciate religious authority. Re-looking at sacred texts and reinterpreting them from a feminist point of view is certainly opening new venues to Moroccan feminist scholars. It is a means of addressing patriarchy from a "legitimate" perspective. This new trend is supported by both liberal and religious feminists. "Modern"-type women's magazines like *Femmes du Maroc* displayed the picture of the first cohort of *Murshidats* (religious guides) on their cover pages. They are aware that it takes a long time, much energy and dedication, but they felt the need to encourage whoever is ready to do it.

Women's entrance in the sacred texts' interpretation and spirituality has revealed that the way Islam has been implemented from the seventh century until now has consistently been geared to serving and consolidating patriarchy through imposing a strict space dichotomy where men relate to the public space and women to the private space (Ahmed 1992). Muslim political rulers have always sought the support of religious leaders to maintain the status quo for fifteen centuries.

It is true that the Age of Enlightenment in Europe, the reforms of Christianity and Judaism, as well as the Industrial Revolution brought about some fresh rethinking of Islam in the nineteenth century. The great reformers of this period, Jamal Eddine Al-Afghani, Rachid Redha, and Mohamed Abdu made genuine attempts to reform Islam and give more space to women in the Arab-Muslim world. However, the painful experience of colonization put a heavy brake on these attempts by pushing Muslims back into a search for identity by going back to orthodox Islam. These reforms are being revived by men and women in Morocco.

Illiterate women and cultural, religious, and communal agency

In spite of a disempowering environment, illiterate, often rural, women, like the literate ones, are not passive; they "fight back" by developing empowering strategies of oral communication through which they express their views of politics and religion. This type of agency is political in the sense that it directly impacts the communities which nourished them.

Illiterate Moroccan women use Berber and/or Moroccan Arabic as a means of religious expression. Their strategies of communication belong to oral genres that constitute part and parcel of Moroccan deep culture. The historicity and dynamism of these genres have guaranteed their survival over centuries. In spite of the fact that Morocco's history has been constructed by men and women, female oral genres have been muted in Morocco's recorded history. Oral female genres are "unofficial" voices that "circulate" as "anonymous" literature in the community without being officially recognized. As such, these voices have been powerful in constructing mentalities but they have never gained social authority. The absence of female oral literature in Moroccan official culture is mainly due to a rigid patriarchal system regulating gender behavior whereby women are excluded from public authority. Paradoxically, the anonymous aspect of oral female literature freed women's self-expression from social constraints and gave it space.

Moroccan women's association with oral languages and literature is related to their strong association with Morocco's overall culture as orality is part and parcel of this culture. Moroccan women's exclusion from social authority legitimizes their central role in the preservation and transmission of private oral languages and the cultural aspects they vehicle. Illiterate women in Morocco use two mediums of orality: traditional skills and oral literature genres. It is through these two mediums that these women mark their presence in the community and it is also through them that they sometimes subvert the roles that patriarchy assigns them. Women's agency in oral literature is often perceived as a "threat" to the male status quo and established order.

It is worth noting that although Islam is scriptural, writing has never been abundant in Morocco. As political and social power has been constructed mainly on the basis of written culture, the Qur'anic scripture has been jealously guarded by those who administered political and social power and orality became reduced to "listening" and "obeying." Consequently, reading and writing became the exclusive prerogative of the ruling elites and listening and obeying the function of the masses, especially women. Women's orality has systematically been relegated to the footnotes of official history as the long silences and gaps in the official history attest.[9] A mixture of misogyny and sexism has been the main cause. However because of these cultural dogmas, orality became a powerful subversive tool in the hands of women: oral literature (folktales, proverbs, riddles, etc.) and oral transmission became loci of able agency. Women in Morocco are so rooted in orality that their true history can be rewritten only from oral sources. Although women's writing traditions have always existed, most of these women today, as in the past, are primarily oral peoples.

The oldest exclusively women's oral texts in Morocco go back to the beginning of the nineteenth century and were named *La'rubiyat* (a metathesis of Al-Ruba'iyat: the classic Arabic Bedouin poetic genre) (Sadiqi et al. 2009). *La'rubiyat* is an exclusively female poetic genre which originated in Fes, Morocco, and was sung and performed until the mid-twentieth century to express women's views of religion as a means of family cohesion.

In spite of its pervasive use, orality was not acknowledged as a worthwhile means of self-expression until very recently with the spread of democracy and human and cultural rights. Indeed, at no point in history have Moroccan scholars come to grips with the truth that orality is the mirror of women's history until modern times where the emerging vibrant literature, female cinema industry, and other media tools are making the best of orality to retrace and relocate women's history in Morocco. Making the journey back in time could not be done without evoking the history of the Berber language and culture. Berbers are the indigenous peoples of Morocco and the entire North Africa west of the Nile Valley. Their history is millennial, pre-dating Islam, Christianity, and Judaism. Berbers are not confined to a geographically continuous region; they are discontinuously distributed from the Siwa Oasis in Egypt to the south of Morocco, and from the Mediterranean to the Niger River. Berbers speak various dialects that form the Berber language, a branch of the Afro-Asiatic language family. The majority of Berber speakers live in Morocco and Algeria. Many Berbers call themselves some variant of the word *Imazighen* (singular *Amazigh*), meaning "free men." The spectacular survival of Berber, a multi-millennial oral language that has never served as the official language of a central power even during the reigns of the strong Berber dynasties that conquered Spain, is largely due to women (Chafik 1982; Sadiqi 1997; Ennaji 2005).

The Berber aspect of Moroccan women is also associated with political leadership which at times constituted a natural mix in North African women's orality. Such female leadership relies more on recognized personal power than on institutionalized authority. Female boldness has often been required to defend personal freedom and self-determination. The most courageous women in Moroccan history challenged oppression. For example, Kahina, whose name means "priestess" or "prophetess," was a notorious Berber queen, army leader, and outstanding warrior who was born in the Aures Mountains in Algeria some time during the 600s CE (Ibn Khaldun 1967). During her lifetime, Arab generals began to lead armies into North Africa, preparing to conquer the area and introduce Islam to the local peoples. Kahina directed the most determined resistance to the seventh-century Arab invasions of North Africa. In about 690, Kahina assumed personal command of the African forces and under her aggressive leadership, the Arabs were briefly forced to retreat. The Berbers of the seventh century were not religiously homogenous. Christian, Jewish, and Pagan Berbers were spread through the region that is now Morocco, Tunisia, Algeria, and Libya. Kahina emerged as a war-leader who could rally everybody during this tense period, and proved amazingly successful at leading the tribes to join together against their invaders. Her reputation as a strategist and sorceress spread and she managed to briefly unite the tribes of Ifrikya, the Berber name for North Africa, ruling them and leading them in battle for five years before her final defeat. Kahina took her own life, and sent her three sons to the Arab camp with instructions that they adopt Islam and make common cause with the Arabs. Ultimately, Kahina's sons participated in invading Europe and the subjugating of Spain and Portugal. Although it is hard for many people today to conceive of such broad female authority, women in the time of the Prophet had the formal power to veto the decision to go to war and Kahina was a warrior who fought to defend her people and their country.

Orality came to play a significant role in Morocco's struggle for independence. Work on the evaluation of the theoretical assertions about the constructed nature of the nation-state in the concrete historical context of Morocco is still lacking. Women's oral texts in this regard bring new analytical methods from social movement theory to the study of colonialism, anticolonial protest, and nation-building, which clarifies the process by which history, culture, religion, and oral tradition were integrated in the construction of modern Moroccan national identity. This method contextualizes the Moroccan case vis-à-vis concurrent anticolonial struggles in other parts of Africa. It also analyzes the roles played by subaltern groups (Berbers, Jews, and women) at the inception of an Arab-Islamic nationalist discourse that subsequently contributed to a political order marginalizing them. Women's oral sources in this respect are primary sources. The colonizers themselves were aware of the importance of such texts as the collections of Berber poetry gathered by Arséne Roux and his collaborators during the 1930s and 1940s show.

For example, the French historian François Reyniers said of Tawgrat Walt Aissa N'Ait Sokhman, a Berber illiterate professional poet who lived at the end of the nineteenth and beginning of the twentieth century, that "she was neither a prophet nor a witch, but she had an imagination that astonished people with its extraordinary power." The French colonizers noticed that women's oral poetry, said in Berber and Moroccan Arabic, carried communal strength and was sometimes used to encourage fighters to stand in the face of the colonizers. This poetry was cherished by people and recited in the whole of the Middle Atlas. Such poetry is crucial for highlighting the Middle Atlas armed resistance. In recent decades, orality has served as an instrument of language loyalty, which has developed into militancy for language and cultural rights.

Oral literature is strong and alive in Morocco. Oral storytellers are seen in the market places and cafes, as well as in homes; the Qur'an is learned by rote, the call to prayer is publicly announced five times a day; and centuries-old poetry is still recited among literate and illiterate people. Oral literature is seen as the most authentic and un-Westernized type of literature in Morocco although, up to recent times, written literature was considered the only prestigious "literary" form. In the present times, oral literature is receiving more and more attention within the trend of the new historicism, which is closely linked to realism and supported by psychological and sociological accounts of everyday facts. Oral literature, such as oral histories and folktales, covers a broad range of social writings (Ong 1982; Kapchan 1996). A growing number of Moroccan intellectuals are reclaiming this literature as a typically Moroccan medium of expression. Moroccan Arabic and Berber are more and more used in public spaces such as the media and TV. The place of Berber in Moroccan oral literature is central given the historicity of this language. Efforts are being made at the highest official level to preserve the Berber oral literature.

The symbolic formations and the systems of representations that are transmitted by oral literature are so revealing that they may be qualified as a new subversive genre (Sadiqi et al. 2009). Oral literature is full of the mysteries that are dismissed by Western modernism: demons and other supernatural agents intervening in the lives of humans, ecstatic dreams, miracle cures, and superstition. Oral literature is continually presented, represented, and exhibited in a recursive way as the images and symbols constituting the core system of Moroccan cultural themes tend to recur in an infinite number of distinct and original expressions, exhibitions, and texts. The representations in oral literature are often combinations of these cultural themes.

Oral literature is generally associated with Moroccan women. Moroccan society assigns the role of guarding oral literature to women and expects them to carry out this role in the process of raising their children by keeping and transmitting the traditions that characterize Moroccan culture and by maintaining and symbolizing these traditions. Moroccan women are conscious of the significance of this role and they use oral literature to express their inner selves (Sadiqi 2003).

Oral literature falls outside the "official" literature of Morocco and is both more complex and less accessible than it. This literature is in most cases produced by poor illiterate men and women who do not have an official voice. It is marginalized because it does not meet the traditional needs of the Moroccan society, among which is using the written medium. From a feminist point of view, women's oral literature highlights the tension between the written and the oral discourses in Morocco and makes ordinary "trivial" texts problematize canonical texts by claiming that just as women have a specific way of writing (in Cixous's sense), they have a specific way of "speaking" and "telling" (Kapchan 1996). This female way of speaking displaces the laws of both gender and genre.

In addition to illiterate professional women poets, ordinary women improvise poetry to decry the effects of colonization. Women's orality as a weapon against colonialism is revisited in present-day oral testimonies which corroborate the angry feeling of the poems. Oral testimonies are equally common oral genres used by women, especially the illiterate.

Women also use orality to invest the powerful field of spirituality and religious authority. Beverly Mack (2004) argues that even those Muslim women who acquire knowledge through the written word often tend to favor oral means of imparting and (re)constructing knowledge. This is certainly true in the case of some Moroccan women who managed to become central for the functioning *zawiyas* (religious brotherhoods) and mosques (Elboudrari 1993; Rausch 2006). A residue of a rich repertoire of women's Sufi didactic poetry is a type of oral texts that women still sing in the south of Morocco. Women's religious and spiritual power elevated them to the status of venerated saints across Morocco, female saints invoke "*baraka*" (a mixture of religious charisma and noble descent) which makes women detain and exercise social authority. In parallel to spiritual agency through orality, women's oral blessings, profanity, curses, insults, etc. are consequential in everyday Moroccan life.

One of the bastions of women's orality is the family. Women in Morocco have always been associated with the family. All of women's family functions have been significant for the family structure; from wives, sisters, female in-laws, to mothers, they are the ones who have been shaping and transforming the deep cultural views and values on the family. The most culturally significant family events, namely, marriage, birth, circumcision, and death, are historically celebrated, transformed, and transmitted by women's songs and rites. Further, the first teachings of Islam are often done by mothers to their children.

Storytelling is another family-related women's oral practice. Possessing the skill of storytelling is an old woman's way of ensuring status within the family and transmitting specific values. The art and technique of storytelling shows older women's dexterity in ensuring dependence and stretching imagination. (For example, old women's folktales ensure their authority over children whose curiosity they keep alive by stopping their storytelling at moments of suspense and resuming the stories the following night.) Storytelling is also a communal participatory experience: women participate in formal and informal storytelling as interactive oral performers—such participation is an essential part of traditional communal life, and basic training in a particular culture's oral arts and skills is an essential part of children's traditional indigenous education on their way to initiation into full humanness.

Women's orality also records powerful stories of family strength and survival. It also records issues of the self and continuity. Lullabies, for example, are an oral genre that has always been associated with rural and urban women across the whole of Morocco. The strong maternal emotions women's orality conveys is proof of its intrinsic relation to women's inner self.

Conclusion

This chapter highlighted the complex nature of the historical and contemporary links between Moroccan women, Islam, and political and cultural agency. These links constitute a source of a constant rethinking process aiming at empowering women in both the private and the public spheres of power. The association of both liberal and religious feminisms with Islamization attests to the power, dynamism, and pervasiveness of tradition (of which Islam and monarchy are part and parcel) in the perception of Islam in Moroccan society. It is this tradition that provides the cultural roots of Moroccan feminism.

Moroccan women's political agency will certainly gain from a return to the cultural roots of Moroccan feminism which reside in the rich oral culture that women have been preserving over centuries and which is re-emerging as an empowering symbol of women's agency. Only future research can uncover this aspect of Moroccan women's agency.

Notes

1 An earlier version of the first part of this chapter was published in *Signs*, 2006. I wish to thank two anonymous readers of this chapter for helpful comments and judicious suggestions. I would also like to thank Elizabeth Matthews for her help in preparing this chapter.

2 Four major languages are used in Morocco: written Arabic, French, Berber, and a spoken Arabic. While the first two are non-mother-tongue written languages that are learnt at school, the latter two are mother-tongues that are culturally conceived as oral languages in spite of the fact that Berber is now taught in some schools.

3 The Moroccan monarchy has solid roots in the socio-cultural make-up of the country; its inception is inextricable from that of Islam in Morocco in the seventh century. The Moroccan monarchy is not only the oldest ruling one in the world, but also the only one in the Arab-Islamic world which has not been removed by colonization. One of the main characteristics of monarchy is its commitment to maintaining a synergy between tradition and modernity, hence its present-day support of women's issues.

4 Radical Islamists constitute danger not only for Moroccan feminists but also for the monarchy.

5 "Comprehensive" means all-encompassing issues that people are concerned about in their life and after their death.
6 The first Moroccan feminist association was created in 1946 under the name of Akhawat Al- Safaa. This association demanded political and legal rights for women. Their *Wathiqa* (The Document) which was issued at the inauguration ceremony is considered the oldest political demand by women.
7 This quote has been translated from French into English by the author.
8 In Morocco, global hegemony is often associated with the U.S. invasion of Iraq and the Israeli occupation of Palestine.
9 See Sadiqi et at. (2009).

3 Assia Djebar and Malika Mokeddem

Neocolonial agents or postcolonial subjects?

Abdelkader Cheref

Introduction

The latest re-examination of Frantz Fanon's work maintains that his ideas are as important nowadays as they were when written. Echoing Fanon, Abdi argues, "today's struggle is not to resurrect the past, but to change the unbearable present and the potentially bewildering future" (1999: 53). Also, to address one of Spivak's queries, "how far should literature be read as sociological evidence?" (2003: 17). I will argue in this chapter that Algerian postcolonial literature deals largely with such issues as representation and heavy-handed nationalism. Under these two headings, literature is generally regarded as a means for social investigation. Moreover, as I show in this chapter, both Assia Djebar and, to a certain extent, Malika Mokeddem explore the status and roles assigned to women. Their respective works examine political issues, especially with regard to women's resistance and representation.

Typically politicized voices, Djebar and Mokeddem systematically engage in the ways in which cultural practices engender inequalities for women in Algeria. For these two women writers – each according to her artistic and political sensibility, are aware that 'decolonization' is not only an individual development in a communal context, but a collective experience as well (Wisker 2000: 80). It is through this perspective that I focus on Assia Djebar's *Vaste est la prison* (1995)[1] and Malika Mokeddem's *Les hommes qui marchent* (1997).[2] My argument is that in these two works, to apply Miriam Cooke's insight, "one can most clearly see the individual creating alternative realities. ... These reflections on personal experience and forays into fiction may provide the blueprint for the future" (Cooke 2001: x). Yet, alternative reality may be separate or irrelevant, as I will show in Mokeddem's work.

The choice of Djebar and Mokeddem can be partly explained by the fact that these two writers are controversial literary figures in Algeria. Besides, their respective works reflect/refract a postcolonial changing society. Unlike the works of some male contemporary writers (Rachid Boudjedra[3] and Wassini Laredj[4]) whose *raison d'être* is to put on show their erratic fantasies, or other women writers (Leila Aslaoui[5] and Latifa Benmansour[6]) who write against their sex and seem to marvel at the socio-political status quo, Djebar and Mokeddem draw attention to the ordeal of Algerian society. Every writer makes use of a different aesthetic and political lens to explore this Algerian reality.

Distinct lives, but not so similar concerns

It was in the midst of the Algerian war of independence that Fathma-Zohra Imalayan (nom de plume Assia Djebar b.1936) launched her literary career with the publication of *La Soif* (1957). Her work has positioned her alongside Sara Suleri (*Meatless Days*, 1989) as a lucid critic of gender, history, and subjectivity in colonial and postcolonial contexts.

To begin with, it is worth noting that Djebar concentrates her efforts on producing texts that bear witness to Algeria's long and rich history of linguistic, religious, cultural, and political diversity, and to the absurdity of attempting to wipe it out, either in the name of Nationalism, Pan-Arabism, or Islam. Literary works such as *L'amour, la fantasia* (*Fantasia, an Algerian cavalcade*, 1985), *Ombre sultane* (*A Sister to Scheherazade*, 1987), *Le blanc de l'Algérie* (*Algerian White*, 1995), *Vaste est la prison* (*So Vast the Prison*, 1995), and *Oran, langue morte* (*Oran, Dead Language*, 1997) epitomize this approach. *Vaste est la prison* is remarkable for its "pluralizing" effects. [7] It takes Abdelkebir Khatibi's concept of "Maghreb Pluriel"(1983) a bit further. It brilliantly maps out the multifarious interactions between the Maghreb and other Mediterranean cultures. It stretches from ancient Greece, Rome, and Carthage, through the period of Arab conquest, the return of the Andalusian Moors, and on into the epoch of French colonial conquest, anti-colonial war and the current state of political violence and subsequent assassination of intellectuals and exile forced on Djebar and many of her fellow citizens.

Djebar has been frequently nominated as a candidate for the Nobel Prize in literature. She taught history for many years at the University of Algiers. She won several international prizes for her significant contributions to world literature. In 1997, she was appointed professor and director of the Center for French and Francophone studies at Louisiana State University. Since autumn 2001, Djebar has been Silver Chair Professor of French and Francophone studies at New York University. Djebar who is already a member of the "Académie Royale de Langue Française de Belgique," became in June 2005 a member of the *Académie Française*. She is the first Maghrebi woman to become an *Immortel*, a lifetime member of the renowned 40-member French academy of letters, instituted by Cardinal Richelieu in 1635, during the reign of King Louis XIII, "to protect and monitor the French Language."

This mark of distinction draws attention to her constant literary importance as Algeria's inexhaustible and most prolific and iconic woman writer. If her acceptance of the appointment has rekindled the disconcerting polemics associated with neocolonialism and "nationalism," besides the issue of Maghrebi writers writing in French, her work powerfully epitomizes her avant-gardism. Djebar's writing resonates with current issues that reflect the course of Algeria's cultural, social, and political changes.

Nevertheless, in the eyes of Algerian government officials, Djebar is a "westernized" expatriate whose feminist books in French misrepresent women's condition in Algeria (Mortade 1971).[8] Without a doubt, Djebar's novels are feminist and significantly analytical of women's condition in Algeria. Her fiction has "broached an area of interrogation . . . that calls into question not only tradition, convention, and religion but the modern uses of power in post-independence North Africa as well" (Harlow 1986: xxi).

Anticipating Spivak, Djebar does not claim to "speak for" the Algerian women, but to "speak next to" the language that would be spoken by "incarcerated bodies," as they first secured their liberty (Grace 2004: 139). For women to liberate themselves from the inflicted silence and the patriarchal chains, they have to "retrieve a voice that has been driven into silence" (Spivak 1988: 122). Both a plainspoken writer and movie director, Djebar, more than Mokeddem, is mainly concerned with women's voice, memory, the position of women in Algerian history, and language.

I should indicate that after Algeria gained its independence, Djebar was severely criticized for writing in French, when Algerian writers were expected to shift to the official language, Arabic. In the 1970s, Djebar started studying classical Arabic to broaden her literary expression. Yet, her long literary silence in the 1970s was, to a certain extent, attributable to her growing interest in non-literary art forms such as movie making, and her recognition that she was not going to be an Arabic-language author. Briefly, her collection of short stories *Femmes d'Alger dans leur Appartement* (*Women of Algiers in Their Apartment*, 1980), is a defining moment in Djebar's career as a writer: "I had just turned forty. It's at that point that I finally felt myself fully a writer of the French language, while remaining deeply Algerian" (1980: 65).

In a multilingual country such as Algeria, Djebar is attentive to the risky stand she takes in opting for the use of French language. In fact, Djebar, following Kateb Yacine, describes her appropriation of French as "one of the spoils of war" (1980: 45), but she has also taken Kateb Yacine's motto a step further. Albeit she writes in French, she is not writing in the language of the "Other" because she has artistically manipulated the French language, giving it the sounds and rhythms of both Tamazight and Arabic. In short, she has "translated" French into her mother tongue (Ghaussy 1994: 460).[9]

Djebar creates some kind of "mutability" in her language—she makes use of expressions that are closely related to her mother's Tamazight heritage, "which crosses cultural divides, and creates 'a continuum of intersections' breaching divides of time, space and gender," (Grace 2004: 231–232). One perfect example of such a strategy is in *Vaste est la prison*, when referring to the cruel nature of the Algerian powers that be, she writes, "Ceux qui commandent . . . ceux qui ont la *Solta!... Dhiab fi thiab!...* Des loups dans des vêtements d'hommes! [Those who are in command ... those who have the *Solta!... Dhiab fi thiab!...* wolves dressed as people]" (1995: 311).

Another perfect illustration is in her previous novel, *A Sister to Scheherazade* (1987) when Hajila is contemplating herself in the mirror: "'The face of sorrow,' you murmur to yourself in Arabic, to your solitary, mute self," (1987: 9). This approach is actually one in which "language is taken to 'bear the burden' of one's own cultural experience … to convey in a language that is not one's own the spirit that is one's own" (Ashcroft et al. 1989: 38). This is Djebar's art and one of her major concerns, French stuffed with her mother tongue's imagery.

Djebar, in conjunction with other women novelists such as Yamina Mechakra, Hawa Djabali, and Nina Bouraoui, "have brought the issues of women's identity and freedom into a contemporary context, in which women seek to define themselves as more than a colonial or patriarchal 'other'" (Grace 2004: 131). As Valerie Orlando states, "these authors find themselves at the intersection of French and North African feminist viewpoints, exposing a complicated world that must be re-negotiated and re-defined" (1999: 20). This re-negotiation/re-definition is the main concern of *Vaste est la prison*.

Using polyphonic discourse in *Vaste est la prison*, Djebar connects her own life as a modern, tri-lingual educated Algerian and postcolonial woman with her female ancestors. In this third book of her quartet, Djebar self-consciously blurs the boundaries between history, autobiography, and fiction. *Vaste est la prison* gives paramount importance to ancestral figures like al-Kahina or Fadhma n'Soumer. Djebar celebrates her literary ancestry by highlighting the impact of Arab and Berber women such as Tin-Hinan and Zaynab Lalla.[10] She also describes the predicament of urban Algerian women who shook off the fetters of colonialism only to withstand the worst of a postcolonial regime that ostracizes and oppresses them.

Like Djebar, Mokeddem's work is also assessed according to its political, cultural, and ideological overtones (Helm 2000: 238). The oldest of 13 children, she was born in 1949, in Kenadsa, a village near Béchar, on the edge of the Algerian Sahara desert and close to the barely visible border between Morocco and Algeria. Her illiterate nomadic family became settled in 1947. Mokeddem spent her childhood in a *ksar*, the traditional Saharan village built of earth. She was raised on the stories of her grandmother, Zohra, who encouraged her schooling at a time when girls were barred from school. She studied medicine in Oran, Algeria, and then left for Montpellier, France, in 1977 where she divided her time between her medical practice and creative writing until 1985 when she decided to devote herself entirely to literature.

Like large segments of the Algerian population, Mokeddem lives in Montpellier. Like most of her female protagonists, she studied medicine. And just like her female protagonists, she is captivated by the Sahara desert, and is repulsed by Islamic fundamentalists who "assassinated her dreams" and her close friends. Though her works seem to echo the tragic socio-political situation in Algeria, she does not appeal, like Djebar for instance, to millions of Algerian men and women.

Unlike Djebar whose main concern is to bring to light "la condition humaine," to quote André Malraux, Mokeddem has won, in the West, much acclaim for her exotic novels set in Kenadsa, "au pied des dunes, aux portes du Grand Erg [by the foot of the dunes, and the gates of the Great Erg]." In her novels, she endeavors to depict the problematical condition of women in contemporary Algeria. An examination of some of Mokeddem's works such as *L'interdite* (*The Forbidden Women*, 1993); *Des rêves et des assassins* (*Of Dreams and Assassins*, 1995); *Les hommes qui marchent* (*The Men Who Walk*, 1997); and *Mes hommes* (*My Men*, 2005) does highlight patriarchy as a dogma embedded in the Algerian socio-cultural structure.[11] However, unlike Djebar, she does not subvert the foundations of this patriarchy.

As Yolande Aline Helm has rightly pointed out, "the gangrene of mentality" remains an abscess in Algerian women's lives and I believe there is so much that postcolonial feminist literature can do to alleviate the Algerian society of its suffering (2000: 221). Djebar's heroines refuse to compromise. They fight and escape from their prison, "so vast" it might be. Nevertheless, Mokeddem's female protagonists concede defeat and consider flight as the only way out, thus creating new hurdles and failing to wipe away the specters and hardships of the past.

This flight is explicitly substantiated in *Les hommes qui marchent*. Unlike Djebar who reveals in *Vaste est la prison* that she "was neither here, nor there … but [she] could not help feeling the clouds getting closer, ushering the tempest" (1995: 59); Mokeddem confesses in an interview to Françoise Germain Robin (1995): "Je suis partie en 1977 [to Montpellier] parce que je suffoquais. J'espérais trouver ici la paix. Mais ce qui se passe là-bas me trouble." ["I left in 1977 because I was suffocating. I thought I would find peace here. But what is happening there troubles me."][12]

It should be noted that *Les hommes qui marchent* spans over 30 years of Algerian contemporary history (1941–1970). It brings together an ancestral narrative, revolving around three generations of Algerian women telling their story, the narrative of colonial rule, and the nationalist movement culminating in the independence of Algeria.

Disenchantment and representation of the subaltern

Djebar and Mokeddem are diversely conscious of their women's predicament; but they know that their suffering is not a trite matter. At the time of colonization, Algerian women were the first victims. For in the colonialist phantasm, as the Algerian scholar Mostefa Lacheraf has unveiled in his study of the colonial immorality instilled in the correspondence of the military officers whose mission was to "pacify" Algeria between 1830 and 1870, to subdue Algerian women meant to control, to a certain extent, all Algerians. Montagnac, one of the most zealous young officers of the Conquest confesses to a friend: "This … is how one must go about confronting Arabs: Slay all the men over fifteen years of age, seize all the women and children, load them on the vessels, [and] send them off to the Marquises Islands or elsewhere."[13]

This is how those who were supposed to be the agents of a grand "mission civilisatrice" considered women. In her analysis of violence against women in Africa, Amina Mama (1997: 48) reminds us that "colonial penetration was both a violent and a gendered process" and that the "colonization process also transformed African gendered relations in complex, diverse, and contradictory ways that we have yet to fully understand" (Mama 1997: 53). Such a predicament has remained engraved in women's psyche just like all the other hardships they have to endure in the name of their own religion. Both experiences have found their way to their literature.

Since the 1960s, there has been an emergence of many new writers and a shift in themes. They revolve around three major considerations: How to depict the newly independent Algerian woman? What to express, and how to articulate it? Now that the struggle against the colonizer is over, these writers are facing themselves. They know that their new function, which is similar to literature's, is to be the driving force for men and women to change the society in which they live. This new literature refuses to perpetuate an anachronistic nationalism that would alienate Algerians from their new reality. The emphasis is on the post-independence socio-political malaise, and the necessity to denounce it.

In her semi-autobiographical novel, *Les hommes qui marchent*, Mokeddem underscores the subjugation of women in post-independence Algeria as follows: "Au lendemain de l'indépendance, la première préoccupation des hommes était encore et toujours de cacher, de cloîtrer leurs femmes. Liberté oui, mais pas pour tout le monde. [Right after independence, the major concern for men was to hide from view and lock away their women. Independence, yes; but not for everybody]" (1997: 246). The foregoing passage vividly illustrates what is really at stake in modern-day Algeria. I agree with Susheila Nasta when she rightly notes in her introduction to *Motherlands*:

> The post-colonial woman writer is not only involved in making herself heard, in changing the architecture of male-centered ideologies and languages, or in discovering new forms and language to express her experience, she has also to subvert and demythologize indigenous male writing and traditions which seek to label her.
>
> (Nasta 1991: XV)

After Algeria's independence in 1962, and when the presumed women's emancipation was not accomplished with the country's freedom, dissatisfaction was the brand name of all the postcolonial governments. David Gordon affirms, "With the dawn of independence," the atmosphere was "confused and economically ominous" and "the expectations of and for women were high. But the force of the legacy of centuries was soon to make itself felt. The gap between promise and reality, law and fact, was to widen" (1968: 61).

In fact, the promise of social justice for women was dropped right after independence in 1962. Thus, this democratic deficit by the country that had played an admirable role in anti-colonial wars worldwide caused an excruciating malaise

(M'rabet 1969). Progressive intellectuals perceive the subordination of women to "tradition," and their subsequent exclusion from public life to be a betrayal both of the women freedom fighters and of the Algerian Revolution itself. When the war of liberation veterans wanted to build an independent state, how far did they include women in the state building process? Women were treated either patronizingly or with outright hostility. There is a deep feeling of disillusionment among the *Mujaheedats* (former women freedom fighters). They are furious to see that the independence of the country has not achieved one of its fundamental goals, i.e. women's emancipation (Benallegue 1983: 25). On the other hand, as Valentine Moghadam has rightly put it, "the fact that women played a crucial role in the revolt did not prevent them from being discouraged, if not barred, from assuming prominence in the public sphere following victory" (1994: 2).

Yet, for Algerian women writers, to conjure the heroic period of the revolution is to emphasize women's role in the struggle. Women want to reinforce their incontestable presence in the community. If this post-independence literature presents some protest overtones, it is because the gap between women's engagement in the struggle and their position in today's society is considerable. It is also because of the frustration at seeing artificial barriers separating the public arena from the domestic space. Baya Gacemi explains this gap in an essay in *Le Monde diplomatique*:

> There has always been a lack of understanding between Algeria and its women. During the 1950s and 1960s, Algerian women were in the vanguard of the struggle for liberation. But, nowadays the relative freedom of the "sisters," famous for having "fought like men," has almost ceased to exist. It began to disappear in 1972 when the *Family Code* threatened to institutionalize male guardianship.
>
> (Gacemi 1997)

In this respect, Catherine Delcroix presents this issue in dichotomous terms (1986: 139). She affirms that "in view of the Algerian woman's higher level of education today, her under-representation can only foster frustration and obstruct the evolution of her personal status, and thus, of her emancipation." Delcroix argues that the traditionalist mentality is as accountable for women's exclusion, as "the ideological system itself, which doesn't sufficiently mobilize the female population for fear of seeing woman transgress her role as guardian of traditional values" (1986: 138–139).

However, Peter R. Knauss's investigations of current male–female relations reveal that the state-backed practices not only emasculate women but also "contain the social consequences of significant changes that have taken place in education and employment" (1987: 137–141). This is in the name of "patriarchy which has become part of the warp and woof of Algerian political culture." This is perceptible in the permanence of traditional social customs ordained by regressive interpretations of shari'a (Muslim canonical law) and promoted by cynical political regimes ever since independence. The constrictive "Family Law" of 1984 has confirmed these disempowering traditions.[14]

Although male legislators claim that this "Family Law" stems from the Qur'an and *sunna*, they have distorted the Islamic foundational texts, i.e., the Qur'an and *sunna*, according to their own interests. The post-independence governments have always chosen to construe Islam in a way that fails to recognize women's rights. For instance, under the Algerian *Code de la Famille* (personal status law), there is no relief out of marriage for a woman whose husband refuses divorce. This is an evident refutation of the Qur'anic verse: "Do not retain them [your wives] by force" (Qur'an 2:231). In reality, the Algerian authorities have made divorce quite trouble-free for men, while making it troublesome for women to get rid of an unbearable marriage. In such circumstances, Mai Yamani's analysis of women in Saudi Arabia seems be just right: "the marriage contract becomes for the woman akin to a form of bondage to her husband that cannot be revoked by her will alone" (Yamani 1996: 17). Here, I can infer that what is valid at the family level is also valid at the national level. However, how is this patriarchy translated into the nationalist discourse?

There is an important literature on the effects of nationalism. Points of view vary. According to Evelyn Accad (1990: 14) many Arab feminists are now conscious that nationalism remains the most pernicious and oppressive factor against women. Novelists like Rachid Mimouni in *Le fleuve détourné* (1982) or Malika Mokeddem in *L'interdite* (1993), for instance, show that the FLN (the National Liberation Front) has cultivated and upheld many of the most reactionary and archaic values of Islamic traditionalism out of opportunistic nationalism. The post-independence FLN-state has simply "turned back the clock on the socially transformative potential the revolution offered" (Grace 2004: 134).

For Mokeddem, Algerians are suffering an acute identity crisis. Algerians have been devalued by colonization, then by the FLN, which discredited the Berbers, the Francophones, and muzzled everybody. In *L'interdite*, Sultana, the female protagonist who bears much resemblance to Mokeddem, is about to be sacked by the mayor from the hospital where she works as a medical doctor. All the women in the hospital challenge the mayor, who represents "le Parti unique," the FLN-state in Algerian politics. The women's representative is a *Mujaheedat* who makes a synchronic and diachronic analysis of the way the Revolution has been confiscated (1993: 242).

However, in her latest autobiographical work, *Mes hommes* (2005), she falls back on the "exotic colonial sub-culture" and does a hatchet job on men, especially her father (Lacheraf 1982: 56). There are actually a lot of men in this autobiography, a brother, a medical doctor, a first love, a brief relationship, failures, and encounters. But the fundamental figure, the first absence, the one who opens the first chapter, is her father. She writes: "My father, my first man, it is with you that I learnt to weigh up love with the gauge of damage and deprivation" (2005: 5).

Without really trying to analyze the root causes of this bias, she seems to forget that her father's behavior is conditioned by a patriarchal structure over which he has no control. Given his milieu, the socio-political situation of Algeria at the time of French colonial rule, his actions/reactions are determined. How can Mokeddem blame a victim for being an executioner? This question and others are worth posing.

A literature soaked in blood

The rise of Islamic fundamentalism in the late 1970s and 1980s, especially with the Islamic Salvation Front (FIS) as a grassroots movement, and the popular disavowal of the corrupt FLN-one-party system, led to a landslide victory of the FIS in the first free post-independence parliamentary elections in December 1991 (Garçon 1989: 6). But the Army toppled Colonel-President Chadli Benjedid (1979–1992), declared a state of emergency, cancelled the elections, incarcerated thousands of Islamists and non-Islamists in "concentration camps"[15] in the Sahara desert, and launched an all-out war to eradicate Islamism but also to curtail the post-October 1988[16] slight and short political liberation.

With a death toll in the order of 200,000 the brutal civil war, triggered by the Algerian Generals and the "Islamist Armed Groups" (GIA), has been going on since 1992 with an earth-shattering impact on literature (Aggoun and Rivoire 2004: 92). Renowned writers and academics such as Youcef Sebti, Bakhti Benaouda, and Tahar Djaout have been the tragic victims of this political violence. Scarcely has a family not been affected by these tragic events. And a lot of novelists (Latifa Benmansour, Abdelkader Djemaï, Habib Tengour), playwrights (Slimane Benaissa), poets (Zineb Laouedj, Rabia Djalti, Hawa Djabali), journalists (Salima Mellah, Malika Boussouf, Baya Gacemi), essayists (Abdelkader Djeghloul, Hafid Gafaiti, Benaouda Lebdaï), and critics (Dalila Morsly, Amine Zaoui, Christiane Achour) have gone into exile.

Currently the army rules the country with a rod of iron and Algerian nationalism has become a tyrannical dogma in the hands of a myriad of corrupt government notables and a reactionary "elite." [17] Besides, the system has domesticated most of the movements of opposition that have surfaced after the October 1988 riots against unemployment and corruption. Yet, Ait Ahmed's party, the Socialist Forces Front (FFS), remnants of the FIS, and very few independent intellectuals embody the only effective opposition to the regime.

I have to point out that in the 1990s, political violence in Algeria has certainly added a layer of brutality to the domestic and institutional violence made against women. Besides, Djebar's writing, more than Mokeddem's texts, denotes a cry of revolt, a quest for buried roots, and a progressive vision for the future that empowers women and gives them a voice. In her Quartet for instance, Djebar shows how French colonialism abused women, how the successive post-independence governments used them, and how the GIA killed them.[18]

The Algerian writers who lived to tell the tale are tormented by the woeful socio-political situation. They feel obliged to couch it on paper and pay homage to those who have been assassinated. Djebar's literary production during these years has revolved around this national tragedy. *Vaste est la prison* (1995) and *Le blanc de l'Algérie* (1995) were followed by *Oran, langue morte* (1997) which is a poignant tribute to the Oran-based playwright, theatre director, and actor Abdelkader Alloula who was gunned down on a Ramadan evening in 1994, on his way to give a lecture on Brecht. Malika Mokeddem, *Des Rêves et des Assassins* (1995), Leila Marouane, *Ravisseur* (1997) similarly to Rachid Boudjedra, *FIS de la haine* (1992) and Rachid Mimouni, *De la barbarie en général et de l'intégrisme en particulier* (1992) have all examined the causes of the political violence and the nature of the warring factions; each according to his/her political color. As an echo to the waging civil war, Susan Ireland, in her article "Voices of Resistance," considers Algerian women as the mythical Scheherazade, "surviving, remembering, and negotiating the impossible choices between destructive patriarchies of a military government and its 'fundamentalist rebels'" (Ireland 2001: 172).

In these circumstances, I believe it is irrelevant to construe Algerian literature as a self-sufficient aesthetical discourse, especially if it involves political polemics in Algeria. I suggest that the literature's nexus to its matrix, i.e., the Algerian society, should rather be substantiated. Now that Algeria has experienced the hardships of a tragic post-electoral process, in addition to the scenes of carnage that have been a consequence of the 1992 coup, and taking into account the dramatic socio-political situation in Algeria, I can simply affirm that the national context substantiates the anxieties traceable in the works of Djebar and Mokeddem. For instance, the issue of domestic violence that Djebar has underscored in *Ombre Sultane* (*A Sister to Scheherazade*, 1987) has taken another tragic dimension.

Violence wreaked on all the Algerian "Hajilas" (Hajila is the heroine in *A Sister to Scheherazade*) by "The Man" in Algeria has taken on an ominous precedent in *Vaste est la prison*, as the novel closes with "Islamic fundamentalists' assassination of Yasmina," a 28-year-old teacher of French and proofreader with the French-language *Le Soir d'Algérie*, a leftist Algerian daily. As it was difficult to roam around Algiers, in the terrible circumstances of June 1994, Yasmina's Polish friend decided to leave the country. On their way to the airport, Yasmina stopped at a gas station. A group of men, in police uniforms, asked to see their papers. When the men took the Polish young girl away, Yasmina opposed them. The men then searched Yasmina Drici's handbag and discovered her press card. Her friend was released on the spot. The next day, passersby found Yasmina's body with her throat slit. Yasmina's ruthless assassination suggests that the brutality facing Algerian women who refuse to give in to silence and subordination is altogether spine chilling.

In her various works, Djebar has depicted a new fearless emancipated woman, a woman-subject whose subversive conduct has shattered the archaic traditions. Her work shows a whole range of representative characters such as grandmothers, students, bourgeois women, intellectuals, and mothers who claim their right to participate in the combat for a better society. Djebar produces a literature that clearly depicts feelings of disillusionment with the nationalist and totalitarian project, a literature that highlights the female character as an "agent de rupture" (Nisbet 1980: 32). This is manifest in all three of Djebar's latest works such as *Vaste est la prison* (1995), *Le blanc de l'Algérie* (1995), and *Oran, langue morte* (1997).

While Djebar dissects the root causes of the Algerian tragedy, Mokeddem is somewhat concerned with some of the effects of this disastrous situation. She has not realized that her exclusive western colonial education, self-imposed exile, and incomprehension of her Algerian matrix, have put her at odds with her nomadic origins. Unequivocally, she has profited from the 1990s tragic events. As Y. B. (himself a journalist whose life has been genuinely threatened), indicates in *Le Nouvel Observateur*, not only are Mokeddem's texts poorly written, but they are also a sheer manipulation of the Algerian Civil War. "But most troubling is that behind this lethargic mediocrity something more serious seems to hide: a perfidy that surfs the bloody Algerian wave. It seemed necessary to me to denounce it once and for all" (1998: 53).

Mokeddem's major concern is not really about women's resistance and self-fulfillment. Unlike Djebar, Mokeddem's primary concern is the Other, i.e., Western readership. An elementary analysis of some of her works reveals the themes and narrative strategies she uses to captivate this readership. In *Les hommes qui marchent*, she provides a clichéd illustration and shallow description of the Sahara desert: "Comment envisager l'écoulement du temps dans un paysage aussi immuable.... Aucune limite ne résiste aux démesures du Sahara.... Ici, l'espace et le ciel se dévorent indéfiniment. [How does one consider the passage of time in such an unchanging landscape.... No border can resist the excessiveness of the Sahara.... Here, space and sky devour each other indefinitely]" (Mokeddem 1997: 8).

Another illustration of the aberrations in this semi-autobiographical work is the reference to Sufi *Hadras*.[19] It is commonly known that in several parts of the Maghreb, the Sufi *Hadras* are exclusively male religious gatherings. Nevertheless, in *Les Hommes qui marchent* Mokeddem writes, "Les hadras sont des réunions de femmes autour de la célébration d'Allah et de son prophète. [Hadras are gatherings of women that celebrate Allah and his Prophet]" (1997: 128).

To exert a pull on her exoticism-hungry readership, and in addition to the voluptuous dances and songs, Mokeddem peppers her exotic erotic postcard, as Malek Alloula would say in *The Colonial Harem* (1986), with *youyous* [ululations] "Youyou, vertige voluptueux du sanglot, cri de l'indicible lancé vers les cieux. [Youyou, the voluptuous vertigo of the sob, the cry of the invincible launched toward the skies]" (1997: 127). This is a perfect example of what Frantz Fanon, Edward Said, and Homi Bhabha have been combating.

Conclusion

Like the Moroccan Khnata Bennouna, the Tunisian Hélé Béji, or the Algerians Leila Marouane and Salima Ghezali, to name just a few, these two writers, namely Djebar and Mokeddem, address the ills of Algeria as a postcolonial Maghrebi nation, attacking the totalitarian Algerian regime, either openly or allegorically.

Not only does the substantial body of texts, produced by Djebar and Mokeddem, explore the role of religion in society and the dangers of radical Islam, but it also denounces the terrible civil conflict that began in 1992 in Algeria, and unveils the effects of patriarchal family structures.

It may well be argued that Djebar's and Mokeddem's work is concerned with the situation of women in post-independence Algeria and with giving them the voice that conservative elements in society would deny them. Moreover, if Djebar, as a voice of and from Algeria, ingeniously and perceptively debunks political amnesia, and established traditionalist belief systems, through a language that is clear-cut and stripped of superfluous phraseology, Mokeddem, oddly enough, adds force to the misrepresentation, misunderstanding, and amnesia that Djebar denounces.

Nevertheless, I suggest, that both Mokeddem and Djebar, despite their fundamental differences, are postcolonial subjects and agents of change in their own right. In the face of Algeria's political and socio-cultural uncertainties, they both contribute to socio-political and cultural change in their own ways. They both fight against exclusion, discrimination against women, violence, and terror; taking into consideration that "literature [plays] a crucial role in the re-establishment of national cultural heritage, in the re-instatement of native idioms, in the re-imagining and re-figuring of local histories, geographies, and communities" (Said 1992: 15).

Notes

1 Assia Djebar, *Vaste est la prison* (Paris: Albin Michel, 1995). All translations from French are my own.
2 Malika Mokeddem, *Les hommes qui marchent* (1990), (Paris: Grasset, 1997). All translations from French are my own.
3 See for instance his novels, *Lettres algériennes* (1995); *Fis de la haine* (1992); *La Pluie* (1987); *L'Insolation* (1972); and *La Répudiation* (1969).
4 See, *Fleurs d'amandier* (2001); *Les balcons des mers nordiques* (2001); *La gardienne des ombres* (1996).
5 See, *Coupables* (2006); *Ce ne sont que des hommes* (2003); *Les Jumeaux de la nuit* (2002); and *Les Années rouges* (2000).
6 See, *La prière de la peur* (1997); *Le Chant du lys et du Basilic* (1990).
7 The novel's title is extracted from the Tamazight song, "So vast the prison crushing me. Release, where will you come from?"
8 Pam Morris has rightly indicated that it is common and useful for failed Third-world governments to accuse "Third-world women who dissent ... of being 'westernized'" (Pam Morris, *Literature and Feminism: An Introduction*, Oxford: Blackwell Publishers, 1994, p. 190).
9 The term Tamazight designates the language of the Amazigh (Berber) people. With its various regional dialects, Tamazight is the native language of the Maghreb. Vast regions in Algeria and Morocco still use it as the only medium of communication and, in recent years, especially after the "Berber Spring" (reference to the demonstrations which took place in Algiers, Bejaia, and Tizi-Ouzou in 1980), there has been a sort of cultural renaissance. Using the Tifinagh alphabet—still used by the Touaregs in the Sahara Desert, Tamazight used to be written in the

past. With Arabization, the Arabic alphabet was used for some time until fairly recently (1980s) when in the midst of a huge controversy figures like Mouloud Mammeri decided to opt for Latin characters. (See, Mouloud Mammeri, *L'Ahellil du Gourara*, Paris: Editions Maison des Sciences de l'Homme, 1995; André Basset, *La langue berbère*, London: Oxford University Press, 1952; Fatima Sadiqi, *Grammaire du berbère*, Paris and Montréal: Éditions l'Harmattan, 1997; Salem Chaker, *Linguistique berbère: Études de syntaxe et de diachronie*, Paris and Leuven: Uitgeverij Peeters, 1995.)

10 In the past, the Maghreb has seen the rise of several female figures such as al-Kahina who opposed the Arab armies in the seventh century AD; the Berber resistance leader Tin-Hinan (fourth century AD), who is believed to come from Tafilalt in the Atlas Mountains of Morocco, and who set an example in indigenous resistance in uniting the Touareg Tribes and founded a kingdom in the Ahaggar Mountains (1,500 kilometres south of Algiers and west of Tamanrasset); Fathma N'Soumer (1830–1873) who fought the French in 1871, and Zaynab Lalla (1850–1904) who ran the powerful Rahmaniya Sufi order in the 1890s in the village of Zaatcha, in the Aures region (Eastern part of Algeria).

11 "The self-sustaining structures of power, by means of which women's interests are always ultimately subordinated to male interests, constitute the social order known as 'patriarchy,' a designation that applies to almost all human societies, past and present" (Morris 1994: 4). Patriarchy is often used as a figure of speech, a paradigm of power imbalance and the cause of the predicament of colonialism and neocolonialism.

12 Françoise Germain Robin, "Entretien avec Malika Mokeddem," *L'Humanité*, 2 October 1995.

13 Quoted by Mostefa Lacheraf, *L'Algérie: Nation et Société*, Paris: Maspero, 1969, pp. 255–256. All translations from French are my own.

14 A benchmark of feminist struggle, Family Law (*Code de la Famille*) has been among the highest agenda items of Islamic and secular women's movements. In 1984, the most reactionary and cynical government of Colonel-President Chadli Benjedid concocted the notorious *Code de la Famille*. Under this law, women remain legal minors; a woman's decision to marry must be authorized by a guardian; and it is tedious and disastrous for women to initiate divorce. Moreover, there is actually no national consensus that Algeria's *Code de la Famille*, as reformed in 2005, incarnates the ideal interpretation of shari'a principles. Algeria has a long time ago thrust aside Islamic law for French-inspired law with the exception of personal status matters.

15 I use this term in reference to the Nazi use of camps to eradicate the Jews, and the Stalinists who also used the gulags in Siberia in order to incarcerate hundreds of opponents such as Alexander Soljenitsyne, André Sakharov, and scores of others. The Algerian *Nomenklatura* is but a Stalinist military clan which has emulated the KGB and the former East German political police, the Stasi. (See Mohamed Harbi, "L'Algérie prise au piège de son histoire," *Le Monde Diplomatique*, May 1994.)

16 The alienation and anger of the Algerian population was fanned by the widespread perception that the government had become corrupt and aloof. The waves of dissatisfaction got bigger on October 5, 1988, when a series of strikes in Algiers degenerated into rioting. When the violence spread to other major cities such as Oran and Annaba, the government declared a state of emergency and began using force to crush the unrest. By October 10, the security forces had restored a semblance of order; more than 500 people were killed and more than 3,500 arrested. The military intervention was traumatic for it was the first time in post-independence Algeria that the Algerian armed forces fired at other unarmed Algerians. What is also referred to as the "Couscous Revolt" was attributed to an unacceptably slow pace of political and economic reform, as well as serious food shortages caused by the 1986 oil price drop and subsequent decrease in hydrocarbon export revenues. Per capita

income dropped from $2,600 to $1,600, unemployment rose to 30 percent, and social conditions deteriorated rapidly. Economic regression blew apart the legitimacy of the state socialism. (See Abdelkader Djeghloul, "Les Risques de la Société à Deux Vitesses," *Le Monde Diplomatique*, Janvier 1989, p. 14. See also my article "Algeria: A Revolution Hopelessly Gone Wrong," *Khaleej Times*, June 9, 2005, p. 12; Rémy Leveau, *L'Algérie dans la guerre*, Bruxelles: Complexe, 1995; Mohamed Harbi et Benjamin Stora, *La Guerre d'Algérie: 1954–2004, la fin de l'amnésie*, Paris: Robert Laffont, 2004.)

17 Lahouari Addi, "Le régime algérien et ses oppositions," *El Watan*, 23 November 1995.

18 So far, Assia Djebar has published three volumes of her Algerian Quartet, *L'Amour, la fantasia* (1985), *Ombre sultane* (1987), and *Vaste est la prison* (1995).

19 One of the most important Sufi rituals is *Hadra* which is regularly held on Thursday evenings after night prayer. The *Hadra* male-only attendees most often stand in a circle and perform collective chanting, centered on praise of the Prophet Muhammad, and supplication to Allah. See for instance, Alan Godlas, "A Commentary on 'What is Tasawwuf?'—An Anonymous Persian Poem," *Sufi Illuminations,* 1996, pp. 63–80.

4 Women and political reform in Israel

Galia Golan

There are many criteria by which a state and society may be determined to be a democracy. Freely elected organs of government, an independent judiciary, rule of law, and pluralism are counted among the main elements. Critical to all of these is the principle of equality, whether the reference is to liberal or social democracy. Neither rule of law nor justice, nor free elections, nor pluralism can be fully achieved without equality of all citizens of a state. Generally equality is interpreted as equality of rights, although just what rights are meant has varied, from the right to freedom from discrimination or persecution, to the right to speak or associate freely or the right to a decent standard of living. Denial of these and other rights to a group, a segment of society, or individuals constitutes a denial of the principle of equality. There is a difference between denial and simply the absence of equality, but a genuinely democratic state cannot be one in which there remain pockets of inequality. By most definitions, and according to most criteria, Israel (within its borders) is in fact a democratic state. It does not officially deny equality to any of its citizens. Yet there are quite large pockets of inequality and large segments of the population that do not enjoy full equality in every sphere, whether as a result of intention or otherwise. It is from this point of view that we raise the issue of women in Israel and the need for political reform to ensure the democratic nature of the state.

The position of women in Israel, both with regard to social and political status as well as actual legislation is generally perceived as quite good, possibly even close to that of the most progressive states. This impression was born of a number of facts and myths. Namely the fact that Israel had a woman prime minister (Golda Meir), women served equally to men in both the pre-state (pre-1948) fighting units and in the Israeli army, and women received the vote as early as the late 1920s (in the pre-state self-governing Jewish institutions). Moreover, the socialist orientation of the country seemed ideologically to ensure equality. Following statehood in 1948, women received full equality under law, including the right to vote and be elected to public office, universal education, and protection from discrimination. Early legislation included a number of laws protecting women's rights in the workplace and in society as a whole (including maternity leave and protection from dismissal for pregnant women and mothers returning to work, and other protective legislation). With rights and laws similar to those in Western

Europe and North America, women in Israel, together with Israeli society as a whole, believed that women were being treated equally and that their status was indeed equal to that of men.

In the early 1970s Israeli feminists began to challenge what they perceived as this "myth of equality" in Israel. They pointed out that the early achievements had not been won easily, and in fact were the result of the quite strenuous efforts of the "first wave of feminism" characteristic of many countries in the early twentieth century (Izraeli 1992). They also pointed out that many of the obstacles and problems women had faced in obtaining their rights from the male elites in the pre-state days were still prevalent in Israeli society, such as the inordinate power of the religious establishment, especially with regard to marriage and divorce. Nor did women in fact have equal rights, even in some cases under law (such as pension regulations) and they certainly could not be considered to have equality of status—be it in the family, in political life, the business or academic world, or almost any workplace, or even the family. Women were far from equal in the army, even with regard to conscription, much less their treatment (subordinate) in the army. Statistically women had never reached more than 10 percent of members of the Knesset (the Israeli parliament); their percentages in managerial positions (public and private sectors alike) were even less; and while their numbers were equal among student bodies in higher education, their percentages in academic staffs were extremely low. Women were concentrated in the lower salary ranks in virtually all professions and sectors of society, barred from lucrative overtime and night work (due to protective legislation) and forced to retire five years earlier than their male counterparts (also due to what had been viewed as protection of women). Women constituted the majority of part-time workers—for whom advancement and higher pay were virtually impossible; salaries tended to differ between men and women even in identical positions; married women could not file an independent income tax return even if they owned their own businesses. Thus there were still traces of the traditional perception of women as "belonging" to the male, who was still considered head of family and whose permission was required for dissolution of the marriage.

Inequality was, of course, relative. Compared to countries in which women did not even have the right to vote, or own property, or travel without male permission, or countries in which arranged marriages, even of minors, were still the norm and men might legally have more than one wife, clearly Israeli women had little to complain about. Israeli society was generally considered to be similar to the non-traditional cultures of Europe and North America. Indeed employing parameters such as percentage of women in the workforce, level of women's education, general standard of living, and length of time since women received the right to vote, Israel was in a very respectable position.

Yet the second wave of feminism of the 1970s began a gradual awakening of women (and some men) throughout the world to the injustices of women's situation, no matter how different this situation might be, in relative terms, from one country or culture to another. The United Nations decade of women beginning in 1975 along with the feminist movements of Western Europe and North America clearly played a large role in this awakening. In Israel the women's movement of the 1920s and 1930s was reborn and feminists became active in the early 1970s.

A critical first step was to acknowledge that equality was indeed merely a myth and recognize the actual situation. The activities of feminist organizations, a government commission to study the status of women, and nascent women's studies programs in the universities undertook these tasks and affected a certain degree of public awareness of the matter. The remaining, no less crucial, tasks were then to identify the causes and hopefully the remedies for the inequalities.

Clearly traditional concepts regarding gender roles were a primary factor. As in all patriarchal societies, a woman's role was perceived in terms of the home and the family, the private rather than the public sector, and even there as an appendage to or subordinate to the male. While not denying a public role for women, or work outside the home or even political participation, this underlying sense of the "appropriate" division of gender roles influenced attitudes and practices. Moreover, as feminists everywhere pointed out, this approach to gender roles was perpetuated and fortified by society, be it the education system (what was taught and even how it was taught), children's stories, literature, along with the media and advertising, or the gendered nature of society's institutions themselves. It should not be surprising that the institutions created and dominated by men would in fact suit the interests, needs, and qualifications of men—as distinct from women. Women as well as men had internalized this situation to the point that discrimination was not even perceived as such but seen, rather, as the natural order of things.

In Israel, however, there appeared to be two additional causes of, and obstacles to the situation of inequality, not necessarily unique to Israel but of central importance. These are the influence and even political power of religion and the religious establishments, and the effects of militarization on the public as a result of the prolonged state of armed conflict. While only approximately 20–25 percent of the population (Jews and non-Jews) would identify themselves as religiously observant, in fact, traditional religious values and customs exist to some degree in far larger percentages among the Jewish and Palestinian (Muslim and Christian) populations, as well as the other religious communities in the country.[1] Among the most observant Jewish (ultra-orthodox) and Muslim populations this can mean the continued practice of arranged marriages, including (illegally) girls as young as 14 or 15. While polygamy was outlawed by the country's earliest legislation, it is still practiced in very limited Muslim circles, as is the practice of honor killings. Traditional ideas of gender roles, particularly regarding the primacy of family and the gender separation of private and public life persist in the ultra-orthodox Jewish community but also leave their trace in simply observant Jewish and Muslim families. However, given the absence of separation of religion and the state in Israel, some of these religious attitudes, Jewish and Muslim, are actually enshrined in law. Maintaining a custom from the period of the Turkish Empire, family law—namely marriage and divorce—are the domain exclusively of the religious courts. There is no civil marriage or divorce in Israel. For both Jewish and Muslim women this has serious ramifications particularly with regard to divorce, as the fate of women and often their children is placed, legally, in the hands of the male partner. The influence of religious circles, which actually have their own often powerful if small political parties, may also be seen in laws connected with abortion or surrogate motherhood and other areas in which the religious have "concerns" directly affecting women. Indeed with regard to abortion, for example, a progressive law passed in the 1970s was almost immediately stripped of its only subjective clause[2] when a right-wing/ultra-orthodox coalition came to power, and the law has been restricted somewhat over the years due to pressure from the religious establishment. Abortion is legal, but only in state hospitals and under certain conditions, subject to a somewhat laborious committee process. Actually, the Israeli justice system has always (consciously) ignored illegal abortion in the country, with the result that women, even before the law was passed and still now, may obtain a safe abortion from a doctor at a relatively reasonable price, if for some reason or choice the legal route to abortion is not an option. Nonetheless, the principle of a woman's right to control her own body still has not been accepted nor found its place in the law.

The militarization of Israeli society due to the prolonged armed conflict has also played a role in the perpetuation and even strengthening of gender inequality in Israel. The conflict has elevated the army to a position of centrality—perhaps the most important institution—in Israeli society. And drafting youngsters at the age of 18 renders it a major instrument of socialization as well. Conscription of women along with men to this institution might, therefore, serve the idea of equality—if in fact conscription were equal. But not only are all Arab women (like all Arab men) excluded from the draft, but also religious Jewish women and even Jewish women who simply declare that they are religious. Moreover, gender relations within the army are far from equal; nor do they provide a sense of equality. The military was and remains a patriarchal institution. The early concept of women as the "mothers" of the national struggle was translated in the army into the idea of providing warmth, a touch of home, serving as a helpmate. Thus until very recently women were not permitted into combat positions—a ban that immediately placed them in an inferior status, limiting their possibilities (be it as recruits or members of the professional army) for advancement and respect. Given these limitations, the duration and nature of the service varied greatly from that of the men, along with the attitudes (internalized by women as well as by men) toward women's service—and towards women. Even recent changes within the army, which we shall discuss below, have not altered the gendered attitudes.

The reinforced concept of gender roles, as well as the values promulgated by the military (manliness associated with strength, power, and domination) play a role beyond the army, in society at large. Professional military leaving the army are often parachuted into top roles in politics, business, government—even academia and, of late, the school system. Their experience as "commanders" is seen to provide them with the necessary qualifications for leadership roles. But the preferential treatment, apparent even in their selection for media and other public roles, is a reflection of the value placed on former military people because of their experience and expertise in the one area most valued by the Israeli public: the area of "security." Security is indeed the major preoccupation for a society engaged in prolonged armed conflict, and the valuation of the qualities as well as institutions and persons associated with security is a significant factor in Israeli life. This valuation begins even before the army, for the Jewish male child is perceived both by his family and society as a future "protector," one who may be called upon to sacrifice even his life for the sake of the country. At the least, he is to play an essential role for Israeli society, and the institutions of the country do much to instill a sense of pride, in both parents and children, in the role the male is to play. Such treatment generally strengthens a boy's self-confidence or self-esteem; it also strengthens his sense of entitlement that tends to be reflected in behavior and expectations later in life. But the same attitude toward men's role in Israeli society not only fortifies the male but also provides him with a significant advantage in society, even beyond the advantages provided by the gendered socialization familiar to other societies.

Reforms

Determining both the situation and, to a large degree, the causes (socialization—social norms and customs, religion, militarization), most Israeli feminists viewed political reform as the key to change. Other avenues were attempted as well, such as impacting on the media and the schools, for example, or changing institutions like the military or the religious establishments from within. And there were those who sought more radical, revolutionary forms of change in the belief that laws and lawmakers represent the current norms of a society rather than the will to change them, therefore societies' norms must be changed before one can think of legislation. Nonetheless, a major thrust was directed at the Knesset in the belief that new laws, which could be upheld by the courts, might set such new norms and thereby change gender relations in society. Courts might also be preferred in order to gain a law or even change a norm, although the decision to approach the courts before or after legislation was often a tactical decision. The choice of legislative change carried with it the need for political change of a broader kind, namely, the elevation of more women, and specifically feminist women, to the legislature. In effect, all three efforts were tried at the same time: new legislation, court cases, and the promotion of women in politics.

In the area of religious oppression, specifically the question of family law, very little progress has been made, although some of the laws in other areas did involve overcoming religious opposition (for example what is left of the abortion law, changes in the national security law and the party financing law, both of which we shall see below). The tenacity of the religious establishment regarding marriage and divorce may best be illustrated by the failure of several attempts to pass a Bill of Rights in Israel or a written constitution. In the case of the former, proposals introduced in the 1990s by Shulamith Aloni first as the head of the Civil Rights Party and then as the head of its successor, Meretz, failed primarily because of its Article 21 dealing with marriage and divorce.[3] The religious parties would not permit the passage of any bill that would alter religious control over these matters. The same problem exists today in the effort to forge a written constitution. And given the nature of the Israeli electoral system, the religious parties have the power to swing the creation of government coalitions in the direction of either of the large parties. As a result, the major parties are unwilling to alienate the religious parties even when out of power. The most that has been achieved are two changes. The first is the possibility for matters of maintenance and custody in a divorce to be decided by the civil rather than the religious courts. This improvement was obtained first with regard to the Jewish sector (family law being under the purview of each religious community). But in 2001 this measure was extended by law to all the religions, so that Muslims and Christians could also turn to the civil courts for these matters. The Knesset debate on the extension of this law to Muslims and Christians, the positions of the political parties, including the parties from the Arab sector, split along secular/religious lines, with secular Arab Knesset members (MKs) supporting the measure intended to augment the rights of Arab women in Israel.

The second reform was the enactment of a series of measures that might be used to pressure a man to grant his wife a divorce in case of repeated refusals on his part. These included the withholding of a passport or driver's license or bank account, or blocking departure from the country, although they have not been particularly effective if and when applied. Other changes were made in the Jewish religious courts themselves (namely the possibility for a woman to represent a divorce-seeking woman before the judge, though women judges are still not allowed). On the whole, however, no change has yet been enacted to resolve the problem of thousands of women unable to obtain a divorce, some of whom have been waiting for many years. And specific efforts to introduce civil marriage and possibly civil divorce have never had even minimal success. One result is that the number of marriages in Israel has declined significantly, as couples choose to live together without benefit of official marriage vows, and others sign marriage contracts or travel abroad for civil marriages. Mixed couples (Jewish-Muslim, etc.) have no choice but to go abroad if they want a marriage ceremony since marriage is possible in Israel only within each religion. Even observant Jews of the Reform or Conservative streams of Judaism are in a similar position if they do not accept the orthodox (or ultra-orthodox) system, which is the only stream of Judaism recognized for marriage and divorce in Israel. Marriages conducted abroad are recognized by Israel, but problems arise if these couples should seek divorce.

While the militarization of Israeli society has not changed, the situation for women in the army has undergone legislative and court action. In the 1990s the National Security Act was amended to allow women into any position in the army. The army maintained the right to determine the suitability of such positions, and regulations rendered women's service in combat positions voluntary rather a choice left up to the army, as in the case of male soldiers. The new law was followed by a court case brought by the same feminists (the Israel Women's Network) who had pushed for the change in the law.[4] This was the precedent-setting case of Alice Miller, a young draftee who had a degree in aeronautics and a civil pilot's license but who had been denied the right to apply to the pilots' training course of the army—an all-male, highly prestigious bastion of combat duty. The Israel Supreme Court ruled that the army's refusal was in violation of the principle of equality and called upon the army to make whatever logistic and other adjustments were necessary to meet the needs of women in the course and in the service. The result was not only the entry of women into the course (and a number of women pilots). Within a few years there were broad changes in women's service, including abolition of the women's corps, introduction of integrated training, inclusion in combat units, and the opening of numerous formerly male positions. Women's service in combat units is on a voluntary basis, thus still not equal to that of men's compulsory service.

Nonetheless, women had sought these changes, and did indeed view them as critical steps toward equal status in this central institution and, therefore, toward equality in Israeli society. Many other feminists felt, however, that the army was an oppressive institution at the heart of militarism, with its values and norms of dominance and violence. As such it was seen as incapable of serving the cause of gender equality.[5] Indeed, research subsequently demonstrated that rather than promote a positive change in gender attitudes, the service of women in combat positions or in positions previously held only by men, tended to reinforce negative attitudes toward women by the women themselves—as they adapted to the male norms of behavior and attitudes, without changing the latter. For example, they might join in the sexist comments or jokes by the men, regarding women as inferior to men—and themselves, presumably, as exceptions that proved the rule (much like the "queen bee syndrome" in politics and other areas). It is conceivable that in the long run, as women's presence in these tasks becomes more routine, and women's numbers there increase significantly, the results will be different. Studies have indicated that greater numbers of women in police forces abroad have actually changed those forces positively. The principle is similar to the idea of a women's critical mass in politics (i.e., sufficiently large numbers of women in order to change the environment, as distinct from the phenomenon of isolated women politicians adapting to male norms in order to succeed in the male environment). The hope is that rather than having the women undergo (negative) change, the army will change, positively, and with it gender attitudes within Israeli society. The opposite, at least, may be true—without change in the army, or more positively, a significant reduction of the army's importance in Israeli society, there is little chance for gender equality in Israel.

Women in the workforce is one area in which a good deal of legislative and litigation progress has been made. As a socialist country, Israel was quite early in providing for the right of women to work (outside the home) and protective legislation. When it was realized, as part of the second wave of feminism, that some protective legislation actually discriminated or worked against women financially and sometimes professionally as well, various laws were canceled and others amended. The three-month maternity leave with pay, for example, ultimately became parental leave at least for part of the benefits, but few families have taken advantage of the law (primarily because of various restrictions built into it) and it has come up for reconsideration. The obligatory retirement of women at age 60 instead of 65 as for men was challenged in the courts in the 1980s, and although the court case was unsuccessful it did lead to a change in the law. That change was then tested in the courts, successfully, so that women might continue to work to the age of 65 if they so choose. Making this optional rather than equalizing men and women's retirement ages (60 or 65 for both, or optional for both) marred somewhat the principle involved, but the new law and the precedent-setting case implementing it, like the Alice Miller case, did move the issue of gender equality further along the road.[6]

Other legislation that promised to bring still more progress was the Equal Opportunity in Employment Law (1988) which legislated against discrimination in employment and in wages (namely, equal pay for equal worth in order to correct inequalities in salaries for men and women in the same or similar positions). A series of laws were also legislated regarding affirmative action in various sectors. These bills began in the mid-1990s with the requirement of "appropriate representation" for women on the boards of directors of state-owned companies. It too had to be tested in the courts, but once that was successfully accomplished, again by the Israel Women's Network, the law was extended to the boards of all public bodies, including by implication local government. The Civil Service went further by instituting the requirement to hire women candidates in cases in which male and female candidates had similar qualifications.[7]

A most significant piece of legislation, relevant primarily but not only for women in the workplace, was the bill against sexual harassment passed in 1998. An advancement over bans on sexual harassment in the earlier Equal Opportunity in Employment Law and various stipulations in the Penal Code, the Sexual Harassment Law is probably the most comprehensive and progressive law of its kind in the world, both in its broad definition of sexual harassment and in its stipulation of punishment, including imprisonment, as a criminal offense. Employers as well as the harassers themselves are subject to punishment if convicted, and employers are required to take certain steps for the prevention of harassment, to appoint a person to receive and investigate complaints, and disseminate information on the law, on what constitutes harassment and on how to file a complaint.

The advances of the Equal Opportunity in Employment Law, as well as the laws on affirmative action and the Sexual Harassment Law were capped in late 2005 by the passage of a law to create an Equal Opportunity Commission meant to oversee all aspects of equality in the workplace and ensure that the equal opportunity law against discrimination is known and implemented. While discrimination on the basis of gender is considered the most prevalent form of discrimination in the workplace, the Commission will deal with discrimination of all types, arising from nationality, ethnic origins, age, religion, personal status, sexual orientation, and political affiliation. The women's organizations had pressed for the creation of this Commission, as part of their (continuing) efforts to obtain an Equal Rights Commission—that is, a body to deal with all forms of discrimination and inequality, anywhere in society, including the family as well as the workplace.

Violence against women is a topic that evoked interest relatively early as it was one of the first issues to be raised by Israeli feminists, but it took some time before changing attitudes were enacted into law. Beginning in the late 1980s amendments were made to the laws regarding rape, for example, recognizing rape in marriage, easing somewhat the demands upon rape victims as witnesses, including the possibility to participate in trials via closed circuit television rather than face their assailants in the courtroom. With regard to battered women, legislation was passed at the beginning of the 1990s allowing for men to be removed from the household, plus restraining orders for a limited amount of time. More recently, there has been a good deal of legislation designed to prevent trafficking in persons, with particular reference to trafficking in women, protection of victims, and bringing perpetrators to trial. Accompanying this legislation, in 2005 a hostel was opened in Tel Aviv for women victims awaiting the trials of their traffickers. In the wake of all of the legislation regarding violence against women, significant efforts have been made over the years to provide appropriate education and training for law enforcement personnel dealing with these issues.

A large number of additional issues were addressed by legislation, such as the recognition of women as heads of single-parent families, government payment of alimony and child upkeep payments, widow's inheritance of half a family's property, equal division of property upon divorce, the possibility of a woman to file an income tax report separate from her husband's in certain circumstances, and more. One important bill under consideration but not yet passed would allow for an income tax deduction for child-care payments (to a daytime nanny or day-care centers).

A different direction with regard to women's rights came in 2005 in the form of legislation designed to promote gender equality in the political and policy-making arena. Building on the United Nations Security Council Resolution 1325 of 31 October 2000, the Knesset passed a law stipulating appropriate representation of women in Israeli decision-making teams, particularly with regard to the resolution of national crises and peace negotiations. While initially formulated and intended primarily for women, in keeping with the UN resolution, the law in fact applied to "various sectors" of Israeli society, with the intention of ensuring representation of minorities (ethnic, national) as well. While somewhat vague, the law established an important principle of participation for women in central matters concerning the country.

Somewhat more concrete, and in part another way of gaining access for women to national decision-making, is legislation intended to ensure women's representation in the legislature itself—and by implication also providing them a role in decision-making. This has come in the form of an amendment to the law on party financing, providing the "reward" of 50 percent more financing for each woman the party elects to the Knesset and with the condition that women constitute 30 percent of the party's Knesset delegation. Although this will not provide equality, it is meant as an incentive to parties to place more women in realistic places on their lists of candidates to the Knesset. This path of augmenting funding (rather than reducing it as in a similar French law, for example) was chosen so as to avoid "punishing" those parties, mainly the religious parties, that tended to have no or almost no women on their lists for religious/cultural reasons. Even so, the religious parties oppose the bill, which nonetheless has passed its first reading in the Knesset, and it may be expected that parties willing to do without the added financing will simply ignore the law (as has occurred in France). Nonetheless, what until now was merely the choice of some political parties, namely the allocation of minimum quotas for women candidates, may now be elevated to a principle of law.

One political party, the social-democratic Meretz has had its own rule that all bodies of the party, including its list of candidates to the Knesset, must be composed of a minimum of 40 percent from each gender. Its constitution states that these percentages must be applied to the top five positions on the list in particular, just in case the party does not win more than five seats. One of Israel's major parties, the Labor Party, traditionally had a 20 percent minimum quota for women, and it has accepted a plan to increase this gradually to 40 percent by the year 2015. However, there is no stipulation that these must be in realistic places on the party list. As a result the party determines a certain percentage (usually two of the first ten places) on an ad hoc basis before each election. The second major party, the right-wing Likud, has also decided before each election to place a certain number of women on their list, usually one in every ten places. The women in the party have been trying to get a 25 percent quota into the party constitution, until now unsuccessfully. No other party has any quota system, even of an ad hoc nature, although there are pressures, sometimes successful, in the small parties to have at least one woman in a realistic place. (There have occasionally been women's parties in Israel, but only once, in the very first elections of the country in 1949, did they manage to get anyone into the Knesset.)

The law calling for 30 percent representation, and the efforts by the left-wing parties to get 40 percent, are the result not only of the demand for steps towards equality, but also designed to obtain what is called a "critical mass" of women in the legislature. Research has demonstrated that when only a small number of women are present, not only do they have no effect on the parliament's agenda or behavior, but often they adapt themselves to the patriarchal customs of this male-dominated institution, even avoiding gender-related legislation in an effort to minimize their gender. The theory, in part proven in some places, is that when there is a critical mass, usually believed to be 30 percent, women do begin to have an effect, at least on the agenda, namely on issues that are raised. In the absence of a critical mass, the numbers of women may be less important than the nature of the women lawmakers themselves. Put simply, feminist lawmakers, even if few in number, may indeed have an effect on the type of laws proposed, if not actually passed.

In Israel it certainly was the case that the election of feminists made an enormous difference even in a Knesset that had roughly the same number of women as the average for Israeli Knessets—in the area of 9 percent of the total 120-person membership. In the Knesset elected in 1992, which included 11 women members (the previous Knesset had had 8), some 104 gender-related bills were proposed, in comparison with only 37 in the previous Knesset.[8] Namely almost three times as many gender-related bills (there were other bills in which women raised gender-related questions even though the bill itself did not deal directly with women's issues). Of the gender-related bills, 70 were proposed by women. Only a small number, 19, of the gender-related bills were passed at the time, and out of these 9 had been proposed by women. The striking rate of increase in women-initiated gender-related legislation was directly traceable to the presence for the first time of a number of feminist legislators. Four in particular, from three different parties (Labor, Meretz, and the former Communists) were responsible for most of the women's initiatives, and on many bills they were joined by two women from the Likud who also were feminists (as well as occasionally by men from various parties). The suggested importance of ideology (feminism) over numbers may be found in the Knesset elected in 2003. A record-breaking 18 women were elected to this Knesset, a large number of them from the right-wing Likud, of whom one, possibly two, might identify themselves as feminists. The election of the Likud women was regarded with some suspicion (relatives of influential party members, for example), but of interest to us is whether this unprecedented large number of women would make a difference. Results of the three years of this Knesset, with 18 women, show that there were only 63 gender-related bill proposals (compared to 104 in the Knesset of 1992–1996), with 32 of them proposed by women (although a record 29 were actually passed—indicative perhaps of the fact that the a large portion of them were proposed by a center party (feminist) MK Eti Livni at a time when the party was a member of the government coalition). The earlier Knesset served four years, the present Knesset only three, which could account for some of the difference in the number of gender-related bills. But the lower percentage, and particularly the fact that most of them were actually proposed by the same women (one from the center party, one from the Likud, and the one Meretz woman MK—all feminists), does seem to support the idea that feminist ideology rather than numbers accounts for the political reforms concerning women in Israel. Nonetheless, numbers do play an educational role, accustoming the public to seeing women in these positions, and it is also possible that when the critical mass is reached, more women MKs will be willing to identify themselves with gender issues and genuinely represent women's interests.

The work of Israeli legislators, particularly the feminists among them (and usually in cooperation with feminist organizations), has on the whole been impressive. Indeed Israel was always relatively advanced when it came to laws on the books—in part presumably because of the dominance for many years of social democratic ideology and parties. This is in keeping with research worldwide that has found that left-wing and centrist parties are more likely than right-wing parties to elect women and deal with human rights issues, including women's issues. Israel would seem to fit these findings, although there certainly have been efforts within the right wing to move in this direction as well. A major problem in Israel today, however, is not so much the legislation or even (most of) the parties, but rather the major problem concerns implementation of the various laws and regulations. In fact there has even been backsliding regarding laws that have long been on the books, such as the ban on dismissing a pregnant worker. As we have seen, in some cases, individuals and organizations have turned to the courts to ensure implementation, and feminist organizations have tried to raise the issue of implementation. The creation, finally, of the Equal Opportunity Commission was the result of such efforts and intended to serve this very purpose of ensuring implementation, at least in matters connected with employment. Other governmental institutions and bodies had been created in the past to deal with women's rights and directly or indirectly promote implementation. The first of these was a National Commission for the Advancement of the Status of Women and the appointment of a woman advisor to the Prime Minister on this subject. They were created by the government, and it is significant that the terminology was "status," rather than "rights." In any case, they were allotted virtually no budget, and it is difficult to say that they accomplished anything, despite the good intentions of many of those involved.

In time, however, the task of advisor on the status of women was created in the Civil Service Commission and the woman, Rivka Shaked, who has held this position (in addition to her regular duties in the Civil Service Commission) trains and oversees a very large number of women who have been appointed, by law, as advisors on the status of women in all government offices, at all levels including local government. At local government level there are also councils on the status of women, usually made up of volunteers acting under the chair of a woman member of the local government. In one case, the city of Herzliya, there is actually a statutory Administration for Women's Affairs (in addition to the advisor) as an integral part of the city government. Introduced by Herzliya's feminist mayor Yael German (of Meretz), the Administration serves as a model that is presently being followed elsewhere in the country.

A Knesset Committee on the Status of Women was also formed, although it was made a statutory committee only after vigorous efforts in 1992 by its chair, Labor MK (then) Yael Dayan, who also had to struggle (once again) to prevent its cancellation years later. Through Dayan's efforts a government Administration (Rashut) for the Advancement of the Status of Women was created in 1999, attached to the Prime Minister's Office. Both the Committee and the Administration were to undertake a variety of measures, among them promotion and monitoring of laws. While the Administration works with an internal council (replacing the earlier National Commission for the Advancement of the Status of Women), the Knesset Committee works with a broad spectrum of feminist and other organizations. Nonetheless, aside from trying to monitor, it has been hard put to ensure implementation.

There are numerous obstacles to implementation of the often progressive laws that have been passed. The very factors contributing to the inequality of women in Israel often serve also as impediments to implementation. Religious elements may find themselves in opposition to feminist efforts, obviously and particularly in the area of family law, but also in relation to abortion, family planning, and various issues connected with women serving in the army. However, on an issue such as pornography many feminists find themselves working hand in hand with the ultra-orthodox. Shortage of money is the obstacle most often encountered, or invoked officially or unofficially. Budgetary considerations are a matter of priorities, and security needs are often cited as a reason (pretext) for budgetary priorities that defer women's interests. Interest groups and interested individuals, usually with political connections, may have a stake in non-implementation of some of the progressive bills on the ledgers, while party politics (particularly between coalition and opposition parties) can of course complicate or impede implementation. There is also bureaucratic inertia or confusion with which to contend, but bureaucrats, along with the police and even judges require re-education and sensitizing to gender-related matters if laws are to be implemented.[9] Finally, prejudice and sexism, if not just plain ignorance—within the government, the bureaucracies, the law enforcement and justice systems, the business community, the political parties, and the public at large—can lead to the total disregard for, non-compliance with, or non-implementation of the best laws in the world. It has been argued that if society is not ready for change, legislation will make no difference, but legislation can make a difference in changing the situation and the norms if monitoring agencies and organizations, the courts, and the public (through education, the media, and NGOs) are mobilized for the task. These are the instruments of a democratic society, characteristic of participatory democracy in particular. And they are quite strong in Israel.

Notes

1 Reference throughout is to Palestinian citizens of Israel, not the Palestinian population of the occupied territories.
2 Abortion was permitted under various objective circumstances such as possible damage to the health of the mother or the fetus. The only subjective clause, the so-called "social clause" that was repealed, permitted abortion for social reasons such as family or social conditions.
3 Similarly Israel signed and ratified the Convention on the Elimination of All Forms of Discrimination against Women (CEDAW) but with certain reservations, particularly to Article 16 regarding freedom in marriage.
4 The IWN was joined in court by the Association for Civil Rights in Israel.
5 Another argument held that the changes affected only otherwise privileged women, Jewish women mainly from the middle or upper class (European origin) since Arab women were excluded from the army altogether and lower class or lower women would not qualify for the new positions. Thus even if the attitude toward some women might change, the majority of women would remain unaffected. Some years ago then Brigadier General Amira Dotan argued that those women, as well as men, serving in the army might be positively affected by seeing women in new, respected positions. She believed that male recruits benefited from role models provided by reservists whom they saw during their service – engineers, academics, artists, professionals, but since women do not do reserve duty (with only few exceptions), women recruits were denied such role models. After General Dotan, nothing was ever done to change this situation.
6 As mentioned previously, Alice Miller (who had a civilian pilot's license from South Africa), was refused acceptance to the Israel Air Force pilot training course, so she petitioned the Supreme Court together with the Israel Women's Network and the

Association for Civil Rights in Israel. The court ruled that, in the name of equality, the army had to make all necessary adjustments to permit women to enter the course.

7 Affirmative action in the Civil Service was introduced for Arabs as well by the same Civil Service Commissioner, Prof. Itzhak Gal-noor.

8 The reference throughout is to private member bills rather than government proposals.

9 Judge Roth-Levy has for a number of years conducted training sessions for judges on gender issues.

Part II

Women's leadership in civil society

5 Women's NGOs and social change in Morocco

Moha Ennaji [1]

Introduction

In this chapter, I deal with gender, activism, and social change in a broader socio-political approach. The emergence of women's NGOs is an answer to the crisis of the nation-state model form of governance. Such grassroots movements are treated as a way to ensure democracy and sustainable development. They create social dynamism through the mobilization and participation of the masses. They also decentralize governance in a more globalized world. Their modes of action raise new challenges for government development policies and open up new ways of thinking about the issues of sustainability.

To understand the significance of Moroccan women's activism, it is essential to relate it to the dialectical relationship between "needs satisfaction" and authority renewal of legitimacy. The approach of "needs interpretation" according to Nancy Frazer (1989) allows for the emergence of the marginalized consciousness whereby the marginalized use different tools and strategies from the dominant group. The idea is to incorporate feminine NGOs taking into account women's own interpretations, needs, and views of gender and development in order to fit local realities and satisfy these needs and demands.

The present contribution deals with the role of women's NGOs in the struggle against gender inequalities. It highlights their agency to consolidate democracy and social justice and to challenge traditional thinking and practices of governance.

The role of women's NGOs

Women's issues and emancipation have recently become an important political topic that attracts the attention of decision-makers, activists, researchers, and politicians. Moroccan women's organizations play a decisive role in the democratization and modernization of society. From the 1970s, women's NGOs have severely criticized the ways in which policy-makers overlooked women's demands for emancipation and gender equity.

At the socio-political level, after the political reforms of the 1990s (re-amendment of the constitution and law on elections), which led to more democratization, a large number of women's associations emerged having a great national and regional impact. As a case in point, we cite the following major associations: *Josour, l'Union Féminine Marocaine,* and *l'Organization Démocratique des Femmes.*

These non-government organizations often have links and communicate as they form networks. However, despite the dynamism of these organizations, women are still disfavored at the judiciary level in legal matters (e.g., in polygamy, inheritance, etc.), as will be shown in due course. By contrast, the conservative forces view women's role to be limited to home, reproduction, and child rearing.

Women's NGOs promote women's emancipation, participation, social mobilization, and associative lobbying that encourages good governance and a culture of responsible citizens, not passive subjects. Women's NGOs should be seen as a way to ensure a dynamic participatory and equitable democracy. NGOs have become real schools of democracy which encourage women's empowerment and participation in decision-making and in public affairs. NGOs have enabled women to critically assess their own situation and shape a transformation of society (cf. Ennaji 2006 and Ennaji 2008).

Women's NGOs are characterized by pragmatism and clear objectives, namely improving women's socio-economic situation, integrating them in development, and ensuring their participation in public life. They adopt strategies and actions which enable them to achieve sustainability through the empowerment of women.

Despite problems related to lack of training, information, and know-how in associative management and initiatives, weak internal as well as external communication, and heavy reliance on international donor agencies as far as financing is concerned, Moroccan women's NGOs strive hard to empower women through mobilizng different actors in civil society, through decentralization and development of the know-how of their members.

The network of women's NGOs is proliferating by the creation of local chapters in each city in the country. International funders like the World Bank, UNIFEM, PNUD, FNUAP, European Commission, and UNESCO sponsor many projects of development; due to their help, these NGOs have organized many seminars and workshops about strategic themes like violence against women, the new family code, fund raising, information technology, literacy programs, etc., the aim of which is to empower women and raise their degree of awareness.

Women's NGOs indulge in diverse activities, and as a result they have so far accumulated a great deal of experience in local development; their experience should be known, studied, and analyzed profoundly to show that Morocco's women are dynamic and problem-solvers (see Mernissi 1989). Women's NGOs attempt to address Morocco's burning socio-economic problems and their root causes explicitly and systematically. Many feminine NGO leaders (like Leila Rhiwi, *Espace Associatif Marocain,* Latifa Jbabdi, *Action de l'Union Féminine*) are among the most influential women activists in the region.

Women's NGOs work in the areas of human rights, women's rights, economic development, education, and health, and also continue to fight the fundamental battles on legislation and democratic checks and balances. Two main types of feminine NGOs can be distinguished. The first type focuses on local development, attempting to improve the deficient government services. Many local associations address concrete problems on the ground using their own means. The second type focuses on advocacy and lobbying with the objective of defending democracy. Human rights groups are the most prominent examples of this second type. They have performed a qualitative leap from the defensive role of denouncing women's rights abuses under the late Hassan II's repressive regime, to a pro-active stance in promoting the values of democracy and human rights. Some of the leading NGOs (namely *Union de l'Action Féminine* and the *Association Démocratique des Femmes du Maroc* (ADFM)) combine the two approaches, for example, by providing counseling to women victims of domestic violence while lobbying for legislative change to ensure better protection of women's rights. These two leading associations originally developed from women's sections of the political left.

Women's NGOs operate independently from political parties and the government; they are politically and financially autonomous from other institutions. However, they at times work hand in hand with democratic parties and government ministries on specific goals and projects like literacy, education, reproductive health, micro-credits, etc. The government usually devotes a budget to NGOs that work actively for achieving gender equity and sustainable development. In 2008, the Ministry of Social Development, Family, and Solidarity led by Nouzha Skalli, a well-known feminist and socialist, distributed millions of dirhams to these NGOs to sponsor their development projects within the framework of the national campaign for human development (INDH). Unlike in many Arab countries such as Tunisia, women's NGOs are also allowed by the government to receive financial aid from foreign organizations and donors.

NGO coalitions on specific issues (human rights, law on associations, fight against corruption, domestic violence, etc.) have become important political agents. For example, the women's movement has proposed amendments to all relevant legislation (personal status code, penal code, nationality). The alternatives they propose receive huge media and public attention. One of the remarkable achievements of the women's movement has been the establishment of a 10 percent quota for representation of women in parliament and 20 percent of the political bureau of some political parties like the *Union Socialiste des Forces Populaires*. As a result, in 2008 we have 34 women in parliament and 7 ministers. Even the religious right and Islamist women's associations have lobbied hard for more representation in parliament. For example, Nadia Yassine, daughter of Cheikh Yassine, leader of the Islamist group *Al Adl wa Al Ihssan*, approved the reform of the Mudawana (family law) in favor of women.

The challenge facing women's NGOs is to elaborate autonomous strategies and to establish themselves as forces for innovation, political pressure, and proposals to push the state to revise its policies. The NGO's autonomy is a basic guarantee for genuine partnership with the state and for cooperation with political parties.

Morocco is perhaps the only country in the Arab world where feminist NGO activists have been able to achieve important civil rights, particularly the reform of the personal status law, the citizenship law whereby a Moroccan woman has the right to pass her nationality to her children, and other policies fostering the integration of women in sustainable development.

Furthermore, over the past two decades over a hundred Moroccan women's advocacy organizations and associations have emerged to combat violence against women, illiteracy, poverty among women, gender-based legal and cultural discrimination, and under-representation of women in policy-making. While the majority of Moroccan women's NGOs are based in big cities like Rabat, Casablanca, Marrakesh, and Fes, women's advocacy organizations have emerged in smaller towns and villages across the country since the late 1990s to address local problems unique to women in their regions.

Historical background of the Mudawana reform

The campaign and struggle of feminist activists and democratic forces in Morocco for the reform of the personal status law goes back to the 1970s. There were many meetings and workshops on women's rights, and a debate was conducted on women in Islam. There was a real concern to join forces to change the Mudawana in favor of women's rights.

As Morocco was facing a financial crisis by the 1980s, the late King Hassan II agreed to implement a program of structural adjustment imposed by the World Bank and the International Monetary Fund. A series of economic and human-rights reforms followed. When parliament started discussing the new constitution, women renewed their fight for equality on two fronts: government and civil society, where they publicized their petition to revise the Mudawana.

In October 1990, a coalition of professional middle-class women, mainly the Union for Feminine Action, led by Latifa Jbabdi, launched a campaign to gather a million signatures on a petition to reform the Mudawana. Their goal was to raise awareness, especially among women, that widespread poverty, illiteracy, and domestic violence stemmed from the Mudawana, which made women second-class citizens.

In 1992, Islamic fundamentalist leaders issued a *Fatwah*, or a religious ruling, against those involved in the struggle to reform the Mudawana. They went repeatedly to the most distant cities in Morocco and to many public places like mosques to incite violence against all those who signed the petition.

An eminent Islamic scholar said: "In our religion, if somebody dares to counter the divine laws that we must interpret according to Shari'a, they must be punished." That is what fundamentalists considered a *Fatwah*, of which they made big media coverage. As the dispute between the women and the Islamists escalated, an unexpected development took place. The Commander of the Faithful, King Hassan II, intervened in a national broadcast on August 20, 1992. He stated: "The Mudawana is my responsibility. I am the only one with the authority to amend the Mudawana." The King also acknowledged that the women had grievances and held a meeting with them in Rabat.

When, in 1992, the King made his statement and recognized the injustices against women, it was a happy moment and a great relief for all women, and for everyone who was fighting for women's causes. After meeting with this group of women representing different political parties and NGOs, King Hassan II brought some of their proposed reforms before the all-male council of *Ulemas* – the panel of jurists and scholars who rule on matters of Islamic law.

Nearly a year later, the King unveiled the reforms approved by the council of *Ulemas*. A husband now needed his wife's permission to take other wives, and a religious judge's approval was required for divorce. A mother over 18 would receive custody of her children, if their father died. As limited as the reforms were, they opened the door to change for the first time in centuries.

However, although the revised Mudawana approved in 1993 still defined women as economically dependent on men, and as emotionally too weak to have the right to divorce, Islamists were unhappy about it. In this regard, Abdelilah Benkirane, leader of the Islamist party (Party of Justice and Development (PJD)) stated in parliament:

> In the past, any man who wanted to marry another woman in addition to his wife, it was easy. Today, he is obliged to take the advice of his first wife and of the judge. Sometimes, that simply pushes the man to divorce his first wife. For us, divorce is a catastrophe. Everyone knows that. Satan is never so happy as when there is a divorce in the family. This is stipulated in our religion. So maybe we have been too carried away with pleasing the Westernized elite which is tied to the West and tied to money.

Despite opposition, women continued to campaign for further reforms of the Mudawana and improvement of their social status. Women's activism increased in intensity during the first socialist government of "Alternance" led by Abderrahman El Youssoufi in 1998. This democratic transition had repercussions on gender dynamics, as was clear in the subsequent reforms. In 1999 the pressure of women's NGOs and democratic parties forced the government to adopt an unprecedented National Plan of Action for the Integration of Women in Development. High on the agenda was protecting women from violence and raising the low levels of female literacy.

This plan of action was a vast program for the integration of women in socio-economic development at the macro- and micro-economic levels. It aimed to promote women's rights on the legal, political, and socio-economic levels.

This program also sought to improve the living conditions of women in order to eliminate any segregation against them and to foster gender equity. In education, the plan aimed to promote the schooling of young girls, increase literacy and promote training and high skills among women. Women's social and legal status was also the concern of the project, which planned to take concrete measures to protect women's legal rights and social interests and encourage their participation in public life.

Concerning their economic well-being, the project aimed to reduce poverty among women by reinforcing their economic role, by ensuring their full participation in the management of human and natural resources, and by supporting institutions and organizations that promote women's emancipation.

This moderate project, which was presented by former State Secretary for Family Affairs Mohamed Said Saadi, was not intended to revolutionize women's rights, but aimed to assert some basic rights for women against discrimination and abuse. However, opponents of the plan saw these changes as a diversion from Islamic moral values.

On March 12, 2000, a supportive rally in Rabat drew hundreds of thousands of people. Islamists organized a counter-protest the same day in Casablanca, with at least as many marchers denouncing what they called the Western nature of the project.

Women NGOs conceived of the Action Plan as a tool to introduce and respect gender equity in all walks of life, mainly in economic projects, politics, education, social policy, and sustainable development in general. They suggested that the reforms be based on the institutionalization of equality between the sexes in rights and obligations, at the social, economic, cultural, and political levels. Thus, the family law, the employment code, the penal code, and other laws must be amended, taking into account the gender dimension. New strategies must be established to protect women from violence, sexual harassment, social injustice, and illiteracy. Feminist organizations also recommended concrete actions and effective campaigns to encourage women's participation in elections.

King Mohammed VI, who made this issue a priority when he reached the throne in 1999, decided to step in, leveraging his status as the country's supreme religious authority. An advisory Royal Commission composed of religious theorists, academics, and women experts was later set up to propose a revised, Islam-derived reform.

In October 2003, the King announced the new family code which he said respected both the Islamic law and the universal declaration of human rights. The reform was unanimously approved by parliament and nearly all Islamist organizations because this time the formulation of the reform was done in such a way that it spoke about family not personal status law, it made both spouses responsible for the household, made marriage legal at the age of 18 for both boys and girls, and made divorce impossible without the decision of the judge, and polygamy highly restricted.

After the suicide bomb attacks by radical Islamists which claimed 45 lives in Casablanca on May 16, 2003, which discredited Islamists in the country, the latter were obliged to keep a low profile. Parliament, the PJD included, voted for this reform although the new Mudawana was similar to the proposed 2000 action plan on most issues.

This time, however, Islamist leaders said the reform was in tune with their ideas. In a statement, the official Islamist party, the PJD, declared that the new family code "constitutes a substantial accomplishment for the entire Moroccan people."

PJD leaders claim the King's reform directly refers to Islam, unlike the earlier proposed reform, which had socialist roots. "The Ijtihad [the reinterpretation of Islamic law] has no limits. We just want to avoid contradictions with Islamic law," said Abdeslam Ballaji, a member of the National Council of the PJD.

Analysts argued, however, that PJD leaders were acknowledging the King's religious authority while also moderating their language in response to May's terrorist attacks in Casablanca. Many Moroccans blamed the PJD for inspiring the May 16 strikes.

Since its ratification by parliament on January 16, 2004, the new Mudawana has been on everyone's lips. In a crowded commercial street in Rabat, the capital, a man loudly complains: "Now I will be commanded by a woman in my home. What do I have left to do in this country now?"

Thus, we can state that women's NGOs have made important realizations, namely the ratification of CEDAW (Convention for Eliminating Discrimination against Women) by Morocco on June 21, 1993,[2] the elimination of the authorization of the husband for practicing a trade activity (1995), or for the signature of a work contract (1996), the revision of the work code and of the penal code (2003), and the reform of the nationality code which now allows a Moroccan women to transmit her citizenship to her children. Yet, the most remarkable achievement is the reform of the family code (in October 2003). The latter code came after more than 20 years of struggle by feminists and women's NGOs. The changes brought out by this code are briefly as follows.

The family is considered to be under the responsibility of both the husband and the wife, while the previous personal status law treated the husband as the only person responsible for the family. The old idea that the wife must obey her husband under any circumstances has been eliminated because the new reform recognizes equality of rights and obligations of spouses. Couples must appear before a judge before contracting marriage and when filing for divorce. The judge has a crucial responsibility in both acts. Women now can marry without the authorization or agreement of their father, while in the previous personal status code, the presence and approval of the father was compulsory before marriage could be ratified. Women now have the right of custody over their children even in case they remarry. In the old law, the mother lost custody over her children the moment she remarried another man.

However, the new family code has its own limitations and imperfections despite its advantages and its positive impact on women and families. I will mention the following limitations. As a case in point, polygamy, although drastically restricted, is legally maintained; "repudiation" (unilateral divorce by the husband) is kept, although under special circumstances. Divorce by compensation is maintained: in case the wife wants divorce, she must pay some compensation to her husband, the amount of which and the deadline of which are determined by the judge. The distribution of property and money accumulated during marriage remains problematic, because the contract relevant to this aspect remains optional, while the women's movement demands that it become compulsory. In case of divorce, the father remains the legal guardian of his children, even if the mother has custody over them. Inequality concerning inheritance is still maintained, whereby a woman inherits half the part of a man, which implies that males inherit the double of females. When there are no males among the inheritors, the females inherit only part of the legacy and the rest goes to the family of the deceased male.

Over the last five years, women's NGOs have intensified their efforts to improve women's living conditions. Thus, many associations fight violence against women, and assist battered women by giving them shelter and legal advice. A network of 17 such associations called "ANARUZ" has been created. This network has organized numerous activities and campaigns to sensitize women and men to gender equality, the promotion of women's rights, tolerance, and citizenship. They have been successful in using the media, especially television, to make their voices heard and to contribute to debate on equality between the sexes. In 1998, the first national campaign against violence against women was organized. This campaign mobilized many government administrations and ministries, as well as civil society. As an outcome of this campaign, the Ministry of Family has adopted a national strategy to combat violence against women, and recently the government has initiated an 800 phone number for women victims of violence who want to seek help or make a complaint about domestic violence. Violence, which was taboo until five years ago, has become a debated topic in the media, due to the efforts of women's NGOs. The silence about violence has been broken, particularly about domestic and sexual violence.[3]

It is worth mentioning that, in addition to women's associations, women journalists and academics have been actively fighting for change through their articles, publications, and research. These top-level actions have boosted the morale of Moroccan feminists in general and women's NGOs in particular and confirmed their legitimate legal demands and concerns, and are recognized as important tools for social and political reforms and for the transformation of gender roles and the implementation of gender equity (for more on this point, cf. Sadiqi and Ennaji 2006).

By and large, the Moroccan feminist movement started to become a locomotive for the democratization of public space and for the protection of women's rights which are human rights, fostering the universal principles of citizenship, equality, diversity, and social justice. The movement has succeeded in empowering women politically, economically, and socially, by encouraging them to participate in public life, pursue their education, and climb the social ladder.

However, there are still limitations and barriers in the path of women's emancipation and legal rights. For instance, Morocco has not ratified some international accords in favour of women's rights, particularly those relevant to prostitution (1949), and the Moroccan constitution does not mention that it is based on any of the international accords and agreements. Similarly, the principle of the quota is not officially recognized in the constitution, which implies that the political representation of women depends on the political wish and decision of political leaders.

We also note the weak commitment of the government to protect women from violence, especially domestic violence, at the legal level, precisely concerning police investigation, sanctions, and legal advice to women victims of violence. It is also noticeable that the new *livret d'état civil* contains four pages for wives, while the revised family code has heavily restricted polygamy. Finally, in the new work code, there is no sanction against sexual harassment, and equality in terms of salaries is not guaranteed; maids, for example, who are generally over-exploited by their employers, are not protected by the new employment code. In the penal code, the notion of rape by the husband is not mentioned for the simple reason that the body of a married woman is still considered a property of the husband.

Although Moroccan women have realized important achievements, women's NGOs have other demands which seek to improve the living standards of women and to establish equality of the sexes in all domains. They demand, for instance, the institutionalization of the quota system, the introduction of quotas within political parties and organizations; they also encourage women to stand for office or elections where possible, and foster the promotion of women in administrations (see Skalli 2007).

However, despite the important reforms brought by the new Mudawana, there are problems relevant to their implementation as yet. Cultural barriers and patriarchal traditions, illiteracy, and lack of information about the new family code prevent women from invoking their rights or reporting crimes against them, such as rape, child abuse, sexual exploitation, and domestic violence. Concerning such cases, lawyers do not often make legal arguments based on international human rights treaties. Similarly, judges often resist relying on international treaties on the pretext that the law enumerating the sources on which they may base their decision does not include international law.

Conclusion

Women's activism has feminized civil society in Morocco due to its greater social involvement in social and political affairs and due to the proliferation of women's associations, and their access to the media. Since the early 1980s, gender roles have been shaken by women's contributions and their participation in the public life motivated by their aspirations for equality and civil rights (Sadiqi and Ennaji 2006).

The feminist and democratic civil society succeeded in reforming the Mudawana, which is no longer considered a sacred text. While in the past, the Mudawana was treated like the holy Qur'an, it has now become more like secular law, more open to debate. Perhaps just as important as reforms of family law are the attempts by women to lift the male control of sacred Islamic religious texts. Increasingly, women in Morocco and throughout the MENA region have called for an opening of these texts to reinterpretation from feminist perspectives. Such critiques as those from Fatima Mernissi, for example, question the use of religion to control women politically, even in Islamic countries that have announced the rights of their populations to universal suffrage. Mernissi (1990) debates "political Islam," as distinct from the right religion of Islam based on the Qur'an and Sunna —in which the oppression of women is paralleled with the repression of the will of the people. Feminist NGOs argue that the door must be open for creativity and scholarly research in matters relevant to the family code and legislations. Women's activism is essential to modernization and democracy, for it is the women's movement that has opened space for civil society and for democratic society. One cannot imagine any true development without the full emancipation of women.

Notes

1   I am grateful to Elizabeth Matthews and two anonymous readers for their judicious comments and remarks which led to the improvement of this chapter. I am also thankful to audiences at Northwestern University and Oldenburg University, where this work was presented in 2004 and 2006 respectively.
2   During the Green March Anniversary, on November 6, 2008, King Mohammed VI declared Morocco's ratification of CEDAW without any reservations; this is an unprecedented decision, given that most Muslim and Arab countries have not ratified CEDAW.
3   A law is being discussed by the Moroccan parliament to counter and punish sexual harassment (see the Moroccan Magazine *Tel Quel,* February 28, 2009).

6 Palestinian women's movements and activism

Islah Jad

Introduction

The study of the Palestinian women's movements is challenging. These movements are faced with two major tasks: continuing the national struggle and participating in state-building while at the same time pressing for women's rights. Like women's movements worldwide, the Palestinian women's movements are faced with both "old" agendas of mobilization and liberation and new ones concerning women's equality and empowerment. Under normal circumstances, it is difficult to straddle these two agendas; all the more so when there is an extraordinary situation in which the state and society are threatened in their very physical existence by the Israeli Occupation. The extremity of the situation became shockingly apparent in March 2002, when women leaders examined the possibility of pouring into the streets to stop the advance of the Israeli tanks re-occupying their cities. The answer was simple but very revealing: "We are not organized," they said.

The era of state-building that followed the signing of the Oslo Agreement in 1993 greatly diminished women's, and other social groups' capacity to mobilize. Israeli harassment and land confiscation discredited the Palestinian Authority (PA) and gave power to the Islamists as the true nationalists. In the Palestinian women's movements, power was granted to new feminist elites working from within civil society in NGOs or from within the PA apparatuses leading to the emergence of "femocrats."[1] This changed the composition and the strategies of what is now categorized as the secular women's movement at the expense of women cadres of rural or refugee background. Islamists are the main contesters of this hegemony. The nascent state structures were ill-equipped to assist in the organization of people's resistance and women's movements, and the emerging "civil society" was not in a better shape.

The Oslo era enhanced a new Palestinian civil society that emerged as a de-politicized arena which, while providing a forum for discussing democratization, human rights, and women's rights, had effectively lost its previous capacity to organize and mobilize different groups, and in particular, women's groups aiming to combat the Occupation. In the meanwhile, the growing power of the Islamists, now taking on the mantle of a national struggle despite their being seen as undemocratic, fundamentalist, and not part of a "true" civil society, added more complication on the possibility of forming a unifying agenda for combating the Occupation or achieving women's rights.

The shift in the role of the NGO sector in the PA era left deep marks on the different forms of women's activism. The change pressured women's movements to shift their agenda from combining the national struggle with women's emancipation into targeting the state to claim women's rights. Many successful women's grassroots organizations were transformed into NGOs or came under the growing influence of NGO practices.

One of my main arguments in this chapter is that the transformation from organizations of mass mobilization into NGOs was ultimately disempowering in that it weakened the mobilizing potential of secular feminist women's organizations and depoliticized their activism. I interrogate the growing trend depicting Middle Eastern women's secular, feminist NGOs as the "modern" and democratic "agents of civil society" (Moghadam 1998: 25; Kandil 1995) and problematize the unqualified and interchangeable use of the terms "NGO" and "social movement" in the Palestinian case, in particular, and in the Middle East, in general (Kandil 1995; Moghadam 1998; Bishara 1996; Beydoun 2002; Chatty and Rabo 1997; Shalabi 2001). Many scholars view the proliferation of NGOs in the Middle East as evidence of a vibrant civil society and paradoxically as counter-hegemonic to Islamist discourse (Norton 1993, 1995; Ibrahim 1993; Al-Sayyid 1993; Moghadam 1998). However little is done to verify and evaluate the impact of the proliferation of NGOs on the empowerment of the different social groups which NGOs claim to represent and in their capacity to present a viable alternative to Islamist groups. Nor are there attempts to verify whether women have succeeded in mobilizing or organizing different groups in pursuit of their rights. Few studies on the Middle East focus on how NGOs affect and interact with other forms of social organization whether in the form of unions, political parties, or social movements involving students, women, or workers.

From "self-help" to "self-government": femocrats between patronage and feminism

One group of players coming into its own with the formation of the PA is that of the femocrats. The Palestinian femocrats are not necessarily feminist, nor are they "employed within state bureaucratic positions to work on advancing the position of women in the wider society through the development of equal opportunity and anti-discrimination" (Yeatman 1990: 65). Most Palestinian femocrats, in particular those in high-ranking positions, are nominated through patronage relations and not for their feminist credentials.[2] However, these women are neither co-opted women who are waiting for the President to give them the *mot d'ordre* to act on his behalf, nor are they innovators; they are somewhere in between. In other words, some of them may try to develop a gender agenda within the numerous constraints facing the PA and their positioning within it, while others may use the gender agenda and their political access to promote their own interests. Thus, patronage per se is not necessarily anti-feminist or against women's representation. As Goetz observes, in Uganda patronage may lead to a situation whereby "high-profile appointments of women to senior civil service positions have significantly enhanced women's presence in the administration" (2003: 110). In this sense, it is safe to denote these women as femocrats since they deploy women's interests and rights, regardless of whether they "truly" believe in them or not, to make a space for themselves within the PA and society.

The Inter-Ministerial Committee for the Advancement of Women's Status (*lajnet al tansiq al wizaria leraf'a makanat al mara'a*) (hereafter referred to as IMCAW) was the locus of femocrats within the Palestinian "state" apparatus until its dissolution and the establishment of the Ministry of Women. IMCAW consisted of women in key positions in their respective ministries, mostly nominated by the President to mainstream gender in their structures.

The success in fundraising and capacity-building was seen as vital for women in IMCAW in proving themselves as professionals; they attempted, it seems, to imitate professional women in NGOs at the expense of their "old" image as militants. As the UNIFEM coordinator puts it:

> The members of IMCAW feel that they need lots of training on capacity-building, they feel they lag behind the skills in the women's NGOs who all know how to fundraise, how to formulate a strategy, how to manage and communicate, they used to be *mere* [stress added] freedom fighters. They did not need to fundraise; they used to get funds through money collections and donations from the Arabs or the Palestinians in the Diaspora. ('Alya, Interview)

Thus, NGOization set the model for the "old" militants and was their path to professionalization. As noted earlier, in the Palestinian Development Plan (PDP 1996–1998), IMCAW was assigned the task of "developing" women, but mainstreaming gender was left without resources. It is not surprising that the committee is heavily dependent on donor aid and that it is functioning as an NGO (or in this case, a GONGO, a governmental non-governmental organization). As such, women were lumped in their gender units in which many activist women were co-opted while gender equity was not integrated into the economic and political agendas of the new "secular" PA. The lack of an overall goal for development-led femocrats in IMCAW to focus on technicalities, such as how many workshops were needed for a mainstreaming plan, thus falling in the trap Goetz warned about when criticizing the notion of mainstreaming as a focus on processes and means rather than ends, leading, thus, to a preoccupation with the minutiae of procedures at all levels, rather than clarity or direction about goals (Goetz 1997).

The confusions and conflicts within IMCAW reflect a similar trend in all ministries and structures of the PA which seriously hinders not only mainstreaming gender but also any serious attempt to sustain development. One can hardly speak of an orchestrated clear national project for change in this case. Incoherent, contradictory, and sometimes conflicting policies and interventions are the rule.

The Ministry of Youth and Sports provides an illuminating example of the slight outcomes of gender mainstreaming. The Ministry's philosophy for a national social agenda for children and teenagers, as seen in its publications and its summer camps, focuses on civic culture promoting basic rights such as freedom of expression, gender equality, democracy, and participation. However, the Ministry was shadowed by another structure linked directly to the President's office and the remnants of the PLO: the Recruitment and National and Political Guidance Directorate which follows a nationalistic agenda for youth focused on "symbolic" military training and political indoctrination in favor of the ruling party and the political leadership. The Ministry and the Directorate represent two different policies with two distinct sets of gender sub-texts. In the Ministry of Youth and Sports, gender issues are integrated more systematically through regulations and programs: equal participation for both sexes in the camps, highlighting gender equality through activities, and through making more efforts at the community level to encourage parents to send their daughters to co-educational camps. As for the Ministry of Youth and Sports, it adopted the "mainstreaming" agenda as if independence was achieved, and new governance structures could take the gender agenda into account.

In the case of the Directorate, gender issues were targeted by including both sexes in the "national agenda," i.e., in the military training camps. Gender issues were not dealt with as a social problem even in the workshops designed for female cadres, but rather as in the old PLO formula, namely, that men and women should both participate in liberating Palestine. The differences between the Ministry and the Directorate highlight the confusion between the national and social agendas. After a few months, the "gender-aware" Minister of Youth and Sports was demoted because of his critical stands on patronage and corruption in the PA. He was replaced by a "religious" figure in order to accommodate the Islamists.

If mainstreaming gender suffered from the conflict and confusion within the PA, women's activism in civil society was in no better shape. The establishment of the PA led to de-mobilization of the General Union of Palestinian Women (GUPW) as well as of grassroots organizations in general and that of Fatah, the ruling party, in particular as is explained below.

GUPW: between mobilization and NGO-ization

The structure of the GUPW, whether in the homeland or in the Diaspora, represents the outcome of the constant political changes which have taken place in the Palestinian political system. Political instability led to the freezing of elections in all bodies belonging to the PLO. The last election for the GUPW was organized in Tunisia in 1985 after the expulsion of the PLO from Lebanon in 1982.

In an attempt to solve the problems posed by geographical dispersion, a new representative body was formed as a reference point for the Executive Committee (*al amana'a al a'ama*). The structure of the GUPW in the Occupied Territories was different from that in the Diaspora due to the circumstances imposed by the Israeli Occupation. The GUPW in the Occupied Territories was banned by the Israeli authority as part of a "terrorist" organization. This led the leadership to function through the body of legal charitable organizations existing in the main cities in the West Bank. Gaza did not join due to the fear that the leader of the Arab Women's Union, Yussra al Barbari, would be deported. The Union could thus not function as a national organization. Soon, most of the charitable organizations involved in "national" activities were shut down, harassed, and the head of the biggest society Samiha Khalil (a.k.a. Im Khalil) was put under town arrest. These acts paralyzed the power of the Union to play a leading role in women's resistance to the Occupation. An older generation of women active in charitable societies was in control of the Union, promising conflict with the new generation of women activists in the grassroots organizations.

New women's committees started to emerge to fill the vacuum left by the Union and political factionalism. The committees brought new blood to the leadership of the Palestinian women's movement but were not allowed by the old leadership to join the underground structure of the Union. Supported by their parties, these new committees started to gain a new and broad constituency due to their success in organizing women. The Union and its leaders were marginalized when these committees and their heads became the uncontested leaders in the street to lead all women's activities in the first Palestinian *Intifada* in 1987.

Empowered by their success, these committees tried for the first time to by-pass the structure of the GUPW in an attempt to create "the Higher Council of Women" in 1988. The attempt was quickly blocked due to fierce opposition from the GUPW and also because of lack of a unifying internal vision about the future role of the Higher Council beyond the first *Intifada*. This failed attempt led to the inclusion of the representatives of these committees in the Administrative Committee (*al-hay'a el-edareya*) of the Union but they were heavily diluted among the larger representation of the charitable societies (there were more than 55 representatives of the charitable societies and 6 for women's committees) (Jad 1990, Jad et al. 2000).

This was the shape the organization had taken when the Executive Committee (EC) and the different bodies of the GUPW arrived in the homeland. As a first step the head of the branch in the West Bank asked the diasporic leadership to include their Administrative Committee (AC) in the leading body of the diasporic leadership in the EC. That request was rejected as "unconstitutional since the members in the EC were elected from the general conference and not nominated" (Rema, Interview). This led to some tension between the two bodies, aggravated by the marginalization of the AC in the coordination committee of IMCAW referred to earlier.

The non-existence of the Union in the Gaza Strip facilitated the creation of a new structure, the GUPW, headed by the powerful figure of Najla Yassine (a.k.a.

Im Nasser) who was the treasurer of the GUPW in the Diaspora and a member of the EC. She had easy access to the President's office and consequently to some resources. The GUPW targeted all women activists in Gaza whether in women's committees, NGOs, or those newly appointed to the public sector. While one of the main issues raised in the West Bank was the independence of the Union from the PA, this was not the issue in Gaza. This could be related to the ways in which new members were recruited. It seems that patronage links, as in the PA, were commonly used in instances varying from distributing food coupons and exemption from membership fees to the provision of aid and social services. The links were also used for the distribution of membership forms to women working in government bodies urging them to join the Union (Mona, Interview). The structure of the GUPW in Gaza was mainly built on the persona of its founder. After she became ill, almost all activities were frozen and the Union proved incapable of competing with the growing power of the Islamists in Gaza.

The establishment of a new structure for the GUPW in the West Bank was less successful for many reasons: the structure of the GUPW in the West Bank was already weakened and the Union, as in the 1930s, was based on members representing their charitable societies rather than on individual members. The average age of the charitable society representatives, their middle class background, and their "do-gooding" approach to women did not help enlarge the Union's constituency. As for the representatives of the women's committees, it is clear that they were too busy with their own committees to invest real efforts in establishing a structure in which they might not gain more power. As the head of the EC stated:

> I keep urging them to put in more efforts, to see themselves in the Union's structure, I need to hand the flag to a new generation but they never listen. It is seven years now since the return of the PA and what we achieved is really very little. We have to set up a new structure, we created a new constituency but where are the other women's organizations?
>
> (Salwa, Interview).

The freeze in the expansion of the GUPW is not only related to the power struggle between the "returnees" and the locals, it is also related to the facts on the ground created by Oslo. When Salwa Abu Khadra, the head of the GUPW and the EC, was faced with persistent criticisms about the lack of new elections she stated that:

> What prevents elections from happening are very real and problematic issues such as the scope and location of the election. The members in the Diaspora cannot all come unless the Israelis grant them permits, and the Israelis don't accept that because of the shaky political situation. We cannot organize elections in the Diaspora as a principle; the Occupied Territories are now the centre of the headquarters of the leadership. Also, it will be very costly to bring big numbers of women representatives from the Diaspora and the Union coffers are empty. And even if they restrict the election to the members living

in the homeland in Gaza and the West Bank, the members in Gaza cannot join because of the siege.

(Salwa, Interview)

The conflict between the diasporic and local leadership of the GUPW reflects the conflict over the role of the Union in its relation to women at the grassroots as well as to its relations with the PA. Since their return, the diasporic leadership announced that the Union is a non-governmental body. However, this leadership and its administrative staff receive monthly salaries and the rent of their luxurious villas is paid for by the PA. This reality was used by the local leadership to challenge their claim of being an NGO.

We follow here (in the West Bank) our internal administrative culture as spelt out in our constitution of charitable societies, according to which an elected member should not get a salary or any financial grant. We consider this as a conflict of interest. Besides, how could they claim independence from the PA as the representative of a group of society while they all get salaries from the PA?

(A, Interview)

Clearly, this financial dependence on the PA is seen as a danger signal that the GUPW has become a mere hack for the PA. This was stated by one of the interviewees also from the local group:

Every time we want to publish a leaflet or a political document, they always insist that we have to add some glorifying sentences about the President; they ask us to display his photos. We are rebellious here; we are not used to that. Also, they object to one of our leaders attending a conference in Amman as one of the signatories of a leaflet published by an opposition group criticizing the corruption in the PA. Of course we have to criticize the government, this is our right, we are not representing the government, we represent our people, our women.

(B, Interview)

The new head of the Administrative Committee is less powerful because of her less well known history of militancy, her being Christian and less political, all factors which have strengthened the control of the returnees over the Union. We should note that this does not mean that women in the local leadership have no power base of their own; they have indeed developed ties with grassroots women's organizations belonging to political parties and women's NGOs and have greatly invested in building a popular base for the Union, especially in rural areas. The second *Intifada* also led to the inclusion of the "local" head of the GUPW in the National and Islamic Leadership of the *Intifada*, considered the highest popular political structure formed by the political activists belonging to political parties, unions, and grassroots organizations.

In conclusion, the above analysis aims to shed light on the internal dynamics of one of the most important Palestinian women's organizations, the GUPW, which has played a leading role in the Palestinian national movement. The fact that the power of a certain elite came from their leading role in the national resistance in the Diaspora did not entail a loss of power when the political system and their locations changed. In an attempt to gain new sources of power new elements have had to be looked for, whether within the new structure of the PA, the old PLO structure, or in society. The women on the EC, as well as some women femocrats (diasporic leadership) are not passive followers of their political leadership. These women realize the gender inequality practiced by the national leadership; they "chose," however, not to protest overtly against this inequality. As Agarwal put it, these women are compliant but not complicit (1997: 25) with political hierarchy. In order to secure their self-interest while appearing to comply with the leadership and with the prevailing patronage norm, they use the same norm to hold their leaders accountable. Compliance with the leadership here is the main strategy for diasporic women leaders to achieve gains; they don't seek autonomy or independence (as many feminists assume) as a pre-condition for women to realize their interests (Peteet 1991; Molyneux 2001).

The case of the GUPW and the gender units reflects how the international blueprints for women and development may not be best equipped to overcome the contradictions in a case like Palestine in which the continuing Occupation is greatly hindering the application of most of the mechanisms for development. All these blueprints assume a situation of political normality and stability, the existence of a state with functioning structures, and a stable and well-defined civil society. The tendency of outside "experts" is to ignore the impact of structural and national instability and to pursue the implementation of previously designed "projects" of mainstreaming gender. However, as I have shown, women in the PA or the GUPW were not mere passive recipients of foreign aid, they also worked to direct aid to increase their gains and to strengthen their negotiating power vis-à-vis the PA and other women's groups in civil society. The increasing power of women femocrats and the diasporic leadership in the GUPW has come to be, as Radtke and Stam[3] show, power "over" other local women's organizations. In what follows I describe how power has shifted to the benefit of expatriate and professional women in the local women's organization of Fatah, the Women's Social Work Committees.

Between state and civil society:
the role of women's NGOs

The role played by Palestinian NGOs before the Oslo Agreement differs significantly from their role in the post-Oslo phase. Before the formation of the PA, Palestinian society was organized in and around political parties and grassroots mass organizations. NGOs linked to these parties under the umbrella of the PLO which encouraged and financially supported the parties and their satellite organizations. While the PLO and its political parties were banned by Israel, their satellite organizations were to some extent allowed to work since they were seen as service provision organizations. Between the end of the 1987 *Intifada* and Oslo, the NGO sector was used as the main channel of foreign aid, a fact which resulted in service delivery at the grassroots level. This included clinics, schools, kindergartens, and income-generating projects. The result was that these NGO actors became important and acquired even more power than their parent parties.

The role of NGOs in the West Bank and Gaza shifted under the influence of the state-building process initiated by the Madrid Conference in 1991. The period from 1988 to 1994 witnessed a proliferation of feminist women's organizations (Women's Affairs Centers in Nablus 1988 and then in Gaza 1989, Women's Study Centre 1989, Women's Affairs Technical Committee 1991, Women's Centre for Legal Aid and Counseling 1991, Women's Study Program at Bir Zeit University 1994) (Jad et al. 2000: 44). The growing number of institutions propagated a new discourse on women and women's status but within the context of a steady decline in women's mobilization. In an unpublished study by an NGO, Panorama, based on five women's mass organizations, it was revealed that their membership declined by 37 percent after 1993 and the new enrolment rate in 1996 did not exceed 3 percent, most of it in the Fatah women's organization (probably for patronage reasons) (Jad et al. 2000: 44).

The effects of the state-building dynamics on different forms of organization in civil society are important in understanding the actual process of demobilization of the Palestinian women's movement. In my view, the dual dynamics of state-building and "NGO-ization" led to more fragmentation and demobilization of all Palestinian social movements. The limited life cycle of "projects" induced fragmentation, rather than bringing about what Tarrow (1994) has called "sustainable networking," whereby ties made with members and organizations are maintained on a regular basis. NGO-ization also has a cultural dimension, as it spreads values that favor dependency, lack of self-reliance, and new modes of consumption.[4] NGO-ization as a process also introduces changes in the composition of the women's movement elites (Goetz 1997) which has resulted, in my view, in a shift in power relations. I use Radtke and Stam's definition of power as the "capacity to have an impact or produce an effect" so that "power is both the source of oppression in its abuse and the source of emancipation in its use" (Radtke and Stam 1994: 8[5]; Rowlands 1998: 14; Agarwal 1997). In Palestine, there is a shift from "power to" women in the grassroots to "power over" them by the new elite.[6]

If the diversity of women's organizations reflects the diverse positions of women in society, it is important to examine how different forms of women's organization reflect different interests (Yuval-Davis 1997; Molyneux 1998, 2001), how these interests are articulated, how these women's activists link to other female constituencies and activisms, and how all these processes are shaped and reshaped in a context of unachieved national struggle and unachieved state formation.

If we compare the size of the older societies and unions with that of the constituencies of contemporary NGOs, one easily notes a decline in numbers. The prevailing structure of NGOs is formed of a board of between 7 and 20 members, and a highly qualified professional and administrative staff whose number is generally small, and depends on the number and character of projects. The practical power of decision-making frequently is not in the hands of the board but rather with the director. The power of the latter stems from his or her ability to fundraise, be convincing, presentable, competent, and able to deliver the well-written reports that donors require. In order to achieve these requirements, communication and English language skills become vital, in addition to modern communication equipment (fax, computer, mobile phones).

As for the internal "governance" of NGOs, a survey of more than 60 Palestinian NGOs[7] reveals that most NGO employees do not participate in decision-making due to "their passivity or their lack of competence" (Shalabi 2001: 152). The "target" groups do not participate in decision- or policy-making either. When administrations were asked why this was so, they answered that they were part of this society, they knew it, and could decide about its needs (Shalabi 2001: 152). In many women's NGOs, the staff has nothing to do with the general budget of their organization, and do not know how it is distributed. According to Shalabi, the internal governance of the surveyed NGOs was "a mirror reflection of the Palestinian political system based on individual decision-making, patronage and clientalism," and the lack of rules organizing internal relations in the organization. In some cases, union internal disputes were settled in a "way very far away from the rule of law" (Shalabi 2001: 154).

The highly professional qualities required of administrative staff for better communication with donors may not directly affect the links between an NGO and local constituencies, but most of the time they do. Referring here to the Palestinian experience, the qualities of cadres in what were known as "grassroots organizations"—the women's committees that were branches of political formations that sustained the first Palestinian *Intifada*—differed considerably from those required in NGO staff. The success of the cadres lay in *organizing* and *mobilizing* the masses, and was based in their skills in building relations with people. They succeeded in this because they had a cause to defend, a mission to implement, and because they had a strong belief in the political formations they belonged to. It was important for the cadre to be known and trusted by people, to have easy access to them, to care about them. The task needed daily, tiring, time-consuming effort in networking and organizing. These cadres knew their constituency on a personal level, and communication depended on face-to-face human contact. But NGOs depend mainly on modern communication methods such as media, workshops, conferences; globalized rather than local tools. These methods may not be bad in themselves but they are mainly used to "advocate" or "educate" a "target group," usually defined for the period needed to implement the "project." Here the constituency is not a natural social group, rather it is abstract, receptive rather than interactive, and the "targeting" is limited by the time frame of the project. This temporality of the project and the constituency makes it difficult to measure the impact of the intervention, and also jeopardizes the continuity of the issue defended.

It is important to notice these differences to help clarify the prevailing confusion between social movements and NGOs, because in order to have weight or, in political terms, power, a social movement has to have a large popular base. According to Tarrow, what constitutes social movements is that "at their base are the social networks and cultural symbols through which social relations are organized. The denser the former and the more familiar the latter, the more likely movements are to spread and be sustained" (1994: 2). He adds,

> Contentious collective action is the basis of social movements; not because movements are always violent or extreme, but because it is the main, and often the only recourse that most people possess against better-equipped opponents. Collective action is not an abstract category that can stand outside of history and apart from politics for every kind of collective endeavor—from market relations, to interest associations, to protest movements, to peasant rebellions and revolutions.
>
> (Tarrow 1994: 3)

The same can be said of women's movements. To put "'women's movement[s]' into context, we have to ask first, what a 'women's movement' is and how can we distinguish it from 'women in movement'" (Rowbotham 1992, quoted in Jackson and Pearson 1998).

There are different views as to what constitutes a women's movement. It could be a mobilizing engine to demand female suffrage, with a leadership, a membership, and diffuse forms of political activity that qualify it as a movement, as distinct from forms of solidarity based on networks, clubs, or groups. And according to Molyneux, it implies a social or political phenomenon of some significance, due both to its numerical strength and to its capacity to effect change, whether in legal, cultural, social, or political terms. A women's movement does not have to have a single organizational expression and may be characterized by diversity of interests, forms of expression, and spatial location. Also, it comprises a substantial majority of women, where it is not exclusively made up of women (Molyneux in Jackson and Pearson 1998: 226).

Thus, it seems preferable to reserve the term "movement" for something larger and more effective than small-scale associations. The typical structure of NGOs debars them from serving as mobilizing or organizing agents, so that however much they proliferate they cannot sustain and expand a constituency, nor tackle issues related to social, political, or economic rights on a macro- or national level. Were they to undertake these aims, they would have to stop being NGOs.[8] When, in 1988, women's NGOs undertook such a national initiative in a model parliament, the constraints of NGOs in mobilizing and organizing became clear.

Conclusion

The emergence of the PLO, a national, secular leadership, especially after the Arab defeat of 1967, played an important role in consolidating Palestinian national identity based on core elements of struggle, return, and sacrifice. However, the new construction of Palestinian nationalism constituted women in contradictory images of the "traditional," "sacrificing mother," whose main role is to reproduce her nation by providing male fighters and of the "revolutionary militant" who should join the struggle hand in hand with her brothers to liberate the nation. This contradictory construction was contested by women activists who started to challenge the prevailing gender order by pressuring their organizations for a more equitable legislation and policies to redress this inequality.

The "revolutionary" era in the Diaspora and the Occupied Territories was an important phase in the development of the Palestinian women's movement during which women's activism was successful in bridging the gap between urban elite women, rural women, and refugees. This linkage was an important shift to wider organization and mobilization for women at the grassroots level and the formation of new cadres, for the first time, who did not come from a middle-class background.

The Oslo Agreement and the emergence of the PA triggered an ephemeral process in which civil society organizations shifted from sustaining their community into claiming their citizens' rights. This shift brought back to the fore the professional urban elites at the expense of the rural and refugee leadership. The merger between the structures of the PLO with the PA led to the marginalization and fragmentation of all grassroots organizations and their elites.

Notes

1   This is an Australian neologism that refers to a feminist bureaucrat and it is equal to the Scandinavian term "state feminist." The term originally referred to women who are "employed within state bureaucratic positions to work on advancing the position of women in the wider society through the development of equal opportunity and anti-discrimination strategies of change. This professionalization of feminism and its incorporation into the state have been significant points of tension for feminists who identify with a grassroots women's movement, and who were able to consider their ideological commitment to be uncompromised by either motives of career advancement or by incorporation into agendas of a state which is still under the control of men. "Femocrats are distinguished from female public servants in non-femocrat positions because the former occupy career positions which feminism has legitimized" (Yeatman 1990: 65).

2   Drawing on a similar situation in Africa, Amina Mama juxtaposes femocracy with feminism. In her view feminism is defined as being the popular struggle of African women for their liberation from various forms of oppression, and "femocracy," described as "an anti-democratic female power structure which claims to exist for the advancement of ordinary women, but is unable to do so because it is dominated

by a small clique of women whose authority derives from their being married to powerful men, rather than from any actions or ideas of their own" (Mama 1995: 41). She wonders whether "femocracy" can result in improvement of the status of ordinary women, can be democratized, and whether state structures act as vehicles for ordinary women's struggles or only serve the elite.

3 For an operational use of the term Radtke and Stam use the term "power over" as a means of controlling power whether to comply or to resist and which might lead to domination (Radtke and Stam 1994: 8; Rowlands 1998: 14).

4 In advertisements in Palestinian newspapers, it is common to read about collective community actions, organized by youth groups who do things like cleaning the streets, planting trees, painting on the walls, etc., and the article is followed by a little icon indicating the name of the donors who funded "these projects." It is also noticeable that many of the NGO activities are held in fancy hotels, serving fancy food, distributing glossy material, hiring "presentable" youth to help organize the event or the activity, which has led to the gradual disappearance of the "old" image of the casual activist with the peasant accent and look.

5 Radtke and Stam and Rowlands differentiate between two types of power: "power over" as controlling power, which may be responded to with compliance or with resistance, which weakens processes of victimization, or manipulation and "power to" as generative or productive power (manifested as resistance and /or manipulation), which creates new possibilities and actions without domination. This power enables the individual to hold to a position or activity in the face of overwhelming opposition, or to take a serious risk (Rowlands 1998: 14).

6 My concern here is to avoid dichotomies such as "traditional" versus "modern," "authentic" versus "Westernized" (Ahmed 1992; Abu-Lughod 1998). My aim is not to judge the NGOs in terms of what class they represent, what Pringle and Watson (1992) call "representation" politics; rather, I intend to underline the fact that women articulate their agendas according to the changing political atmospheres in the country. This adaptation is a form of agency given the difficult situation in Palestine.

7 Cf. Jad (2004).

8 In the middle of a recent debate in Egypt on *khul* (a woman's right to be divorced if she gives up her financial rights), a prominent feminist activist was asked if her center was taking part in the debate. She replied, "We don't deal with such 'projects.'"

Part III

Women and legal reform

7 Tunisia at the forefront of the Arab world

Two waves of gender legislation

Mounira M. Charrad[1]

Introduction

Beginning in the 1950s and continuing thereafter, Tunisia has implemented gender legislation expanding women's rights in several areas, especially in family law. A steady stream of reforms has followed the first and ground-breaking phase, which occurred in the mid-1950s, at the time of the formation of a national state in the aftermath of independence from French colonial rule. The promulgation of the Tunisian Code of Personal Status (République Tunisienne 1997) in 1956 constituted a radical shift in the interpretation of Islamic laws with regard to the family and set a stage for further developments. Another major phase occurred in the 1990s with reforms of citizenship law as embodied in the Tunisian Code of Nationality (République Tunisienne 1998). As a result of these two major phases, Tunisia has been at the forefront of "woman friendly" legislative changes in the Arab-Islamic world and is widely recognized as such (see for example Nazir and Tomppert 2005).

When we consider reforms of family law, three key questions come to mind. What is the substance of the new laws, and what rights do they confer on women? What are the socio-political conditions that make the reforms possible or encourage policy makers to make them? Once new laws are promulgated, how are the provisions put into practice, and what effects do they have on the lives of individual women? At a time when issues of women's rights are not only highly debated, but also sometimes violently contested in Muslim countries, the Tunisian case requires examination. The consistency in gender legislation over half a century is itself a remarkable development. This chapter documents the two major phases of reforms in favor of women's rights in Tunisia and outlines the conditions that permitted or encouraged the continuity over the last half century. While the third question is beyond the scope of this chapter, the discussion focuses on the first two questions.

The first wave of reforms transformed the legal construction of gender roles within the family (Charrad 2001: 219). The second wave redefined conditions for the transmission of Tunisian citizenship (Charrad 2000; Moghadam 2005: 295, 297). The evidence suggests that different political configurations were conducive to reform in different periods and that a careful analysis of the political forces at work is necessary to develop an understanding of each particular reformist phase. In painting social change in broad strokes, I see the initial and pioneering phase of the 1950s as a reform from above resulting from the actions of a newly formed national state interested in building a new society at the end of colonial rule. By contrast, the role of women's agency came into play in Tunisia starting in the 1980s and became more robust in the 1990s. From the 1980s to today, women's rights advocates have contributed to the making of gender legislation either through direct involvement in the committees preparing the laws or by indirectly putting pressure on the power holders, neither of which was present in the 1950s.

How Tunisia compares with other Arab countries

Scholars and activists have agreed on the extent to which the Tunisian Code of Personal Status (CPS) has expanded women's rights when compared to the situation *ante* and to developments in other parts of the Arab-Islamic world. For example, in November 2006 the Library of Congress in Washington, D.C., organized a symposium to commemorate the fiftieth anniversary of the promulgation of the Code of Personal Status (U.S. Library of Congress 2006). During the symposium, I heard Justice Sandra Day O'Connor describe Tunisia as a model for other countries in the Islamic world regarding gender legislation. In advocating the Tunisian example for Palestinian women's rights in the future and in considering countries with a Muslim majority, A. K. Wing and H. Kassim (2007: 1551–1552) write: "Along with Turkey, Tunisia has taken the most secularized approach to women's rights in majority-Muslim countries." Referring to the Arab world, L. Labidi remarks that "the [CPS] has been a beacon and a source of hope for other women's movements and governments in the region" (2007: 7).

In a similar vein, V. M. Moghadam notes: "Tunisia's 1956 personal status code, the Code du Statut Personnel, afforded women full and equal rights and remains one of the most progressive family laws in the Arab world today" (2005: 295). A Tunisian woman journalist declared: "The dispositions of the Code are revolutionary relative to the laws of personal status in countries similar to ours" (quoted in Charrad 1998: 74). A Tunisian woman active in politics echoed the statement: "The Code of Personal Status is a cutting edge body of legislation that many countries envy. I just came back from a meeting in an Arab country and I realized that, as soon as people speak about Tunisia, they speak about the Code of Personal Status. It is an excellent thing" (quoted in Charrad 1998: 74).

In an extensive survey of women's rights in the Arab World, Freedom House compared countries on several dimensions related to gender (Nazir and Tomppert 2005). It ranked Tunisia number one regarding women's legal rights (Nazir and Tomppert 2005: 25). Table 7.1 shows that Tunisia ranks highest with its score of 3.6 out of 5 in the categories of non-discrimination and access to justice and 3.4 in autonomy, security, and freedom of the person. The first category assesses women's equality under the constitution, protection from gender-based discrimination, citizenship rights, equality in the penal code and criminal laws, and women's legal identity. The second category refers to family laws and equality within marriage, freedom of religion, freedom of movement, and freedom from gender-based violence (Nazir and Tomppert 2005: 1–14).

Table 7.1 Final ratings chart

	Non-discrimination and access to justice	Autonomy, security, and freedom of the person	Economic rights and equal opportunity	Political Rights and Civic Voice	Social and Cultural Rights
Algeria	3.0	2.4	2.8	3.0	2.9
Bahrain	2.2	2.3	2.9	2.1	2.8
Egypt	3.0	2.8	2.8	2.7	2.4
Iraq	2.7	2.6	2.8	2.2	2.1
Jordan	2.4	2.4	2.8	2.8	2.5
Kuwait	1.9	2.2	2.9	1.4	2.8
Lebanon	2.8	2.9	2.8	2.9	2.9
Libya	2.3	2.1	2.3	1.2	1.8
Morocco	3.2	3.2	3.1	3.0	3.0
Oman	2.0	2.1	2.7	1.2	2.1
Palestine	2.6	2.7	2.8	2.6	2.9
Qatar	2.0	2.1	2.8	1.7	2.5
Saudi Arabia	1.2	1.1	1.4	1.0	1.6
Syria	2.7	2.2	2.8	2.2	2.3
Tunisia	3.6	3.4	3.1	2.8	3.3
UAE	1.7	2.1	2.8	1.2	2.3
Yemen	2.4	2.3	2.3	2.6	2.1

Source: Nazir and Tomppert 2005: 25.

The initial step: Code of Personal Status of 1956

Promulgated in the aftermath of independence from French colonial rule, the Code of Personal Status (CPS) redefined relationships within the Tunisian family. The particular historical conditions during the emergence of the Tunisian state in 1956 help explain the reformist policy. I have discussed these conditions in detail in previous work (Charrad 2007 and 2001: 201–215). It suffices here to give an overview of the 1950s to show the continuity in gender legislation between then and the 1990s. The CPS was part and parcel of a larger state-building program that aimed at developing a modern centralized state and at marginalizing tribal or kin-based communities in local areas. The newly formed national state was able to make radical reforms of family law in part because a modernizing faction faced no political challenger at the critical moment when it took the reins of power in 1956. Defeated in factional conflicts during the anti-colonial struggle, the political groups that could have spoken for a conservative interpretation of Islamic law and blocked the reforms had lost all political leverage at that particular time (Charrad 2001: 209–211).

The CPS represented an aggressive top–down reform. The executive branch of government under President Bourguiba initiated it immediately after the achievement of national sovereignty, at a time when electoral politics did not exist, and then, he presented it for ratification to a supportive national assembly controlled by members of the winning Bourguiba faction. The CPS was not a victory of feminism. It was the victory of a government strong enough to place a claim on Islam and enforce a reformist interpretation of the Islamic tradition. Like other world religions, Islam offers many possible interpretations and systems of meaning, as demonstrated by Clifford Geertz (1971). In Islamic texts, arguments exist both for and against legal innovation. Members of the 1956 government introduced the CPS as a new phase in Islamic innovation, similar to earlier phases in the history of Islamic thought. Rejecting dogmatism, they emphasized, instead, the vitality of Islam and its adaptability to the modern world.

Although it is tempting to interpret the reforms of the 1950s as feminist, the temptation must be resisted because this would amount to reading motives into the 1950s as a result of the debates of the 1980s and 1990s. When women were politically active in the 1950s—and some highly educated women were—they defended nationalism rather than a feminist cause centered on issues of women's autonomy and gender justice. The reforms were prompted by a nationalist agenda to build a new sovereign nation equipped with a modern state. There can be several discourses of contestation and liberation in a given country with a different discourse occupying center stage at different times. During struggles of national liberation—as in Tunisia in the early to mid-1950s—feminism tends to take a back seat to nationalism.

In brief, the CPS reformed marriage, divorce, custody, and to some extent, inheritance (Chamari 1991; Charrad 2001: 215–232; Bessis 1999). On all of these dimensions, it expanded women's rights by eradicating some of the most patriarchal arrangements of the legislation previously in force. In one of the boldest moves in the Arab—Islamic world, especially in 1956, it abolished polygamy. It radically transformed divorce by eliminating the husband's right to repudiate his wife and allowing women to file for divorce. It made divorce a matter for the courts. It gave women and men the same rights and obligations with respect to both initiating a divorce and paying its cost to the other party. It also established the principle of alimony and increased women's rights to child custody, while maintaining men's advantage through guardianship.

The best known aspect of the CPS is the outright abolition of polygamy. Even though in Tunisia, as in most of the Arab–Islamic world, polygamy could only be practiced by men able to support two or more wives and their children, polygamy was nevertheless a constant threat for women. Tunisia is the only Arab–Islamic country to make a second marriage null and void, as well as to make any attempt to take a second wife, while already married, punishable with a fine and imprisonment.

Although regulations on divorce may appear, at first glance, less dramatic than those on polygamy, they have far-reaching implications on gender roles and family dynamics. They contribute at least as much as the reform of polygamy to transforming the legal construction of the family. The Shari'a, or Islamic law, was in effect in Tunisia prior to the reforms. A comprehensive ethical and legal system embedded in the original texts of Islam, including the Qur'an, the Shari'a gives a man the right to divorce his wife at will, even though it depicts divorce as abhorred and only tolerated by God (Charrad 1994: 54). Although the Shari'a constitutes a common legal and ethical umbrella for the Islamic world as a whole, different countries and regions historically developed their own interpretations and schools of law.

Prior to 1956, the Maliki school of Islamic law applied to the overwhelming majority of the Muslim population in Tunisia. In part for reasons of political expediency, the French colonial state had left Islamic family law untouched. In the Maliki school, a repudiation required only the presence of two witnesses and no judicial intervention for the termination of marriage by the husband. Furthermore, the wife had no judicial recourse. She could turn to her family or community to put pressure on the husband not to repudiate her. But that is a different order of intervention from the role of a judicial authority. By contrast, a woman could appeal to a religious judge and ask for a divorce only on highly limited and specific grounds.

The CPS abolished the man's unilateral right of repudiation by establishing the principle of equal divorce rights and obligations for men and women. It introduced the necessity of judicial intervention in all cases: "No divorce shall take place save before the court," reads Article 30 (République Tunisienne 1997: Art. 30). The CPS also makes it possible for women to get a divorce and gives them the same rights and obligations as men in this respect (Chamari 1991). It states that the party not desiring the divorce, man or woman, should get compensation.

Presenting a new conception of divorce, the CPS requires the party wanting the divorce to go to court, go through a session of reconciliation, reflect on the situation, and consider the possibility of having to make a payment to the other spouse. A new law, introduced in 1981, addressed post-divorce issues. It increased a mother's custody rights by making her automatically the guardian of a child in case of the father's death, something that had not been true earlier.

While it is undeniable that women made immense gains through the CPS, the limitations of the new family law should not be overlooked. The CPS granted women considerable autonomy from husbands and male kin. At the same time, however, it maintained gender inequality by leaving a woman's share of inheritance as half of that of a man's, by granting fathers greater rights regarding guardianship of children, and by requiring that a wife should obey her husband.

In sum, relative to Maliki law previously in effect, the CPS brought major changes that expanded women's rights, even though it did not eliminate gender inequality in family law. By requiring judicial intervention in divorce, abolishing polygamy, and increasing women's custody rights, the legal reforms embodied in the CPS lessened the prerogatives of men in marriage and gave more protection to women in the family. This was pioneering legislation in the Arab world in the 1950s.

The second major wave: reforms of 1993

The second major wave of reforms occurred in 1993 under the government of President Ben Ali who succeeded President Bourguiba in 1987. The remarkable difference between the two waves of reform resides in the role of women's activism in the latter. In contrast to what happened in the 1950s, women's associations emerged and the feminist discourse came to the forefront of public debates in the 1980s and 1990s. This was a period when women's rights advocates made their voices heard (Brand 1998; Zoughlami 1989).

One of the greatest changes of 1993 concerns women's citizenship rights as defined in the transmission of nationality to their children (Charrad 2000: 75-79). I use the terms "citizenship" and "nationality" interchangeably in the following discussion. A consideration of nationality rights raises the question of the conditions for membership in the community of citizens. The Tunisian Code de Nationalité (République Tunisienne 1998) was promulgated in 1957, revised in 1963, and revised again in 1993. As with other codes of citizenship, its purpose is to delineate the conditions for membership in the community of citizens within the nation-state. Like the codes of many countries in the world, it combines elements of *jus sanguinis*, the right of blood, and elements of *jus soli,* the right of soil, in the attribution of nationality rights. Whereas *jus sanguinis* confers nationality through blood descent, *jus soli* means that people born within the national territory are nationals.

Unsurprisingly, in Tunisia, as in other Maghrebi countries, the patrilineage has historically had primacy as a determinant of nationality in that membership in the political community of the nation-state flows directly from male descent or patrilineality. *Jus sanguinis* through fathers is unconditional. The Tunisian code states: "Is Tunisian: ... the child born of a Tunisian father" (République Tunisienne 1998: Art. 6). Since paternal filiation serves in all cases as a source of nationality rights, fathers have a definite advantage. A Tunisian father thus automatically passes nationality to his children regardless of whether the children were born on Tunisian national territory or abroad. A child whose father and grandfather were born in Tunisia also is Tunisian (République Tunisienne 1998: Art. 7).

The reforms of 1993 made mothers a source of *jus sanguinis*. For the first time a Tunisian woman could pass her nationality to a child born abroad, regardless of the nationality of the child's father: "Becomes Tunisian ... [if he or she meets all conditions imposed by the Code and makes the request] within one year before reaching the age of majority, a child born abroad from a Tunisian mother and a foreign father" (République Tunisienne 1998: Art. 12). Widely applauded in Tunisia and elsewhere, the 1993 provision has granted a critically important citizenship right to women. In introducing matrilineal descent as a legitimate and sufficient reason for *jus sanguinis* regardless of *jus soli*, the provision of 1993 challenges the special status of patrilineality as the source of membership in the political community. Calling into question the privileges of the patrilineage, the provision is an important step toward allowing women to become equal citizens in the nation-state.

The conditions that surrounded the reforms of 1993 were significantly different from those that prompted the CPS in the 1950s. In the 1990s, women's associations played a major role in creating a climate in which women's rights and women's issues were prominent (Brand 1998: 220–246). The reforms of 1993 are best understood within this context. Ever since the achievement of national sovereignty in 1956, the country had invested heavily in education, including the education of women, thus creating a new segment of educated women in the population (Centre of Arab Women for Training and Research 2001). Partly as a result, a woman's movement developed starting in the late 1970s and increasingly in the 1980s.

During the academic year 1978–1979, a group of students created a club for the study of women's conditions and named it the Club Tahar al Haddad, after the Tunisian legal scholar who was a pioneer in discussing the conditions of women in the 1930s (Zoughlami 1989: 444). The charter of the Club Tahar al Haddad included the following objectives: to show women that they were still often treated as unequal in practice despite the existence of new formal rights in the law; to support women and encourage them to participate actively in the economic and cultural development of the country; and to direct women's struggle not against men as such, but against social practices that place power in the hands of men (Zoughlami 1989: 445).

The creation of the Club Tahar al Haddad was a monumental step towards the further development of women's associations in the country. It grew into a forum where women academics, lawyers, journalists, and other professionals met regularly for discussions and often heated debates. They called themselves "the daughters of Tahar al Haddad" and developed a sense of solidarity. What unified these women was a passion for the issues addressed in their meetings, ranging from national politics to personal issues.

Several other women's organizations emerged from this period onward (Zoughlami 1989: 444–447). In 1983, a women's section was formed within the main trade union, the Union Générale de Travailleurs Tunisiens (or General Union of Tunisian Workers) and called itself the Women at Work Commission. The mandate of that section was to call attention to any concern that might be specific to women workers. A group calling itself NISSA, and publishing a magazine of the same name, released its first issue in 1985. The magazine addressed many themes, such as international solidarity among women or women's unpaid "invisible" work. One theme figured prominently: the ongoing defense of the Code of Personal Status and the necessity for Tunisian women to remain vigilant against the danger of losing the fundamental rights they had gained in family law.

More associations developed in the late 1980s (Labidi 2007: 15–17). Most, if not all, declared their unrelenting commitment to defend the CPS. They became the watchdog of gender legislation. The Association des Femmes Tunisiennes pour la Recherche et le Développement (AFTURD) (Association of Tunisian Women for Research and Development) included mostly women working in professions such as journalism, secondary school and university teaching, engineering, medicine, and law, with the majority employed in the public sector. The AFTURD organized workshops and conferences, in addition to launching research projects studying women. Created in 1989, the Association Tunisienne des Femmes Démocrates (ATFD) (Tunisian Association of Women Democrats) combined an agenda for the society at large with a focus on women's conditions. A sign of the prominence gained by women's associations in the late 1980s, the ATFD was invited to join in the signing of the "Pacte National" (or National Covenant). This was a form of moral agreement initiated by the government and involving various political constituencies in the country following the change of regime from Bourguiba to Ben Ali in 1987. Other women's groups came into existence in major political parties and in more informal venues such as religious groups, small leftist networks, and the business community. Examples include the Tunisian Association of Mothers, the Association for the Promotion of Women's Economic Projects, the Association of Women's Activity for Sustainable Development, and Women in Science (Labidi 2007: 16).

All these associations served to focus attention on women's issues. While some might have been more vocal than others, together they generated a sense that, not only should the CPS be protected, but that women's issues had to remain at center stage on the agenda of national politics. Furthermore, this was a period when Islamic fundamentalism appeared as a growing political threat in Tunisia and internationally. The Tunisian government was inclined to reach out to women's rights advocates as one source of support.

Conclusion

This chapter has discussed two major waves of gender legislation that have expanded women's rights, one regarding family matters and the other regarding citizenship. Even though women have made immense gains through those reforms, important dimensions of gender inequality in the law remain to be addressed in Tunisia. During a visit in the summer of 2007, I heard the discourse of women's rights advocates now focusing on three particular areas of concern. If they remarry after a divorce, women who had custody of their children can lose it because of the remarriage itself. Issues of domestic violence remain insufficiently addressed in legislation. Finally, inheritance continues to be unequal between men and women —who generally inherit half as much as men in similar family situations.

We can draw some lessons from the Tunisian experience. It shows that different socio-political configurations may be conducive to legislation expanding women's rights. The first wave of such legislation took place in a period of nation building when a primary objective of the nationalists was the creation of a modern state in the newly sovereign country. Occurring in the absence of a feminist movement, reforms of family law in the 1950s were part of a broad program of social transformation pursued by a nationalist movement holding the reins of power. In the second phase of the 1990s, women's voices were heard. The proliferation of women's associations created a general climate of visibility for women's issues.

Furthermore, because women already had significant legal rights in the CPS, they could turn their attention to other matters or refinements of the original CPS. The second phase of reforms cannot be understood except in continuity with the previous phase.

The Tunisian experience also suggests that "woman friendly" reforms matter a great deal, even when they are top–down and even when they are initiated by power holders in the absence of feminist pressures. They are important because, even if they fail to have the intended effect on jurisprudence, which they may or may not for different groups, they nevertheless generate a new climate in which the next set of debates will take place. Further, a woman friendly gender policy made in the absence of pressures from below, as in the 1950s in Tunisia, may contribute to the emergence of a social movement. It may give it a powerful rallying cause, as in the 1980s and early 1990s, when women's rights advocates defended the rights gained in the 1950s and had a say in the reforms of the early 1990s.

The issue of continuity should also be considered from the perspective of the power holders and their inclination to make reforms in different periods. After the initial step had been taken and opponents to reforms had been silenced in the aftermath of independence, the Tunisian state had greater leverage for further reforms because it did not have to confront the kind of anti-reformist opposition that often arose in other Muslim countries. Once Tunisia became identified with woman friendly legislation earlier than other countries in the Arab-Islamic world, it became a matter of national pride and international recognition to continue on that path.

Even though a return to the situation *ante* is always possible in principle, it would entail considerable social and political costs, both nationally and internationally. The two waves of major reforms of the 1950s and 1990s propelled Tunisia to the forefront of gender legislation in the Arab world. One can reasonably expect that it will retain its place for the foreseeable future.

Note

1　This chapter was initially published as "Tunisia at the Forefront of the Arab World: Two Waves of Gender Legislation" by Mounira M. Charrad, *Washington and Lee Law Review*, Vol. 64 (2007): 1513–1527. It is reprinted with permission from the *Washington and Lee Law Review*. An earlier version of this research was presented at the Symposium on Gender-Relevant Legislative Change in Muslim and Non-Muslim Countries, Lexington, Virginia, March 30–31, 2007, jointly sponsored by the Islamic Legal Studies Program of Harvard Law School and the Frances Lewis Law Center of the Washington and Lee University School of Law. I wish to thank Penny Andrews, Zaina Anwar, Louise Halper, Ziba Mir-Hosseini, and Adrien Wing for their valuable comments. I appreciate the careful editing of Kim Herb and Megan Reed of the *Washington and Lee Law Review*. Translations of French texts are by the author. Lisa Manning of the Washington and Lee School of Law confirmed the translation of French sources used in this chapter.

8 Feminism and family law in Iran

The struggle for women's economic citizenship in the Islamic Republic

Valentine M. Moghadam

"We have a strong feminist movement in Iran that is opposed to unjust laws. This movement has no leader or office, but exists in many women's homes. For this reason it cannot be eradicated. If one person is arrested, another woman comes in her place." [1]

Since June 2005, Iranian women's rights activists have held several public protests against religiously based laws and policies that subordinate them to the men in their families and that ban them from high decision-making positions in politics and the judiciary. The emergence of the feminist movement in Iran, suppressed since its initial flowering in early 1979, was a response to political opportunities afforded by the reformist presidency of Mohammad Khatami, albeit a relatively late response. On the eve of new elections and Khatami's departure from office, Iranian feminists demonstrated for women's rights, signaling to the new leadership their determination for reform of the country's highly patriarchal family laws. [2] However, in the context of a new presidency—that of the highly religious and very socially conservative Mahmoud Ahmadinejad—the 8 March 2006 rally for women's rights was physically attacked by police and vigilantes, as was the protest of June 12 2006. Several of the organizers and other well-known figures of the women's movement received prison sentences.

In response to state repression, Iranian feminists changed tack and in August 2007 launched the One Million Signature Petition Campaign. [3] Activists have been taking their campaign for the one million signatures door to door, to classrooms, and in stores, obtaining signatures from housewives, shopkeepers, and students to end discrimination against women in the family laws, penal code, and other polices. The campaign is also conducted through the Internet, and has been supported by expatriate Iranian feminists as well as transnational feminist networks. [4]

The purpose of this chapter is to explicate what the Campaign—and the broader feminist movement of which it is a part—is targeting. Iran's Shari'a-based family law is similar to family law in other Muslim-majority countries, but also has specificities.

Family law in the Muslim world is a social policy intended to regulate family life according to the norms of the Shari'a, or Islamic law. It is also a key ingredient of the state's gender policy. Family law is meant to ensure the rights and responsibilities of family members, especially those of the head of the family; and it aims to guarantee security to the wife in the event of divorce or widowhood. The content of family law varies across Muslim countries, depending on the particular school of Islamic jurisprudence in place, and depending also on the nature of the state and social structure (Charrad 2001). Hence the enormous gulf between the legal status of women in, for example, Tunisia and in Saudi Arabia.

Most feminist critiques of Muslim family law have focused on the civil and political aspects of women's forgone human rights. Shirin Ebadi—who is a veteran lawyer and served as a judge prior to the Islamic revolution—has often has pointed out the injustice and absurdity of a legal system whereby her testimony in court would count only if supplemented by that of one other woman, whereas the testimony of a man, even if he were illiterate, would stand alone. But family law also has implications for women's socio-economic participation and rights. Together with the region's political economy (oil revenues and the rentier state), Muslim family law may be a major contributing factor behind women's relatively low levels of labor force participation, employment, and earned income.

In this chapter I cast a critical perspective on those aspects of family law that undermine women's economic independence and empowerment. Focusing on Iran, I also point out the divergence between aspects of Islamic family law, on the one hand, and the social reality and women's own aspirations, on the other. Patriarchy is in crisis in Iran, which suggests that some aspects of the family law are irrelevant, anachronistic, and moot. But the transition from patriarchal to egalitarian family dynamics and gender relations, I argue, cannot come about as long as women's access to paid employment remains limited. It should be noted that while women make up 33 percent of professional and technical workers, they comprise just 16 percent of the total paid labor force in Iran (according to the 2006 census), because of their exclusion from many occupations in industry and services. Through a focus on Iran's family laws, this chapter helps explain why.

Some features of Muslim family law

In its ideal-typical form, the broad features of family law are the following. The highly formal Islamic marriage contract requires the consent of the wife, and in some countries women may insert stipulations into the contract, such as the condition that she be the only wife or that she may be entitled to a divorce if her husband takes a second wife without her consent (An-Naim 2002). Marriage, however, remains largely an agreement between two families rather than two individuals with equal rights and obligations. Moreover, marriage gives the husband the right of access to his wife's body, marital rape is not recognized, and a wife is required to obey her husband (Shehadeh 1998; Welchman 2001). Children acquire citizenship and religious status through their fathers, not their mothers. Muslim women are not permitted to marry non-Muslim men. Women have the right to own and dispose of property, but they inherit less property than men do. Non-Muslim widows cannot inherit from Muslim husbands. Muslim family law—like Shari'a law in general, from which it is derived—distinguishes principally between women and men and between Muslims and non-Muslims. Men have more rights than women, and Muslims more than non-Muslims.

The principle of patrilineality underlies those provisions that give men legal guardianship over their children and custody in the case of divorce. It also explains why Muslim men may marry non-Muslim women (because they confer their nationality and religion on their children) whereas Muslim women may not marry non-Muslim men. Even so, inter-faith marriages are difficult in the Middle East, and usually the non-Muslim wife is the one who converts.

The practical implications of Muslim family law are that the UN's Convention on the Elimination of All Forms of Discrimination against Women (CEDAW), which has been signed by most of the countries in the region, is a mere formality because of the nature and type of reservations that governments have entered. Most of the reservations pertain to articles in the Convention that call for women's equality within the family and equal nationality rights for women—and these reservations have become a source of contention between the state and women's rights activists.

Reform of family law has gained urgency because of the aspirations of increasingly educated and employed women in the Middle East and North Africa (MENA) and because the family laws that are in place are in striking contradiction to international human rights instruments—many of which have been signed and ratified by MENA governments—as well as to the discourses and objectives of "global feminism," especially as they have evolved since the 1995 Beijing conference (Moghadam 2005). In some countries, the family law contradicts constitutional guarantees of equality (e.g. Egypt) or provisions in the Labor law that stipulate the social rights of working women. It is also in need of reform because of its divergence from the social realities and actual family dynamics of many MENA countries. Finally, in some cases, new and more women-friendly governments have put the reform of family law on their agenda (e.g., the case of Morocco at the turn of the new century).

Significant reforms to Muslim family law were adopted in a number of countries between the 1950s and 1970s and again in more recent years. In 1956 Tunisia banned polygamy and repudiation and gave women the right to divorce; Iran's Family Protection Act of 1967 and 1973 gave women greater rights with respect to marriage, divorce, and child custody. And the former People's Democratic Republic of Yemen (PDRY) (then known as "the Cuba of the Middle East") adopted an audaciously egalitarian family law. Iran's reformed family law, however, was abrogated after the 1979 Islamic Revolution, and the PDRY's was dissolved when the country merged with the North in 1990. None of the family laws in the Middle East are gender-egalitarian, although Tunisia's comes closest, as a result of amendments in the early 1990s. Egypt's family law now allows women to seek a *khul* divorce, an option not available to them previously, and since 2000 wives no longer require the written permission of their husbands to travel or obtain a passport. In 2003–2004, the reform of Morocco's Mudawana, among the most conservative in the Muslim world, was the result of a ten-year-long campaign on the part of women's rights organizations, along with a change in the nature of the state (Sadiqi and Ennaji 2006).

The family laws in the Islamic Republic of Iran consist of articles in its Civil Code that are based on the Jaafari Shia interpretation of Shari'a law. They replaced the Family Protection Law of the Pahlavi era, which sought to enhance the status of women in the family by giving them more say in marriage, divorce, and child custody. Having abrogated that law in 1979, the Islamic state in Iran introduced a number of provisions pertaining to women, men, and the family that remain highly problematical, despite some reforms in the early 1990s.

Socio-economic implications of family law

Muslim family law is based on the principle of patrilineality, which confers privileges to male kin. Provisions regarding obedience, maintenance, and inheritance presume that wives are economic dependents, thus perpetuating what I have called the "patriarchal gender contract" (Moghadam 1998). In particular, Muslim family law prevents women's economic citizenship by constraining their participation and rights.

In this respect, both national laws and international laws are contravened. Muslim family law negates constitutional guarantees of equality, official pronouncements on the need to enhance women's social participation, and worker rights under labor legislation. Muslim family law also contravenes the UN's International Covenant on Economic, Social and Cultural Rights (ICESCR), which is the main framework of economic citizenship. The ICESCR prescribes the right of people to a freely chosen job; equitable and equal wages for work of equal value; dignified working conditions for workers and their families; professional training; equal opportunities for promotion; protection for families, especially for children; maternity protection; protection of boys, girls, and teenagers against economic exploitation. However, in most MENA countries, women are required to obtain the permission of father, husband, or other male guardian to undertake travel, including business travel. In Iran and Jordan, a husband has the legal right to forbid his wife (or unmarried daughter) to seek employment or continue in a job. Although wives (at least those who are educated and politically aware) may stipulate the condition that they be allowed to work in their marriage contracts, many wives make no such stipulations, and courts have been known to side with the husband when the issue is contested (see, for example, Sonbol 2003: 89–99). Inasmuch as Muslim family law and norms in many countries prevent women from applying for or staying in a job without permission of father or husband, and in some countries certain occupations and professions are off-limits to women, this denies women the right to enjoy the ICESCR's provision for "a freely chosen job."

The unequal inheritance aspect of Muslim family law compromises women's economic independence but is a sensitive issue; it is seen on one level as a divine imperative revealed in the Koran and on another level as an important part of the patriarchal gender contract whereby women are provided for by their fathers, husbands, or brothers. Sons inherit twice as much as daughters, but they are also expected to look after their parents in old age.[5] Polygamy is not practiced widely in MENA, but it does occur, along with divorce. A deceased man's inheritance and his pension are divided among his widows, children, and other relatives that he may have been supporting. As a result, many widows receive insignificant pensions. Sonbol reports that this is recognized to be a problem in Jordan (see Sonbol 2003: 110–111). The situation is exacerbated in a country like Egypt where, as recently as 2000, over half of the female population did not hold an identity card—which is required to apply for a pension or social assistance, to withdraw savings from a bank account, or to sue for land ownership. Hence, "poverty is more often found among unmarried, divorced, widowed and abandoned women than in any other social group" (Loewe 2000: 3). Even though Islamic norms and some laws require that fathers and husbands financially support their daughters and wives, it is also the case that divorced, widowed, or abandoned women without access to jobs or a steady source of income, especially among the low-income social groups, are often left in a state of impoverishment.

In some ways, Muslim family law may be seen not only as a pre-modern or pre-feminist code for the regulation of family relations, but also as a way of retaining family support systems in the place of a fully functioning welfare state predicated on concepts of citizen contributions and entitlements. The welfare of wives and children remains the responsibility of the father/husband. When a woman seeks a divorce or is divorced, her maintenance comes not in the form of any transfers from the state, and even less in the form of employment-generating policies for women, but in the form of the *mahr* that is owed to her by her husband, or (in the Islamic Republic of Iran) the *ujrat-ul-mithl,* which is the monetary value of the domestic work she has performed over the years.

The Islamic Republic of Iran

The Islamic Republic of Iran's very ambitious constitution of 1979 requires the government to provide full employment to its citizens, including (presumably) women citizens. But this constitutional guarantee has been undermined by (a) poor economic conditions, inadequate domestic and foreign investments, and subsequently low levels of job creation, (b) a preference for investments in capital-intensive, male-intensive sectors such as oil, gas, and nuclear energy, (c) a constitutional clause extolling the virtues of motherhood, and (d) the ubiquitous Islamic criteria, including the fact that under the Islamic Republic's Shari'a-based civil code, women cannot seek jobs without the approval of their fathers or husbands.

After the revolution, a massive ideological campaign was launched to tie women to their family roles, and the new Islamic family law restored men's rights to polygamy, unilateral divorce, and automatic custody of children after divorce. In matters of inheritance, women became severely disadvantaged. For example, a man inherits all his wife's wealth, but she is entitled only to one-fourth (if he has no child) or one-eighth (if he has children) of his movable property and of the value of his estate. This pertains to cases of permanent marriage; partners in a temporary marriage receive no inheritance.[6] In polygamous marriages, wives must divide among themselves the allotted inheritance, which—according to Article 942 of the Civil Code—can never exceed their designated fourth or eighth. Article 1117 of the Civil Code stipulates that a man has the right to prevent his wife from employment "if he deems such employment would be at variance with their family interests and values." What follows is a critical assessment of some key aspects of the family law in the Islamic Republic of Iran that are targeted by women's rights advocates within Iran and in the diaspora:

"Minimum age for marriage: The civil code provides that marriage contracted before puberty is invalid *unless authorized by natural guardian* with the ward's best interests in mind. When authorized before puberty, minimum age is nine."[7]

Children's rights advocates in Iran point out that the law therefore permits sex with a girl-child. A reform to the family law during the presidency of Mr. Khatami raised the minimum age from 9 to 13. This aspect of the family law is in clear contradiction of several international conventions; in the Convention of the Rights of the Child, for example, where a child is defined as a person under the age of 18 (Article 1), it is noted that the State has the responsibility to protect children from all forms of exploitation, including sexual (Articles: 34, 35, 36).

It is important to note that this particular legal provision does not necessarily reflect the social reality of family life and women's positions in Iran. There is a large gap between what the law permits and what actually occurs in the society. Although the law allows a girl of 13 to be married, the mean age at first marriage among women was 22.4 in 1996 (up from 19.9 in 1986), and among men it was 25.6 (up from 23.6 in 1986). The increase in mean age at first marriage applied to both rural and urban men and women.[8] Women's rights activists in Iran therefore call for family law reform to conform to the social reality and to international standards by raising the minimum age and prohibiting marriage of the girl-child.

"Temporary Marriage: permitted; must be for fixed time period."

Temporary marriage is a contested area not only for lawmakers but also for some Iranian feminists. In the early 1990s, then-president Hashemi Rafsanjani announced that there was nothing wrong with temporary marriage. A negative reaction ensued and the president added that he only referred to temporary marriage as a good solution for war widows. During the presidency of Mr. Khatami it was suggested that temporary marriage was salutary for young people who for different reasons (such as financial difficulties) were postponing marriage. Shahla Sherket, editor of the Islamic-feminist magazine *Zanan*, argued: "First, relations between young men and women will become a little bit freer. Second, they can satisfy their sexual needs. Third, sex will become depoliticised. Fourth, they will use up some of the energy they are putting into street demonstrations. Finally, our society's obsession with virginity will disappear" (Sciolino 2000).

However *sigheh* remains a social taboo and the general reaction to *sigheh* is the stigmatization of women who engage in the practice. Historically women who agree to *sigheh* do so out of financial need; in most cases the man is married and much older than the woman. Moreover, the institution of *sigheh* is clearly biased in favor of men. A married/single man can have as many *sigheh* as he likes, while a woman is required to be unmarried and can only be *sigheh* to one man.

While some supporters of temporary marriage have suggested that temporary marriage can prevent the spread of sexually trasmitted diseases, one analyst categorizes prostitutes and *sigheh* wives together: "The majority of the prostitutes and *sigheh* wives in Iran exchange sex for survival. Being uneducated sex workers, they accept risky sex behaviors easily. *Sigheh* wives are an important source of infection. The very high rate of persistent infection despite standard treatments is disturbing. Our ideal is a world in which nobody is obliged to enter commercial sex work" (Zargooshi 2002).[9]

"**Polygamy**: a wife may obtain divorce if her husband marries without her permission or does not treat co-wives equitably in the court's assessment."

Here inequality is clear since polygamy is the prerogative of men. Although a woman legally can file for divorce if the husband marries another woman without her consent, in practice this is not easy. In many cases the wife is financially dependent on the husband, and due to the laws regarding guardianship of children, in the case of divorce she will most likely lose the custody of her children.

That Iranian law still permits polygamy not only flies in the face of international standards, it also is clearly disconnected from the social reality and actual practices of Iranian society. By all accounts, polygamy is almost non-existent in Iran. And yet the law remains and official channels seek to promote it. Iranian feminist Parvin Ardalan has described how women activists launched a protest campaign against state television, controlled by hard-liners, which aired a series called "Another Lady," in which a woman introduces her friend to her husband for marriage. "The gathering on April 28, 2004 in Tehran [was] a voice of protest against the trampling of our rights and promotion by television of polygamy."[10]

In 2007 the Ahmadinejad government sent a bill to the Majles (parliament) that would allow a man to take a second wife without informing the first wife. This bill was considered appalling not only by feminist activists but also by a wide spectrum of Iranian society including several enlightened clerics. At the time of writing (December 2008), the bill is still under review by the Judicial Commission of the Majles.

"**Obedience/Maintenance**: subject to classical conditions; a wife who is not *nashiza* [disobedient] may take the matter to court if her husband refuses to pay maintenance and the court will fix a sum and issue maintenance order, arrears of maintenance to wife have precedence over all other liabilities against husband. Under Article 11.v, a husband must maintain his wife in return for his wife's obedience. In temporary marriage, the wife is entitled to maintenance only if the contract stipulates such; a husband may deny his wife the right to work in any profession 'incompatible with the family interests or with the dignity of himself or of the wife;' wife's refusing conjugal relations where husband has contracted venereal disease not deemed disobedience."

Women's rights activists consider that this law undermines all norms and objectives of women's human rights, while also commercializng marital relations.

Although the definition of "disobedient wife" is fluid, one expression of disobedience is to withhold sexual services from one's husband—unless the husband has venereal disease, or if the *mahr* has not been paid, in which case the denial of sexual services is justified and not considered disobedience.

Ziba Mir-Hosseini (1996) explains the obligation of the man and the woman in the Shia marriage contract in the following way:

> With the marriage contract, a woman comes under her husband's *isma* (authority, dominion and protection), entailing a set of defined rights and obligations for each party; some have a moral sanction and others have legal force. Although the boundaries between the legal and the moral are hazy, it can be said that those sanctions with legal force revolve around the twin themes of sexual access and compensation, embodied in the concept of *tamkin* and *nafaqa*. *Tamkin* (submission, defined as unhampered sexual access) is a man's right and thus a woman's duty; whereas *nafaqa* (maintenance, defined as shelter, food and clothing) is a woman's right and a man's duty. A woman becomes entitled to *nafaqa* only after the consummation of marriage, and she loses her claim if she is in a state of *nushuz* (disobedience), (while she has the right to refuse sexual access until she receives it in full). It is essential to note that a woman retains full control over disposal of her property and management of her affairs. The contract establishes neither a shared matrimonial regime nor reciprocal obligations between spouses; the husband is the sole provider and owner of the matrimonial resources and the wife is possessor of her own wealth. The only shared space is that involving the procreation of children, *and even here a woman is not expected to suckle her child unless it is impossible to feed it otherwise.*"

> (emphasis added)

Here Mir-Hosseini is referring to Article 1107 of the Civil Code, which states that "the wife's living expense includes shelter, clothing, food and furniture that are commensurate with her status, which may even include a maid in case she is used to having one or she needs one due to illness or incapacity." According to Article 1176 of the Civil Code, "The mother is not obliged to suckle her own baby unless the baby can not be fed by any other means." Article 1199 further emphasizes that "the responsibility for children's expenses lies with the husband. After the father's death or his inability to meet his children's expenses, such responsibility has to be shouldered by the husband's father or grandfather. If these relations are dead or unable to provide for the children's expenses, the mother will be responsible to do so." And according to Article 1206 of the Civil Code, "A wife can claim all the previous non-payments by lodging her complaint at a court, and in case of bankruptcy of the husband, this is considered a prime debt which must be resolved before other settlements have been made."

The law regards the husband/father and his male kin as those primarily responsible for the maintenance of the wife and children. Not only is the wife "maintained" by her husband (in return for her "obedience"), but providing for the living expenses of the children lies with the husband and the wife *has no financial obligation towards her own children.* Although proponents of this law/norm feel that it is a special privilege granted to women (e.g., Mehrpour 1995), in fact it reinforces the notion that the mother is not the guardian of the children and is herself economically dependent. Two other institutions and norms do the same— the practice of *mahr* and the *ujrat ul-mithl.*

"Post-Divorce Maintenance/Financial Arrangements: 1992 Amendments extended divorced wives' financial rights from maintenance during *idda* and deferred dower, to the right to claim compensation for household services rendered to the husband during marriage *(ujrat ul-mithl)."*

The Shia version of wages for housework, *ujrat ul-mithl* is considered a major achievement by the advocates of women's rights in Iran. For example, Mir-Hosseini (1996) argues: "by introducing the concept of alimony for divorced women in the form of *ujrat ul-mithl,* and substantially restricting men's right to repudiation *(talaq)*, the 1992 Amendments break new ground in divorce provisions of the Shia school of law: they limited men's ability to act capriciously, and protect women against such insecurity by providing them with some financial support."

The law mandating wages for housework in the event of divorce was passed by the Majles in late 1992. The regime's Islamist women supporters played an important role in the adoption of this policy—largely because of their dismay over the ease by which men could divorce their otherwise good Muslim wives. As believing women, their protests and recommendations were delivered in a religious idiom. Hoodfar explains:

> Islamist women activists argued that women, like all other Muslims, are entitled to the fruit of their labour on the grounds that Islam is against exploitation; that in Islamic tradition wives have no duties to their husbands beyond being faithful and are not required to work in their husbands' homes, to the extent that women are not even obliged to breast-feed their children without payment from their husbands. Therefore, because all women do, in fact, work in their husbands' homes, they are entitled to the fruit of their labour!
>
> (Hoodfar 2000: 311)

Given that in the United States and Britain, feminists have urged the courts to enforce fathers' support of their children and even appropriate the wages of delinquent fathers toward that end, one might think that the Islamic Republic of Iran is ahead of the game. But the reasoning behind the two systems is different (even if the Anglo-American divorce and child-custody regime have many problems of their own). First, a wife is entitled to maintenance and post-divorce alimony only if she is deemed to have been obedient and without fault. If she is deemed by the court to be the guilty party, she forfeits the compensation and is not entitled to any share of marital assets (unless her husband has voluntarily placed them in her name). Second, in the Anglo-American case, both parents— custodial and non-custodial alike—are regarded by law and custom as equally responsible for the care and support of their children. In contrast, the principle of patrilineality prevails in the Islamic Republic; responsibility for support lies with the father, who is also the legal guardian and the custodial parent after divorce.[11] As we have seen, the mother has no obligations toward her "own" children, and need not nurse them, let alone financially support them. She has no obligations toward the household and need not even engage in housework. Her chief responsibilities—in return for maintenance—are sexual services and childbearing for her husband.

Third, while feminists have long called for the recognition of women's reproductive labor (care work and domestic labor), many would argue that the solution does not lie in measures that would privatize such compensation—as *ujrat ul mithl* does—but rather in compensatory measures by the state, such as more extensive maternity leave, quality childcare facilities, and allowances for mothers. These are, for example, among the social politics of the Nordic welfare states. It is, in any event, difficult to imagine how *ujrat-ul mithl* could be calculated.

Women are also disadvantaged in the inheritance laws. The Civil Code stipulates that women's share of inheritance is half of men's share, and it is explicitly based on the Qur'anic verse "God has ordained that amongst the children, the son's share is double the daughter's." According to one account, "A husband's share of inheriting his wife's wealth, depending on whether his wife has borne children for him or not, is one-half and one-fourth whereas the wife's share would be one-fourth and one-eighth, respectively" (Mehrpour 1995: 58). What justifies the wife's lesser shares? It is "the marriage portion and provisions of women's living expenses by the husband" (ibid.), which, as we have seen, are conditional upon the wife's good behavior.

We can conclude that in the Islamic Republic of Iran, women's social rights and economic citizenship have been constrained in various ways. First, under the strict confines of the law, they are relieved of any responsibility for—or rights to —the household and the care of children. Second, their share of inheritance is less. Third, they have been legally barred from being judges. Fourth, a woman does not have freedom of mobility—she needs the written permission of her husband or guardian in order to travel or obtain a passport, whether for business purposes or for pleasure. Fifth, in many cases, an unmarried woman needs the permission of a male relative for work. Though a married woman does not require her husband's permission to work, he can legally put limitations on the type of work she can or cannot do. Once again this is in contradiction with Article 6 of the ICESCR:

The State's Parties to the present Covenant recognize the right to work, which includes the right of everyone to the opportunity to gain his living by work which he freely chooses or accepts, and will take appropriate steps to safeguard this right.

124 Valentine M. Moghadam

Maternalist politics or economic citizenship?

Since its inception, the Islamic Republic of Iran has designed social policies and legal frameworks toward the persistence of the patriarchal gender contract, women's economic dependence, and inequalities in economic citizenship. As we have seen, the Civil Code stipulates that a husband is responsible for the upkeep of the family. Supporters of the Islamic state's family law may exclaim, with approval and pride, that "According to the Iranian legal system, women are not legally obliged to do any household activity. Even the wife's suckling of her own child is not one of her responsibilities" (Mehrpour 1995: 60). However, they are blind to the larger implications of such a "right" on the part of the wife and mother —which is to exempt her from any labor whatsoever other than sexual services to her husband, and therefore to deny her any economic citizenship or agency. As we have seen, in the event of divorce, "when the wife *is free from any blame or fault*, [the husband] is obliged to pay a lump sum to his wife, which payment is in addition to his obligations on marriage portion [*mahr/mehrieh*], recompense of the wife's past services in married life, and alimony payment during the specified time after divorce when she is religiously prohibited from a new marriage" (Mehrpour 1995: 61).

Supporters of the Islamic Republic's legal and social policy frameworks insist that

> men and women are entitled to equal rights in possessing and executing the privileges of their legal capacity, and as such there is not distinction between men and women. All the means and tools by which men can obtain economic resources are legally at the disposal of women as well. ... The only limitations on the employment of women concern jobs which defy family values and interests.
>
> (Mehrpour 1995: 61)

This is not entirely accurate, since the Islamic Republic has placed other limitations on women's employment, such as banning them from certain occupations and professions. There are no limitations on men's employment— other than, in recent years, to define the field of gynecology (but not obstetrics) as a female profession. The state's approach toward women and the family contradicts not only the norms and objectives of gender equality as these have evolved since the late twentieth century, but even the state's own constitutional emphasis on the "rights and dignity of motherhood" (Moghadam 2006). Feminists have noted that despite its "motherist" discourse, the Islamic Republic of Iran has in practice devalued motherhood through the articles on women and the family in the Civil Code. In particular, feminist lawyer Mehrangiz Kaar has highlighted the wide gap between the Islamic state's formal praise for mothers and Iranian mothers' lack of legal protection, such as the right to custody of their children, the right to open a bank account for their children, and control over their own bodies (Kaar 1996). Her articles in the women's magazine *Zanan*—which came to exemplify the Islamic feminist perspective in the 1990s—concentrated on women's legal rights and the need for reform. Others called on women to engage in *ijtihad* (independent reasoning and interpretation) to claim their rights on behalf of their status as mothers (Gheytanchi 2001: 566). *Ujrat ul-mithl* was one such example of women's *ijtihad* to further their social rights. Another was to argue that in cases of divorce, the courts should calculate the wife's deferred dower (*mahr*) according to an index updated for inflation (Poya 1999: 101–102).

Not all Iranian feminists supported the new policy, and many felt ambivalent about the use of the discourses of republican motherhood and the rights of mothers under Islam. Although the law clearly benefited women and increased the "cost" of divorce to men, *ujrat ul-mithl* was functional for the Islamic Republic in that it carried no financial implications for the state, it reinforced women's maternal roles, and there was no onus on the government to provide employment opportunities or any other social assistance to divorced women. Moreover, as we have seen above, these entitlements are due only to wives who are deemed to be not at fault in the case of divorce (see An-Naim 2002: 110). This type of maternalist policy, therefore, could be seen as reinforcing the patriarchal gender contract rather than expanding women's economic citizenship.[12]

The Islamic state in Iran continues to insist that women have achieved a high legal status within the family and in the society. And yet a bill that would have allowed women the same inheritance rights as men was rejected as contrary to Islamic law by a large majority in the Majlis in 1998 (Shahidian 2003: 222). Later, the Expediency Council and Guardian Council turned down a parliamentary bill to award a temporary stipend to widows disadvantaged by inheritance laws from their late husbands' estates. In frustration, Mehrangiz Kaar wrote in *Zanan* (cited in Gheytanchi 2001: 573):

> In the beginning of the Persian new year, I am listening—in the midst of political battles in Iran—to understand who I am and what are my rights which I have lost under the name of motherhood. Women are asking one question: under the contemporary legal system of Iran, are women citizens or possessed objects? I hope you understand that when a victim—at the peak of her suffering—speaks of injustices and objects, a historical event proceeds. Take her seriously!

Kaar's observation and prediction was quite prescient, because several years later, the Iranian feminist movement burst onto the political scene in Iran. The movement—and specifically the One Million Signatures Campaign—has targeted, *inter alia*, the issues of child custody, inequitable inheritance laws, and the obligation of a wife to secure her husband's permission before taking a job outside the home. Nobel laureate Shirin Ebadi similarly has observed a discrepancy between the stated objectives of some of the laws and policies of the Islamic Republic of Iran, and their real objectives and implications:

> Priority is given to the betterment of women's status throughout the country, given their supreme dignity and the Muslim woman's fundamental role in strengthening the foundations of the family, as well as strengthening social, scientific, and artistic projects.
>
> A closer look at the place of women as viewed by cultural policymakers will reveal their emphasis on family values; a woman's independence, her social situation, and the discriminations levelled against her are never at issue. Policymakers view women as wives and mothers, who need cultural reinforcement and guidance to better fulfil their domestic roles.[13]

If the Islamic Republic of Iran's policies have sought to valorize motherhood and domesticity through such redistributive/allocative measures as pensions for mothers of martyrs, compensation for housework, and the sharing of marital property in the case of divorce by the husband (the extent and efficacy of which remain unknown), most Iranian women seem to be more interested in the reform of family law and in increasing their economic and political participation. Indeed, like MENA feminists in general, Iranian women's rights activists, while not discounting the economic value or cultural capital of *mahr* and *nafaqa*, prefer a discourse emphasizing civil, political, and social rights that are in line with international standards, notably CEDAW. Such are the objectives of the One Million Signatures Campaign and other feminist groups in Iran.

Conclusion

Sylvia Walby's theory of the shift from the private patriarchy of the family to the public patriarchy of the state appears to explain some developments in Iran (Walby 1991). Socio-demographic changes such as the increase in the age at first marriage; lower fertility; growing educational attainment and tertiary enrolments; and rising divorce rates—all these signal changes in the nature of family dynamics and women's positions within marriage, despite the fact that women are still legally disadvantaged. The legal disadvantage is rooted in the patriarchal nature of the state and its institutions, such as the legislature, the judiciary, and state-owned media.

Patriarchy is in crisis in Iran, due to the increased educational attainment of women, changes in family structure, and the emergence of a feminist movement determined to effect social reform. Many writers have emphasized the presence of assertive women active in the public sphere; a growing proportion of women enrolled in universities; a prodigious women's press; a large number of non-governmental organizations staffed by women; and a dramatic decline in fertility. But patriarchal attitudes and practices still govern the lives and life-options of low-income urban and rural women. Beneath the veneer of a dynamic civil society lies a socio-economic base of profound inequalities, high unemployment (especially among women), low salaries, inflation, economic stagnation, corruption, and serious social problems such as drug addiction, prostitution, divorce, runaway teens, a shortage of affordable housing, domestic violence, and an alarming brain drain. Along with other civil society actors, the women's movement is targeting these social and gender injustices, although the political-juridical structure prevents these issues from being properly addressed and resolved.

In particular, the transition from patriarchal to egalitarian gender relations—whether in the home or in the wider society—cannot occur until women have achieved economic independence. That goal is elusive as long as women's access to paid employment remains limited. Institutions such as *mahr* and *ujrat ul- mithl* not only perpetuate the patriarchal gender contract, they also concentrate the burden of responsibility for women's well-being within the family. This relieves the state of any obligation to provide for the welfare, empowerment, and equality of its women citizens—an obligation that it would have to face if it signed CEDAW.

As a key element in the Islamic state's gender policy, Muslim family law requires a major overhaul if all women are to achieve equality and security within the family and the society. Also needed is consistency in Iran's approach to its international obligations, and harmonization of its laws with international standards and norms as enshrined in the international human rights instruments. But can this be accomplished in an Islamic Republic? And will the women's movement—currently a major force for democratization and cultural change—succeed in breaking through the formidable institutional barriers?

Notes

1 Remarks made by Shirin Ebadi, Iran-born 2003 Nobel Peace Prize laureate, at the first international conference of the Nobel Women's Initiative, May 29–31 2007, Galway, Ireland. The remarks were made just before the screening of a video on women's protests and the One Million Signature Campaign, on May 30. Observations by the author.
2 In Iran, there is not one body of laws known as the Family Law or Personal Status Code (as in North Africa) but laws pertaining to women and the family in the country's Civil Code.
3 This strategy was adopted from the successful Moroccan feminist campaign of the early 1990s, which canvassed a million signatures to petition the monarch to amend Morocco's patriarchal family law. In 1993, King Hassan agreed to some amendments, but a more comprehensive reform came about ten years later, under a new king and new government.
4 For details on the One Million Signatures Campaign, see http://www.change4equality.com/english/. Another feminist campaign, "End Stoning Forever," may be found on http://www.meydaan.com/English/aboutcamp.aspx?cid=46. A third feminist site is the "Feminist School", found on http://feministschool.net/campaign. These sites are maintained in Iran.
5 Middle-class women's rights activists who are professionals and are also looking after their parents would like to see this aspect of Muslim family law changed in part to reflect the changing social realities.
6 Temporary marriage, known as *sigheh,* is an Iranian Shia phenomenon.

7   All references taken from the on-line database of Emory University's Islamic Family Law project, under the direction of Abdullahi An-Naim.
8   http://www.unescobkk.org/ips/arh-web/demographics/main.cfm. UNESCO's demographic profile for Iran, 2003.
9   Dr. J. Zargooshi is a researcher in the Department of Urology, Kermanshah University of Medical Sciences, Iran.
10 http://www.iranian.ws/iran_news/publish/article_2203.shtml.
11 Small children are usually left with their mother after divorce, only to be returned to the father at puberty.
12 Yesim Arat (2000: 278–279) reports that a similar debate took place in Turkey, when women's groups proposed that an amendment to the civil code allow women to select the option of sharing assets acquired during the marriage. Some feminists opposed this measure, fearing that women would continue to see housewifery as an attractive prospect, decline to work outside the home, and continue their economic dependence.
13 Shirin Ebadi, *Women's Rights in the Laws of the Islamic Republic of Iran* (2002), reproduced in the Iranian on-line feminist journal *Badjens*. http://www.badjens.com/ebadi.html (last accessed December 20 2004).

9   The legal status of women in Egypt

Reform and social inertia

Hoda Ragheb Awad

Introduction

Despite the undeniable strength of traditional Islam today, both as a religion and as a font of legislative and judicial authority, a number of legal reforms have been introduced in the Muslim countries. The reforms are always expressed in terms of an Islamic framework, not in terms of secularization. No Arab country has created a non-confessional state. Islam is the state religion everywhere except in Lebanon. What reforms have been adopted are always presented by the legislators themselves as new interpretations of the Shari'a, an adaptation of the Holy Law to the modern conditions which have so transformed the family, especially in urban areas where the extended and multiple family group has given way to the nuclear family. Although women are still dominated within the nuclear unit, they do occupy a more important position. The reforms are thus a belated and timid acknowledgment of what has already happened.

Unlike most Arab countries, Egypt is an old nation, whose identity has never really been threatened, despite the Ottoman, French, and British presences. This is probably why, as early as the turn of the century, Egypt developed an enlightened intelligentsia who broke away from the doctrinaire teachings of Al-Azhar, the great Islamic university, and turned to study the new thinking from the West, which they eventually adopted as their own. Early in the century, in 1923, a woman member of this intelligentsia, Hoda Sharawi, publicly removed her veil and established a feminist movement which enjoyed the support of political, social, and even religious reformers. The latter felt that the degradation of Egyptian society stemmed from the isolation of women. The movement's actions were entirely oriented towards the emancipation of women, with the removal of the veil as its symbol. In the early 1940s, Hoda Sharawi founded the national Union of Arab Women. Even earlier, in 1920, working women had organized themselves and forced the government to pass the first laws regulating women's employment in factories (mainly textiles) and commercial establishments. Until then they had been made to work 15 to 16 hours for low wages (Minces 1978: 95). Thanks to their struggle, they obtained better working conditions and salaries.

The same feminist movement called for the creation of schools and the development of education for girls. By 1928, despite public opposition, young women were admitted to the university.

Similarly, as early as 1925, the traditional Egyptian form of repudiation was outlawed (Badran 1991: 76).[1] From that time onwards, all the legislation has been geared toward discouraging repudiation and divorce. The Egyptian legislature was also quick to ban early marriage, young people having reached the age of consent, were allowed to marry without requiring the permission of a guardian or parent. In other words, Egypt reformed its laws to bring about a gradual recognition of women's rights long before most other Arab countries did. The new reforming legislation nonetheless remained firmly within an Islamic framework. Without going into details, it is worth noting that Nasser's rise to power reinforced the reformist tendency, as Egyptian women won the right to vote and run for political office in 1956 (Egyptian Constitution 1956). That same year, free education was instituted for both boys and girls. Due to the shortage of teachers and buildings, mixed education became the rule in state schools. Later, co-education, which had originally been prompted by lack of facilities, became the Ministry of Education policy, in an attempt to change and "modernize" the attitudes of both men and women.

Despite the reforming legislation, women used to complain that the long-promised improvement of women's status had not been properly implemented. Their demands were finally met in June 1979, despite the strong opposition of the "Muslim Brotherhood," which is particularly powerful in Egypt.

The new reform further restricts men's rights to repudiate their wives. From now on, a man is required to inform his wife that she has been repudiated, which was not the case before. Similarly, a man must inform his spouse if he takes a second wife. The economic constraints imposed by the new law are also likely to discourage men who are thinking of repudiating their wives or taking a second bride. If a man repudiates his wife, he will be obliged to pay her maintenance and compensation; for instance a wife with children can expect to retain occupancy of the family home. Furthermore, the State Bank will provide financial support to the repudiated spouse by paying her advances on the maintenance payments which will later be deducted from the ex-husband's salary.

Custody of the children, which used to be granted to the mother only until the age 9 for girls and 7 for boys, has been extended. Girls now stay with their mother until marriage and boys until they are 15 years old. However, the legislators did not insist that divorces be decreed by a tribunal. They accepted the 1931 law which required that the proceedings be registered by a departmental official; this was a major advance at the time but seems sadly out of date nowadays.

When it comes to reforms of the marriage laws, to women's right to divorce, *khula'* (divorce on demand), and contraception, Egypt certainly does not lag behind the other Arab countries. The legislation has long striven to keep abreast of social changes. True, polygamy is still allowed, but only 3 percent of all marriages are polygamous (Karam 1998: 99). The justification offered is that polygamy is a lesser evil than divorce; the children continue to have a home and even the women are thought to prefer sharing a husband to not having husband at all. Legislative reforms to upgrade the status of women in all spheres of life are still subject to further studies inside the Parliament. It is important to present a survey on the legal codes that impacted the status of women in Egypt.

The religious and political impact on personal status law in Egypt

As has been stated above, a new era had started after the Egyptian Revolution of 1952, based on the socialist ideology that necessitated the participation of women in the process of development. Thus, the new political atmosphere gave legal rights to women in all domains of life, namely the political, the economic, and the social. These rights were stated in the Constitution of 1956: the rights of women in education, work, and the political vote as well as to become a candidate. Despite the fact that Islamic legislation, Shari'a, was not the main source of legislation, it was considered "a source," as stated in Article 2 of the Constitution of 1956. The new reforming legislation nonetheless remained firmly within an Islamic framework. Egypt reformed its laws to bring about a gradual recognition of women's rights long before most other Arab countries. Men and women move side by side without any apparent problems, even at work. However, despite the reforming legislation, women used to complain that the long-promised improvement of women's status had not been properly implemented. Thus, no doubt, Egyptian women's status, on paper, had greatly improved, but in practice laws were far in advance of people's thinking. Unfortunately, keeping women in a permanent state of dependency is still seen as the best guarantee against decadence. This state of dependency reflects the patriarchal nature of the society that is reinforced by all agents of socialization: family, school, peers, religious institutions, media, and political leaders. Nevertheless, women's demands were finally met in June 1979, despite the strong opposition of the Muslim Brotherhood.

The position of the Muslim Brothers has been adopted and continues to be so by representatives of the religious establishment and other conservative elements in society, thereby reflecting the influence the Muslim Brothers have in shaping the content and structure of the mainstream Islamic discourse. The Muslim Brothers' violent tendency in the 1940s and 1950s is largely overlooked by most Egyptians; that particular aspect of the movement in history is seen as being part of the resistance against the British and other imperialist forces. Their initial claim of peaceful advocacy, which has been used to reaffirm their position since the early 1970s, is the aspect that most people remember. Also, in comparison with other groups, the Muslim Brothers are perceived as rational and moderate. This allows them to provide many of the so-called traditionalists, as well as the general public of Muslims, with a frame of reference for the Islamic order.

Following Egypt's defeat in the 1967 Arab–Israeli war, disillusionment with the performance of Nasser's regime set in. A wave of religiosity swept through Egypt, encompassing both Muslims and Christians. Claims that the Virgin Mary had appeared above the Cathedral of Zeitoun came alongside a widespread feeling that the defeat was the result of having abandoned faith in favor of human-made ideas and belief systems. In the same vein, some have noted that the 1973 victory was explained to have resulted from the return to religion. It was this general mood of religiosity, coupled with state encouragement, which led to the emergence and growing influence of the Islamic groups (*Jamaat*), and their proliferation first within and then beyond national universities. In his fight against remnants of the Nasserist regime, President Sadat achieved noticeable headway by allowing the Muslim Brothers to reissue their monthly publication *El-Dawa* (The Call), and by giving the Islamists a free hand on university campuses.

From the 1970s onward, the relationship between the regime and Islamists began to deteriorate. The first confrontation between them occurred in 1974 when a group of cadets from the Military Academy (MA) attempted a take-over of the academy. The event, which was aborted, was planned as a precursor to a coup d'état, which the cadets perceived as necessary in order to reinstate Islamic rule. The MA incident was followed in 1977 by a confrontation with the group known as *Jamaat El-Muslimin*, otherwise known as *El-Takfir Wal-Hijra* (Repentance and the Prophet's Migration). The deterioration of relations also encompassed the *Jamaat*. Weary of their influence, the state began to curtail their activities and disallow the wearing of female *niqab*, which had begun to spread in Egypt. Although the general trend is towards women's liberalization and greater equality between men and women, many active educated young women are putting on the veil again, of their free will. Visitors to Cairo are usually intrigued by this curious phenomenon. In fact, this new behavior, which might be called "'anti-feminist,' may well turn out to be a sort of feminism in reverse" (Ibrahim and Hopkins 1996: 178), with a political connotation as well as a moral one. The political aspect of these women's attitude is clear. Their position is similar to that of the Muslim Brotherhood, to whom they are in no way hostile.

The shift from state economy to market economy

The socio-economic changes in Egypt during the last two decades impacted the family structure, particularly women's status. The increasing "feminization" of the Egyptian family is a result of male migration to urban areas within Egypt or to neighboring Arab countries, or to the west. Many men left their wives in charge of the household while they were away. While finding this pattern of life very stressful, at least initially, many Egyptian women have developed a sense of efficiency, autonomy, and independence. In the early 1990s, as husbands returned home and tried to resume their traditional power in the family, gender conflicts erupted. Consequently, there was a need to amend the established laws concerning family code or the personal status law to cope with the changing circumstances of the status of women in terms of marriage, divorce, custody, and inheritance. In 1997, a new bill was issued, Law 44, which gave the wife the right to ask for divorce if she discovered that her husband is married to another woman and refused to live with a second wife (Lila 2000: 53).

Legal reforms were met with opposition, especially when they fell within the realm of Shari'a. For example the opposition to Law 44 of 1979 amending the Personal Status Law of 1929 is a case in point. Also opposition to what was referred to as Jihan's law (ardently supported by the then First Lady Jihan Sadat) was most vehement among the Islamists, both establishment and opposition. They perceived Mrs. Sadat's attempts to reform the Personal Status Law as the ultimate proof of a conspiracy against Shari'a. Adding to the intensity of their opposition was the fact that the decree was passed during the summer recess of Parliament, thereby casting doubt on its constitutionality. In fact, the law was declared unconstitutional in 1985 by Egypt's Higher Constitutional Court. Law 100 of 1985, which subsequently replaced it, did not add much to the 1929 Personal Status Law (Guenena and Wassef, 1999: 100-105).[2] The minor changes that were introduced did not come close to those secured by Law 44, nor did they reflect the efforts toward greater equity exerted by Egyptian women throughout the century.

Gabhat Al-Azhar (the Al-Azhar Front) was established in 1969 as part of Al-Azhar University. Its mission was to protect religious education against attempts at co-optation by the general curriculum. Over the years the *Gabha* came to represent the Muslim Brothers (albeit informally). While a number of the *Gabha* members are active in the Muslim Brothers association, the association has enjoyed the sympathy of non-affiliated individuals as well.

The renewed vitality of Islam as an alternative to secular ideologies has been explained as due to a number of economic, political, and social factors. Economically, the open-door policy (*infitah*) of the 1970s was perceived as a threat to the middle class, the key strata in Egyptian society. The rank and file of both militant and non-militant Islamic activists come from the middle class. They are the government officials and professionals who lost the edge they had gained during the socialist Nasser era to the new class of businessmen and entrepreneurs that began to emerge in the mid-1970s. Conspicuous lifestyles and excessive consumerism appeared, contrasting with the low key, largely unobtrusive ways of living that had prevailed throughout the 1950s and 1960s.

More importantly, the younger elements of the middle class felt they had been short-changed. Young and educated in Egypt's most prestigious universities, they had all the attributes of a professional elite, but none of the opportunities or rewards they had been led to expect. On the political front, the rapprochement with the United States and the subsequent peace treaty with Israel were decried by many in the middle class, who accused Sadat's regime of having sold out to the enemy. Egypt's loss of the leadership position in the Arab world was perceived as too high a price to pay for the return of the Sinai.

As a result of emigration to the oil-rich Arab countries after the 1967 war, Egyptians were exposed to new values and practices, many of which were absorbed into their lives upon returning to Egypt. Even the practice of Islam was affected by their stay in the more conservative Arab countries. Consequently, much of the polemic of the Islamists, including issues related to morality, the family, and gender relations, is derived from or based upon interpretations and practices of Islam that are not the usual moderate ones for which Egyptians are renowned. Today, Egypt is in the throes of an economic adjustment program. Its costs are high and its benefits have not yet trickled down to the middle and lower classes. Consequently, there is a pressing need to redefine the personal status law.

Redefinition of women and the family: personal status law

When drafting laws earlier this century, a compromise was reached: secular law was used in civil, commercial, and penal codes, while the family and the governance of the personal lives of men and women remained under Islamic law. As a result articles of personal status codes often conflict with the constitutions of Arab countries. While the latter guarantee equal rights for all their citizens, the former extend privileges to men, rather than women in the family (in the areas of marriage, divorce, and child custody). The family is often identified as a primary location of women's oppression. Given that the personal status law organizes the relationship of marriage through all its stages, it has a tremendous impact on gender and power hierarchies within the family. It was issued in 1925 as Law 25, and then amended in 1929. More recently changes have taken place in 1979 and in 1985. In general, the personal status laws dealt with women as part of the regulation of the organization of the family, not as individuals with their own separate or equal rights (Hussein 1985: 229–232). This was in direct contrast to the changes taking place for women in the realms of education and work. The entire mechanisms of society could alter but the patriarchal family unit was guarded from any such change. Polygamy is still the legally and religiously sanctioned right of Muslim men. This is in direct conflict with the Egyptian National Charter (1962), which claims that the family is the first cell of society and therefore, in the national interest, it must be afforded all means of protection. Women's needs and demands were short-changed yet again. Even when a faction within the government attempts to institute some reforms, the remainder of the government will often give in to the more conservative strands of public opinion. This normally happens regarding women's issues, but with other policies the government often enforces laws regardless of public protest. Unfortunately, most of the compromises and concessions seem to take place in the domain of and at the expense of women's rights (ibid.).

Egypt's personal status laws present a particularly egregious example of discrimination. The discriminatory personal status laws governing marriage, divorce, custody, and inheritance in Egypt deny women many of the rights protected under international human rights law. Throughout the Middle East and North Africa, these laws have institutionalized the inferior status of women essentially as legal minors and their placement under the eternal guardianship of male family members. These laws "deal with women as part of their own separate or equal rights" (Saleh 1977: 81).

Despite the advances women have made in Egypt in other areas, such as education and access to the public space, the law remains relatively unchanged and continues to undermine women's full personhood in society. Personal status laws have been the most resistant to change, because in Egypt, "women are perceived as the bearers and perpetuators of cultural values and social mores," which "increases the resistance to any change in their status or the laws that govern their lives" (Guenena and Wassef 1999: 100).

Personal status laws for Muslim Egyptians rely predominantly on Islamic law (Shari'a). These religious-based personal status laws violate equality provisions in Egypt's Constitution because, as one scholar has noted, "while the Constitution guarantees equal rights for all citizens, the family (in the areas of marriage, divorce, inheritance, and child custody) denies these rights to women."

All the three of Egypt's presidents since independence, Gamal Abdel Nasser, Anwar Sadat, and Hosni Mubarak, despite remarkably different political orientations, were, to different degrees, public proponents of women's rights. However, they all shied away from directly addressing the stark gender inequality codified in Egypt's personal status laws, which dates back to the 1920s as stated above. Despite their varying efforts to advance Egyptian women's status in the public sphere, they implicitly left the personal status laws in the hands of the religious establishment, which was willing to ensure the religious character of the state by preserving male dominance at home. These contradictory tendencies have resulted in the very anomalous situation of Egyptian women, who, even though they have gained more public rights in education, work, and political participation, still confront serious forms of gender inequality in the family such as arranged marriage, divorce, house of obedience.

Divorce is the dissolution of the marriage contract. A man's right to divorce his wife without witnesses or recourse to a court is sanctioned in Shari'a (Islamic legislation). Law 24 of 1920 states that if a husband is unable to support his wife or if he suffers from an irreversible illness, a woman has grounds for divorce. However, divorce still remains a male "utterance" in private and not a reality debated in a court of law. When these laws were being revised in 1929 to insert the amendment that a man could not pronounce himself divorced from his wife in a moment of duress, and that a wife could ask for a divorce, women could be granted a divorce if they could prove that their current marital situation was in some way harmful (*darar*) to them.

Unfortunately the final judgment was left to male judges who might or might not be sympathetic to women. Of course, the repercussions of divorce affect women from various classes in radically different ways. From the early decades of the century until today, the reality is that alimony or compensation are rarely paid to the wife, who is left to fend for herself and her children.

Custody, a mother's right to keep her children until they are of a certain age, was extended from ages 7 for boys and 9 for girls in 1929 to ages 10 and 12 respectively in 1979. However, in both cases the judge is allowed to exercise his discretion in extending the duration of custody. Should the mother remarry, she loses custody of her children, while the father never loses that right. Again the realities of this law affect women differently depending on socio-economic factors: a wife's recourse to the legal system is an expensive and time-consuming option, making it virtually inaccessible to poor women. Moreover, even if there were gender-sensitive laws, the general lack of legal literacy among women is an impediment to the attainment of their rights, as are the biased attitudes of male judges.

Bayt al-taah (house of obedience) is not derived from or related to the Qur'an (Islamic Holy Book) or *Sunna* (the practice of the Prophet), yet it is law. The idea of *bayt al-taah* is inextricably linked to a man's right to demand obedience of his wife. The origin of *bayt al-taah* is the belief that a wife must remain in the conjugal home and obey her husband in exchange for his financial support. Should she leave the conjugal home (hence disobeying her husband) then he has the right to order her back, either to their home or to another that fulfills certain criteria. The criteria for this abode are that it should normally be a suitable healthy place for the family, duly equipped and furnished and not shared with other families. It is advised by the law that neighbors should be near enough to be able to hear the scream of the wife and therefore be witnesses on what takes place between the married couple. This stipulation offers a hint about the nature of the relationship between the spouses, especially when the husband forces his wife to return to him and obey his commands against her will. *Bayt al-taah* has been used by men as a loophole to avoid alimony payments to the wife: if the wife refuses to go to *bayt al-taah* then she becomes deviant (*nashez*) and forfeits her right to alimony upon divorce. The "Women's Union," known as the EFU, formed by a number of educated upper- and middle-class women, campaigned for the abolition of *bayt al-taah* in the 1920s but was unsuccessful. There was an amendment to the *bayt al-taah* law on 13 February 1967: a Ministerial order was issued that prohibited the use of the police to bring a woman back to the house. Attempts to abolish it have continued through the decades to no avail. This situation is sanctioned by society, protected by legislation, and apparently exempt from change because it is falsely ascribed to religion.

Feminists' perceptions of women's problems came from their own experiences. Hoda Sharawi's marriage in her early teens to her cousin, a man much older than she, served as a reminder of the negative implications of marriage at a young age. In the 1920s, the EFU petitioned the government to set a minimum marriage age. Parliament acquiesced and set the minimum marriage age for girls and boys at 16 and 18 respectively. Unfortunately, at least for girls, this law is rarely enforced and falsification of the necessary documents is easily achieved. Moreover, as usual, a law governing minimum marriage age affects segments of society differently. It is supportive for middle- and upper-class families who want to continue the education of their daughters. The law also encourages the completion and attainment of school degrees for boys (at age 18), whereas girls' education can be curtailed earlier (at age 16), implying that it is of secondary importance. The dangers of early childbearing and the problems of access to health care are exacerbated by this law. Thus due to the influence of the cultural heritage, reform within the family was not sufficient; women wanted access to public life within society. To realize equal rights and equal citizenship, women needed education, the right to work in the profession of their choice, and the right to vote. Denied these rights and life options, they were homebound within a domestic power hierarchy. This hierarchy was rarely favorable to them as they were always social dependents.

The legacy of the nineteenth century was the creation of a dichotomy of cultural outlook produced by the introduction of a state school system modeled on European lines and the expansion of the missionary and foreign community schools, superimposed on the religious Kuttab system. The religious schools continued to provide rudimentary education for the masses in the form of the threes (reading, writing, and arithmetic), while the modern government schools provided secular European-style education for the existing and aspiring elite. In 1873 the first state girls' primary school was created, teaching its pupils religion, mathematics, history, geography, and home economics. However, girls were not entitled to sit for a final examination until 17 years later. Qasim Amin's nationalist and emancipatory discourse propagated education because it enhanced women, but only to produce better children in service to the nation, not to grant women greater life opportunities. Women themselves espoused this discourse; some genuinely believed in it while others used it as a loophole to get what they wanted.

While the post-revolutionary government (1952) encouraged women to obtain education and seek employment, the Egyptian National Charter (1962) sent contradictory messages. It told women that the family was their primary concern, and that they alone were to preserve the national tradition within society. In 1963 laws were passed to promote the idea of equal pay for equal work and equal right to promotion between men and women.

In 1962 a woman named Hekmat Abou Zeid was appointed Minister of Social Affairs. During this time, the socialist government was still sending mixed messages to Egyptian women. During Sadat's rule (1970–1981), a new Constitution was passed. According to Article 11 of that Constitution:

> the State guarantees the reconciliation of woman's duties toward her family with her work in society, and her equality with man in the political, social, cultural, and economic fields of life without prejudice to the principles of Islamic Sharia.

Men's duties to that family are not mentioned and women are painted as torn between their primary concern (the home) and their adopted environment (work outside the home). Furthermore Article 9 states that: "The family is the basis of the society founded on religion, morality and patriotism."[3]

This is a line from a song by Sayed Darwish entitled *Banat al Yom* (Today Girls) from the early decades of this century. His music was exceedingly popular for its passionate nationalism. The family is at the base of the society and is shaped by religion, ethics, and nationalism. The state pledges to preserve this genuine character of the Egyptian family, the customs and values it represents, and to generalize them to the rest of the society. Given the emphasis of Islam on women's roles as wives and mothers, grounding women within the religious and nationalist framework was highly constricting. Interestingly enough, a strand of nationalist thinking looks upon women as the producers of good sons that will add to the nation's glory, not unlike the previous stance.

By 1957, modest changes occurred in the new constitution to enable Egyptian women to participate in the political arena. Accordingly, two women were elected to the National Assembly. Armed with the right to vote, women felt that the door was open. However, the 1960s and 1970s were ambiguous decades for women's rights. There was a general silencing of all groups, including women's organizations, perceived to be too political.

During the 1970s, First Lady Jihan Al-Sadat's voice dominated, but her position as the President's wife often worked against what she tried to achieve. Women who were not part of the official regime, like Nawal El-Saadawi (whose feminist organization was eventually closed down), were silenced. However, the United Nations Decade for Women (1975–1985) began to revitalize the issue in Egypt. This coincided with increased disillusionment from unfulfilled promises over women's rights, whether from the government or other movements that proposed alternative systems. The rise of Islamism also forced middle-class women to organize themselves in opposition to its socially restrictive goals. But the question still remains: How are Egyptian women faring today and what is being done to improve their lot?

Egyptian women today

As has been stated above, Egyptian women have struggled throughout the last century to establish their presence as full-fledged partners with men in the public sphere. Their presence outside the domestic sphere has increased as a result of numerous factors, namely education, economic necessity, and the will of the political elite; but most importantly as a result of their own efforts.

Any threat to the gains women have made constitutes a legitimate cause for concern for both women and men who believe that the wellbeing of society cannot be achieved or maintained through politics of exclusion. Consequently, while the post-revolutionary government assumed a comprehensive transformation that would encompass women, it has been noted that women's liberation has never come to assume the primacy of political or economic liberation. Women's particular concerns have been, and continue to be, subordinate to those of society, the nation, and development. Also, Egyptian men like their counterparts in the West have resisted the process of redefining gender roles and allowing women more equity. The growing presence of women in the public sphere has not been paralleled by more equity in the employment market. After the 1952 revolution, however, opportunities opened up for women, allowing them more space in the public sphere. Nevertheless, for a number of reasons, including male unemployment, women's participation in the labor market has remained modest. The percentage of women in the labor force in Egypt has risen somewhat over the last decade; in 1995 the percentage of women working for wages (not family workers) stood at 21 percent of urban women, 11 percent of rural women.

Article 14 of the 1971 Constitution gives all citizens equal access to public employment irrespective of gender. Law 137 of 1981 allows women to work at night in hotels, theaters, and airports as long as adequate protection is provided (a rather ambiguous clause that is largely ignored). Despite such increases in women's labor force participation, women's average wages are approximately one-third lower than those of men. On the whole, women hardly ever reach leadership positions, and when they do, the occurrence is viewed as an anomaly. Moreover, women's representation in labor unions remains insignificant; only 621 women belong to labor unions compared to 17,441 men. This suggests that women do not perceive unions as beneficial to their interests. Women's business initiatives and acumen are constrained by their entrenchment in the domestic sphere, restrictions on their mobility, and by their lack of exposure to information about loans and training opportunities. Consequently, small, traditional, home-based enterprises are often women's only alternatives. This is especially true among women from the middle and lower socio-economic strata who, instead of reallocating the income from these enterprises to the expansion or upgrading of the business, are often required to use it for household and other emergency purposes. Moreover, the skepticism surrounding women's business abilities often works as a deterrent to their entrepreneurship. The discouragement of women's economic role is legitimated by the prevailing value system and associated norms. These values and norms denigrate women's labor and contrast it to women's domesticity, which is generally commended and, in the case of the Islamists, sublimed. The perpetuation of the image of the house as a woman's kingdom is part of the resistance of society to women's emancipation. Moreover, women who have ventured into the public sphere have often been blamed for much of the violence inflicted upon them, both in the workplace and on the street, while domesticity has been presented as the way for women to preserve their dignity. Women are also subjected to other difficulties that further their isolation from the public sphere. Working hours that are incompatible with family obligations and inappropriate modes of transportation are among the many factors that women encounter in both private and public sector employment. The following letter, cited from a female government employee, illustrates the institutional obliviousness to the multiplicity of roles that women play:

By Force...Not By Choice: It is true that the evening shift at the Registry office is optional and not mandatory, yet this is only in theory. The reality is somewhat different. Women represent approximately 80 per cent of all employees at the Registry; consequently, whoever refuses to work in the evening is deprived of the additional income which is in fact a major source of income for most of us. Moreover, the way the shifts are organized from 8:00 am to 2:00 pm and from 5:00 pm to 8:00 pm make it impossible for us to go home and come back. Most of us live in remote areas, and the traffic does not help. By the time we go home, it is already time to leave for work. What about our children? How are they supposed to fare during our absence? We would prefer to work one long shift from 8:00 am till 4:00 or 5:00 pm so that we can fulfill our obligations both at work and at home. We hope that the Minister of Justice will understand our conditions and that he will be receptive to our suggestions.

Women and political participation

Political participation and representation are issues of concern for Egyptians regardless of gender. The apathy characterizing participation in the Egyptian political process has been noted by many scholars, but a discussion of this apathy is beyond the scope of this chapter. However, despite a general lack of political participation and representation, the situation among women is dismal. The marginal presence of women in Parliament has become evident since 1990, when the law setting a quota of seats reserved for women was declared unconstitutional. The idea that politics is a male preserve is inculcated into women from childhood and throughout adolescence, via a conservative discourse that portrays different roles and obligations for each gender.

While the 1956 Constitution asserts equality between women and men in the exercise of their political rights, women's registration to vote in electoral ballots is optional while men's is obligatory. In the mid 1990s, the level of women's registration remained less than 10 percent. The actual participation of women in parliamentary elections was only 6 percent in 1990 (Abou Zeid 2000: 177–188).

Family opposition, limited knowledge of the law, and scarce resources combine to discourage women from entering the political arena. A research project based on case studies of women parliamentarians indicated that family support has been a crucial factor in determining the course of women's political careers. These women, however, are exceptions.[4] The political game is a dirty and rough one, in which men—as the supposed stronger species—are more apt to engage. Further, when campaigning in elections, women's effectiveness is limited as they tend to abstain from raising or engaging in debates related to gender issues for fear of compromising their chances of being elected. The reluctance of political parties to support women from their own ranks also restricts women's candidacy in elections. Awareness of the constraints to women's political participation has prompted the formation of a program of action to enhance their participation in decision-making processes. A workshop was held prior to the 1995 elections in order to formulate an electoral program for Egyptian women.

One survey of action-oriented interventions designed to enhance the socio-economic status of Egyptian women recommended that a center for supporting women candidates be established. It also recommended that the laws affecting women's political participation be revised, and that women be trained in leadership skills in order to serve as leaders for poor communities.

Women and equity as interpreted by legislators

Another area in which women have not been treated equitably is the law. While contention has been strongest regarding the family and nationality laws, women are also short-changed in the penal code. Though much of the discrimination that takes place is due to the interpretation of the text and its application, which are left to the discretion of a predominantly male judicial body, there is also a differentiation between genders in the body of the text. A notable example is the difference in the penalty for the murder of one's spouse upon discovery of adultery. Whereas men are given a light prison sentence (not more than three years) for murdering their adulterous wives, women are often sentenced to hard labor for life for murdering their unfaithful husbands. This difference is justified by the widespread attitude that a man's honor is dependent upon his wife's virtue. Consequently, his violent reaction to his wife's adultery becomes excusable, especially if committed in the heat of the moment.

The interpretation of the text also presents problems. Although rape itself is penalized, forced or non-consensual marital intercourse is not considered by the law to constitute a criminal offense. However, a study conducted by the New Women Research Center and El Nadim Center found that 93 percent of the women in the sample considered intercourse under such conditions as rape.

The fact that 46 percent of the men in the sample said they are entitled to force their wives into intercourse reveals the discrepancy between their worldview and that of women. The penal code is also applied differentially by gender. In cases of spousal battering, the punishment is usually harsher for a woman who beats her husband than for a husband who beats his wife. This research project is an initiative of the Ibn Khaldoun Center for Development Studies and El Nadim Center and New Women Research Center (1994: 38–39). By law, husbands are entitled to physically punish their wives in case of disobedience (*masseya*) so long as no permanent damage is inflicted, yet women are not allowed similar provisions. The difference in penalties exacted from each gender reflects the preeminence of a value system in which the purity of women is assigned utmost importance, and men's sexual latitude is tolerated. Moreover, the supremacy (*qawama*) of men over women is accepted with varying degrees among Egyptians of both genders. For example, the 1995 Egyptian Demographic and Health Survey found that a not insignificant number of women, especially among lower and middle income women and those residing in rural areas, believed that wife beating was justified under certain circumstances.

Another contentious legal point is the nationality law. The 1975 Law 26 stipulates that an Egyptian woman married to a non-Egyptian man cannot confer her nationality onto their children. Yet, if the father is unknown, the children are registered as Egyptian citizens. Men do not face the same problem: non-Egyptian wives can apply for Egyptian nationality two years after marriage, and their children are automatically registered as Egyptian citizens at birth, regardless of their mother's nationality.

The social, political, and economic implications of this law extend far beyond the blatant differentiation between men and women. One implication is that the offspring of Egyptian mothers married to non-Egyptians are deprived of all the rights and privileges of Egyptian citizens. They cannot vote, serve in the army, or be employed in the government. They are required to obtain residence visas and work permits. They register at schools and universities as foreigners and, consequently, pay fees that are much higher than they would otherwise pay as Egyptians. The economic burden that this law entails is often shouldered by the mother who is forced to resort to extreme measures to bear the costs involved. Moreover, the preventive and hence protective aspects of the law are emphasized and presented as justifications for the persistence of discrimination. Suggestions for reform remain unheeded. Consequently, the nationality law remains a main item on the agenda of Egyptian feminists, together with the personal status law. Despite decades of active lobbying, the government has resisted changes in the personal status law, so much so that the law has been described as the ultimate mainstay of control as manifested in the new marriage contract.

The Personal Status Law and the new marriage contract

O mankind, we have created you male and female and appointed you races and tribes, that you may know one another. This verse from the Qur'an has often been cited to legitimate the complementarities of the genders. Equality such as that sought by the amended Personal Status Law 44 of 1979 and the proposed new marriage contract have been the subject of fierce resistance from both secular and religious establishments. When President Sadat issued the presidential decree known as Law 44 (or Jihan's law), it was met with vehement resistance from all factions of the political spectrum. The secularists opposed it on procedural grounds because parliamentary approval had not been secured, and the religious establishment, the opposition, and other conservative forces opposed the law on the basis that it did not conform to Shari'a. The main supporters of the amended law were its initiator and patron (Mrs Sadat) and a group of feminists who celebrated it as a victory crowning their long struggle for a less discriminatory personal status law. The law did not receive adequate support from society at large, but especially from men, for a number of reasons. Most importantly, the amendments had economic implications that favored women; in addition, both men and women refused to relinquish the tradition of men's superior hold over women.

Under the amended law, a woman obtained the right to ask for a divorce on the basis of injury (*darar*) within one month of being officially notified of her husband's marriage to another woman. After this month, she could no longer claim injury; thus in case of divorce, she loses her rights as stipulated by law. The main advantage of the amended law was that it gave women the right to refuse being part of a polygamous relationship, without being legally and materially penalized. Prior to this amendment, women were often not notified of their husband's second marriage; and if they objected and asked for a divorce, they lost their rights to alimony and to remain in the marital home as long as they retained custody of their children, in addition to any other material compensation stipulated in the marriage contract. The law also curtailed another practice called *bayt al-taah* (house of obedience).

The widespread objections to Law 44 resulted in its reversal and the subsequent reinstatement in amended form as Law 100 of 1985. The new amendment made Shari'a the sole basis for personal status legislation rather than being one of its foundational bases. Thus Islamic law became the one and only frame of reference for matters pertaining to personal status. The idea of the new marriage contract was conceived in the mid-1980s; however, due to opposition, it has not yet come into effect. Apart from requiring a medical examination before marriage, the new contract contains no compulsory clauses. Aspiring to more equity within the institution of marriage, this new contract provides a checklist, which includes many issues. The existing marriage contract allows for the inclusion of conditions agreed upon by the partners; however, the fact that it does not include a checklist intimidates women and discourages them from establishing themselves on a more equal footing within marriage. For example, among the most contentious issues of the new marriage contract is that it allows both spouses the right to divorce (*esma*). Other possible clauses relate to ownership of the furniture and conjugal home, as well as the right to education and travel. The new marriage contract has been decried under the pretext that it would lead to the disintegration of the family and an increasing rate of divorce. A well known proverb is often cited in rebuttal to the proposed contract: *Al-markeb eli leha rayessin teghraq* (A ship with two captains sinks). Most vocal women's organizations in Egypt (cf. Chapter V "Strategies of Resistance," in Guenena and Wassef 1999) focus on research, monitoring, advocacy, counseling, and service provision. The effectiveness of their work on the ground is limited due to legal, as well as institutional constraints. Law 32 of 1964, which regulates associations, has been criticized for restricting the ability of NGOs to address community concerns because of excessive regulations that limit their ability to act in a timely manner. For example, while religious NGOs have the freedom to mobilize funds through alms (*zakat*), non-religious based NGOs are not allowed to solicit funds unless they obtain special permission to do so from the Ministry of Social Affairs.

Opposition to reform of the personal status law and the marriage contract is embedded in ignorance of the law, as well as in conservatism. For example, most Egyptians do not know that the existing marriage contract does not oppose the inclusion of provisions such as sharing the right to divorce. Moreover, practices that the proposed changes are designed to curtail are justified in a patronizing manner. The gist of such justifications is that protection of women, family, and society is incumbent on men and that polygamy, *bayt al-taah*, and male monopoly over the right to divorce are mechanisms that enable them to fulfill this obligation. Resistance to Law 44 took many forms. While some were able to vocalize their opposition, the majority expressed their standpoint by circumventing the law (men) or by choosing not to exercise their rights (women). For example, some men avoided notifying their wives of their second marriage, and some women, upon being informed of their husband's second marriage, chose not to exercise their legal rights. The conservative tendencies of the Egyptian middle class have been explained as the result of their exposure to rigid interpretations of Islam, either directly through migration to the oil-producing Gulf countries during the late 1960s and the 1970s, or indirectly through contact with returning migrants. Consequently, the manner in which opposition to Law 44 and to the new marriage contract was expressed can be said to reflect the changed circumstances and worldview of the middle class. This conservatism of the middle class is accompanied by a focus on gender relations and sexuality.

A number of Egypt's laws and certain provisions in its Constitution maintain and perpetuate women's unequal status. Article 40 of the Constitution states: all citizens are equal before the law; they have equal public rights and duties without discrimination due to sex, ethnic origin, language, religion, or creed. Yet, Article 11 of the Constitution places certain limitations on women's enjoyment of their rights. So, although Article 11 explicitly refers to women's equality in the "political, social, cultural, and economic spheres," it leaves room for the denial of these rights if they are interpreted to be at odds with Islamic jurisprudence.

Although women have nominal equality in Egyptian society, numerous laws directly violate these Constitutional guarantees. Under Article 4 of ministerial decree No. 864 (1974), an Egyptian woman may not be issued a passport without the prior written consent of her husband or his legal representative (Chamais 1987: 79). The law also allows the husband to reverse this consent at any time. Under decree, a husband can prevent his wife from traveling, even if he had given his consent to her obtaining a passport or making previous trips. Although there was a proposal to change this law in 2000, the Egyptian government decided to drop this provision from the draft law just before passage, reportedly as a concession to religious conservatives, despite the fact that Muhammad Sayyid Tantawi, the Sheikh of Al-Azhar University, had supported the new law even with this provision. Despite a 2003 reform to the citizenship law, Egyptian women still have an unequal right to pass on their nationality to their children if they marry foreigners.

Provisions of the penal code also discriminate against women. Egyptian law imposes harsher penalties for women committing adultery. A wife is penalized for two years, whereas a husband is penalized for no more than six months. For adultery, the evidentiary standards are different for women and men. While a wife is penalized for committing adultery anywhere, a husband must do so in the marital home in order for such an act to be considered adulterous. The murder of a wife (but not a husband) in the act of committing adultery is considered a misdemeanor.

The Egyptian women's movement, considered by many to be the forerunner of the Arab women's rights movement, has been actively working to repeal discriminatory laws and advance women's status in Egypt for decades. The various regimes, of both left and right, which have succeeded one another in Egypt over the last 20 years, have all sought to modernize structures and attitudes by passing laws or decrees, including some which have allowed women greater autonomy vis-à-vis the family and men in general. The real problem has been one of information, of making sure that the laws were known and enforced. The initiative for change particularly in the legal codes comes from above. This modernization, from which the notables and their wives have benefited most, was clearly the product of the West's impact on the Egyptian ruling classes, who saw it as a new means of enriching themselves and, eventually, of developing the country.

Women's rights are often the main battleground for the ongoing confrontation between successive Egyptian governments and those seeking to increase the Islamic character of the Egyptian state. This has led some observers to mark the 1980s and 1990s as the beginning of Egyptian women's endangered rights. Successive Egyptian governments have routinely compromised certain rights to appease religiously conservative elements in Egyptian society. For example, the government of the late Anwar Sadat decided to amend the Egyptian Constitution in 1980, in order to make Shari'a "the principle source of Egyptian legislation." In this constrained environment, any departure from conservative interpretations of religious text by women's rights activists has resulted in a backlash. Egyptian women who have raised concerns about women's status, particularly within the family under Egypt's Shari'a-based personal status laws, have been accused of being "pro-western (i.e. feminist, liberal, or secular), antagonistic to Islam, and influenced by leftist ideologies."

Women's issues were almost absent in the political discourse of the ten candidates contesting in the last presidential elections, despite the fact that women constitute 41 percent of the national votes. One woman, Ashgan El Bihiri, a lawyer, who dared to join the presidential contest, made an application, but was rejected on the grounds that she nominated herself without being affiliated to any political party.

Almost the entire political discourse of the political parties failed to address women's rights and problems. According to the candidate of the "New Wafd" party, women already have received their rights, and there is no discrimination against them. As for the candidate of "El Ghad" party, Ayman Noor, he suggested the establishment of a ministry dedicated only for women's issues. In general the political support of the political parties and the candidates for women's issues was very poor in order to win the support of the Islamic conservative trends. Even in media campaigns for the elections, women's issues were not addressed as of public interest or concern, instead they were marginalized. Only the ruling party gave solid support to women in many areas—social, economic, and political—because it controls the necessary institutional equipment.

In general, the presidential campaigns have not highlight the importance of women's participation for public opinion. Current governmental practice denies Egyptian women the opportunity to become judges. Women's exclusion from the bench is not codified in any law (religious or secular) or in the Constitution, but is simply a matter of standard practice based on stereotypical and biased views about women.

The question that comes to mind is: Could the issue of women's equality be achieved by presidential decrees, constitutional articles, or should it be supported by the civil institutions, such as professional syndicates, political parties, non-governmental organizations, and intellectuals? The answer to this question could be a relevant topic of further research work on the issue of gender equality.

Notes

1 The changing conditions of women in Arab society have affected the whole contemporary family institution. In urban areas, marriage is becoming less arranged and more based on individual "romantic" selection.
2 The minor changes that Law 100 included were that the wife has the right to ask for divorce if her husband marries another woman without her consent and this second marriage harmes her physically and psychologically. The problem with this law is that the first wife has to submit to the court an alibi to prove that she was harmed physically and morally in order for her to receive a divorce.
3 According to the permanent Egyptian Constitution of 1971, in Article 9, the state is keen to preserve the genuine character of the Egyptian family—with what it embodies of values and traditions—while affirming and developing this character in relation to Egyptian society.
4 The project for supporting women candidates was initiated by the Ibn Khaldoun Center for Development Studies in 1995, and is designed to provide women with such support.

Part IV

Women: social, cultural, religious, and symbolic change

10 Algerian women as agents of change and social cohesion

Zahia Smail Salhi

In a one woman show staged right in the midst of the decade of terrorist violence in Algeria, Fadhila Assous makes the FLN (*Front de Libération Nationale*: National Liberation Front) party representative address a group of women in the following terms: "Dear Women, dear mothers, dear sisters and dear wives. Be women! Always and forever remain women! Give us many children. Sweep your floors and polish your furniture. Make us good soup, and if you have time weave the wool and make some rugs."[1]

This statement clearly defines the expected role of Algerian women by the male elite and designates the private sphere of the family home as the women's space, while preserving the public sphere as the male's domain.

It is important to emphasize that the discourse of the Islamists vis-à-vis women's roles is not very different from that of the FLN; the leaders of the FIS (*Front Islamic du Salut*: Islamic Salvation Front), often called for the return of women to their homes to produce good Muslims; "Women should go home and leave their jobs for the thousands of young unemployed men. They waste their time, spending their salaries on make-up and dresses," stated Abdelkader Moghni, an FIS imam.

Such rhetoric not only coerces women and excludes them from the public sphere but also undermines the vital roles played by women in Algeria throughout history in order to effect fundamental change in society. As such Assous's play, *Al-Basma al-Majruha* (*The Wounded Smile*) comes as an alternative to the discourse of both the FLN and the Islamists. It demonstrates the courage of this female/ feminist voice who challenged the silence that was imposed on the country by the Islamic fundamentalists who stifled all types of liberal expression, and reveals the determination of Algerian women to continue their struggle to retrieve their citizenship rights by repealing the Family Code that was imposed on them in 1984. Most importantly, however, this play reminds women of the revolutionary roles they played in the not-too-distant past during the Algerian struggle for national independence, and stimulates them to maintain their roles as agents of change and social cohesion.

It is the aim of this chapter, therefore, to demonstrate that despite great resistance from patriarchy, Algerian women have always played major roles in effecting change in their society. Their new roles during the struggle for Algeria's independence engaged the whole society in a process of change and evolution, and their resistance to the retrograde forces of Islamic fundamentalism and the barbarity of terrorist violence was vital for keeping the country alive, and for keeping their demands for their citizenship rights a priority.

The birth and development of the Algerian feminist movement

The Algerian feminist movement was born in the 1940s while Algeria was a French colony. To better understand this movement it is very important to underline the conditions under which it emerged.

Several sources testify to the extreme violence associated with the conquest of Algeria by the French armies in 1830. Unable to crack down on the Algerian resistance, the colonial forces resorted to a policy of exterminating entire villages, expropriating their land and capturing their women and children as part of war booty.

As to the fate of the captured Algerian women, I would like to quote General Montaignac's letter to his mistress in the metropolis:

> In a letter you asked me what happens to the Algerian women we capture; some we keep as hostages and the rest are auctioned to the troops like animals. In the operations we have carried out during the last four months I have witnessed scenes that would melt the hardest heart if one had time to let them! I witnessed it all with a frightening indifference. Kill all men over the age of fifteen; take all women and children and put them on a ship for the Marquisa Islands or some other destination.
>
> (Bennoune 1999: 40)

General Canrobert testifies to the disastrous effects of a terrible and barbaric war which provoked a deep sense of demoralization among the French soldiers, who slit the villagers' throats, stole their possessions, and raped their women (Bennoune 1999: 46). Captain Lafaye, another officer who took part in the conquest, reports: "We burnt down a village in the Khremis, of the Beni Snous tribe. Our soldiers did not spare the lives of the elderly, the women or the children … the most hideous thing is that the women were actually killed after being dishonored" (ibid.).

Rape here was disseminated as an act of violence performed by a dominating colonial power on the dominated colonized women. It was practiced as a punishment not only against the victims of rape but also on their men-folk whose honor was tarnished. In most cases the victims were raped in front of their parents, and the rape was perpetrated as an act of dominance. As such "the bodies of women became political signs, territories on which the political programs of the rioting communities of men were inscribed" (Veena Das 1996: 1).

Transforming the bodies of the colonized women into arenas of violent struggle granted the honor of the male kin of the victim more relevance, and the trauma greater poignancy. What became the central feature was not the violence done to women but the wounded honor of the family or even the whole tribe. This resulted in women's seclusion and total exclusion from public life.

In rural areas where women used to work in the fields things had to change too, as a result of colonization. On the one hand the best arable lands were expropriated by the settlers, and on the other hand men preferred not to allow their women to work for the settlers as daily laborers to safeguard the family honor.

The ultimate result was an increase in the degree of poverty among Algerian families who often relied on the labor of their male members. Tensions grew among family members as life consistently became unbearable for the great majority of Algerian households; men who were regularly exploited at work and humiliated in the public sphere, often poured their frustrations and anger on their partners at home and much of the mistreatment they underwent at the hands of their French employers they replicated on their women folk, which put women in the awkward condition of being the colonized of the colonized, undergoing a double sense of humiliation and alienation, as both the public and private spheres became hostile to them.

It is also worth commenting on the demeaning attitude of the French colonists towards native women, whom they viewed either as exotic objects as in the case of colonial media,[2] or as human things; they named all native women 'Fatmas', to the extent that the name of Fatma became synonymous with house maids.

The colonial condition of the country resulted in the dramatic deterioration of the condition of women both in the rural[3] and urban[4] centers. The colonial presence of the French increased veiling, seclusion, and unequal treatment of women often as a reaction against colonial rule and Western ways. As such, within the domestic realm women maintained an identity strongly resistant to colonial influences and became the guardians of tradition and cultural values. On the other hand the home became a place of safety, a refuge where the man, constantly undermined by colonialism, could regain his pride and identity.

The colonial French administration quickly became aware of this important role played by women, and having given up hopes in assimilating the Algerian men they deployed great efforts for the assimilation of the Algerian women, whom they considered as the repositories of the Islamic cultural values of Algeria, as well as the axis around which the whole society revolved.

In his book *L'An V de la révolution algérienne*,[5] Fanon states: "To convert the woman, to win her to foreign values, to rescue her from her status, is both a means to have full control on the man and to have the practical and efficient means to demolish Algerian culture" (Fanon 2001: 20). He demonstrates that the more the French tried to assimilate the Algerians, the more the latter resorted to the veil and seclusion of women. He explains how the French tried to culturally dominate Algerian society through targeting its women:

> The colonial administration could then define a precise political doctrine: if we want to hit Algerian society in its deep contexture, in its resistance strategies, we must start to conquer the women; we must go and find them

behind the veils under which they conceal themselves and in the houses where
the men hide them.

(Fanon 2001: 19)

As such the condition of Algerian woman became the theme of many 'humanistic'
French actions. Their declared aim was to defend and rescue the humiliated,
marginalized, and secluded Algerian woman. They went on describing the
immense opportunities denied to her by the Algerian man who transformed her
into a static object, by completely isolating her and even dehumanizing her.

At this stage the "woman question" attracted the interest of the Algerian
nationalist parties such as the PPA (*Le Parti du Peuple Algérien*: The Party of the
Algerian People) and the MTLD (*Le Mouvement pour le Triomphe des Libertés
Démocratiques:* The Movement for the Triumph of Democratic Freedoms), who
had initially believed that there was no genuine women's question for as long
as Algeria was not liberated; both parties put Islam at the base of their political
strategy, and as such it was judged almost indecent to speak about the rights of
women, as the prime concern of all was to fight colonialism.

The UFA (*Union des Femmes d'Algérie*: The Union of Algerian Women) was
thus created in 1943 under the aegis of the PCA (*Parti Communiste Algérien*: the
Algerian Communist Party); the sole Algerian political party to believe in equality
of the sexes. In its first congress in 1944 the PCA deplored the miserable condition
of Algerian women, and set up an agenda to make women aware of their lot and
suggested possible solutions such as education among rural and urban girls.

Between 1944 and 1951 the UFA gathered some 10,000 to 15,000 members,
and issued its own journal known as *Femmes d'Algérie* (Women of Algeria).

The tragic events of May 8, 1945, which followed the massive popular
demonstrations of Algerian people in which women participated in huge numbers,
changed the mood among other political parties vis-à-vis the cause of women;
for the first time in modern Algerian history women from all ranks took part in
political demonstrations and moved to the forefront of the nationalist opposition
to French colonialism.

The PPA (*Parti du Peuple Algérien*: the Party of the Algerian People)
declared that "it should work towards the improvement of the general level of
awareness among Algerian women so that they could be brought into the national
struggle" (Daoud 1996: 134). For this purpose it created the first feminine branch
in Algiers to bring together prominent women like Nafissa Hamoud and Fatima
Benosmane.

A genuine debate on the condition of women started and various surveys were
conducted among the members, which revealed their conflicting views; on the
question of the veil, for example, 60 percent of the members think that education
results in unveiling, 20 percent of which were calling for complete unveiling while
17 percent were against unveiling (Daoud 1996: 135).

July 2, 1947, saw the creation of AFMA (*Association des Femmes Musulmanes
Algériennes*: The Association of Muslim Algerian Women) by Mamia Chentouf
and Nafissa Hamoud. The program of this association was mainly social as it

helped the families of the May 1945 victims, tended the sick, and distributed clothes and food to the poor. They also spread political consciousness among ordinary people, whom they encouraged to educate their girls as well as boys. Together with the UFA they led a genuine and strong social program reaching both rural and urban areas and resulting in tangible changes.

It was this political and social work that prepared women for the challenges posed by the Algerian struggle for independence, while the widespread view is that they emerged from the shadows of their homes to suddenly become war heroines of the 1954 revolution and take on new roles.

The struggle for national independence and the roles of women

With the outbreak of the armed struggle, the leaders of both feminist associations joined the ranks of the freedom fighters and called for their members to follow suit. Nafissa Hamoud, the leader of AFMA, was the first woman doctor to join the freedom fighters in 1955, and was followed by Fatima Benosmane, the leader of the UFA, who was arrested and tortured in 1957. Their example was followed by several female nurses who responded to the call of the FLN, and female university students, following the May 1956 strike organized by UGEMA (*Union Générale des Etudiants Musulmans d'Algérie* : the General Union of Algerian Muslim Students).

There were 49 women among the 1,010 first *moudjahiddine* (freedom fighters), according to a census conducted in August 1956 during the Soummam[6] congress (Daoud 1996: 138). By the end of the revolution the number of *moudjahidat*, women freedom fighters, amounted to 10,949, of whom 1,755 were in the ranks of the ALN (*Armée de Libération Nationale*: National Liberation Army). To this number was added the great number of the *fida'iyat* [7] which amounted to 2,388 women. The role of the latter group was to assure liaison between the various factions of the ALN/FLN, to smuggle arms, and money, and to facilitate the movements of the *moudjahiddine,* especially in urban centers, where women's roles were of paramount importance. Under their veils they hid messages, money, and weapons, and dressed as Europeans they entered the European quarters and deposited explosives during the battle of Algiers. They also washed, knitted, and sewed the fighters' clothes, cooked their food, and at times hid the fighters in their homes. For this massive participation in the revolution the FLN declared officially, "Algerian women won their rights by their participation in the war."

Joining the revolution meant an extraordinary move for Algerian women from the private to public sphere. The spirit of the revolution inhabited the souls of women and empowered them to defy major social taboos. On the other hand the society itself seemed to have taken a pragmatic view on the way things were progressing. Joining the ranks of the revolutionaries was not seen as breaking the code of honor, although most often the young women who joined the revolution did so without the consent of their parents, especially in the case of university students.

In much amazement on the new roles played by these revolutionary women, Frantz Fanon remarks:

> Carriers of machine guns, hand-grenades, hundreds of forged identity cards, or bombs, the unveiled Algerian woman swims like a fish in the Western waters. The military, the French patrols smile at her as she passes, compliment her on her physical appearance , but no one suspects that in her briefcase lies the machine gun, which in a short while will be used to shoot four or five members of a patrol.
>
> (Fanon 2001: 41)

He explains in great detail how the revolution gave women more confidence in themselves, and how it helped to rid them of their previous fears as they entered the European quarters.

The participation of "the new Algerian woman in the revolution" was quickly exploited by international media and the whole world was moved by the heroic stories of women like Djamila Bouhired, Djamila Boupacha, Baya Hocine, and others who stood unabated in the face of the most hideous forms of torture. Humanists and left-wing activists from the whole world sympathized with their cause, and French writers like Simone de Beauvoir, Jean Paul Sartre, Gisèle Halimi,[8] and others criticized the colonial policy of France in Algeria.

Women's participation in the war of independence was a major vehicle of change not only in so far as the roles of women are concerned but in the way these women challenged the forces of patriarchy, changed the concept of honor, and most importantly in the way they helped change world opinion towards the Algerian revolution.

The contribution made by women to the Algerian revolution ranged from fighting alongside the men, planting bombs in urban quarters, carrying weapons, nursing the sick and wounded in the *maquis* and, above all, keeping the revolution moving forward. The Italian-Algerian film, *The Battle of Algiers*,[9] is one of many creative works to depict women during war-time, rarely seen, and it shows the extraordinary courage of the Algerian women in particular.

The rebellion of Algerian women had two fronts: it was simultaneously a rebellion against the colonial occupation and against the restrictive attitudes of traditional Algerian society. Women's new status as warriors not only altered the patriarchal concept of the division of labor between the genders, but also challenged the wider power of patriarchy, threatening to erode its power and privileges. Rejecting their restrictive roles as mothers, wives, and daughters in the private sphere of the household, women took on active roles in a wide public sphere. Their work was described by Fanon as the hallmark of a national revolution's potential to liberate women.

Women in post-colonial Algeria

In 1962 Algeria achieved its independence after a long and ruthless war that lasted for almost eight years. Women's work was fundamental to the struggle for national liberation and, therefore, equally important to their own liberation. With this is mind, it is interesting to compare how far patriarchal values were challenged both during the revolution and later in post-colonial Algeria. Would the spirit of the revolution survive in the post-war period, and would women maintain their agency and power of decision making in so far as their lives were concerned? Would they continue their activism and become real agents of change in post-colonial times?

Woodhull observed that: "At the time of the Algerian revolution and at the time of independence the emerging nation still held the promise of social equality for women, whose fundamental role in the war had been recognized by the National Liberation Front"(Woodhull 1993: 10).

In the early years of post-colonial Algeria two ideological factions were soon to be identified, one liberal and the other conservative. While the liberal faction believed in the promotion of women's rights and their integration into the government's program for the advancement of the whole society, the conservative faction called for cultural authenticity and the revival of Islamic cultural values.

It is undeniable that the war of national liberation severely disrupted the religious and cultural values of Algerian society; for the length of the war, whole villages were displaced, social roles were shifted, and the whole society was subjected to traumatic military violence. Similarly, the end of the war brought about a major move towards putting back things in their original order; where they should have been prior to the war.

Interestingly enough, the roles of women were seen at the top of the list of things that should be restored to their original places. In a society where cultural values had been dislocated for so many decades by the forces of occupation women were quickly identified as the repositories of these values and the guardians of traditions and customs, all fundamentally important components of the Algerian national identity.

The roles played by women prior to the revolution as guardians of cultural values in the private spheres of their homes were commended by the conservatives as being the main factor of resistance to the French campaign of acculturation. They extolled the work of women in this domain and gave this role prominence over their role in the armed revolution, which, at best, was seen as a necessity imposed by war circumstances. There was consensus among almost all factions that once the war was over, women should return to their homes and assume their traditional roles.

Concurrently with such views, however, the first government of independent Algeria included women in its program to mobilize various sectors of society in support of socialism. In 1962 the government created the UNFA (*Union des Femmes Algériennes*: National Union of Algerian Women), as a state-affiliated and controlled organization which rallied Algerian women to the national program for the advancement and progress of women. The union held its first march on the International Women's Day in 1965, with the participation of almost 6,000 women.

It is important to point out, however, that the UNFA never captured the feminists nor did it reach out to the masses whether in urban or in rural areas. It remained a formal state organization which did not work for the interests of women in a country where much was needed to be done among the masses of an illiterate and often ignorant female population.

An important question to pose, however, is how did Algerian women whose analysis and praxis of women's liberation were so advanced, react to the creation of the UNFA and how did they respond to the increasing restrictions on their lives and the lives of their daughters in the aftermath of war?

While some female war veterans decided to return to their homes considering that their role was over, some others and mainly the educated ones took on positions or jobs, and were sidelined by either government or society. Many of them were repudiated by their husbands who in the aftermath of the war and after taking important positions in government decided to go for younger and educated wives who were good enough to attend reception parties.[10] In fact this was almost a trend in the 1960s. Buthaina Shaaban reports the testimony of a woman war veteran, who describes this as common practice:

> This was very common. In fact, it was the norm. There were lots of men who married their women comrades in the mountains. Once they came down, however, and got a good position or good jobs in the towns they divorced their comrades and got married to younger, more presentable, women. As women we paid the price from every point of view, and now they won't allow us to put our own laws on the market. I am convinced that all men are aware that women understand things a lot better than they do. That's why they feel inferior to us and instead of having the courage to face us they try to keep us down. How long it will take us to outwit them, just as we outwitted the French, I don't know. Not very long, I hope.
>
> (Shaaban 1988: 200)

With very few exceptions, soon after independence Algerian men obliterated the strong ties they forged with their female compatriots during the revolution and denied them their basic civil rights. Most Algerian men have always seen the liberation of women as neither specific nor a priority. Similarly, therefore, they do not acknowledge the need for a women's movement which is seen as secondary next to the endless list of priorities faced by the country and government.

As a result, women felt a deep sense of betrayal and bewilderment, as if the years of the revolution were a short-lived dream of an ideal world where women were valued for the roles they were able to play, and a world where men and women worked side by side for a common noble goal. Many women wondered why such camaraderie could not continue in the post-colonial period when the country needed both its men and women to build itself as a modern state whose revolutionary past could have served as a platform for development and societal cohesion.

A wide feeling of disillusionment reigned among women and progressive men who all admitted that the revolution had failed. Such feelings were to deepen with the growth of a big gap between official discourse and what actually takes place in society. Gradually women's positions shifted from being active participants to passive and silent victims. On the political front no female members were elected to the National Assembly under Ben Bella,[11] and no women sat on any of the key decision-making bodies.

In society however, mothers encouraged their daughters to have an education; overall enrollment at all levels of schooling has risen sharply, and the numbers of school girls represent more than 40 percent of students.

Boumedienne's rule and the position of women

President Boumedienne took over the reins of power in 1965 after an organized coup that removed Ben Bella. His time was known as a revolutionary time that brought about an egalitarian socialist rule which aimed at integrating all factions of society into its developmental program. As early as 1967, 99 female candidates were elected to communal assemblies (out of 10,852 positions nationwide), and in 1976 the National Charter, which was adopted by a countrywide referendum, constituted the supreme source of the nation's policy and the laws of the state. It gave high priority to the integration of women into the national program of progress and development and went far in guaranteeing equality between men and women. The adoption of the National Charter was quickly followed by the 1976 National Constitution which championed the equality of the sexes and guaranteed women's freedom of movement, and following in the steps of the Algerian revolution it promoted women's emancipation.

The 1976 Constitution deplored the condition of women and insisted on the restrictive role of feudal ethics. It emphasized the efforts of the state in granting women their political rights and exalted the socialist regime adopted by the government as a democratic movement which would promote justice, strive against backward mind-sets, and promise to change the justice system in women's favor.

In this same period Islamism was constantly putting pressure on the socialist state. The desire to Islamize Algerian society from above was set in place by a whole series of measures and initiatives. Stora demonstrates that "in the twenty years following independence, religion was used as an instrument to contain possible advances in the secular and democratic currents, and, above all, as a weapon for the legitimatization of power" (Stora 2001: 171). The Islamist movement that began in the 1970s operated underground while exercising a lot of pressure on government, especially in areas related to women such as family planning and abortion. Muslim activists exercised increasing pressure on women by harassing those they felt were inappropriately dressed, and intimidating working women.

Bendjedid's rule and the institution of the family code

The Islamists gained increasing influence under the rule of Chadli Bendjedid who succeeded President Boumedienne after his death in 1978. As early as 1980 a ministerial decree prohibiting women from traveling unaccompanied by a male relative was passed by the FLN. The first time such an arbitrary decision became public knowledge was when a group of women who were enrolled in universities abroad were stopped at the airport and were prevented from joining their universities. Although these women attempted to trigger a public scandal, the echoes of this event were only timidly reported in the Algerian daily *El-Moudjahid*[12] and the weekly *Algérie Actualités*.[13]

A group of women, including many university students, signed a long petition and requested to meet the minister of the interior. On March 8, 1980, a huge demonstration was organized on the occasion of International Women's Day, demanding that the decree which hampered women's freedom of movement be definitely abolished. This resulted in the ministerial order being cancelled (Messaoudi and Schemla 1998: 49).

In 1981, the government was preparing a pilot study of the *code sur le statut personnel* i.e., Family Code, which was backed by conservative Islamists. The news was announced in the newspapers, which reported that the code in question was a clear setback for women. Outraged, hundreds of women activists in Algiers staged a sit-in in the offices of the UNFA. They demanded to see the classified text of the pilot study in question. The women representatives of the UNFA replied that Algerian women were not aware of their rights and had, therefore, nothing to discuss (Messaoudi and Schemla 1998: 49).

The outcome of this incident was the ultimate rupture between the women of the UNFA and the independent feminists who, despite the repressive measures adopted by the Islamists and the government towards them, were determined to continue the fight for the rights of Algerian women. A number of new women's groups emerged including the Algerian Association for the Emancipation of Women and the Committee for the Legal Equality of Men and Women.

In my view it was only at this stage that a real feminist movement took root in post-colonial Algerian society. Buthaina Shaaban reports the testimony of an Algerian woman regarding the role of UNFA, describing it as "the only women's organization in the country, which does absolutely nothing for women.... [The] U.N.F.A. is an official organization; that is why it doesn't do anything which the government might dislike" (Shaaban 1988: 188).

On October 28, 1981, a "Hundred Angry Women" as announced by the daily *El-Moudjahid,* demonstrated in the streets, expressing their wrath at the government's decision to debate the code in secret. On November 16, 1981, 500 women gathered in front of the National Assembly as it met for a plenary session. Khalida Messaoudi testifies:

We had gathered more than ten thousand signatures of support from all over Algeria. Along with two friends, I marched into the assembly chambers. Rabah Bitat, the assembly president, was obliged to adjourn the session. The assembly leaders skillfully manipulated the situation: we were given four days to make propositions for amending the text. ... The movement became divided at that point: there were those who wanted to accept the deal, and those who rejected it.

(Messaoudi and Schemla 1998: 49)

Despite this division which, on the one hand, demonstrates the vulnerability and weakness of the movement and, on the other, its immaturity, Algerian women activists continued their fight for women's civil rights.

The year 1982 was considered important in the history of the secular feminist movement in Algeria. It was when the women war veterans, who had led the fight for liberation within the FLN and helped carve a new Algeria out of the old French colony, joined the young feminist activists and voiced their rejection of the government's deal. In the words of Khalida Messaoudi "the old *Moudjahidat* joined us, the young, as a bloc, for the first time. Thirty of them decided to join the fight against a government that had completely betrayed them" (Messaoudi and Schemla 1998: 50).

Marie Aimée Hélie Lucas states with much regret: "I have been blindly nationalist in the past." She explains, "In Algeria, many of us, including myself, kept silence for ten years after independence, not to give fuel to the enemies of the glorious Algerian revolution; by so doing we have merely given those in power time to organize and strengthen, allowing them, amongst other things, to prepare and enforce discriminatory laws on women."

Lucas explains what caused Algerian feminists and war veterans to observe silence and inaction for so many years. She says, "I will certainly admit that Western right forces may and will use our protests, especially if they remain isolated. But it is as true to say that our own rightist forces exploit our silence," which resulted in the male supremacy in all state affairs on the one hand and the weakening of the position of women on the other.

The urgency of the matter resulted in the young feminists seeking the help and support of the female war veterans whose historical legitimacy afforded them respect and status. The young and the old generations of Algerian women gathered in front of the main post office in Algiers, and voiced their protest against the introduction of the Family Code. The demonstrators carried slogans reading, "No to silence, Yes to Democracy!" and "No to the betrayal of the ideals of November 1, 1954!"

The women veterans pass on the message to the younger generation of feminists; the fight for freedom, justice, and democracy is not over. They insist that they should follow in the steps of their mothers; "How dare they throw this rubbish at us again! You have to fight, my girls. You just have to fight, even against the men closest to you. The battle has to be fought and won" (Shaaban 1988: 194).

It has to be emphasized at this point that these marches and demonstrations are important highlights in the annals of civil disobedience in post-colonial Algeria; they were the first women's demonstrations for twenty years since independence. Lucas explains, "Usually any kind of demonstration is just crushed, but this time we had in the front line six women who had been condemned to death under the French, so the police didn't beat them. It was good tactic."

Here again women are regaining terrain as agents of change not only in so far as recording their disobedience to the state, but also by demonstrating a new pattern of resistance and solidarity. Furthermore, their action, together with the events of the 1980 Berber spring, made visible the plurality of Algerian civil society.

In addition to the demonstrations the women veterans put an end to their silence; they wrote to the minister of veterans in protest against the Family Code and wrote to the minister of justice and the president insisting that they had not fought for such a deal! The state was truly frightened and the president stopped the proposal. Lucas reports; "we thought it was a big victory, and anyway the first one since independence. Then what happened was that everything was very quiet, after 1982, and then we heard that this proposal (or another like it) was still there, and could be passed at any time."

On June 9, 1984, the Family Code was enacted as Law no. 84-11. Algerian women were in deep shock; they considered this act as barbaric and a second betrayal by the neo-patriarchal state of Algerian women. At this stage it had become clear that the state had preferred to compromise with the conservative Islamists and that women had to constitute themselves as an opposition to both the state and the Islamists.

The main provisions of the Family Code

The 1984 Family Code reproduced provisions of Islamic Shari'a law. Among these provisions:

1 Women have no right to marry but can only be given in marriage by a matrimonial guardian (Article 11).
2 Women cannot divorce their husbands and can only obtain divorce by submitting to the *Khol'a* practice which stipulates that they should give up their legal rights or claims to alimony. Men can divorce as and when they want (Article 54).
3 Women are given the role of procreators, making it their legal duty to breastfeed their children and care for them until adulthood (Article 48).
4 Women must obey their husbands and respect them. Women can only work if they are granted permission, and must respect as well as obey husband and in-laws (Article 39).
5 Women are given custody of their children; boys till the age of 10 and girls till marriage. If a woman has no guardian, the man will only support her if he can. This means if the husband owned only one house, the divorcee and the children will have to end up being homeless. Furthermore, a divorcee is not

permitted to take her children abroad or get them onto certain school activities without the father's signature (Article 52).

6   The family code institutionalized polygamy and made it the right of men to take up to four wives (Article 8).

In short, the Family Code is a piece of legislation that decrees men's superiority and codifies women's subordination. The code makes women minors under the law, treats them as non-citizens, and defines their role primarily as daughters, mothers, or wives. The first few years that followed the implementation of the code demonstrated that it is central to women's problems. Not only because women felt deeply disadvantaged and devalued in society, but most importantly it made divorce a simple matter for men, and a disastrous occurrence to women; wives and mothers have no right to the family home, since this is automatically awarded to the husband. Moreover, the state does not provide housing or financial support for divorced mothers. Consequently, in the absence of assistance from their relatives, divorced women often find themselves living in the slums, in sheltered corners of public car parks or often roam the streets with their children.

One positive element that was triggered by the institution of the Family Code is the rebirth of independent women's organizations working underground. Women's associations include SOS Women in Distress which gives refuge to battered women, divorcees, and abandoned women with children. SOS aims to rehabilitate and empower women by helping them find employment so they can go back to society.

It was only after this major setback that women came to realize that they should no longer rely on the state nor trust the government that had betrayed them and condemned them to institutional injustice and humiliation. Messaoudi testifies:

> I had the feeling that the deepest injustice had been perpetuated. We had been had, totally had, and we could do nothing but bang our heads against the wall, because we knew that this text was going to structure the entire society from that point on. For me, the whole business had really opened my eyes: The traitor in this story was the Algerian state.
>
> (Messaoudi and Schemla 1998: 55)

This opinion of Messaoudi is shared by many other women who have come to comprehend that they were misled for so many years by the concepts of nationalism, and that the revolution had used them but did not help them to liberate themselves as citizens of an independent state. Furthermore, women were always made to believe that the nation came first and that calling for women's rights was a betrayal of the state, that feminism was a Western notion not to be followed in the developing world, and that feminists were often used by the West against Muslim countries.

Marie Aimée Hélie Lucas explains this state of affairs in the following terms:

We are made to feel that protesting in the name of women's interests and rights is not to be done now (it has never been the right moment: not during the liberation struggle against colonialism, because all forces should be mobilized against the principal enemy: French colonialism; not after independence, because all forces should be mobilized to build up the devastated country; not now that racist imperialist Western governments are attacking Islam and the third world, etc...) defending women's rights "now" (this "now" being ANY historical moment), is always a betrayal-of the people, of the nation, of the revolution, of Islam, of national identity, of cultural roots, of the Third World ... according to the terminologies in use.

On the notion of nationalism and its relation to women, Lucas explains that the narrow approach adopted by developing countries towards nationalism is very effective especially in the case of Algeria where, at the outbreak of the revolution the women's movement was not fully developed and was weak ideologically; the urgency of liberating the nation took priority over the liberation of women who automatically assumed that the two processes went hand in hand. At the eve of independence Algerian women found themselves in the position of losing ground to their male compatriots, whose camaraderie and trust built up during the years of struggle against colonialism they still relied on. Women did not wait for long after independence to feel the consequences of their misplaced trust; one woman reports; "Our only regret is the loss of that absolute equality achieved during the revolution; as far as that's concerned, we seem to have moved backwards rather than forwards" (Shaaban 1988: 199).

Another remarks; "Our return to 'the inside' didn't begin in 1962, but, rather, before independence. Little by little, during the war, the F.L.N. removed us from the real fighting zones and sent us to the borders or overseas. Our role was defined from that moment on. We didn't have any place in the world of the 'outside'" (Messaoudi and Schemla 1998: 51).

These testimonies consolidate Partha Chaterjee's statement that "The story of nationalism is necessarily a story of betrayal" (Chaterjee 1993: 154). She explains that "nationalism confers freedom only by imposing new controls, defines a cultural identity for the nation only by excluding many from its fold, and grants the dignity of citizenship to some because others could not be allowed to speak for themselves" (ibid.). In so far as Algerian women are concerned I would argue that they were not armed with a strong feminist ideology to help them challenge or reject the dominant male discourse. In the early years of independence the nation was engaged in an arduous quest for national identity and religious authenticity which allowed the neo-conservative discourse to take prominence over other discourses including the leftist and feminist discourses. Interestingly enough, while the leftist discourse was being pushed out on grounds of "imported ideologies" and "Westernism," the left used the same accusations against women.

This situation also explains the lack of support for women in their opposition of the Family Code from the left, or indeed from any other male groups.

Messaoudi asserts: "Men were painfully absent from our struggle. This reinforced my conviction that Algerian women could expect salvation only from themselves" (Messaoudi and Schemla 1998: 56).

This in turn, led to the establishment of strong bonds between the women of Algeria; the generation of women who fought the war of independence, and I have to add that by now these women have almost become fictional figures that the younger generations could not see or hear for the twenty years or so after independence, and the younger feminists who had no links with the UNFA and who only became visible in the public sphere through their defiance and their rejection of the code. This union is to become the foundation of a new feminist movement whose main platform is the repealing of the 1984 Family Code.

Social unrest and political reform

In the mid-1980s Algeria experienced a deepening economic crisis mainly manifested through high unemployment rates together with shortages and the soaring of the prices of basic consumer goods. This situation was made worse by the huge drop in world oil prices in 1986, which caused the country's economy to collapse. A sense of anger and frustration became widespread among the poor and working classes who developed a perception that the government had become corrupt; "The social compromise established under Boumedienne's regime was broken. The widening gap between rich and poor, the austerity programs which affected mostly the poor and the lower middle class coupled with the impudent exhibition of wealth by the *nouveaux riches* who made their fortunes with the assistance of high officials and/or the underground economy, exacerbated social tensions in the country" (Zoubir 1993: 87).

On the October 5, 1988, the waves of discontent expressed initially through a series of strikes and marches degenerated into widespread riots which the government met with violent repression resulting in the killing of around 500 people and the arrest of more than 3,000.

Such stringent measures resulted in more anger and resentment. The youth movement triggered protests and demands for change from many other groups. Seventy Algerian journalists published a declaration in which they denounced the ban on reporting and condemned the restrictions that were imposed on freedom of speech. They also denounced the violence, torture, and arbitrary arrests used by the state. The Algerian League for Human Rights denounced the practice of torture, while the doctors who saw the results of torture and the ruthless repressive measures undertaken by government forces became the principal driving force behind the creation of the National Committee against Torture. The women's groups expressed their full support for the youth movement and called for the recognition of democratic liberties. In short, the whole political system was coming under sustained attack; the 1988 revolt was an expression of "a crisis of confidence in the state's ability to include all of its citizens in its socio-economic program of development" (Lazreg 2000: 59).

In order to save his government Bendjedid addressed the nation on October 10, and gave promises of economic and political reform, which he launched in November of the same year. A new constitution, drafted and approved by referendum in February 1989, guaranteed Algerian citizens freedom of speech, association, and assembly (Article 39), and recognized the right of the citizens to create political associations, meaning political parties (Article 40). This constitutional amendment brought an end to the one-party rule and brought to the fore a new model of social organization based on citizenship rights in lieu of an abstract notion of development. According to Lazreg, "The 'discovery' of citizenship is a powerful tool of protest in the hands of political opposition groups and social groups such as women, traditionally excluded from the full enjoyment of their political rights. It opens up a new era of inquiry into the many dimensions of citizenship and their culturally specific expressions as well" (Lazreg 2000: 58). In so far as Algerian women are concerned this new situation becomes very interesting as on the one hand women enjoy political citizenship while on the other hand they are denied their civil rights under the Family Code. This disjuncture between political and civil citizenship, "has prevented Algerian women from fully participating in public life and from achieving autonomy in the conduct of their private lives" (ibid.: 60).

This condition was made even more precarious with the emergence of the Islamists as political parties despite the fact that the law on political associations prohibits the foundation of parties set up exclusively to campaign on religious, linguistic, or regionalist issues. Several parties that should have been banned under this law were recognized by the government, hence the recognition of the Islamic Salvation Front (FIS), whose leaders never supported democracy, but repeatedly asserted that once in power they would fully implement Shari'a law.

The leaders of the FIS unequivocally declared that they would repeal the republic's Constitution and ban secular political parties; "Ali Benhadj repeated *ad infinitum* that democracy was incompatible with Islam and was *kufr* (blasphemy) because it placed the power of the people over God's power over the people" (Al-Ahnaf et al. 1991: 87).

Through their use of populist rhetoric to express their outright hatred of the regime, the FIS posed itself as the strongest alternative to the FLN. It recruited widely among the unemployed and poor factions of society and used the mosque as a space for propagating their extremist views, especially vis-à-vis women whom they put at the centre of their populist propaganda; over and over again they portrayed women as needing male protection and reiterated that the safest place for them was the home. Women should not go to work, as their prime duty is "to produce lions to fight for the cause of Islam" in the words of Ali Benhaj. Young men were made to believe that employed women were less moral, and female employment caused male unemployment. In a nutshell: "women have become one of the wrongs to be righted as a matter of duty to God" (Lazreg 2000: 67).

Resisting terrorist violence and continuing
to repeal the Family Code

Although women's organizations have now been recognized,[14] and have gained access to a wider audience thanks to the liberalization of the media, feminist groups and organizations became alarmed, and were particularly worried by the propaganda that members of the FIS had started to direct at young people.

On the March 8, 1989, during a gathering to celebrate International Women's Day called by the Association for the Equality before the Law between Men and Women, members of the association emphasized the "sub-minor" status of women, and declared, "the Family Code stands in absolute opposition to our aspirations for justice, equality and democracy: that it constitutes the primary obstacle to the full development of the Algerian woman and of the society as a whole."[15] Women's status as minors under the law prohibits the whole society from progressing into a democratic society, and makes them extremely vulnerable in front of the campaign of intimidation started by the FIS members against them.

As early as the 1980s, women became aware of the threat of Islamic fundamentalism, not only to women but to the whole society. Before even becoming a political party Islamists imposed veiling on women, forced segregation between boys and girls in some schools, and deprived school girls from physical education. They attacked women on the street for dressing up 'indecently' and threw acid on their bodies. They intimidated people on beaches and swimming pools and interfered with cultural life in general.

The government made no retort in face of these early signs of fascism. In fact the whole society allowed itself to become more and more intimidated by the Islamists who did not refrain from gaining and occupying more terrain in the public sphere, giving themselves the right to control it according to their new ways. Louisa Ait Hamou explains the reasons for this in the following terms, "The one-party state co-opted conservatives, and later, Muslim fundamentalists, to safeguard their interests and stay in power. Various governments have many times made compromises and sacrificed women's rights and safety to keep peace with the fundamentalists" (Ait Hamou 2004: 118).

It is in fact this silence and sometimes the complicity of the neo-conservative state that encouraged the fundamentalists' attacks against women. Such attacks escalated quickly into outbursts of brutality in 1992, soon after the government cancelled the electoral process, which could have taken the Islamists to power legally in 1991, and declared the FIS illegal.

At this stage the Islamist political movement turned into several armed movements such as the AIS (*Armée Islamique du Salut*: Islamic Salvation Army) and the GIA (*Groupe Islamique Armé*: Armed Islamic Group) as well as other appendices of the FIS. Such groups issued death threats against the intelligentsia, government security workers, and feminist activists and leaders of the likes of Khalida Messaoudi whom they sentenced to death in 1993. She testifies, "Over the loudspeakers, whose monotonous echoes penetrate into the very centre of the surrounding houses, imams would hurl curses at me, describe me as 'a woman of delinquent morals' and a 'danger to the morality of women,' and warn those women who might be tempted to follow my example" (Messaoudi and Schemla 1998: 87).

This savage war was not only directed against all that represented the Algerian regime but against the civilian population. It took the form of bombings, village massacres, beheadings, abductions, and rape which escalated into organized femicide.

It soon became obvious that women were at the top of the terrorists' agenda and that their bodies were primarily targeted as symbols; lists of women to be killed were pinned up at the entrance of mosques, women who worked in government offices were threatened and killed, women who owned shops such as hairdressers, beauty salons, Turkish baths were not spared and in some instances were forced to close their businesses. Women teachers were beheaded in front of their pupils, women related to government officers or security workers were also targeted. In remote areas whole villages were massacred, young girls were kidnapped, gang raped and turned into sex slaves, divorced women or widows who lived alone were also targeted.[16] Women's bodies were mutilated and abused, with their genitals often amputated.

Ait Hamou describes the horror as follows, "Women were attacked in their homes, brutally beaten, abducted, raped, taken as temporary wives of the 'emirs', or as slaves. They were shot dead, torn apart when they were pregnant and their fetuses smashed on the walls" (Ait Hamou 2004: 120). Such horrors were constantly making the titles of tabloids in the 1990s, and many pondered on the Islamists' femicide. In the words of Khalida Messaoudi:

> At the heart of their way of life, their mindset, their imprecations, and their savagery, I perceived a constant obsession, of the kind that is symptomatic of madness: an obsession with women. The truth is; no other theme looms as large as this one does in the ideology of the FIS. ... According to the fundamentalists, women are the root of all evil. Or, rather, the salvation of the *oumma*[17] [*sic*] lies in women's submission to the wishes of the imams.
>
> (Messaoudi and Schemla 1998: 100)

In fact, in their constant quest for equality and civil rights women were seen as the first enemies of the Islamic *Oumma* (nation) as conceived by the fundamentalists. Women's demands for the abolition of the Family Code, which the fundamentalists see as not strict enough in its observance of the Shari'a, represented a subversion of the Islamists' social order which is based on patriarchy. Furthermore, targeting women's bodies demonstrates that gender is at the core of the issue of Islamic fundamentalism and inflicting violence on their bodies is a means of controlling women and terrorizing their community.

Nevertheless, in their attempt to confine women to the private sphere, Islamists' violence was making them more visible and more central to the fight and resistance against their barbaric acts.

Women as agents of change and social cohesion

In the midst of what is seen as a barbaric war against civil society which by its end at the turn of the twenty-first century resulted in the loss of over 200,000 lives, Algerian women stood unabated against the retrograde forces of terrorism. Trapped between the dictates of an infamous Family Code and the barbarism of the Islamic fundamentalists, women were not prepared to submit to the threats of the terrorists or to give up their struggle to repeal the Family Code.

Their new struggle took a dual course; on the one hand they adopted resisting strategies to the destructive powers of Islamic terrorism by simply continuing to lead "normal" lives despite the atmosphere of war. They continued to go to work and do their daily errands. They continued to send their children to school, and female teachers who were not sure of returning to their homes in the evening continued to attend to their duties. They persisted in going to hairdressers and beauty salons and they continued to find ways to celebrate births, weddings, and their children's birthdays and school achievements. In brief, these women stood for life and for the continuance of life in Algeria despite the roaming danger of death in an extremely dangerous and hostile environment. This in itself is an extraordinary act of resistance and societal cohesion.

On the political front, despite their status as victims of terrorist violence women became more active than ever before in their society. They engaged in consolidating their roles as agents of change and resistance to the Islamist movement. On January 2, 1992, women were the first to stage massive demonstrations against the FIS and their victory of December 1991 across the major cities of the country. They called for the cancellation of the electoral process in which many women's voices were taken by the FIS through the proxy vote, and warned of the danger of Algeria becoming an Islamic republic. Their banners carried slogans which read, "No Iran, No Kabul, Algeria is Algerian," "Algeria: Free and Democratic," "Let's save the principles of the republic."[18] Their numbers amounted to thousands; their aim was to occupy the public sphere which the Islamists were trying to dominate, but more importantly to manifest their refusal of a fundamentalist rule which they saw as a threat not only against women but also against the whole society. Such demonstrations became a kind of routine to show that Algeria was not to submit to terrorist violence.[19]

Several feminist groups started organizing themselves and working together to change the awareness of women's issues in Algerian society and provide women with the knowledge that will enable them to counteract fundamentalism and produce a counter discourse. This was made possible by their brave occupation of the public sphere through demonstrations and organized public meetings. In these manifestations they displayed the photographs of the victims of terrorism, they shouted anti-fundamentalist slogans but more importantly the victims of terrorist violence and survivors of rape courageously testified to the media about the hideous act of gang rape to which they had been subjected.

On the social level women organized many charitable organizations to help survivors of rape who were rejected by their families because of the shame they allegedly brought to them. These organizations took care of the children of the women and girls who were forcibly impregnated by the terrorists and pressed the government to permit abortion in such occurrences.

On the cultural level, women continued to celebrate International Women's Day, during which they staged a mock tribunal against terrorism, showed films and staged plays such as the *Wounded Smile* by Fadhila Assous, and other plays that highlighted the dangers of fundamentalism, glorified women's courage and women's contribution to society, and more importantly raised the morale of women who could not be blamed for the dire situation of the country. Such plays highlighted the importance of women's solidarity networks and the importance of the active participatory roles which they have yet to play. This was happening at a time when cultural life in the country had come to a standstill.

At international level, new concepts have now crystallized in place of the old; women are now prepared to take their cause beyond the frontiers of their country and communicate with other women, which prior to the 1990s was still seen as a betrayal to the nation:

> One of the worst legacies of 'specific socialism' (Algeria's isolationist version of the creed) has been the distrust towards the global women's movement and of progressive and human-rights organizations. Among the consequences of this separation from the outside world was the inability of Algerian women to link the rise of Algerian fundamentalism with the situations of women in other parts of the Muslim world, especially Iran.
>
> (Mahl 1995: 2)

Algerian women forged solidarity networks with other women globally but particularly with those living under Muslim laws. In 1995 they joined the Maghreb Egalité Network, which was a great opportunity to communicate with the women of the Maghreb on various issues concerning them but especially to discuss a shared strategy to fight the Family Code.

Joining such groups and networks also allowed Algerian women to secure the support of many Western countries whose media have often portrayed the FIS as victims of the undemocratic Algerian state who crushed their victory by cancelling the electoral process in 1992. The main aim of Algerian women was to create an alternative and counter discourse to that of the FIS and demonstrate to world opinion that the FIS used democratic means to eradicate the nascent democracy in Algeria. Feminists publicized FIS leaders' statements against democracy[20] as widely as they could, presenting themselves as an alternative voice to that of the state which lost its credibility on an international scale.

Furthermore, women published academic articles and books, often in many European languages to reach European readers with the truth about fundamentalism in Algeria; a good example is Khalida Messaoudi's book, *Une Algérienne debout*. Published by Flammarion in 1995, it sold 100,000 copies in France alone. In 1998 the book was published in English as *Unbowed: An Algerian Woman Confronts Islamic Fundamentalism* by the University of Pennsylvania Press, and was subsequently translated into Italian, German, Norwegian, and Turkish. The book tells the reader "the story of an Algerian woman held hostage by terror and a woman who has refused to be restrained … Messaoudi gives a first-hand perspective of the situation in her homeland" (book cover). The book is in fact a testimony about the atrocities committed against women and civil society in Algeria. Based on personal experience it demystifies world views about the FIS.

Once again it was women who created an alternative political discourse at international level by testifying to terrorist violence and by speaking at meetings and conferences organized by the UN and human rights NGOs.

The Family Code twenty years on

In 1999 President Abdelaziz Bouteflika was elected as the new head of the Algerian state. He promised to bring about peace and social justice to a country torn by terrorist violence. He also promised to promote the cause of Algerian women and include them in his program of economic reforms.

Although these reforms were slow to come women have never forgotten their agenda but at the same time trusted the good will of the president, who often repeated that mentalities were not ready for major changes to the Family Code, and that regardless of the code women who made up 52 percent of the Algerian population should continue to occupy the public sphere, through their jobs and through their work in society.

Although I criticized this position in a previous publication, I now understand what Abdelaziz Bouteflika meant. In a society such as Algeria women can only get their rights through a tactful revolution. He rightly sounded the position of the conservative members of government vis-à-vis the implementing of any changes to the Family Code or indeed to the status of women, let alone abrogating the Family Code.

Yet, again a real and tangible change was taking place in society for the advantage of women. Several taboos started to disappear and mentalities, though slowly, are surely changing especially towards women working outside the home and the type of work they do.

The decade of terrorist violence has been a decade of profound social changes in Algeria; while many might have thought that women would have been intimidated from the public sphere, on the contrary, they have occupied many new and uncustomary positions. Furthermore, the new dress codes adopted by many in the form of a head scarf and long skirts/trousers allowed women more mobility in the public sphere.

In an article for the *New York Times*, Michael Slackman lists some figures that show these changes, "Women make up 70 percent of Algeria's lawyers and 60 percent of its judges. Women dominate medicine ... Sixty percent of university students are women. ... In a region where women have a decidedly low public profile, Algerian women are visible everywhere" (Slackman 2007). Furthermore, these women have a political and/or religious discourse which the women of the 1960s did not have. The Algerian sociologist Fatima Oussedik confesses, "We in the 60s, we were progressive, but we did not achieve what is being achieved by this generation today" (ibid.).

It has to be added that the provisions of the code were disintegrating as real-life practices threatened to relegate non-operational ones to oblivion. The challenges imposed on Algerian society by the economic crisis of the 1980s together with factors imposed by the general failure of the Algerian male caused by high rates of unemployment, high school dropouts and failures among boys, the failure of the FIS as an alternative to the FLN, and the surge of fleeing the country seeking better opportunities abroad among young males, enabled women to quickly overtake the space left by men and therefore step into various fields which were traditionally known as male domains, especially in the field of agriculture and engineering. Women accepted all sorts of jobs regardless of what the society used to think if a woman was a cleaner, nurse, hairdresser, or even a waitress.

Militating for the cause of women is also no longer a taboo; massive numbers are now joining women's organizations to press for the changing of the Family Code. They rallied around a new organization called *Collectif 20 ans barakat* (20 years is enough!), whose sole platform is the repealing of the infamous code. These women were especially stimulated by the changes to the Moroccan Family Code in January 2003, which made them more determined than ever before to continue their struggle to achieve full citizenship.

Ourida Chouaki, the coordinator of the *Collectif 20 ans barakat* campaign in Algeria speaks of the various means they have used to raise awareness among women about the dictats of the 1984 Family Code. For this purpose they used public lectures, conferences, a poster competition for adults and children, but most importantly the Internet as an alternative to television to reach as many people as possible in a country as vast as Algeria.

In the summer of 2004 the government appointed a commission made up of lawyers, activists, and academics to draft a proposal for the amendment of the Family Code. Despite the fact that President Bouteflika insisted that the proposed reforms did not target Islamic law but rather social customs that have become codified, Islamist parties such as the MSP (*Mouvement pour la Société et la Paix*: Movement for Society and Peace) provoked a strong opposition to the changing of many essential articles in the code but especially the article concerning the requirement of having a matrimonial guardian.

After lengthy heated parliamentary debates, on November 22, 2004, a preliminary draft of amendments to the Family Code was presented to the Algerian government who examined and approved the changes.

Although these changes were seen as timid and derisory by many feminist groups and organizations, I believe that they are a step towards further changes to be imposed by the major transformations that are taking place in society at an astonishing speed.

Conclusion

To conclude, the institution of the Family Code in 1984 and the decade of terrorist violence have been strong wake-up calls for Algerian women and caused a relaunch of the feminist movement and solidarity networks among women of all ranks and generations. Terrorist violence has taught women a political lesson; women's organizations have developed new strategies by working at the grassroots level and helping women through the work of organized women's groups such as *SOS Femmes en Détresse*, RACHDA: *Rassemblement contre la Hogra et pour les Droits des Algériennes*, *Réseau Wassila*, and others.

Working closely together through organized networks and civil society organizations is seen as an effective means of changing the lives of women, and liberating the capabilities of these women through education and employment as well as through their participation in political, economic, and social development ultimately results in social change.

Women continued to occupy the public sphere, to participate in politics and occupy key positions in government. They stood for the principles of the Algerian republic against the destructive work of the Islamist terrorists and have proved once again that their work and contribution is essential for their own development and for the progress of the nation. This new generation of women is not to be intimidated or to be sent back to their kitchens; their political awareness has developed and matured. Through a quiet revolution these women have built their capacities to promote change and deconstruct a prevalent patriarchy, through their continuous and stubborn fight to repeal the Family Code.

Notes

1   Excerpt from the play *Al-Basma al-Majruha*.
2   For more details see Zahia Smail Salhi, "Representations of the 'Femmes d'Alger' in French Colonial Media," *Middle East Journal of Culture and Communications*, 1(1), 2008.
3   In his novel *La Colline oubliée* (*The Forgotten Hill*), Mouloud Mammeri accurately describes the dire conditions of the rural women in the Kabyle region in North East Algeria. He starts the novel with the statement: "Spring is often short-lived in Kabylia and so is the spring of young Kabyle girls," as they are thrashed into the hard life of becoming young women at a very early age. The novel describes the poverty and humiliation lived by the couple Ibrahim-Sekoura, and the *mal-vie* lived by all the villagers as a result of being colonized.
4   In his novel *La Grande maison* (*The Big House*), Mohammed Dib describes the prison-like life of urban women in Tlemcen, a city in West Algeria. Dib portrays the big house (*Dar Sbitar*) that shelters several families as a big prison whose inhabitants

suffer from various ills including hunger, disease, anxiety, and boredom. For more details see, Zahia Smail Salhi, *Politics, Poetics and the Algerian Novel* (Edwin Mellen Press, 1999).

5 All quotes from this source are my translations.

6 The first congress of the FLN.

7 In the Algerian context, unlike the Palestinian case, this word is used for the civilian workers of the resistance. Their work was mainly liaison, providing food and shelter for the armed resistance, etc. The local word used is *musabilin* meaning: they put their lives at risk for serving the revolution.

8 Halimi, Gisèle, *Djamila Boupacha: The story of the torture of a young Algerian girl which shocked liberal French opinion*, London: Cox and Wyman, 1962.

9 Gillo Pontecorvo, *The Battle of Algiers*, 1965. See also, Youssef Shahin, *Djamila Al-Jazairiya* (The Algerian Djamila).

10 Moroccan female novelist Leila Abouzeid portrays a similar story of betrayal in her novel *Year of the Elephant: A Moroccan Woman's Journey Towards Independence*, trans. Barbara Parmenter, Texas: University of Texas Press, 1989.

11 First Algerian president. He was deposed by President Boumedienne in 1965.

12 *El-Moudjahid:* a daily national newspaper in French.

13 *Algérie Actualités:* a weekly national newspaper in French.

14 Several women's organizations have now been recognized, the best known are:

- AITDF (*L'Association Independente pour le Triomphe des Droits des Femmes*): Independent Association for the Triumph of Women's Rights founded and led by Khalida Messaoudi.
- *L'Organisation de 'égalité devant la loi entre les femmes et les hommes*: Association for Equality before the Law between Men and Women.
- Women's organizations affiliated with the *Front des Forces Socialistes* and *le Parti Avant-garde Socialiste*.

15 Feminist declaration on March 8, 1989, in "Algiers, WAF Articles", *Journal* no. 1, p. 15.

16 In the southern Algerian town of Ouargla, a group of fundamentalists set fire to the house of a divorced woman living alone with her children, resulting in her 3-year-old child burning to death.

17 *Oumma: Umma*, the nation.

18 Such slogans were repeatedly shouted at subsequent demonstrations such as that on October 25, 1993. Such slogans demonstrate women's awareness of the replications of Islamic fundamentalism at the international level. They also demonstrate a will to link the women's movement in Algeria to other women's movements internationally but most specifically with women living under Muslim laws. See http://www.newint.org/issue270/270edge.html (accessed 21 December 2005).

19 For more details see *Shadow Report on Algeria to CEDAW*, submitted by International Women's Human Rights, Law Clinic and Women Living under Muslim Laws. http://www.nodo50.org/mujeresred/argelia-shadwreport.html (accessed 30 June 2004).

20 As an example, this is what the two main Algerian fundamentalist leaders/co-founders of the FIS party had to say, even long before the December 1991 elections were cancelled in Algeria, about their programme and democracy: "I do not respect either the laws or the political parties which do not have the Qur'an. I throw them under my feet and I trample them. These parties must leave the country. They must be suppressed" (Ali Belhadj, *Alger Républicain*, 5 April 1991), "Beware of those who pretend that the concept of democracy exists in Islam. Democracy is Kofr" (Ali Belhadj, *Le Matin*, 29 October 1989). Quoted in Mariemme Hélie-Lucas, "What is your Tribe? Women's Struggle and the Construction of Muslimness", WLULM: Dossier 26, October 2004, p. 26.

11 Women in Turkey

Caught between tradition and modernity

Fatma Umut Bespinar

Introduction

In Turkey's history, the concepts of "tradition" and "modernity" have constituted
the parameters conditioning political discourse since even before the beginning of
the Republic. The search for Turkey's future direction has constantly oscillated
between those who want a path compatible with the "authentic" values of the
past, and those who urge that we scrap the past in order to "reach the level of
a contemporary civilization," i.e., who advocate for Turkey to adopt Western
ideas, institutions, and way of life. In this dialectic, everyday practices, including
issues related to women, have become crucial. Both Kemalist reforms based
on Westernization and other, countervailing ideologies, such as the pro-Islamist
political movement, devote considerable attention to women's issues. Women's
issues—by which is meant their public presence, education, employment, suffrage
rights, and regulations about clothing, family roles, and sexuality—have always
been central to conservative as well as to modernist political ideologies, starting
from the Tanzimat Period and continuing right up to today. The conflict of
approaches to women's issues in Turkey has generated abundant research (Baykan
1990; Tekeli 1986, 1995; Sirman 1989), with the focus usually concentrated on
the tension between Kemalist and Islam ideology (Durakbasa 1988; Arat 1995).
However, less research has focused on the transformation of politics and changing
nature of debates on women's issues in the politics between the 1990s and the
2000s.

Unlike other chapters of this volume dealing with women's capacities, this
chapter takes into consideration the limits women faced in changing the socio-
political milieu of Turkey between 1990 and the present (2008). The period
between 1990 and 2008 is distinguished from previous periods by two trends: the
first is that the power dynamic between the traditional factions in Turkish politics,
roughly the modernizers and the traditionalists, has been re-configured, and new
actors and centers of power have emerged. Since the early 1990s, a number of
national and international actors with conflicting women's rights agendas and
priorities have become pivotal to the debate on women's issues in Turkey. In
addition to the Turkish state and Turkish political organizations, the European
Union, the Convention for Elimination of All Forms of Discrimination against

Women (CEDAW) and international women's NGOs have increasingly tried to influence women's rights policies. The second trend, deriving from the first, regards the status and mode of the debate on women's issues. The discussions changed in accordance with the differing socio-political priorities. These priorities have been constructed and strengthened in the Turkish political battlefield based on binary oppositions such as "authenticity" and "modernity."

In this chapter, I examine this changing playing field. Although the number of actors and agendas increased in the period from 1990 to the present, the opposing "sides" relating to the public role of women became ever more distinctly polarized. This chapter analyzes how women and issues directly related to them are prioritized and defined by the actors of local and international politics and further shows how women are objectified in debates on issues relating to them. The nature of the debate has crystallized around certain themes, such as the issue of *turban* (veiling) in different political and historical contexts, the criminalization of adultery, and the project-based approach towards women's problems. The criterion I have used for my selection of women's issues is the presence of many actors involved in the debates over these issues. This study is based on in-depth interviews conducted with personnel, volunteers, and beneficiaries of women's nongovernmental organizations (NGOs) in Istanbul, Turkey, in 2005, supplemented by a content analysis of newspapers, and a reading of sections of the Turkish Constitution and the Civil and the Penal Code relating to women. The main questions guiding this chapter are as follows: What are the main characteristics of women's issues in the last decades in Turkey? What are the power dynamics among the main social actors in these debates? What changes in the themes debated and the discourse used have occurred during the twenty-first century? What are the limits/capacities of women's activism on these issues?

After briefly discussing the structural dynamics shaping women's issues, I look at changing components of women's issues, using persistent and newly emerging themes as the focus of my analysis. I first provide a brief background on the social dynamics affecting women's issues between 1990 and 2008, leading into a discussion of three issues that have generated the most discussion in the Turkish media and political circles: the changing debate on veiling (*turban*) in the last two decades, the struggle over the law to criminalize adultery, and finally the limits and problems of projects-based approaches to women's problems. In conclusion, I briefly draw the commonalities of these dominant themes in the debates on women's issues in Turkey between 1990 and 2008.

Changing components of "women's issues" in Turkey

When we look at specifically women's rights and reforms, Turkey is an interesting case, having a long progressive history of women's rights, but also retaining many values and practices that reinforce unequal gender roles, with women losing out in terms of rights, property, and salary. The equal status of women, including their public presence, education, employment, and suffrage rights, was one of the hallmarks of Turkish modernization (Kandiyoti 1987, 1991). The discussion of women's issues in Turkey[1] has evolved through phases which, though conflicted within themselves, are distinct and a continuation of each other. In the first phase, which started with the establishment of the Republic of Turkey in 1923, the goal was to create the "new and modern Turkish woman" as a part of the Westernization project. The second phase was experienced in the years following the 1980 coup d'état. In the 1990s, socio-political transformations ensuing from the end of the Cold War order again changed the actors and issues. Women who had been in the periphery became visible in this phase. These women are outside the "modernization" project; their identity and/or their socio-economic positions made it difficult, if not impossible, to be the object of "modernization."

Westernization became more salient as the direction for Turkish development with the establishment of the Republic of Turkey. The multiethnic, religiously institutionalized Ottoman Empire was transformed into the secular nation-state, which was based on Turkishness as an identity. In the first years of the new nation, the break with Islam and the Ottoman past was realized through the abolition of the Caliphate and the Shari'a, the adoption of the Swiss civil and the Italian penal codes, and the replacement of the Arabic alphabet with the Latin one. The creation of the "new woman" was also a part of the Westernization project. In Mustafa Kemal's words, "The path that we are to follow is the path to make the great Turkish woman a partner in all our endeavors, the path that we walk on through life together. She is a man's partner, friend and helpmate within our scientific, ethical, social and economic life" (cited by Gologlu 1972). Women's roles were to be enlightened comrades of men as educated wives and mothers. Rights offered to women through Kemalist reforms were symbols of the break away from Islamist rule and institutions. In this phase, the participation of women in the social sphere through education and employment was encouraged. Education was regarded as the main emancipatory tool to transform women's subordinated social position (Tekeli 1995). Kemalist reforms and secularism were perceived as the most important guarantee for women's rights. Women's associations founded after the 1950s were active along lines determined by state policy. The patriarchal essence and implementations of these reforms were not questioned.

It is paradoxical that the second stage of women's issues took place in the post-military intervention period, which stifled all other kinds of political organization. Political activities, particularly left-wing movements which were socially and politically influential in the pre-1980 period, were silenced by the military intervention. The feminist movement was one of the social movements that developed in spite of the anti-democratic social atmosphere. Questioning the separation between private and public aspects of life was another characteristic of the second stage. The discovery of a public interest in the organization of the "private sphere," which arose out of issues such as domestic violence and the legal equality of women and men in marriage, marked this second stage. The feminist movement revitalized itself through grassroots movements and feminist journals, consciousness-raising meetings conducted in homes, and public campaigns (Tekeli 1995; Timisi and Agduk Gevrek 2002). Women also coordinated numerous larger meetings such as the First Women's Congress in 1989 to discuss their problems. Feminist organizations on several occasions effectively conducted public protest campaigns to change some provisions of the Penal Code.[2]

The third phase in the Turkish discourse on women's issues started in the 1990s. Global social transformations, such as increasing emphasis on ethnic and religious identities and decentralization through social projects of organizations with conflicting interests, coincided with socio-economic transformations experienced in Turkey. In this context, new actors emerged, new positions on women's issues were expressed, social actors who were not visible in the earlier social sphere started to demand their rights, and new backing for the claims of previously overlooked groups was available through project-based organizations. In addition to the national actors, the international and intergovernmental actors and norms such as those set by the European Union, the Convention for Elimination of All Forms of Discrimination against Women (CEDAW), and international women's NGOs have increasingly become important contributors to public discussions related to women's rights in Turkey. In the Constitution and in the new Penal and Labor Codes, provisions have been adopted regarding gender equality, primarily to appease the European Union, which Turkey hopes to become a part of. Although there are important legal improvements, the effects on rights for the majority of women remain largely unchanged due to inconsistent enforcement.

The rising power of pro-Islamic parties since the 1990s is another social transformation which shapes debate on women's issues in Turkey. According to Islamic newspapers and magazines which have become widespread since the late 1970s, women's main social role is motherhood; their social position should be limited to the home (Günes-Ayata 2001; Acar 1995; Arat 1995). After the victory of the Welfare Party (*Refah Partisi*—RP) in the 1995 elections, such arguments become widespread not only in the media, but also in the political arena. RP leader, Erbakan, for instance, stated in his speeches that women should work no more than twice a week or eight hours outside the home, since their work can be only complementary to that of their husbands' (Günes-Ayata 2001). The use of derogatory language for certain groups of women such as women participating in the labor market became common in political speeches during the coalition years of the RP and the True Path Party (*Dogru Yol Partisi*—DYP) (Günes-Ayata 2001). The increasing reference to instantiating an Islamic order in Turkey began to create nationwide disturbances, which in turn led to the covert military intervention that occurred in February 28, 1997, when the RP was thrown out due to violations of the Turkish Constitution. After the Constitutional Court outlawed the Welfare Party in 1998, the Virtue Party (*Fazilet Partisi*) was established with more or less the same cadres.

The Justice and Development Party (*Adalet ve Kalkinma Partisi*—AKP), which emerged after the closures of the Welfare Party in 1998 and the Virtue Party in 1999 using a new set of tactics and slogans to distinguish itself from these parties, started to govern the country in 2002. Although the programs of these parties have similar conservative values with regard to the family and women, AKP has been more careful in publicizing views on women's issues. As Insel (2003: 304) argues, the approach to women's issues is framed in terms of protecting "peace in the family." The women's organizations of the AKP have also expressed their preference for staying home, including working in "home-offices" as more "appropriate" for women.

Although the AKP government attempts to reconcile international and intergovernmental agencies and norms on women's issues, its conservative practices related to women issues are visible in Turkish society. The discourse favoring the social segregation of women and men,[3] discrimination against women in hiring for state employment,[4] the discussion on changing childcare and pre-school education from a full day to half a day, the cancellation of affirmative action in highly gender-segregated jobs such as the cadres of judge and prosecutor,[5] and the discussions on the criminalization of adultery exemplify the conservative practices of the AKP government.

Themes in the discussion of women's issues (1990–2008)

Specific controversies exemplify the larger issues at play in the Turkish socio-political arena. I will look at three of these: (1) the debate on veiling (*turban*) in the last two decades in Turkey; (2) the debate on adultery in the parliament in 2004; and finally, (3) project-based approaches since the 1990s aimed at emancipating women.

The debate on turbans *in the last two decades*

The *turban,* which veils all hair and the neck, has become an important issue since the 1980s as pro-Islamic women university students fought for the right to wear it to protest against the regulation banning it. Since the 1980s, the right of a woman to be turbaned in any public venue has become one of the most divisive social issues. Pro-Islamic ideology, which had been encouraged by the Turkish state since the 1950s, and the rise of conservative right-wing parties, resulted in an increasing number of informal Qur'an courses and religious training vocational schools (*Imam Hatip Liseleri*). The large enrollment in religious training vocational schools in the early 1970s led to the emergence of many female university students with *turbans* demanding their educational rights in the 1980s. Finally, in 1989, the Constitutional Court decided that the *turban* was contrary to the principle of secularism.

Göle's (1992, 1996) and Ilyasoglu's (1994) studies examine the increasing number of women with *turban* in the metropolitan areas of Turkey in the late 1980s and early 1990s. The *turban* is interpreted as a symbol of urban Islamist lifestyle, distancing itself from traditional and secular ways of life at the same time. Göle's and Ilyasoglu's studies were the first sociological attempts to understand the polysemy of this new phenomenon. The female university students and professional women wearing *turban* exerted, through this act of civil defiance, pressure on the strict rules of the secular state and its institutions such as universities and state offices, and became the new social actors of the time, using civil rights techniques normally associated with the left. Göle (1992, 1996) interprets young university students' *turban* as a "hybrid" symbol, located neither in tradition nor in the Western mode of modernism. Interviews with university students showed that, far from being a continuation of traditionalist mores, these women were breaking away from the "socially accepted" tradition of their families. Göle argues that young women, who come from traditional families living in the rural provinces of Turkey, actually chose the *turban* as a quintessentially urban phenomenon. Distancing themselves from the traditional style of clothing, such as headscarf, was very important for these university students. They did not wish to be a part of the "ignorant" masses, who experienced Islam through hearsay. Women who regarded themselves as "enlightened" and "intellectual" are "not simply passive conveyors of the provincial traditional culture; they are, rather, active and self-asserting women who seek opportunities in modernism" (Göle 1996: 92). In this sense, veiling has become a radical Islamic symbol which exacerbates the tension between traditionalism and modernism. While Ilyasoglu (1994) regards the veiling of professional women as an attempt to articulate modernity, in which upwardly mobile women hold themselves apart from what is "traditional" by defining their own modernity, Göle (1992, 1996) argues that veiling is a hybrid form.

Turban continues to form a crucial part of the debate about women's issues in Turkey. Although the *turban* is still an important social and political symbol in Turkish society, its social meaning and presence in the middle of unequal power relations of different social actors has recently changed and is open to new changes. With the electoral success of Islamist parties such as the Welfare Party (*Refah Partisi*) in the early 1990s, the meaning of *turban* has extended from just being an identity tool of young university students to become a symbol of rising political Islam in Turkey. After images of numbers of women wearing *turban*s in public meetings of the RP and FP, Merve Kavakçi, the first woman parliament member wearing *turban,* was elected from the FP in 1999. Since then, the *turban* has assumed a highly charged political meaning. There is a shift from the "oppressed" (*mazlum*) image of female university students standing in front of universities protesting against not being allowed to enter to the "aggressive" image of Merve Kavakçi as she pushed the limits of the secular regime. Although she was elected in her *turban*, she could not take the oath of office in the Parliament due to the strong opposition from the Prime Minister and parliamentarians from other political parties.

An interview conducted with Kavakçi shows the significance of *turban* to her identity.[6] When journalist Nursel Dilek asked if anyone in the Parliament supported her taking office in her *turban* in the Parliament, Kavakçi mentioned two leading FP Parliament members—Tayyip Erdogan who became prime minister in 2003 and Abdullah Gül who was prime minister between 2002 and 2003 and who became president in 2007. While Tayyip Erdogan could not guarantee her party's support if she insisted on entering the Parliament wearing a *turban*, Abdullah

Gül suggested tying her headscarf under the chin. As Ms. Kavakçi said, "This suggestion sounded funny to me. I said 'No, brother. That would be very ugly, like wearing a wig.' His concern was my being accepted in that way."

The Turkish media focused on whether Merve Kavakçi's *turban* was authentic or representative of Turkish tradition and values (Özyürek 2000). The discussion on authenticity and tradition mostly regards the *turban* as a symbol of fundamentalist Islam that does not belong to the Turkish tradition and history. The distinction between the headscarf which is tied under the chin and the *turban* was very clear to Ms. Kavakçi; for her the headscarf was ugly and like a wig. In the days following her attempt to participate in the swearing-in ceremony with a *turban*, this distinction got blurred. As a political maneuver, she argued that she was against the distinction between the headscarf of Anatolian women, which is accepted as a symbol of tradition and authenticity, and the *turban*, underlining the common ground between headscarf and *turban* as both fulfilling religious beliefs.

The discussion on the *turban* has always been focused on many dichotomies such as modern/tradition, authentic/counterfeit, public/private, and the people vs. the elite. Another dichotomy often mentioned is the one between the state and the nation. In these debates, the regulations of state and state institutions are portrayed as keeping the *turban* out of public institutions and limiting it to the private sphere of the home and the street. The issue of the *turban* brought up the status of the Grand National Assembly of Turkey, and whether it represents the nation as the most supreme state institution. The Civil Servants Law (the 7th Clause, Number 657) bans wearing the headscarf in government administrative offices and in the Parliament.

This discussion between nation/people and state foreshadowed the candidacy of Abdullah Gül for the presidential election in April 2007. Ilyasoglu (1994) recognized the *turban* was a symbol of the rising power of the counter-elite in Turkey when the issue first arose, and it has since become the symbol of the Islamist elite gaining power in the economic, social, and political arenas. For the first time in history the prospect loomed for a first lady to be wearing the *turban*. In statements following the announcement of his candidacy, Mr. Gül said that his wife's *turban* is her personal choice and added that everybody should respect her freewill. The main political debates thereafter have swirled around his wife's *turban* and the legitimacy of her representing Turkish women with her head covered. Another significant discussion in the current political season has renewed the story of Mrs. Gül's application to the European Court of Human Rights (ECHR) after she was not allowed to register in the university in 1988 due to her *turban*.[7] After Mr. Gül became the foreign minister, she retracted her application one month before the court decision supporting the university. Mrs. Gül's *turban* was also a part of the public debates behind her husband's withdrawal from the presidential race, which fomented the political crisis between secularists and Islamists around the general elections in 2007.

The general elections in July 2007 resulted in an increase in the power of the AKP in the Parliament and the political arena: AKP received 46.6 percent of the votes, gaining 340 of the 550 deputies in the Parliament. With the aid of another right-wing party in the Parliament, Mr. Gül was selected as president in the third round of the balloting on August 28, 2007. Debate on his presidency has revived discussion of his wife's *turban*. Both international and national media, politicians, civil society leaders discussed Mrs. Gül's *turban* as a symbol of the conflict between modernity and tradition, or Islam and secularism. The rumor on Mrs. Gül's commissioning the fashion designer Atil Kutoglu to "modernize" her *turban* and her dressing style became part of the intensively charged political debates.[8] While debates on Mrs. Gül's style and *turban* achieved media saturation, political debates on female *turban*-wearing university students became dominant in the Parliament between political parties and members of the Higher Education Council during 2007 and 2008. Formulation related to *turban* resulted in changes to Articles 10 and 42 of the Constitution.[9] These political maneuvers have increased tension between different segments of the society by heightening the political polarization. These debates reflect the tensions between secularism and Islam, modernity and tradition, and people and state, putting women in the middle of all these tensions.

Debates on the law criminalizing adultery

The law criminalizing adultery is another public issue of the 2000s in Turkey. This debate reveals a new set of power dynamics between international bodies such as the EU, the pro-Islamist party, AKP, the feminist associations, and the media that did not exist before 1990. The European Commission recommended the adoption of a new Turkish Penal Code to replace that of 1926, which was patterned after the Italian Penal Code. Although previous governments had made several amendments, one of the main obstacles to Turkey's membership in the EU remains the sexist articles in the Penal Code: for example, reducing punishment in "crimes of honor." In the adoption of a new Penal Code in 2005, the AKP attempted to include a clause criminalizing adultery. The constitutional court abrogated the clause on adultery several years ago due to the lack of equivalence between men and women in the definition and punishment of the so-called crime. In the face of opposition from the EU, lobbying feminist organizations, and the media, Prime Minister Erdogan stated that this clause, based on the sensibilities of the Turkish people, should stand and the European body should not meddle in Turkey's domestic affairs. This issue aroused such international and national furor that it put AKP in danger of losing "important political goodwill at home and abroad." [10]

The AKP's argument in attempting to include this amendment was "to strengthen the family and to protect women." Another argument was that most women supported criminalization of adultery. Conservative deputies defended this amendment by arguing that it is based on Turkish cultural values and tradition.[11] A significant characteristic of the proposed clause was that it would have exempted men with long-established relationships. In practice, it would have allowed men multiple religious marriages, and, thus, reinforced sexist implementations. As a result of pressure from the EU and other interest groups, the proposed law criminalizing adultery was ultimately dropped. Discussion on adultery is an example which demonstrates how AKP is zigzagging between its conservative base and the pressures of the EU.

Debates on adultery have also been discussed in the framework of certain binaries such as: people/state, common people/elites. As Tepe (2006: 21) argues, the AKP claims "full knowledge of society's needs and desire." There are two problems in this claim: first, Aydin and Çakir (2007) show that the assumption of a set of shared social values is problematic. Second, AKP's self-identification as the voice of the Turkish people has been challenged. When the AKP attempts to criminalize adultery and thus earn political support from its conservative base, it presents this attempt as a part of its mission of reflecting the entire people's unheard needs which have been neglected by the elites and state for a long time.

Turkish society's traditional roots have been always a part of the legislative regulations on women's sexuality. Women's reproductive rights, adultery, honor crimes have been defined and constructed in the legislative context by taking the "traditional sensibilities" into account. The emphasis on "tradition" and "social sensibilities" has been used in the justification of the sexist clauses in the Penal Code on abortion, adultery, and honor crimes in both the Ottoman Empire and Turkish Republic (Miller 2007). However, the meaning of "traditional sensibilities" is ambiguous enough to be open to political manipulation. In any case, sexist practices should be eliminated from the legal system instead of codified within it.

Project-based approaches to women's problems

Project-based approaches towards women's civil and economic problems have become influential in developing countries from the 1980s (Harrison 1997). Since the 1980s, due to the increase in international interest rates and the following debt crisis, Turkey as well as other developing countries have employed structural adjustment policies (SAPs) dictated by the International Monetary Fund and the World Bank and geared toward cutting government spending, privatizing state-owned companies, and downsizing many state services. Structural adjustment policies transformed "the state-managed approach of socio-economic development" into a "project-based approach of socio-economic development" through decentralization processes. Projects conducted by non-governmental organizations are gradually supplanting the basic services of health, training, and education, once provided only by the state. The 1990s saw an increase in the number and scope of social projects aiming to emancipate rural-to-urban migrant women who have settled on the peripheries of big cities or women from rural areas of Turkey such as the eastern and southeastern regions (Kümbetoglu 2002). Women's issues have become critical as the neo-liberal discourse has expanded its critique of state-sponsored command and control systems. Agenda-oriented NGOs, with support from international organizations, have become powerful lobbyists. The socio-structural problems women face are now being approached through projects conducted by non-governmental organizations. With increasing migration and a changing social structure in both the big cities and the southeastern region of Turkey, middle-class women from urban centers have engaged in projects to emancipate their sisters by teaching Turkish, literacy, and other skills. Starting in the 1990s, projects based on skill development such as carpet-weaving courses or cooking classes have opened not only in the rural areas of Turkey but on the outskirts of big cities.

With the decline of the social state and vanishing welfare provisions, "project-based development" is assumed to compensate for the lack of the state in the lives of citizens who are systematically excluded from segments of labor markets, service provisions, and political decision-making mechanisms. Since Turkey became a candidate for membership in the European Union in 1999, "project-based development" has increasingly become widespread, mainly supported financially by the European Commission. The priorities and expectations of the European Union become the criteria for funding. In these projects, not only priority issues but target groups are specified according to the agenda of institutions providing financial support, including the European Union and local organizations. These projects are set up with the specific mandate of alleviating the unemployment and illiteracy of women as well as domestic violence against them.

Moreover, mainstream socio-economic development projects, common until the 1990s, articulated certain issues such as domestic violence and women's access to their legal rights, subjects which were ignored during the "state feminism" period. It is worthwhile to evaluate the social pros and cons of these projects. Feminist women who developed "consciousness," liberating themselves from patriarchal assumptions about their bodies and other constraints in their everyday lives, as well as their sexuality, started to connect with "other" women on the peripheries of urban centers or in rural areas of Turkey. Although this connection is important and promising for both sides, the differences make it difficult to "listen" and "understand" each other. Class, education, way of life, cultural values, identities, and even language differences make women's connection to each other problematic. The nature of these relations is always open to asymmetrical power dynamics since there is one group that is supposed to be able to "help," while the other group is constructed from the beginning as "needy."

In the interviews I conducted with NGO personnel, volunteers, and the women who are the beneficiaries, the problems each experiences show expected variances. For the personnel of women's NGOs, the main problems are always identified as the bureaucratic barriers of state institutions and the strict rules imposed by their financial supporters. Increasing competition among local and national NGOs for international funding, such as that provided by the European Commission, forces locally produced project proposals to be geared towards the procedures and expectations of the European Union. Writing grant proposals is a complicated process for the majority of NGOs, whose coordinators argue that they spend most of their time and energy fulfilling the strict requirements of the projects.[12] Especially for small civil organizations with limited budgets and low technical skills, trying to adhere to the strict procedures of the European Community's Turkey Pre-Accession Financial Assistance Program is discouraging. While the

European Union's expressed aim is to foster "pluralistic democracy" through the participation of civil actors, this becomes difficult as the bureaucracy gets in the way. A coordinator of an NGO that specializes in helping women attain skills to become economically active argues:

> During the proposal stage, we had too many problems with rigid procedures and requirements to be able to receive financial support. In the implementation process, we experienced difficulties with the state bureaucracy. To find a way, we needed to learn the unwritten rules, which make the procedure less forbidding and everything faster. The necessity to be expert at English report writing is another difficulty small organizations face. We need to have a group of experts who only work on these complex procedures or we need to find a professional grant proposal-writing agency, but their services are too expensive.

Diverse and heterogeneous populations are often melded into a few "target groups"—mainly categorized as "Southeastern women," "urban poor women," and "women who are victims of violence." Although it is important to approach women who have similar problems with combined projects, sometimes these predefined categories are far from capturing socio-structural realities. International priorities play an important role in the definition and selection of target groups. The shift from the coherent, long-term policies focused on structural change to projects which are usually short-term and remedy-focused affects the efficiency of the services. A volunteer of an NGO focusing on improving urban poor women's living conditions in Istanbul states:

> These projects emphasize the need to "increase the awareness" of poor women. Therefore, they only give our organization money for projects in which we collect women in a seminar room and teach them their rights: employment rights, sexual rights, reproductive rights, so on. ... This is very important, don't misunderstand me, but please tell me, what is the meaning of increasing awareness without changing the situation? Women are learning their rights, but there is a huge unemployment problem and lack of opportunities in this country. Women ask us after completing the seminars, "Now that I have learned that as an independent woman I can work, I want to be economically independent. How can I find a job?" I can't give them an answer. This is the worst part of my experience as a volunteer. Without doing anything to change the situation, what is the meaning of awareness?

Women who are defined as "target groups" of these projects also have certain problems. Some of them underline the "uselessness" of these projects, others complain about the attitudes of the volunteers toward them. Certain women stress the critical attitudes of the volunteers as limiting the effectiveness of their outreach. In Esma's words:

> They [the volunteers] see me as an ignorant woman; I can feel that from their manners, even from their looks. Everything of mine is under their judgment; my clothes, my children, even the bruises on my arm.

Although women volunteers asked her about the bruises on her arm with the good intention of understanding if she is a victim of violence, their attitude hurt Esma's feelings. The relationship between the "helper" and the "needy" is problematic and open to misunderstandings, hidden injuries, and abuse. Selda underlines another aspect:

> They [the volunteers] favor some women. They do not treat us equally. I do not know exactly what the reason is, but if the volunteer is from somewhere and there is a woman here from the same region, they get along very well. I know some volunteers favor some women.

While the old structurally based projects, directed by the state, turned out to be systematically discriminatory against certain groups, the project-based approach, too, has suffered from forms of discrimination.[13] The new forms of clientelist relationships can spontaneously or systematically change according to the context. "Target" women have to develop certain strategies to maneuver within these unequal relationships. Religious identity, region of origin, or other characteristics of women can all factor into an unequal provision of the resources.

Concluding remarks

In this chapter, I have focussed on the debates concerning women's issues in Turkey in the last two decades. In Turkey, as well as in the rest of the less developed countries, local and international macro-economic, political, and legal structures have operated convergently to transpose women's issues to forums that did not exist in the past, or have changed dramatically between 1990 and 2008. This has changed, in turn, both the kinds of activism and the discourses in which women are featured. Global transformations such as decentralization and an increasing influence of religion in the political arena, especially in but not only limited to Middle Eastern countries, have also become visible in the socio-economic and political climate of Turkey. Since the beginning of the 1990s, a politically active Islam, the influence of international political bodies such as the IMF, the World Bank, and the EU, and the changing focus on women's issues brought about by project-based approaches have been the main transformations experienced in Turkey.

With the victory of the right-wing pro-Islam parties such as the Welfare Party (*Refah Partisi*—RP), the Virtue Party (Fazilet Partisi—FP) the Justice and Development Party (*Adalet ve Kalkinma Partisi*—AKP), traditional and patriarchal values with regard to the family and women have become more visible in the media and in the political arena since the 1990s. The opposition to these traditional values, emanating from secular political bodies including most of the other political parties and some civil organizations, has also had a shaping influence on the public debates. The European Union's regulations have brought about a different set of arguments to women's issues, as well. Despite conservative trends, certain provisions have been adopted regarding gender equality, if primarily to appease the European Union, which Turkey hopes to join. Indeed, women's NGOs fight for women's rights through lobbying activities and mobilization in the media. Besides, women's issues are being handled through disparate "socio-economic development projects" instead of holistic and coherent social policies. Particularly, women's clothing, public/private sphere and family and sexual rights have become important parts of the debate in the determination of new directions for Turkey in the twenty-first century. In this sense, the different actors on women's issues swing like a pendulum between inconsistent discourse and policies.

The problems of women who are on the periphery politically, socially, and sometimes geographically have started to be visible in the mainstream debates on women's issues since the 1990s. The changing social structure due to rural to urban migration since the 1960s resulted in the transformation of the socio-economic and political dynamic in Turkey. The social problems of women who are recently urbanized or rural have started to become an important part of the debates on women's issues. The headscarf, honor killings, or female suicides are not only of recent origin; however, these issues, being transformed in the new socio-political context, have become much more central to the media and public discussion of Turkey's present and future.

As Leila Ahmed (1992) discusses, women in Middle Eastern societies are limited by the discursive universe in which both modernizing forces and Islamists became entrapped. Middle Eastern political experiences are complex and plural in nature based on the diverse pattern and pace of modernization, and interpretations of Islam. Turkey, much like Egypt and Tunisia, experienced an Islamic resurgence in the 1990s, which increased the political tension among diverse political actors (Esposito and Voll 1996). The tension between "modernity"/ "tradition" and "elites"/ "common people" is visible in all three themes discussed in this chapter, while the definitions of these concepts appear differently to the different social actors and political positions. Women's clothes, social life, education, employment, and sexuality are discussed in the framework of these binaries.

Within this context, some of the practices related to women are regarded as backwardness or an emblem of cultural authenticity. Both positions are equally limiting to women's agency. Both "authentic Islam values" and "modern Western values" are reified and represented as monolithic categories in the Turkish political arena. These binaries remain although the social and economic landscape changes. In other words, structural binaries still govern the overall strategic shifts in the political positioning of the "traditionalists" and the "modernizers." However, as power dynamics have changed in the last decades, women are now subject to the political power of new actors, which, in turn, confront women with new problems and limits. Women's agency is limited in this dichotomous framework where women are objectified in the framework of "authenticity" and "modernity." Their issues have become strategic tools not for their empowerment but for the political actors to gain maneuvering room in the political arena. This dichotomy is caused and reinforced by the absence of a coherent gender policy focusing on women's empowerment in Turkey. Patriarchal gender regimes do not allow women to be full and equal members of society. The lack of specific legal provisions, coherent gender policies, and clear-cut legislation are far from encouraging women's rights in the context of their social, political, and economic rights. The changing power dynamics between these actors make women important political negotiation pawns and even more vulnerable to new discriminatory practices.

Notes

1 Tekeli (1995) underlines the importance of the feminist movement experienced through women's associations, magazines, and journals after the second constitutional period from 1908 in Ottoman society. Unlike "state feminism" which developed after the nation-building process, this first wave of feminism was developed through grassroots movement of well-educated and middle-class women.
2 Article 438 of the Penal Code, which was about decreasing the penalty for rape when the victim is a sex worker, was changed following the efforts and campaigns of feminist groups.
3 The segregation is not limited only to the workplace, but also in recreational areas in Siverek and Konya, and even in shopping areas in Erzurum, Radikal, August 19, 2006.
4 The first criterion for state job openings is to be a male. See http://www.bianet.org for the similar news on gender discrimination in the job application process.
5 June 16, 2006: http://www.ucansupurge.org/index.php?option=com_content&task=view&id=3113&Itemid=76
6 *Aksiyon*, No. 631, January 8, 2007.
7 The ECHR became an influential body in the discussion of the *turban* in Turkey. A university student, Leyla Sahin, applied to the ECHR, arguing that the disciplinarian action taken against her for attending classes wearing a *turban* is against human rights. However, the ECHR in 2005 decided that this practice is not a crime against human rights. It confirmed that wearing a headscarf is against the principle of secularism in the Turkish Constitution and would cause pressure on those who do not wear a *turban*.
8 Both national and international media covered this rumor; some examples: "First Lady Seeks Political Redesign," Helena Smith, August 20, 2007, *The Guardian*; "First Lady Fashion for Hayrunnisa Gül," August 21, 2007, *Sabah*; "Four Creations Signed by Atil for Hayrunnisa Gül," August 25, 2007, *Milliyet*; "Turban Formulas for Cankaya," September 13, 2007, *Aksam*.
9 The changes adopted consist of adding the following sentence to Article 10: "Organs of the state and administrative authorities are obliged to act according to the principles of equality before the law in all their transactions." Article 42 is amended to include: "No one can be denied their right to attain higher learning on the basis of reasons not clearly formulated in writing by law. The limits of the exercise of this right are determined by law." This section and the first article of the Law No.5735 dated 9/2/2008 is amended to include "and in benefiting from all public services"

following the phrase "all transactions"; however, the addition has been cancelled by the Supreme Court decision dated 5/6/2008 (E.:2008/16, K.:2008/116).

10 *New York Times*, September 16, 2004.

11 *Sabah*, September 2, 2004.

12 Some 58 women's associations have sent a joint petition to the European Commission requesting changes to the complex nature of EU project procedures and requirements (http://www.stgm.org.tr/eng).

13 The legislative changes, although they are far from establishing gender equality in many senses, have not been effective for all classes and all regions of Turkey. Ilkkaracan and Ilkkaracan (1998) show how the Kemalist reforms aiming to make women equal citizens to men have failed to be influential in the economically and socially less developed regions of Turkey, such as in the southeastern cities, and even in the peripheries of Istanbul such as Ümraniye. Empirical research has shown how women are far from reaching their citizenship rights such as in civil marriage, inheritance rights, education rights, the decision-making power on employment, participation in political life, and physical mobility both in urban and rural areas. Women's class position is very important to determine their life chances and the resources available for them to be "capable" in accessing their rights.

12 Women and language in Tunisia

Raoudha Kammoun

Introduction

It took sociolinguistics a long time to realize that the gender variable was as significant as other variables. For many decades it was ignored, not seen as scientifically grounded and deserving attention; those who focused their study on this aspect were not taken seriously. In the beginning, studies on variations were the domain of dialectologists and as they were all male, all the respondents and participants they referred to were consequently male, and this had an immediate impact on results. "The Great Dane" as Jespersen is called, embracing the Deficit Theory, contributed to this delay when he asserted that women read more quickly than men because their heads were empty, and that the best way to learn a foreign language was to read books written by women because of their simple words and basic language, which he described as the indispensable small-change of the language.[1] His writings were definitely innovative in Europe in the 1920s as little else had been written at that time, and though his beliefs on women's use of language seem entirely farcical nowadays, his declarations were quite influential and had a great impact for several decades on academia all over the world. Nonetheless, the profound social changes that affected many countries and led to an increasing awareness of civil and human rights and also a more conscious feminism pushed Western academics to reconsider their position regarding women.

In 1975, Robin Lakoff exposed the existence of differences between the language of women and men. She based her results, very much in line with Jespersen's theories, on American subjects. She posited that women use excessively polite and euphemistic language and a variety of "powerless" linguistic strategies such as empty adjectives, hedges and tags, hypercorrect grammar and precise pronunciation and of course "mild" forms of expletives, if not a total avoidance of coarse terms. Lakoff concluded that all these characteristics meant that women had no sense of humor, either in telling jokes or understanding punch lines. These observations still find support from contemporary researchers, in gender studies as well as in humor studies. More recent research has centered on the interaction between males and females, and gendered conversations have brought to light more specific female features (such as the fact that men interrupt women more than women interrupt men, and that men always tend to compete for the floor whereas women tend to be active listeners (Fishman 1980) as they try to ensure that the conversation proceeds smoothly). Along with the classic overt and covert prestige, women are status-conscious and strive for overt prestige, hence using more standard forms of language than men (Fasold 1990). Another famous researcher and a student of Robin Lakoff's was Deborah Tannen, an interactional sociolinguist; her famous *You Just Don't Understand: Men and Women in Conversation* (1990) argues that women and men live in two different worlds made of different words, with men using language primarily to protect their independence and negotiate status, whereas women use language to seek confirmation and forge intimacy. In her "subcultural" approach, Tannen believes men and women's misunderstandings and communication deficit to be due to the different way they use and view language. This attitude attracted enormous criticism; some considered her approach reflected miscommunication and misunderstanding among speakers from different ethnic, racial, and national communities, whereas others considered Tannen's misunderstandings as conflicting instances between subjects having unequal, not different, positions.

Over the past fifty years, a growing interest in feminine language has been noticed, more particularly since the 1980s when gay and lesbian movements started to gain popularity and made tangible breakthroughs benefiting women's studies, and often extending to gender and queer studies. Not unexpectedly, gender studies witnessed a broad upsurge first in the U.S.A., then in Northern and Western Europe, lately in Southern Europe and presently, very timidly, in the Arab world. When women are still struggling for the right to vote or to drive a car, one understands why gender studies are totally absent from the curricula in most Arab countries, where this issue is still considered of minor importance and as having a West-imported content. Morocco has broken the ice, thanks to Fatima Sadiqi, the first female linguist in the Arab world to tackle the issue of women from a gender and language perspective. Egypt also offered research openings to Niloofar Haeri. Both carried out surveys and insightful research and are, currently, in the vanguard of gender studies in the Arab countries.

Among Arab countries, Tunisia, considered in many ways the most liberal and advanced in terms of women's rights, where laws and reforms in favor of women have constantly been encouraged and reinforced, faces a contradictory reality and witnesses inherited social and ideological impediments reflecting male conservative mentalities and diehard stereotypes.[2] Many believe that the gender problems that exist in Tunisia stem from the uncertainties created by Tunisia's extremely rapid development which did not allow for a mature, digested transformation and resulted in paradoxes, contradictions, and a divide between facts, actual reality, and data. An example of this paradox, despite women's comfortable status in Tunisia, is that no academic institution or university offers the possibility of studying gender and language or gender studies.

However, although the issue of "language and gender" has become increasingly accepted over the last thirty years or so, it is still regarded as at best a woman's subject of study, a trivial area of research. Even recently, we have not heard of one man seriously engaging in gender and language studies except when gender research involves more than the traditional male/female duality.

How has women's language been perceived so far?

Scientifically, no serious research or experiment has proven the superiority of men over women regarding linguistic competence or language acquisition. Sociolinguistically, all languages and varieties are equal, and value judgments such as hierarchizing superordinate or subordinate varieties are social phenomena with no scientific value. In male-dominated societies (the overwhelming majority of societies), women's speech is considered inferior because women are seen as inferior persons with subordinate status. Many sociolinguists explain gender-linked differences as a consequence of male dominance. Long considered inferior and deficient, in the same way as their language, women internalized a strong sense of gender identity, which affected their linguistic behavior and communication strategies; if women are thought to lack assertiveness and directness in their speech, for example, it is because they are constantly interrupted by males in conversation (Sadiqi 1995).

The first declarations on women's language were impressionistic and intuitive (Lakoff 1975) and were not based on empirical studies and surveys. Soon, hasty and biased conclusions defining women as immature and not fully fledged language users and confirming the long-standing dormant stereotypes emerged. But socioeconomic progress and the liberation of women and moral values led to an unprecedented interest in women's language, testifying to an irreversible momentum that has speeded up in recent years.

Most recent research has shown the importance of variables in the study of genderlect, such as social class, age, level of education, culture, religion, and civilization, and challenged previous research as male-centric and typical of the white, middle-class American and Western mentality.

I have attempted in this chapter to highlight some aspects of the language of women living in the urban area of Tunis, hopefully to contribute more data to the gender realm and more particularly to the area of genderlect within the Arab world. I prepared a questionnaire with seven questions in order to elicit empirical data and avoid intuitive, personal, and often subjective views (see p. 211). The methodology used was based on a questionnaire (in French and English) submitted to 50 women and 50 men living in Tunis, but who had come from different geographical regions, rural and urban, mountainous, Bedouin and coastal. The age of the informants varied between 22 and 70. They came from different social categories and walks of life and had various professions: teachers, managers, journalists, secretaries, broadcasters, home helps, bartenders, public sector workers or "fonctionnaires," and some university students.

Gender and language in Tunisia

There has been very little interest in women's language in Tunisia. Statistics on women's issues generally are very rare. They are unavailable or nonexistent on subjects such as violence against women, for instance, because disappointing results or conclusions might thwart the unrelenting and unyielding official efforts to maintain and present an optimistic image of Tunisian women.

Tunisia is a bilingual and diglossic society. Classical Arabic is the official language but is the mother-tongue of no-one in Tunisia (or in the whole Arab world). It is not the means of communication of the Tunisian people, who use Tunisian Arabic as a lingua franca, one which only exists in an oral form. Bilingualism operates between Arabic and French and diglossia deals with two varieties of Arabic, Modern Standard Arabic and Tunisian Arabic. Modern Standard Arabic is mostly used in the written media, official documents, and the religious field. It is taught at school but ebbs and flows in the still on-going campaign of Arabization, which often reflects the government's ideological and political stance, which mostly reflects the country's overall economic climate.

Many studies have been dedicated to Classical Arabic and MSA (Modern Standard Arabic). Very few researchers (mostly dialectologists, stigmatized and isolated) have dealt with people's everyday language of communication, which is considered inferior to MSA and to Classical Arabic (the language of the Qur'an), of which it is regarded as a corrupted version. Added to the fact that Tunisian Arabic, like other Arabic dialects, is considered scientifically unworthy of study, half the population (clearly not the most privileged and most visible half) is believed to use an even less respected variety, which many claim justifies the absence of dialect studies and gender studies.

Most of the widespread beliefs about gendered features apply to Tunisian women: women "gossip" but men talk "shop," women are less assertive and make excessive use of euphemisms. However, other speech characteristics widely related to gender talk cannot be identified or acknowledged within Tunisian society, due to geographical, historical, linguistic, socioeconomic, religious, and cultural differences. Talkativeness, for example, is said to be characteristic of women, but it also applies to Mediterranean males; both men and women spend a lot of time talking in the region, the weather not being a particularly discouraging factor. Moreover, Tunisia belongs to the Arab and Muslim world, where traditions of orality and story-telling have always played a great role in everyday life. Oral habits were enhanced by traditional family styles and patterns (the extended family) which favored the oral style. In addition, fifty years ago, when the country became independent, the vast majority of the people were illiterate. Nowadays, though the total adult literacy rate is 74.2 percent and though women outnumber men in higher education, the percentage of readers is quite low by Western standards. The majority of the population, especially the younger generation, hardly ever buy a book, preferring to sit in cafés and talk, with the high unemployment rate among university graduates generally serving as an excuse.

Other characteristics as, for instance, women's tentativeness and hesitancy shown in the excessive use of tag questions, have no equivalent in the different varieties used by women, whether prestigious (Classical Arabic) or less prestigious (Tunisian Arabic), or French, where the equivalent tag "n'est-ce pas?" has a different meaning, more rhetorically and stylistically based than gender-based.

Moreover, being a diglossic society, where the standard language is not spoken, Tunisian women cannot be expected to use more standard forms than men to achieve a status that is denied to them, conforming to a belief widely shared in the Western world.[3] The concept of standard variety is not easily applicable to the different Arabic varieties, since there is only one variety (Classical Arabic) which has a codified grammar, glossaries, and written status. Therefore, although women have been shown to use more standard variants than men in Western speech communities, Tunisian women cannot speak more standard forms than men, for the standard variety is confined to written and formal contexts.[4] Standard Arabic use is context-based rather than gender-based. No empirical studies have been conducted to show that, in the same situations and with the same level of education, women are more or less standard than men.

Some sociolinguists from the Arab world believe that women use less Standard Arabic than men because of their limited access to education. Women's literacy rates vary from one Arab country to another (Yemen 28 percent, Morocco 40 percent, Tunisia 65 percent, Qatar 85 percent) and, as mentioned above, the use of Standard Arabic depends on particular contexts, generally more open and accessible to men than women. Classical Arabic is then believed to be a males' variety because fewer women are allowed access to it, and also because Tunisian women (and Arab women in general) have always been and still are (though to a lesser degree nowadays) excluded from religious settings and public religious practices. Furthermore, the canonic literature, also in Classical Arabic, is male-specific, and women, considered unfit for religious functions and prerogatives, "compensate" by developing oral competence (aided by the traditionally feminine characteristic of story-telling) both in Spoken Arabic and French. In the latter, women display a far better pronunciation than men because they consider French to be the language of modernity and emancipation; a concept closer to their hearts than to men's, and also because of their qualities such as patience and perfectionism that are seen as intrinsic. Consequently, Tunisian women use code-switching (French and Tunisian Dialectal Arabic) more often than men and so become catalysts and agents of linguistic change and also of sociocultural change and the secularization of Tunisian society.

While Haeri (1996), studying the Cairene variety, takes issue with the high/low dichotomy of Arabic speech communities and opts for "standard" in the sense of "normal" or "expected" rather than "standardized," Sadiqi (1995), working on Moroccan Arabic, refers to nonstandard Arabic as "çrubi" language, generally avoided by women, having "a negative connotation outside the countryside. It is perceived as 'rough', 'uncivilized' and 'uneducated'" (ibid.: 69). In the

Tunisian setting, the "*çrubi*" (a word that has no equivalent in the Tunisian dialect) is the language of the people living in rural or Bedouin areas, generally recognized through the g/q phonemes.[5] This variety is gaining tremendous ground and wider acceptance, and is increasingly less stigmatized. It often expresses a feeling of pride and identity, mostly due to the increasing settlement of formerly Bedouin communities on the outskirts of the capital and other big cities. Other characteristics not systematically applicable to Tunisian women are excessive use of polite forms or prestige forms due to social, cultural, and linguistic differences. Tunisian society is undergoing a shift in its politeness system and civility rules concerning naming strategies and also conventions of anti-formality. As for the issue of women and cursing, which I will discuss below, we are witnessing an increasing degree of linguistic violence and boldness expressed in sexual coarseness in public contexts involving both women and men, though it is less accepted when coming from women.

Analysis and interpretation of the data

Surprisingly, women were much more motivated by and showed more interest in the questionnaire than men, asking more questions, disagreeing sometimes, often justifiably, about the way the questions were formulated, and insisting on writing long, explicit, and detailed answers. Conversely, men were often doubtful and reticent about the questionnaire and made flippant remarks or gestures or told stories of a facetious nature, which were meant to be playful and humorous, but which I used to elicit additional information. Collecting the data was difficult since some respondents, strangely all male, lost the questionnaire, never answered, or were somewhat inquisitive. Others called it a "trap they would never fall into" and wondered whether they would have to write down their names or could remain anonymous and if the answers would be published. Some promised to think about the allegedly "tricky" questions but never returned the answers.

The answers to questions are calculated in percentages and are analyzed and assessed, sometimes confirming general and widely shared Western assumptions, but in some cases contradicting them and providing data to enlarge the spectrum of variables for gender study.[6] According to Holmes (1998), whenever there are limits to the applicability of generalizations, they should be refined, while rigorously confining the area to which they apply, and not regarded as useless just because some exceptions are identified.

The data obtained from the questionnaire may be categorized into three major themes: (1) the way male/female linguistic differences are perceived (Questions 1 and 2), (2) the way women's language has changed over the years in terms of traditional cursing, obscenities, and use of French (Questions 3, 4, and 5), and (3) the applicability to Tunisian society of widely held long-standing gender-role stereotyped attitudes, such as that women accept being interrupted more readily than men and that women linger over details (Questions 6 and 7).

Male/female linguistic differences

In order to find out how these linguistic differences are perceived and experienced by men and women, informants were asked the following question: (1) Do you think that there are words or expressions that only men use?

The answers did not reveal any unexpected or striking data, for most informants consider cursing, vulgar words, and blasphemy as typically male (75 percent of female informants (FI) and 65 percent of male informants (MI)).[7] Only 15 percent and 22 percent respectively do not believe that there are male/female linguistic differences. The others have no opinion. It is interesting to note the dominant and automatic answer that vulgar words and blasphemous expressions are characteristic of men's linguistic behavior, excluding all other variables such as age, occupation, field of interest, level of education, etc., and that regardless of how highly educated and respectable men may sound or look, once they get furious they all use terms "from waist downwards;" a word-for-word translation from Tunisian Arabic. Some respondents remarked that in some very masculine and macho contexts, expletives are highly valued, symbolizing power and considered a sign of masculinity. Many male respondents were terrified by the idea of listing male vulgar words, but reassured when they were asked about female expletives (Question 4), believed to be softer and innocuous. Some expressions formerly used only by men are nowadays common in women's speech, such as *berjuliya* (seriously or honestly, by male standards) or *?rrabbi!* (interjection of anger and exasperation).

The majority of respondents have a very firm, almost immutable, opinion about male language, with cursing and vulgarity seen as its most typical and widely acknowledged aspect, hinting at times at its representing an exclusive, private domain and at the difficulty of becoming a member of this community. It is interesting to notice the higher percentage of FI—75 percent (as opposed to MI 65 percent)—who consider blasphemy and cursing as typically male language and make no allusion to the religious register, generally a males' speciality, or to Standard Arabic, generally related to men's use, hence confirming our hypothesis of the non-applicability of women's greater use of Standard to Tunisian women.

Having, then, established that both men and women informants believe that men have specific expressions or style, Question (2) should come as a counterpart: Do you think that there are words or expressions that only women use?

The answers to this question were more consensual, with an even higher percentage among women. Indeed, 80 percent of FI and 75 percent of MI think women have special expressions that men never use. There seems to be an accepted range of illustrations. Both cite the same expressions, imprecations, and female insults. The most common is *Woh!* (an interjection of surprise close to "What!" or sometimes "My goodness!"), which is used by all women, whether old or young, working or non-working, modern or traditional. Expressions belonging to the feminine cursing repertoire such as the famous *Ykeb saçdu* ("down on his luck") tend to be less popular among younger girls and educated women. As for expressions of admiration such as *Yçaqqad, Yhabbel,* or *Yoqtel* (metaphorically said of a person or thing that is absolutely gorgeous, literally leading to psychological disorder, madness, or death), their popularity among women is pervasive, allowing for more coinages. Only 25 percent of MI and only 20 percent of FI think that women do not have special expressions.

Moreover, according to the answers obtained, Tunisian women make more important use of diminutives, often endearingly [ex. *xbayza* ("small loaf of bread"); *bnayti* ("my little daughter")]. But this tends to be associated with the older generation, non-working or lower working-class women. Similarly, women change their intonation and pitch to higher frequency levels when addressing children. Some MI pointed out that women's speech is sometimes indirect, with implicit meaning, particularly in women not in paid employment with a limited education, who use indirectness to manipulate their husbands to buy them things they need or approve some activity they have planned.[8]

Thus, it is clear that the great majority of informants do believe there is a language typical of Tunisian women and that men would not venture to use it lest they be called effeminate or humiliatingly accused of enjoying all-women gatherings, which are considered the "appropriate" setting for gossip, or displaying emotion and oversensitivity through feminine expressions (cursing, or ways of addressing or naming through diminutives or intensifiers). This idea correlates with Sadiqi's (1995) statement that Moroccan women make great use of intensifiers which express their emotions.

Women and linguistic change

Within the broad scope of feminine language, and having noticed that cursing was systematically mentioned, yet with reserve, Question (3) seems to shed more light on this aspect. When asked "Do you think that women curse *(?dça)* more than before?", 90 percent of MI said that women curse in the traditional way much less than before and some of them think that women's cursing has been replaced by swear words. Only 10 percent think that women still curse, particularly older women with a limited degree of literacy. Up to 96 percent of FI think that women used to curse but no longer do so because they have left the traditional home and moved into the public space; 4 percent think that women who still curse are generally illiterate and from lower social and economic categories.

It is necessary to clarify the Tunisian cursing tradition, which is typical of women's language. Its usage is strictly oral, familiar, informal, and it is socially and morally stigmatized. Its forms come in single word interjections or vindictive idiomatic expressions, pronounced in a beseeching tone, calling upon god or the holy saints. Several examples of such expressions were given and seemed to amuse all the respondents, men and women alike, as recalling bygone times and older generations. An example was *Yaç tihelek latibralek!* ["May you be stung [by a scorpion] (not mentioned but implicitly understood, as a scorpion is associated with wickedness, poison, and death) from which you will never recover."]⁹ By uttering such rhyming interjections, generally angrily, women punish or take revenge on the subject of their hostility or anger, thus transcending feelings of helplessness and powerlessness.

Nowadays, with gender empowerment, this form of speech has almost disappeared, giving rise (according to certain respondents) to more brazen and obscene expressions, which used to be in the men's repertoire, generally in public spaces. Today, women's traditional cursing has become the subject of ridicule and mockery. The answers to Question (4): "Do you think that women use more swear words than before?" elucidated this linguistic behavior which had long been considered male-specific. Some of the MI consider the increase in the use of expletives in women's language as the natural consequence of women's liberation and their working alongside men (39 percent). According to them, women curse more because it provides a powerful identity source; they want to assert their presence, and to confirm their equality with men, using this way of speaking as an act of defense. They add that women used to have their own spaces, which they now share with men. The hardships of life and stressful work make women use more obscene words regardless of class and origin. Some 29 percent insist that the social and intellectual factors are decisive and warn that in all-women groups, women have a repertoire of even more crude feminine expletives; 18 percent consider that this phenomenon affects society as a whole, which has become more violent and aggressive, with unisex trends in fashion and habits, and an increasingly uniform language, particularly among the younger generation where speech differences are viewed as less differentiated and more uniform, whether in terms of obscenities, newly coined words, or semantic neologisms.¹⁰ New linguistic styles and novel words and expressions, so fashionable and so dear to youngsters (including expletives), are coming into usage, though these are not appreciated by older people, and affect indifferently young girls' and boys' linguistic behavior. With geographical mobility and more job opportunities, the words and expressions in vogue reach all regions and social categories; regional or class specificities tend to level off, aided by the mass media and popular radio and TV channels which adopt the "new wave" language, a standardized version with massive code-switching with French, in order to sound open-minded and modern, while optimizing the listenership or viewership.

Though expletives and obscenities do not shock so much nowadays, they still constitute a linguistic taboo in Arab societies and are seen as much more morally reprehensible when the users are female; people say that nowadays there are no moral values and that women have lost their femininity and modesty and no longer worry about men's reactions, since they blatantly curse in the street and in schools and universities (14 percent of MI). Some of the respondents deplored the masculine, vulgar attitude of women who react like men in situations of anger or conflict, though they are expected to display more self-control and remain silent. It is interesting to notice that some MI consider the same reaction more vulgar when it comes from a woman, hence clearly expressing a difference and a language hiatus based on gender. Maybe the only domain that remains more masculine is the use of expletives, or the sole female linguistic aspect is typically female cursing.

As to FI, many (46 percent) consider women's increasing use of swear words to be the result of several factors (rapid social and economic change, the liberation of women's minds and bodies, and access to work in an increasingly hostile and violent environment in a short period). Some young respondents answer enthusiastically regarding this characteristic as no more than "a banal and hackneyed social phenomenon." They insist that expletives serve a cathartic function. They would like to break from the stereotypical image of woman: "It is the only way to express my anger; one does not particularly enjoy being girly."[11]

Quite a few FI (44 percent) believe that women do not use more swear words nowadays. Some consider that women, formerly socially and economically invisible, have now gained more public space and therefore more opportunities to speak and to be heard. Ten percent believe the use of expletives is closely related to women's social class and intellectual level.

Summing up, we could argue that male answers did not show a particular dislike of women's use of expletives. Arguments tended to express a surprisingly wide acceptance of linguistic change and an understanding that societal change is bound to be accompanied by a gender role change, shuffling the traditionally established separation of spaces and repertoires. For many years bygone sociolinguistic studies have presented women as more conventional and more conservative regarding linguistic change and licentious language (Trudgill 2000; Coates 1993), with the traditional argument that femininity, softness, and prudery are inherent to women's nature, or more "daringly" invoking their subordination (Lakoff 1975). Conversely, men were granted license to violate the rules of proper speech and viewed as linguistic outlaws and innovators (Jespersen 1922). Many answers to women's use of expletives (Question 4) countered these beliefs. Both MI and FI broke with conventional opinions and strengthened more recent sociolinguistic research, which asserts that women's language, including their nonconformity and unconventionality, had never been studied seriously.

Lately, women's education in Tunisia, a crucial factor of their empowerment, has diminished the divide between them and their male counterparts and is reducing linguistic differences between the sexes. This change in attitude, whether linguistic or social, has displeased many, especially older people who defined their male identity and built their power and hegemony on women's docility and subservience. Men's acceptance of women's linguistic change, particularly toward a more masculine pattern, should not be considered as a sign of open-mindedness and approval but rather as a reluctant acknowledgment of failure and perhaps of powerlessness, the inevitable price to pay for a modern and liberal society. Men would have preferred women to stick to their old linguistic behavior, leaving expletives and blasphemy to men. Confronted with new and different roles, imported from the West, some Tunisian males, including the younger generation, explain it as the result of French influence, and regard young women with contempt and disdain particularly when their "bartered image" is European and is conveyed through the language of the French settler.

The relationship between Tunisian women and the French language resembles that in Algeria and Morocco. To Question (5): "Do you think that women use more French words than men in their conversation?", a great number of FI (47 percent) and 32 percent of MI said that women use more French or more code-switching with French. This correlates with Sadiqi's (2003) statement that code-switching is associated with women rather than with men. Both genders give the same reasons: women use more French words than men to look or sound classier, cultivated, trendy, or "with it," sometimes out of bragging or snobbery. Twenty percent of MI attribute this to the widely held assumption that French is an easier language for women to express their feelings (Trabelsi 1991: 92), because of the absence of cultural taboos and the weight of tradition which are lexically and semantically embedded in the local language. Speaking in French implies identifying with another language and culture as more open and more liberal. Some 25 percent of MI and 14 percent of FI consider it a question of social class, region, social status, and level of education. Among the women's answers, 5 percent think women use French to hide their regional, in other words rural or Bedouin, accents, 7 percent to compensate for feelings of inferiority, and 1 percent as a strategy of politeness. Of MI 14 percent think that French has a firm foothold in the country's administrative and business sectors, where the use of French is required, despite all attempts at Arabization. Finally, 9 percent of MI and 26 percent of FI do not think women use more French than men nowadays; they think it was true twenty years ago but is no longer the case today, now that the standard of French has seriously deteriorated, sparing neither men nor women.

This question was intended to verify the extent to which Tunisian women care for overt prestige, as they are generally believed to. The answers show that Tunisian women are concerned about their social image, especially when they have important social status. Status is often enhanced through the use of French or code-switching with French. This definitely concerns women aged over 30, for the younger generation seems less concerned about French. Twenty years ago, the use of French revealed a great deal about the socio-cultural status of women in Tunisia, but nowadays young people seem to be turning against it, for psychological, cultural, and political reasons.[12] Unlike the situation in Morocco, where English seems to be acquiring a great role and status in society as a whole and among youngsters in particular, or in Lebanon, where the use of English has skyrocketed to the detriment of French, the younger generation in Tunisia, let alone the older, does not seem to pay special attention to English, both women and men. Today, what characterizes young women's speech with regard to French and also in terms of social prestige is their heavier use of code-switching, performed in an increasingly fragmented way, based on French words used separately, scattered here and there and not on phrasal segments (as used to be the case many years ago). Young working women make extensive use of code-switching, particularly in the workplace, perhaps to sound more assertive and professional.

Gender stereotypes

Stereotypes stem from social reality, cultural representation, and behavior. Their perpetuity thus seems predestined. If gender-stereotyped language and behaviors are finally changing in the West, mostly thanks to the feminine "jihad" against sexist language and behavior, the situation in the Arab world seems disconcertingly to be lagging behind. Surprisingly, there is considerable divergence between conventional stereotypes and the reality of women's speech in Tunisia. It is widely acknowledged that Arab societies are positively biased toward men and negatively biased toward women, not only in the West, but also inside the Arab world. We have thus attempted to verify how widely some popular stereotypes are accepted in Tunisia. One stereotype is that women are interrupted by men; Zimmerman and West (1975) see this as a means of exercising power. The second stereotype is that women's speech is over-detailed and redundant. Thus, to Question (6): "Do you think that women are easily interrupted by men in a conversation?", almost half the MI (45 percent) answer vehemently that it is impossible (one called it a tour de force) to interrupt a woman and much easier to interrupt a man, because women are authoritarian and need to impose their opinion due to a certain feeling of inferiority.[13] Others think women refuse to be interrupted because they are afraid of losing their train of thought; only 21 percent of MI believe women accept being interrupted by men almost instinctively because they have internalized a feeling of inequality. They explain this by the fact that the concept of manliness is still an agent of authority, compelling a woman to resort to silence, especially when the discussion is animated. Some 9 percent think that women are easily interrupted because they are very talkative and need to be reminded to stop repeating themselves; 14 percent put forward a different reason: women accept being interrupted because they are more flexible, adaptable, peaceful, and less aggressive.

Conversely, 12 percent notice a great change in women's behavior and hesitate to give categorical answers, suggesting that every woman is a particular case and there are as many answers as there are women. A business woman with many responsibilities will not be interrupted as often as a textile worker. Social factors, socio-economic background and social status strongly determine a woman's language and linguistic behavior and the male response to it.

The great majority (81 percent) of FI gave a negative answer; many consider the issue as not gender-based, but varying from one person to another, depending on the context and the situation (addressing a boss, a sick father, or a janitor). They ascribe the interrupting habit to cultural and traditional factors, for Arab societies have long been patriarchal, had oral traditions organized hierarchically, and were not particularly acquainted with principles of etiquette and turn-taking. Traditionally, the first to speak was the last, the one entitled to such a role— generally the patriarch or someone (elder son or uncle) with equal economic and moral power. Modern rules for speaking roles and politeness strategies in conversation are recent and concern mainly urban areas and the upper class. Fifteen percent of FI consider women to be more easily interrupted because they have a higher sense of communication and persuasion; at the end of conversation they will diplomatically state their opinion, convinced that the last phrase or idea is the most important and remains longest in the interlocutor's memory. Only 4 percent consider this a habit caused by an early education in submission and subservience.

We might argue, here, that the preconceived idea that women accept being interrupted due to their lack of assertiveness, self-confidence, and feeling of insecurity is quite different from current reality. It is confirmed by the majority of informants that the stereotype remains but does not in fact reflect how mixed group conversations actually occur. If researchers, particularly male, continue to posit that women are more often interrupted than men, and that they are linguistically and socially disadvantaged, this simply reveals, implicitly or unconsciously, their longing that this were still the fact.

Today, the difficult conditions of life, the deep change in social and family structures, and the stressful atmosphere in which Tunisian women live, whether at home, outside, or at work, have made them not only less resigned but more aggressive and anxious; many constantly talk about their unhappiness, in an impassioned tone, discouraging all attempts at interruption, as they might, in heated conversations, indulge in using expletives and hurtful retorts (see answers to Question 4). This change in linguistic behavior affects most social classes, but particularly women from the working class and underprivileged categories, generally with limited literacy, as they are more vulnerable to socio-economic disorder. Such women have no status to protect or social image to preserve, and their language is often riddled with obscenities and blasphemous expressions which they utter without thinking (see Stapleton's (2003) and Hughes's (1992) statements about lower-working class women and swearing, who consider that "it's not swearing to them" because "it forms an integral part of their body" and is "part of (their) everyday talking").

Another stereotype traditionally associated with women is their strategy of making a short story long by including every possible detail. Answering Question (7) "Do you think that women give more details when relating an event?", 57 percent of MI unhesitatingly reply that this characteristic is typically feminine and look down on it. Diverse reasons were invoked, among them women's innate talkativeness, desire to put on a show, hypersensitivity and emotiveness, women's love of trivialities, a very vague notion of time, and having more time than men to listen to details, to convince and to repeat themselves. More positively, 29 percent think women have a high sense of exactitude, probity, and forbearance, are particularly observant and keen on explaining events in detail, and have a high sense of perfection and a tendency to analyze rather than synthesize. Socio-economic background may be a determinant factor in women's discourse genre, and their professional environment can be very influential; 14 percent cite the example of lawyers, journalists, or teachers (male or female) who talk a lot due to the nature of their profession.

On the other hand, FI see women as perfectionist and meticulous (42 percent). They believe that women value details and precision, insisting that the quality of a human relationship depends on the importance one gives to details (men are always in a rush and consider them trivial). Some think that the abundance of details provided by women reflects the fact that women have an associative memory, a richer vocabulary, and a higher sense of duty. Conversely, 55 percent consider the use of detail as a way to hold the interlocutor's attention, or that they love to listen to themselves. Half the women respondents believe that women care for details because of hypersensitivity and gossip in general, and as a result tend to be superficial or shallow and ignore or perhaps forget the core. Only 3 per cent do not believe women give more details in general.

The questions dealing with women being interrupted by men and the excess of details in women's talk raised the most heated discussion and questioning; some male participants suggested combining the two questions, commenting "humorously" that "too many unnecessary and irritating details make one want to interrupt the never-ending monologue."

This characteristic is peculiar to conservative societies and certainly perceptible in Tunisian and Arab countries in general. Women have performed their traditional roles of mother or housewife for centuries, developed a unique oral culture among themselves, enjoying the telling of folktales and folksongs in their free time, with special emphasis on minute and meticulous storytelling, keeping the unraveling of the plot as far away as possible, holding back the ending of the tale with extra suspense devices. Fifty or so years ago, the women's world revolved around domestic chores and child rearing and occasionally marriages or funerals. The endless details of preparing and celebrating different kinds of ceremonies were left to the women and considered of little importance. New and different lifestyles and social and family patterns have emerged, forcing everybody to take up a new, unassimilated gender role and position, but also carrying on old perceptions and conservative attitudes. With women working outside the home as modern educated persons, their old, traditional, and undervalued role of housewife has not been replaced or lightened. Their increasingly cumbersome tasks induce regret for bygone times. Even the highly educated or upper class women do not seem to have forgotten or discarded their feminine habit of gossiping. In all-female groups, women who show composure at work and use silence as a form of rhetoric may turn into completely different persons, laughing and uninhibited.

Another silence strategy used only by women is associated with mourning rituals, more common in the countryside. When women come to offer their condolences, they sit quietly for hours, weeping every now and then, and looking compassionate and full of grief and sorrow, even if they have never met the departed. When they look up, it is only to make sure no woman is violating the rules. Men, generally in another room or a cool patio, chat about life and world issues. Using silence as rhetoric, women share sorrow while preserving the image of a respectable, sensible person. This habit is more observed in rural areas, where women are more self-conscious and care more about their reputation than in cities.

Men behave more naturally and worry less about their image, since society is traditionally more permissive and tolerant with them.

A fast-growing society and gender perception

For centuries, women from all over the world have been denied social status and deprived of a public face and the prestige and power related to privilege. Women had inferior roles and positions, their activities were restricted to domestic chores and child rearing. The situation of Arab women changed slowly, and still today the differences from one Arab country to another are enormous. The first attempts to educate women ensured the continuity of the women's traditional roles, focusing essentially on manual work and infant and child care and only concerning urban areas. In the case of Tunisia, the early political decision to provide mass education allowed women to have access to education, which led to profound changes in the gender role system, the entire social structure, and (inevitably) language use. The laws on women's rights helped change how women were conceptualized in everyday language. Six or seven years ago, the concept of equality with men was replaced by that of partnership; the slogan "We have gone past the stage of equality, now we are dealing with women's partnership" was constantly mentioned and has been taken up by the media. Women's emancipation achieved more in theory than in practice, since more than the simple enactment, the implementation of law is needed to change the way people think, has always represented a source of pride which the government constantly highlights nationally and internationally, even when it is used to short-circuit embarrassing questions (generally related to democracy and human rights) or to combat religious extremism. Women's rights and female success are manipulated to hide shortcomings which, with unceasing media overkill, have become part of everyday speech, "deadwood" discourse, or what is commonly called in Tunisia *"langue de bois,"* voided of its substance and sublimated in harsher non-verbal behavior. This leaves decades of gender misconception and gender-biased attitudes untouched and "immaculate."

Tunisian women have equal access to school, and a high rate of literacy allows them to be socially and professionally active. They are encouraged to join the workforce as a bastion against extremism. Although large numbers of women are active in the workforce, their presence in politics and on decision-making bodies is negligible.[14]

Women's swapping the private space for the public one, deserting traditional women's places, disrupted the public/private space dichotomy. The abrupt change in socio-economic structure and organization affected both males' and females' general and, inevitably, gender language.

Many proverbs, idiomatic expressions, and maxims that reflect society's negative opinion of women no longer match the fast-changing society and seem to be disappearing along with the older generation. We can cite previously popular proverbs and idioms rarely used now and totally unknown to anyone under 30:

Ya jeyba l banat, ya hezza l ham lel mamet! ("You who have had daughters, you will be carrying problems till death!") or the following: *?ðrab l qattusa, titrabba laçrusa!* ("Hit the cat, and the bride will learn the lesson," which suggests obedience to the husband by the wife), or the old saying *ʃ art l ça:zeb çalhaj- jela: walli sbiya w nexðek* ["The bachelor's condition for marrying the widow: Be virtuous and I will marry you" (used about a situation requiring impossible conditions)]. It is interesting to note the widow element (widows were socially denigrated and stigmatized) transferred to the divorcee's condition many years ago. Nowadays, with the increasing rate of divorce and the average marrying age for girls nearing 29 in cities and 31 in villages, the stigma has fallen on single girls and seems to be much softer for divorced women. Many Tunisian girls prefer to marry and then divorce rather than remain spinsters, because society's attitude toward unmarried girls is very harsh: they are depicted as unfit for marriage since no man has found them suitable, "they missed the boat," or as is popularly said *baburha zaffar* ("Her boat left the shore") or *ðafreteʃʃi:b* ("She braided gray hair"). All these sayings in Tunisian Arabic, as well as others referring to women, are becoming less popular because unmarried or divorced women now have various alternatives and also because these expressions are oral, preventing them from being hoarded as a cultural and linguistic heritage for future generations.[15] Some may be sarcastic and slightly humorous: *χanha ðreçha, qalet siħruni* ("She fell flat on her face, so she said she's under a spell"), where the woman explains her failure by pretending she has been enchanted.

Celebrating women and lovers in popular songs and poetry is more down to earth today. One famous song dating back to the 1960s, called "Women," starts with a laudatory prelude:

> ?nnisa ?nnisa
> Alla yχalli ?nnisa
> ?nnisa huma l mefteħ
> Welli yħeb yçiʃ merteħ
> yqul yçayiʃ ?nnisa

> Women, Oh! women
> God bless women
> Women are the key
> And whoever wishes to live in peace
> Must say bless women.

Women's language and socio-economic status

In the questionnaire, many respondents mentioned the education/language relationship. Women's language and education are closely knit. If some gender-stereotyped forms of language or speech still exist, it is particularly in the rural areas where the percentage of educated women is lower than in urban areas. In

Tunisia, the level of education is highly correlated with the chances of having a job; rural women's jobs, limited to working in manufacturing or agriculture, do not improve their social or economic status. Social status and class, generally related to urban settings, hardly play any role in rural areas where different social categories do not exist.

Language reflects social class and education. Upper class and higher education have never been so correlated due to the decline of public higher education and the state school system. Women with high socio-economic status have a linguistic behavior and social attitude that reflects their profession, rank, or class, clearly revealed in their speech. A woman's condition imperatively designs and patterns a woman's language.

As to social class and women's language, the only feature that stands out is the use of French. The higher the class, the more French women and also men use (see Appendix for answers to Question 5). The large middle class and the new demographic composition of cities (due to the shift from the countryside to the big cities) has had a direct effect on regional and social linguistic differences, which are tending to level off, eliminating specific lexical, semantic, and phonological features.

Educated and professional women in Tunisia, such as businesswomen or managers, have opted for silence as a new communication strategy. Silence serves as a form of control and also as a subversive strategy. Female gossip and talkativeness have long been depreciated by men and are today also by women. (This correlates with women's low opinion of garrulity and gossiping: Question 7.) Many women abandoning this "hateful" habit, adopt men's attitude of silence. They have noticed that being terse and laconic brings more respect and credibility. In training sessions and communication courses or self-help books, more women, especially in the workplace, are encouraged to deal with conflict by deploying self-control, with brief unemotional comments. Apparently, this has proved worthwhile. Women are now interviewed, asked to sit on various commissions, and presented in the media as a very efficient model to follow.

While women have gained in authority and power, it has been through changing their verbal and non-verbal behavior, adopting men's linguistic norms and strategies and adjusting to their general behavior, in order to gain social approval and the sanction of moral authority.

In Tunisian society, when men happen to gossip and make slanderous remarks (a recent, more common phenomenon in all-male groups, as well as in mixed groups), they are sometimes compared to women (see answers to Question 2) and are subject to joking remarks on their manliness; women are said to talk less nowadays because they are too busy to chat. Women are still considered as chatterboxes and gossips, but men's gossiping and chatting is ever blatant. In urban, and more critically rural, areas, the number of cafés has become an indicator of unemployment. Many young men, mostly unemployed, but also nostalgic for "May 68" idle intellectuals, tittle-tattle all day long, and gossip about the latest spicy stories or jokes or bet on the coming weekend's soccer games. In their way of reading the world, they claim to know how to end the war in Iraq and the

Palestinian conflict, and when the audience is gone, cards and dominoes take over. Young women, on the other hand, work in factories for long hours to feed sometimes several families, where they are allowed to only exchange brief words concerning their work. This recent change in gendered behavior affects the linguistic behaviors and practices of both men and women. But although die-hard stereotypes are dying out, this change in language and strategies will not necessarily grant women empowerment, privilege, authority, and influence.

Gender differences in terms of address

Naming strategies and ways of gender addressing have changed now women are more educated. The classic "madame" and "monsieur" are widespread, surpassing the domain of spouses. "My husband" or "your husband," "my wife" or "your wife" are now termed respectively as *lmonsieur mteçi* or *lmonsieur mteçek* and *lmadame mteçi* or *lmadame mteçek*. Such forms of address are increasingly common in urban areas where *el mra* ("the woman"), as in for instance *jib l mra wija tçaaʃa baħðena* ("Bring the woman and come over for dinner"), has become *jib l madam wija tçaaʃa baħðena* ("Bring your wife and come over for dinner"). The word *mra* ("woman") sometimes carries a derogatory connotation in use but not in its definition in general; the saying *lmra mra werajel rajel* ("A woman is a woman and a man is a man") implies a woman is inferior and should not compete with a man's superior status. For this reason, resorting to French allows both Tunisian men and women to get rid of their inhibitions when dealing with a taboo area to which women belong, and is also a way to show modernity and open-mindedness. This correlates with the results of Question 5.

When addressing a woman or a man in normal circumstances, variables such as age, sociocultural status, rural or urban areas, and of course degree of acquaintance and formality should be considered.[16] Terms such as *xuya* ("brother") or *ʔuxti* ("sister") are used to communicate in formal situations (supermarket, service station, public administration, etc.) to maintain social norms and conventions.

In rural zones, relationships are more informal and more natural and do not conform to any hierarchical or institutional level. Men and women address each other using first names informally and publicly, also between couples "Oh Wife!" or "Oh Husband!," particularly when old age, a factor of respect, very important in Arabs' naming strategy, is not involved. If the woman is not acquainted with the man, he will simply say *Ya mra!* ("Hey woman!") but there is no real reciprocity, for a woman will then reply *Ya baba!* ("Hey old man!").[17]

Tunisian Arabic has no active *tu* and *vous* distinction as French has; using the French *tu* in formal settings to address a man or a woman should not be interpreted as impolite or inappropriate, but reflects incorrect use of (declining) French coupled with a linguistic interference from Arabic.

With women more visible in public spaces, and relatively more self-assured, addressing and naming seem to be the same for men and women. Conversely, non-verbal communication seems to reveal deeply ingrained prejudice; smiling, frowning, chuckling, grasping the upper arm of a woman to help her cross the street, a vague toss of the head as a greeting, etc. represent a discriminatory or sarcastic undermining. Police women handling a traffic jam, for example, still provoke mocking smiles and denigration from male and also female citizens; the public space is traditionally reserved for men, a place of power and male authority that has been universally internalized. A woman bus driver and, to a lesser degree, a woman taxi driver stopping at a bus stop provokes a lot of frowning, and worried looks exchanged in search of support or solidarity.

In terms of politeness, social norms have changed along with the old polite forms of speech. The traditional belief that women's speech is more polite (due to the way they are brought up and educated) no longer corresponds to reality. Tunisian's societal structure is less built on social and class hierarchy, being a republic and not a monarchy (as is the case in Morocco or other Arab countries where women's speech is more deferential). Not only do women use less polite speech today, due to less conventional social interactions, but they may misunderstand the appropriate register for a particular context, confusing formality, informality and tact or serious interaction with banter, or regular professional remarks with personal vexations. Men can also be confused in personal or professional relationships, but when conflicts arise with a woman, the interpretation takes a gendered turn, and the reasons are attributed to female hypersensitiveness, incompetence, lack of judgment and experience or socialization.

The linguistic behavior of the entire Tunisian society has changed. There is much less courtesy and deference and more verbal violence.[18] This linguistic change is causing profound feelings of uneasiness, particularly regarding women's change of linguistic behavior, which has overturned several gender stereotypes; the result has been a much less respectful attitude toward women in terms of civic and social rules and conventions.

The fact that women are increasingly present outside the home has caused great annoyance among males, who have been disturbed in their conceptions of gender roles, and have responded to this rapid change in social and linguistic behaviors with intransigence and intolerance. Women's occupation of public or men's space was perceived as an aggression, and a hostile attitude. Men felt their domain was being invaded by these inferior creatures, who competed with them on their own battlefield. Still nowadays, especially in rural areas and lower-class neighborhoods, women do not hang around in the street aimlessly. If they happen to be out there, it should mean they are on their way to work, to shop, or to visit a relative. Wandering around, or walking at a slow pace, leads to systematic harassment, since it is interpreted as an invitation.

Many young women also feel as uncomfortable as men in a disappointing world where speeches on human rights, democracy, and social justice have made wearing the veil a new communication strategy. Many think that by wearing the veil they are more respected in the street and are no longer harassed, even late in the day. Men's language changes and becomes more respectful. The feeling of having their manhood publicly teased vanishes. The myth that men are unable to control their sexual impulses in the presence of females found a perfect remedy in controlling women's body by excluding them from the public space. Now that women's bodily presence seems to be irrevocable, some men in Tunisia have come to a form of compromise between the conservative and the modern via veiled women who, as they (men) prefer to believe, no longer constitute a threat or a "fitna."

The revival of the veil being recent, veiled women's language has not been studied yet, though their behavior, socially and linguistically, tends to show assertiveness and vigor. They are more vocal, show no excessive shame, and look more assured, though they systematically confuse "gender equality" and "gender equity." Whereas "equality" is the fact of being equal in rights, status, advantages, etc. as a human and a citizen, "equity" means fairness, and from an Islamic perspective it means being treated in conformity with Qur'anic tenets and giving women the rights to which they are entitled. It is interesting to note that lately veiled women are sometimes brash, on the defensive, insolent, and bold, probably because they are still in the process of identifying their new gender identity, which many refuse to associate with the traditional dark stereotypes of veiled women produced and presented by the media. These women use a different language; formerly established women's expressions like freedom, emancipation, and independence have given way to self-fulfillment, self-respect, serenity, and wellbeing.

What we can deduce so far is that the so-called emancipation of the Tunisian woman depends on women's empowerment through social and professional parity generally and also at individual level, to reach a real partnership on an equal basis.

When major decisions are taken in the public sphere, where women are not welcome and where their freedom of movement and speech are still subject to restriction, it is unlikely that the hopes and promises (of physical, linguistic, psychological, professional, and social autonomy) will be realized.

General conclusion

It is not in the least surprising that only recently the gender variable has become apparent, long after factors of age, profession, region, and ethnicity, and the controversial social class variable. If it took so long to study gender language in the West, it is no wonder it has just begun to arouse interest in the Arab and Islamic world. Tunisian society is undergoing profound social changes and new lifestyles. When participants were asked to answer the questionnaire, almost all of them had ready answers at the outset, but soon qualified them and expressed unease saying: "It depends on the person ... you can't lump all women or all men into fixed categories!"

The general impression we got from the answers given, especially by men, is that they seemed to waver, and many added postscripts. Some were adamant about gender differences but thought that larger surveys involving all social categories and different regions would be more reliable. Others seemed to be looking for a self-satisfying answer, in that they expressed worry about their own male identity in such a rapidly changing world, where the preservation of identity and cultural specificities seems increasingly jeopardized. On the other hand, female respondents were more sure of their answers and some believed Arab men to be more at a loss in today's society than women, because men still have to prove they are men in order to conform to a more demanding life in a society that no longer requires traditional manly qualities, whereas women are exempted from this pressure.

Language and gender and gender studies must not be treated as *sui generis* in the abstract. Even when gender is studied from an Arab perspective, the socio-cultural context of each country must be taken into consideration. In our study, the questionnaire was conducted in Tunis, the capital, the largest urban area, which has experienced a massive drift from the rural areas over the last ten or fifteen years. Studying language and gender in Tunis must take these population movements into account. Rural areas should be investigated because in Tunisia, as well as in the whole Arab world, the rural/urban dichotomy, unlike in some Western countries, is closely associated with poor/rich, literate/illiterate, conservative/modern, privileged/underprivileged dichotomies. Rapid urbanization, reducing the rural population to 37 percent, has had a greater impact on women than on men, causing a greater divide between the urban or modern, and the rural woman. As a consequence, women belonging to one category or the other develop different relations with space, traditions, education, gender identity, and language.

According to Sadiqi (2003: 1), when we study gender, we need to focus on four sets of factors: (1) the large power structures of the culture, (2) social, (3) contextual, and (4) identity variables. She insists that "the dynamics of multilingualism, reading of religion, illiteracy and orality" be taken into account, in order to avoid Western ethnocentric paradigms of feminism (ibid.: 314).

Gender differences in language use in Tunisia are not as pronounced as is popularly believed. Most Tunisian men and women believe that the woman's role is fundamental and that the family's good balance depends on the wife's support, participation, and contribution, whether psychological or economic, or both, but men need to be reassured, though virtually and fictitiously, that they are the sole masters on board, confirmed in their so-called superiority. Paradoxically, though nobody believes in this make-believe, everyone insists that it is indispensable to the equilibrium and stability of society as a whole.

However, many changes, whether social, economic, or cultural, that Tunisian society is undergoing are the consequence of a gender role change, whose repercussions inevitably affect language use in all its varieties. The feminization of the teaching profession has had a direct impact on language. From kindergarten to university, women teachers are the agents of language change, not only from a linguistic perspective through class interactions but also through the positive roles they play, serving as models for girls, especially in the rural areas, and encouraging them to study further.[19] While playing a key role in challenging gender-stereotyped designs, female teachers become crucial agents of change. Other professional sectors, such as health and medical domains and institutions, are experiencing the same type of changes with 40 percent of doctors and 72 percent of pharmacists being women.

Women have also entered the less "noble" professions. Hardships and financial difficulties have pushed women to work outside, in places traditionally reserved for men. Obviously, such choices are not the result of Tunisian women's empowerment, self-dependence, or initiative but rather of the difficulty of finding a job when skills and qualifications are limited. Bar and cabaret waitresses are increasingly numerous because women accept lower wages and longer working hours and never complain. Middle-aged, even in their sixties, more and more women of Bedouin origin who had moved to the capital work as street sweepers. They work in teams but are not allowed to sing at their workplace as they used to back home when harvesting wheat or spinning and weaving wool. In this particular case, such public workplaces and displacements inevitably change their language and behavior.

In this study, we have dealt with various parameters and discussed linguistic practice related to men and women from different socio-economic categories, walks of life, regions, ages, professional fields, etc. and the way rapid social and economic changes have affected their perception of language, identity, stereotyped-gender roles and attitudes, etc. The most important idea revealed by the answers and analyses is the enormous gap between figures and facts, between legislation and the daily reality, between statements and actual practices. Tunisian women do enjoy great power, and their speech is particularly forceful, often contradicting established beliefs on gender, yet they have not gained acknowledged authority, inside and most importantly outside the home, i.e., in the public arena where the game is harsher and tougher. So far, most progress has been legally instigated by government officials and many women (and also men), particularly in rural areas, are unaware of their statutory rights, and their behavior regarding gender relations and gender and language does not concord with the law on gender issues. There is a danger that the situation will not change and may deteriorate, considering the pervasive and rampant effects of biased non-secular movements and projects.

In fine, the insights gained from this study must be seen as pertaining to a specific community having its own features and idiosyncrasies, one that belongs to the Arab and Islamic world but which has close historical and cultural ties with the West. Such a community has specific processes but should find parallels and resonances in other Arab communities and societies, and though we consider the city of Tunis as a good case study, representing both urban and rural areas and containing more than one-fifth of the whole population, differences do exist among different local communities which share values and everyday social practices where negotiations of gender identities perceptible through specific linguistic practices could be examined within a "localized" context, whereby more tangible and insightful contributions can be gained (see the "communities of practice" (CoP) concept by Eckert and McConnell-Ginet 1992, 1999).

Arab women, in our case Tunisian women, do not reflect a homogeneous community; analyzing the interaction between gender and other variables such as age, class, ethnicity, relationships, or saliency (Sadiqi 2003) within a community of practice where its members strive to shape and perform their (always gendered) identities will certainly highlight different gender perceptions and is clearly a challenging area for further research.

Notes

1   The Deficit Theory considers women's language as an essentially "deficient" version of men's language.
2   The legal position of Tunisian women is the best in the Arab world. Juridical equality is recognized between men and women. The "Code du Statut Personnel" (CSP) or "Code of Personal Status" includes, inter alia, the regulation of marriage, the abolition of polygamy, the duty of mutual respect between spouses, the possibility of choosing one's spouse, guardianship awarded to the mother in the event of default by the father, etc.
3   It is interesting to note that in her *Sociolinguistic Market* (1996), Haeri clearly demonstrates that the Cairene, the variety spoken by all Cairenes, accomplishes all the functions associated with the Standard variety. She takes issue with the traditional H/L dichotomy of diglossic settings and considers the Cairene variety to stand for the standard language.
4   According to Labov, women tend to be hypercorrect in their use of standard language and are therefore initiators of linguistic change.
5   One of the main characteristics of the Bedouin variety is the use of the g phoneme, where the urban variety uses the q phoneme, ex: *golt* ("I said"), *goffa* ("basket") / *qolt*, *qoffa*.
6   See the Appendix at the end of this chapter for the questions and answers to the questionnaire.
7   Henceforth, FI and MI respectively.
8   Tannen points to indirectness as giving rise to misunderstanding in conversation between men and women. In Arab societies (less true nowadays), women's indirectness is viewed as a sign of shrewdness, sensitivity, and politeness. Women are thought to use the indirect style when addressing their very busy and self-absorbed husbands, thus showing that they cleverly consider their request as not a right but rather a favor if accepted.
9   It is interesting to note that animals like scorpions, snakes, and vipers form the ingredients of a long list of women's curses; all of them come in rhyming expressions and all with the hope of causing great harm and damage to the cursed object. These curses used to be very frequent in women's daily speech, but are hardly ever heard nowadays, especially in urban areas (which represent 63 percent of the whole country).
10   Apparently, women or young girls increasingly use men's expletives but not vice versa. Uniformity in the use of expletives seems to be occurring through a male alignment or adjustment.
11   The comment was given in French. "*C'est la seule manière d'exprimer ma colère; ça ne m'amuse pas d'être féminine!*"
12   This is clearly analyzed in a 2001 study which argues that "students acknowledge a low level of competence in this language, saying that only few among them can answer the teacher's questions, and generally do so in single words, while *Baccalauréat*-level students recognize that they find it difficult to write French in subject-specific exams. Students, in general, report that they participate very little in class … and, when they do, they use TA (Tunisian Arabic) almost exclusively" (Daoud 2001).

13 One male respondent, after reading the questionnaire, turned to me and said, "I know you want me to give answers corresponding to the cultural stereotype, that women have a different language and that their speech lacks firmness, etc. Well, let me tell you this, maybe woman's language in Tunisia is devalued (isn't that the answer you expect!), yet it is assertive and quite forceful (I am sorry to say that! But you don't have to mention it)."

14 Some 22.75 percent of the members of the Chamber of Deputies, 17 percent of the Chamber of Advisors, and 24 percent of the diplomatic corps are women. Presently, there are two women ministers and five secretaries of state.

15 Many of them are hardly ever used; such as *Kayd r rjel Kaydayn w kayd n nsa settaʃ,* which means that men's wickedness is worth two whereas women's wickedness is worth sixteen: women are believed to be eight times more wicked than men. This was probably inspired by a Qur'anic verse *?nna kaydakunna* □*aði:m* "Terrible is your wickedness" (Verse 28 in Surat Joseph where Al-Aziz (Joseph's Egyptian master) angrily accused his wife of lying after realizing that Joseph's garment was torn from behind, proof that Al-Aziz's wife had tried to pull him toward her as he was trying to run to the door, rejecting her sexual advances). This verse is often taken out of its context and used, as an erroneous and decontextualized Qur'anic reference, to refer to all women with no distinction whatsoever.

16 Normal situations exclude street harassment, flirting, quarreling, reprimanding, etc.

17 *Ya* is a vocative used when addressing a person, generally translated by *Oh!* or *Hey!*

18 Many MI expressed resentment about women's behavior, saying women have grown discourteous, and giving examples of women addressing them "with their huge black sunglasses on," or crossing the street in non-pedestrian areas asserting their priority as women.

19 Fifty-one percent of basic education instructors are women, 48 percent of secondary education teachers and 40 percent of university lecturers (http://www.tunisiaonline.com/). Along with the communicative role that language plays, objective elements (social, cultural values, and principles) and also subjective ones (ideologies, beliefs, and personal feelings) may be transmitted and suggested through this channel and bring to the fore, more importantly among male students, various alternatives to current gender-stereotyped attitudes and linguistic behaviors.

Appendix: questionnaire and results

(1) *Do you think that there are words or expressions that only men use? If yes, give examples.*

Responses	FI	MI
Vulgar words and blasphemous expressions are typically male	75%	65%
There are no male/female linguistic differences	15%	22%
No opinion	10%	13%

(2) *Do you think that there are words or expressions that only women use? If yes, give examples.*

Responses	FI	MI
Women have special expressions such as imprecations and female insults	80%	75%
Women do not have special expressions	20%	25%

(3) *Do you think that women curse (?dça) more than before? If yes, give examples.*

Responses	FI	MI
Women curse in the traditional way less than before	96%	90%
Women still curse, particularly older women with a limited degree of literacy and generally from lower socio-economic categories	4%	10%

(4) *Do you think that women use more swear words than before? If yes, give examples.*

Responses	FI	MI
Women use more expletives than before because of their liberation and rapid socio-economic change	46%	39%
No, they are simply more visible in society	44%	--
Society's linguistic behavior, including women's, has grown more violent	-	18%
Yes, because they have lost their femininity and modesty	-	14%
Social status and education are determinant factors in women's use of expletives	10%	29%

(5) *Do you think that women use more French words than men in their conversation?*

Responses	FI	MI
Yes, to sound classier, cultivated or out of snobbery	47%	32%
Yes, to express their feelings (absence of taboos)	--	20%
Yes, to compensate for feelings of inferiority	7%	--
Yes, to hide their rural or Bedouin accents	5%	--
Yes, as a strategy of politeness	1%	--
No, they do not use more French than men today. This was the case many years ago	26%	9%
Social class, region, social status, and education are determinant factors in women's use of French	14%	25%
French has a firm foothold in many sectors despite all attempts at Arabization. (Both genders are concerned.)	--	14%

(6) *Do you think that women are easily interrupted by men in a conversation?*

Responses	FI	MI
No, because they are authoritarian, due to feelings of inferiority	--	45%
No, the issue is not gender-based. It depends on the context and the situation	81%	12%
Yes, because they have internalized a feeling of inequality	--	21%
Yes, because they have a higher sense of communication	15%	--
Yes, because they are more flexible, peaceful, and less aggressive	--	14%
Yes, because they are very talkative and must be interrupted.	--	9%
Yes, due to a conservative education	4%	--

(7) *Do you think that women give more details when relating an event?*

Responses	FI	MI
Yes, because of women's talkativeness, hyper-sensitivity, and superficiality	55%	57%
Yes, because women are observant, meticulous, and have a tendency to analyze rather than synthesize	42%	29%
Yes, but their professional environment can be very influential	--	14%
No, they do not give more details in general	3%	--

13 Women, education, and the redefinition of empowerment and change in a traditional society

The case of Oman

Thuwayba Al Barwani

Introduction

Education is the single most important and consistent factor in the empowerment of women, irrespective of race, religion, or culture (UNDP 2002, 2005). While there is an ongoing debate regarding the definition of empowerment and whether or not Eurocentric definitions (which typically emphasize independence from and equal rights to men) truly represent the aspirations of women in all societies, the critical importance of education in empowerment remains largely uncontested. Similarly uncontested is the belief that education empowers women to challenge themselves to take roles and responsibilities that enable them to be a catalyst of change in their homes, communities, and for some, the nation at large.

Over the past several years, Arab nations have been pressured to focus on issues related to women, mainly in response to several consecutive reports, such as *Towards the Rise of Women in the Arab World* (Arab Human Development Report 2005), that have called for reforms to change the plight of women in the Middle East. When considered within the widely applied Eurocentric framework of empowerment, Arab women are largely thought to lag behind in all four generally accepted measures of empowerment, namely education, health, employment, and participation in society. However, while this may be generally true of many Arab nations, it does not necessarily present a true picture of all Arab nations. One reason for this may be the definition itself: women in some Arab nations may find empowerment not in independence per se or advancement in the workplace, and the like, but via other avenues such as social and political participation within the parameters acceptable in their specific contexts that are typically ignored in current definitions. If so, their role in and influence on their societies (and thus level of empowerment) could be grossly underestimated.

Indeed, Sheikha Mozah bint Nasser Al Missned,[1] a wife of Hamad bin Khalifa Al Thani, the ruler of Qatar, argues that the debate over women in the Middle East depicts women in a timeless battle against the oppressive traditions and religions of the region (Al Missned 2007). She contends that this debate, while ignoring larger socio-political realities, has swung dangerously between two poles, namely patronage and apologist. The first view follows the line of colonial feminism, which is a movement to save women of the Middle East from the miseries of oppression, subordination, and discrimination. Al Missned goes further to say that this view perceives an endless clash between women's liberation and religious dogmatism, which is seen as the stumbling block for Arab women in their quest for freedoms and rights. Over time, the empowerment of Middle Eastern women has not only become politicized and an international issue, but has also been used as a bargaining chip for widespread political reforms in the region. Countering this debate, Al Missned argues, is a growing branch of radicalism that denies problems with women's issues in the region. This apologist view claims that the return of true Islam will guarantee women's rights, and feeds on the belief that women's rights are simply a pretext for a secularist agenda to annihilate the identity and religion of the Middle Eastern people (Al Missned 2007).

The present chapter attempts to dispel some of the aforementioned misconceptions about Middle Eastern women in traditional Arab societies, as well as redefine and contextualize empowerment, by tracing the journey to empowerment of Omani women as an example, and assessing their roles as agents of change despite their strong commitment to the preservation of their culture, traditions, and heritage. That is, despite the differences in perception of empowerment among Arab scholars and the traditional way of life that governs Arab women, they have in many ways made significant contributions to their societies. Future efforts in the advancement of Arab women should thus seek to balance institutional and/or global goals with women's personal goals.

This chapter highlights these issues as they relate to Omani women. Interviews conducted with Omani women combined with analyses of previously published statistics were used to develop an alternative interpretation of empowerment—one that is flexible enough to accommodate different values, principles, and priorities.

Definitions of empowerment

Women's empowerment is often taken to denote their sense of self-worth, their right to have access to opportunities and resources, their independence and freedom to make decisions about important issues that affect their lives and their ability to influence the direction of change (United Nations Population Information Network 1995). Zuhur (2003: 17), on the other hand, defines empowerment as "a condition in which women hold or are in the process of obtaining educational, legal and political rights that are equivalent or nearly equal to those of male citizens." She goes much further to include the ability to work and advance in any chosen career; possess economic rights to own and dispose of property; obtain bodily rights (control over health and fertility and the right to prosecute those who commit domestic violence, rape, harassment, or other violations against them); and even gain legal rights that accord women certain advantages, such as quotas in hiring, education preferences in areas where women have historically lacked access, and/or differential rights such as paid maternity leave.

Although Zuhur's definition is far more extreme, both are based on feminist ideals that are essentially Eurocentric. The issue thus becomes: Do either of these definitions represent the ideals that Arab women seek? In an attempt to contextualize empowerment and at the same time answer this question, the interviews in the present study used Zuhur's definition as a prompt to solicit reactions from women regarding various issues that are often used to gauge empowerment. These include their positions on issues such as Hijab (wearing a veil), polygamy, arranged marriage, freedom, and equality, among others. However, because it is important to consider their responses within a historical as well as modern context, these data and the related discussion are presented after providing the basic background and current statistics-based evidence of empowerment among Omani women.

Omani women: the journey to empowerment

A number of Muslim women have visibly participated in public life since early history. Professor Mohammed Akram Nadwi, a Muslim scholar at the Oxford Centre for Islamic Studies, has conducted extensive research on the contributions of women scholars in the Middle Ages. He alone has identified a staggering 8,000 women who not only transmitted Islamic Hadith[2] and Fiqh[3] but also made laws as jurists, and taught both male and female students. Names such as the Prophet Muhammad's own wives Khadija,and Aisha and Umm al-Darda, a prominent jurist and a respected scholar of the Islamic sciences, are among those who played major and very public roles in Islamic history (Nadwi 2007) .

Indeed, the history of Oman also includes its share of women noted and recognized for their various contributions to public life. To name a few, based on Al Balushi (2000), Seyyida Moza bint Al Imam Ahmad bin Said was a top military strategist in the early eighteenth century, while Seyyida Khawla bint Seyyid Said bin Sultan, the daughter of the Sultan who ruled Oman from 1856 to 1875, was a known thinker, planner, and the most reliable member of the ruling family. Shamsaa bint Al Alama Said bin Khalfan Al Khalili was a well-respected scholar and thinker in Islamic jurisprudence who was consulted to interpret some of the most difficult issues of the early nineteenth century. Aisha bint Sheikh Issa Al Harthy was a famous poet of her time. Al Ghalia bint Nasser bin Hmeid played a major role in national unity and social cohesion in Oman in the early 1900s. The list is long and diverse, and continues from the noted late-nineteenth-century book author Seyyida Salma bint Sultan Al Seyyid Said bin Sultan to the more contemporary scholarly contributions of Nagiya bint Amer Al Hijriya, Sheikha bint Hilal Al Hinaiya, and Nasira bint Suroor Al Riyamiya, to mention only a few.

It is clear from this historic account that Muslim women in general, and Omani women in particular, began the journey to—and indeed achieved—empowerment many centuries ago. Why, then, do many Western writers continue to describe Omani women as Phillips (1966: i) so succinctly put it: "In terms of personality, of economics and civics, there are no women in Oman. Women exist in numbers always greater than men but their existence is domestic." A closer look may paint a different picture.

All of the above-mentioned women were clearly educated and cultured, and had important responsibilities and roles in their society. They were certainly empowered. What may not be so obvious, but is also important to note, is that all of these women operated actively within the parameters of their religion and social norms, and their contributions were supported and encouraged by male members of their families and of their respective societies as a whole.

Modern Oman has produced similarly powerful women. A number of factors have been proposed to explain how these women achieved their level of empowerment, the most significant of which are political will, positive legislation, Oman's seafaring history that has exposed Omanis to different cultures, and the tolerance of the Ibadhiya sect of Islam which is the dominant religious sect[4] in Oman (Al Barwani 2000). Most likely, a combination of these factors provided an enabling environment that opened doors for women to operate naturally and confidently in the external arena while also maintaining their modesty and femininity. Thus, to truly assess the empowerment of modern-day Omani women, it is necessary to consider the social, cultural, economic, and even political environments of the recent past and into the present.

Indeed, the modern journey to empowerment of Omani women parallels a socio-economic journey that began in the early 1970s and continues to this day. When the current Sultan of Oman, Qaboos bin Said, took over in 1970, he promised to transform the country from its present stagnation to its past glory, while also making the best use of modern government apparatus, modern technology, and a market economy to ensure the sustainable development and progress of the Omani people. So it was with this spirit that a new era began – a journey that implemented the wisdom of maintaining a delicate balance between modernity and tradition. To this date, the best description of Oman is that of a nation that is modern yet overtly proud of its unique identity, which is embodied in its rich culture and heritage.

Governmental leaders recognized from the outset that investment in the wellbeing of the citizens was the only way to ensure sustainable development. To this end, they began implementing a series of five-year development plans (starting in 1975[5]) that aimed to balance economic and technological advancements with improved social conditions including measures to ensure gender equality. Each of the six plans thus far implemented has achieved this objective. Even from 1999 to 2003, despite periods of decline in oil revenues (the nation's largest source of income), the government continued to increase spending in the social sector. For example, education funding increased 9.4 percent on average annually during this period and accounted for the largest share of the budget among the civil ministries. At the same time, health expenditures increased by 5.0 percent annually on average (UNICEF/Government of Oman 2005).

This successful system of development, and in particular its emphasis on social advancement and gender-sensitive development policies, no doubt created the nurturing environment necessary for women's empowerment. The following sections briefly summarize the governmental regulations, initiatives, and legislation that set the stage for women within each measure of empowerment (i.e., education, health, employment, and participation in society). Pertinent statistics that evidence the progress of women over time are also presented.

Women and education

The government's commitment to provide equal opportunity to education for girls dates back to the early 1970s when Sultan Qaboos bin Said addressed the nation and vividly established his position on the issue of equal rights to education. For example on the occasion of the seventh national day celebration he said: "The ultimate aim is that every boy and girl in the Sultanate shall receive a minimum of 9 years of education. We have directed that no effort is to be spared to achieve this aim" (Ministry of Information 1995: 62) Since then, a sustained national commitment to education equality has led to a rapid expansion of access to education for girls. For instance, in 1970, Oman did not have any public schools for girls. By 1976, a full quarter of all public education institutions were all-girls schools; by 2002, the number had increased to about 43 percent; and the most recent data show a stable proportional increase.

Equally significant were the increases in female student enrollment rates compared to those of males. The percentage of female students in general education increased from 12.7 percent in 1972 to 33 percent in 1981 and 48.6 percent in 2002. Again, the trend appears to be continuing to this day, with the most current data (2005 and 2006) showing steady increasing rates of enrollment for girls. Table 13.1 shows the enrollment rates of both male and female students between 2000 and 2005 for three different educational levels (Ministry of Education 2006a).

Over time, female enrollment increased across all educational levels, and showed the largest increase at higher levels of education. Moreover, in both the 2003/2004 and 2004/2005 school years, the participation rates of female students exceeded those of males at all three levels. Female students also tended to have lower dropout and repeat rates, and longer persistence rates (Ministry of Education 2006).

A UNESCO report named Oman one of the top ten countries making progress in closing the gender gap in education. In fact, a gender analysis of educational efficiency indicators revealed a reversed gender disparity in favor of girls and showed that, overall, girls take on average 11.3 years to complete the 9-year basic education cycle while boys take 13.9 years. Various other measures of learning achievement also indicate overall higher performance of girls (Al Barwani 2003). For instance, in a study, female students in grades 4, 6, 9, and 10 consistently outperformed males in all content areas tested (Ministry of Education/UNICEF 2000).

These data indicate that female students have not only dramatically increased in enrollment over the years, but have also begun to outperform males in most subjects. An analysis of recent dropout and repetition rates in government schools

Table 13.1 Enrollment according to educational level and gender from 2000 to 2005 (as percentage of total enrollment)

Educational level	2000/2001		2001/2002		2002/2003		2003/2004		2004/2005	
	Girls	Boys	Girls	Boys	Girls	Boys	Girls	Boys	Girls	Boys
Cycle 1 grades 1-6	89.2	90.2	91.2	91.6	90.1	91.1	89.2	89.0	89.8	89.7
Cycle 2 grades 7-9	71.0	69.1	70.9	69.4	72.4	71.1	70.1	69.2	73.5	72.4
grades 10-12	57.7	46.5	61.8	51.8	65.2	54.9	62.5	53.7	62.0	53.5

(Ministry of Education 2006) reveals that boys have higher rates at all grade levels (almost twice as much as those of girls).

These trends in enrollment and performance are similar in higher education. For example, female students accounted for 54 percent of the total number of students enrolled in higher education institutions in 2005/2006. Moreover, they consistently outperformed their male counterparts. A good example of this can be seen in the graduation statistics of Sultan Qaboos University (SQU),[6] where females have consistently had higher graduation rates, lower dropout rates, shorter completion rates, and overall higher levels of performance for the past decade. Table 13.2 lists the graduation statistics at the university for the past 15 years. As can be seen in the grand total column of the table, a transition from overall male superiority to female superiority occurred between 1993 and 1994.

When SQU, Oman's first university, opened its doors in 1986, it immediately began experimenting with the coeducation concept. Both male and female students were admitted to degree programs on the basis of their high school exit exam results. With each successive year, the number of female students who qualified for admission to this prestigious institution increased. Although this was a positive development for female students, it created a number of challenges that called for the government's intervention in order to ensure equal opportunity for male students.[7] This switch in focus from aiding females to aiding males leaves no doubt of the profound impact improved education opportunity had on women's empowerment—at least among the educated.

Nonetheless, the picture is very different among the adult population. Efforts to eradicate adult illiteracy in Oman were initiated in 1973, when a national plan was developed that recognized that women comprised roughly 50 percent of the Omani population, and that having high female illiteracy would likely jeopardize the government's social and economic objectives. It was imperative, therefore, to ensure greater female participation in literacy programs, especially for those who did not have an opportunity to learn to read and write before 1970 or lived in areas that were not easily accessible.

Table 13.2 Sultan Qaboos University graduation statistics according to gender and type of degree

Year	Diploma (two-year program)			Bachelor			Master's			Grand total (larger numbers in bold)		
	Male	Female	Total	Male	Female	Total	Male	Female	Total	Male	Female	Total
1990				160	123	283				**160**	123	283
1991				282	207	489				**282**	207	489
1992				290	268	558				**290**	268	558
1993				323	314	637				**323**	314	637
1994				359	402	761				359	**402**	761
1995				307	432	739	14	10	24	321	**442**	763
1996				281	454	735	2	8	10	283	**462**	745
1997				327	542	869	2	5	7	329	**547**	876
1998				429	579	1008	11	2	13	440	**581**	1021
1999				524	600	1124	14	3	17	538	**603**	1141
2000	87	98	185	497	574	1071	9	2	11	593	**674**	1267
2001	117	133	250	566	732	1298	22	20	42	705	**885**	1590
2002	120	249	369	581	613	1194	64	47	111	765	**909**	1674
2003	286	477	763	718	755	1473	59	46	105	1063	**1278**	2341
2004	207	374	581	742	905	1647	53	39	92	1002	**1318**	2320
2005	121	272	393	837	1090	1927	57	33	90	1015	**1395**	2410

While great progress has been made in the effort to eradicate illiteracy in general (Ministry of Education 2006), the rates of female illiteracy continue to be higher than those of males. Table 13.3 compares the census data on illiteracy between 1993 and 2003.

It is also clear from the table that the 30–39 years age group has the highest level of illiteracy for both males and females. Illiteracy statistics from the Technical Office of the National Population Committee (Ministry of National Economy 2006) indicate, however, that the level of female illiteracy continues to increase in older age groups.

Oman's latest five-year development plan calls for reducing illiteracy by 100,000 individuals by 2010. In 2003 and 2004, 117 literacy centers were operating in Oman with a total enrollment of 6,622 students, 94 percent of whom were females (Ministry of Education 2003, 2004). With the establishment of the "learning village" initiative in 2004, a program that mobilizes local volunteers to address illiteracy in their own communities (developed by Oman's Ministry of Education in collaboration with the Arab Bureau of Education for the Gulf States), the number of adults enrolled in this program almost doubled within a short period of time. In addition to battling illiteracy, the initiative aims to raise social and economic awareness among participants and foster a spirit of civic cooperation by encouraging locals and non-governmental agencies to work together. It is worth noting that the volunteer teachers are typically young, recent high school graduates, and predominantly female.

Table 13.3 Illiteracy rates in Oman in 1993 and 2003 by age group (as percentage of total populace in each respective group)

Age group	1993			2003		
	Female	Male	Overall	Female	Male	Overall
15-19	8.4	2.1	5.2	2.5	1.2	1.8
20-29	32.5	6.6	19.2	5.6	2.0	3.8
30-39	75.1	26.6	51.9	32.7	6.2	19.4
Total population	**53.9**	**28.9**	**41.2**	**29.4**	**14.6**	**22.0**

Women and health

As with all other social services, Oman was a latecomer in the provision of health services to its citizens. The development of the health sector in Oman started in 1970 with two 12-bed hospitals and no more than 12 doctors.

The period between 1976 and 1990 saw the implementation of the first three five-year development plans, which concentrated on the establishment of basic health infrastructure. During the fourth, fifth, and sixth plans, the Ministry concentrated on health development in compliance with international indices.

The government bears the largest proportion of health expenditure in Oman. In 2000, the government covered more than 80 percent of the total health expenditure, which accounted for about 2 percent of the national GDP. As a percentage of total public expenditure, health-related expenditures rose from 2.4 percent in 1980 to 3.9 percent in 1990 and 5.5 percent in 2000; the rate of increase seems to have leveled off, as there was a slight decrease to 5.4 percent in 2003.

The huge government commitment to improve standards of health care is reflected in the overall improvement of most of the main health service indicators (Table 13.4).

In addition to dramatic improvements across all of these indicators, Oman achieved nearly universal coverage of immunization against the three major child-killing diseases. Moreover, there were marked increases in the number of hospital beds and medical and paramedic personnel per every 10,000 people.

After education, health is often considered the second most important indicator for assessing the progress of nations regarding the empowerment of women. In general, improved health enhances empowerment.

As summarized above, the past three decades have seen significant progress in health care services in Oman in terms of quantity as well as quality. A fair share of these services have particularly benefited women, resulting in improved life expectancy at birth and maternal and child mortality rates. Indeed, the maternal mortality rate decreased by nearly 6 percent between 1990 and 2000, while female life expectancy increased markedly and steadily from about 49 years in 1970 to 61 years in 1980, 71 years in 1990, and 74 years in 2000 (Ministry of National Economy 2004).

Table 13.4 Health indicators by decade from 1970 to 2000 (as percentage of total populace for each category)

Indicator	1970	1980	1990	2000
Crude birth rate	N/A	50.0	44.7	32.6
Crude death rate	N/A	13.2	7.6	3.7
Infant mortality rate	118 per 1,000 births	64.0	29.0	16.7
Under 5 mortality rate	181 per 1,000 births	86.0	35.0	21.7
Stillbirth rate	N/A	16.6	13.2	10.0
Maternal mortality rate	N/A	N/A	22	16.1
Life expectancy at birth				
Male	46.3	58.5	67.1	72.5
Female	48.5	61.2	71.0	74.3
Total	47.4	59.8	69.0	73.4
Contraceptive prevalence rate	N/A	N/A	23.8	30.8
Births attended by trained health personnel	N/A	60.0	90.0	93.8
Infants with low birth weight	N/A	4.2	8.7	8.1
Children suffering from malnutrition	N/A	N/A	12.8	15.0

Moreover, according to a reproductive health survey conducted by the Ministry of Health (2000), 97 percent of women aged 15–49 years received pre-natal medical care mainly by trained health workers, and 99.3 percent of them received care at a government health facility. These data indicate that not only has female health improved dramatically over time, but these improvements can be largely attributed to governmental investment in the health care sector as well as direct governmental health services.

However, the progress made in education also seems to have had a significant impact on women's health (and related socio-demographic indicators), which in turn appears to have indeed augmented women's empowerment. For example, a survey of Omani families conducted by the Ministry of National Economy (2003), found a substantial trend towards later marriage among Omani women, especially among educated and urban females. Other findings of a study conducted by the Ministry of Social Development (2003), also suggested that more educated parents generally favored smaller family size. However, perhaps the strongest evidence comes from data on fertility rates, which are often used as a proxy indicator for empowerment. The same survey found that fertility rates differed significantly among women of different educational levels, where illiterate women were more likely to continue to have children past the age of 35 years than were literate women. In addition, fertility rates in general dropped dramatically by 60 percent between 1987 and 2004. Recent statistics of the Ministry of Health indicate that fertility rates are continuing to decline with current rates reaching 3.19 (Ministry of Health 2007). This may be attributed to the delay in marriage, delay in reproduction, and/or women's engagement in formal employment.

Employment is discussed in detail in the following section, but it is important to note here that women have played obvious roles as agents of change in the health sector not only via formal employment as medics, paramedics, and health-support workers but also by their contribution to health advocacy, especially in rural areas. Close to 5,000 women nationwide volunteer to support health awareness initiatives in child health, maternal health, nutrition, hygiene, birth-spacing campaigns, and so forth. Volunteers feel empowered by their acquisition of new skills and knowledge, greater engagement in the community, and an opportunity to meet with women from around the country. As one volunteer put it, "This is the foundation for constructing the future of our country" (UNICEF 2005: 100).

Women and employment

The improvements in educational access for women have not yielded equally satisfying results in labor market participation. However, importantly, their economic participation rates have steadily increased over the past decade. For example, in 1993, 6.7 percent of females aged 15 or older were employed; that number increased to 10.1 percent in 1996, 10.8 percent in 2000, and 18.7 percent in 2003 (Ministry of National Economy 2003).

The female share of the total Omani labor force also increased from 17.6 percent in 2000 to 22.2 percent in 2003. This increase has been largely attributed to the increasing rates of female access to education, as female economic activity is positively correlated to educational status. Moreover, the female Omani workforce tends to have a higher level of education than that of males. For instance, results of the labor force survey of 1996 highlighted that almost three-quarters (71.2 percent) of economically active Omani females held a certificate from secondary school or higher. Of these, two-thirds (63.6 percent) were employed either as professionals (40.2 percent) or as clerks (23.4 percent). Furthermore, the highest rates of economic activity among Omani women in 2003 were found among those with a Ph.D. (95 percent), a Bachelors degree (93.6 percent), Higher Diploma or Master's degree (89 percent), followed by a certificate from secondary school (36 percent) or preparatory school (7.3 percent) and finally illiterates (3.5 percent).

Chatty (2000) reported that illiterate women tend to seek employment in simple, unskilled occupations, and that the single highest regional percentage of women engaged in elementary occupations is found in the Dakhiliya region, a stronghold of Omani tradition. Further, she found that women with elementary occupations tend to be older (with 85 percent aged 30 or older). Overall, these findings seem to indicate that illiterate, rural Omani women also seek employment even if they have to travel away from their homes to search for such employment.

The bulk of Omani female civil servants work in the health and education professions. This is due in large part to government efforts to provide health and education for all, coupled with the drive to nationalize employment in these two fields. That said, women are increasingly competing for (and successfully obtaining) professions in areas such as engineering, marketing, banking, law, academia, and other such fields once considered exclusive to males. It is also becoming more common to see Omani women in the armed forces, the police force, radio, television, reporting, and other jobs once considered unsuitable for females (Chatty 2000). Indeed, Omani women seem to be pushing the frontiers of cultural acceptability, often as a result of economic and sometimes political necessity. Table 13.5 shows the employment statistics for the public sector between 1985 and 2003.

As is clear from the table, women still constitute a much smaller, though growing, proportion of public sector employment. Growth in female employment in the private sector is even slower. In 2003, for example, females represented only 18 percent of the total workforce in the private sector (Ministry of National Economy 2003). This may be due to any of several factors, including long working hours and/or more working days that are not attractive to married women with families; unavailability of private sector jobs in regions outside of Muscat (the capital of Oman); unattractive salaries; and unfriendly working environments/ conditions.

At the same time, however, more and more young women are taking up clerical and front office jobs that were once dominated by expatriate males. Similarly, women are beginning to venture out on their own to establish small businesses such as tailoring and textile shops, beauty salons, driving schools, clothing outlets, perfumeries, cafes, kitchens for preparing traditional Omani foods, day-care centers, play schools, fashion design boutiques, and so forth. As more women have become successful in the market, and other women have witnessed their success, they have become increasingly confident and have begun to invest in bigger businesses such as private schools, small and medium manufacturing companies, service companies, travel agencies, restaurant chains, and many other similar businesses (Ministry of National Economy 2003; Ministry of Social Development 2007).

Nevertheless, women still represent a very small percentage of economically active Omanis, the conventional definition of which excludes students, housewives, retired persons, social income recipients, and those unable to work (Chatty 2000). It is thus important to note that, according to this definition, important agricultural and animal husbandry work of women in rural and Bedouin communities is likely seriously underreported. Finally, considering the huge

Table 13.5 Public sector employment from 1985 to 2003

		1985	*1990*	*2001*	*2003*
Number of employees	Male	30,941	47,293	46,381	51,886
	Female	2,831	20,946	10,678	27,213
	Total	33,772	68,496	57,059	79,099
Percentage	Male	91.6	69.4	81.3	65.6
	Female	8.4	30.6	18.7	34.4

strides made in women's education, these employment statistics may suggest that a large number of educated Omani women may ultimately decide to be stay-at-home mothers.

Thus, the effects of education on women in the labor market have been mixed. What cannot be denied is that progress, though slow, has been made, and educated women have become empowered within the workplace.

Women and participation in society

There are no legal restrictions that forbid women from occupying senior posts in the Oman government. As a matter of fact, the first senior appointment of an Omani woman (as the Undersecretary for Development) took place more than 15 years ago. It is now estimated that women occupy 11.5 percent of the upper management posts in government agencies (Ministry of National Economy 2006). In 2003, the first Omani woman was given ministerial rank and appointed as president of the General Organization for Traditional Craft industries (a non-cabinet post). Since then, the portfolios for higher education, tourism, and social development have been given to women. At the moment, Oman boasts four female ministers, one female undersecretary, and four female consultants.

Similar gains in political participation were made in 1994, when women were granted the right to vote and to run for office. In keeping with the democratic process that Oman initiated, women have been encouraged to run as Majlis Ashura[8] representatives of their own jurisdictions. Competing equally with men, two women in the Muscat Governorate won their elections and were voted into office in 1994, 1998, 2002, and 2004. However, in the last elections held in 2007, no women were elected in any jurisdictions.

Despite strong media campaigns and voter education programs launched by the government to encourage women both as voters and candidates, women have been unable to break through the cultural barriers in regions other than Muscat. This has mostly been attributed to a lack of confidence in their own strengths, a lack of exposure to election procedures, and a lack of support from female voters.

The picture is very different in the Majlis Adowla (State Council). This legislative body comprises 71 appointed members, and nearly 20 percent of them are females. Although this percentage may seem low by international standards, Oman's female representation is better than most other Arabian Gulf Cooperation Council states or even other Arab countries that have longer histories of parliamentary tradition. Omani women are also increasingly working in the diplomatic corps. Oman now has 20 female diplomats and two female ambassadors representing the country in the most powerful capitals of the world.

Omani women's participation in society, however, goes beyond formal employment. Over the past 35 years, women in Oman have organized themselves into women's associations that are actively involved in providing various services to their communities.[9] The services normally include child care facilities, training programs, fundraising, advocacy, income-generating projects to support needy women, and other activities that support the work of government agencies. In addition, Omani women are active in non-governmental organizations that serve the disabled and low-income families, among other social groups, as well as professional organizations that serve a number of special interests. Oman currently has 31 centers that care for disabled children located in most of the major population centers of Oman. In these facilities, women comprise 99.9 percent of the volunteers and administrative and technical support staff (Ministry of Social Development 2007).

Thus, like employment, women have just begun to reach important milestones in their participation in society, none of which would have been possible without the inroads established by improved education access.

Women and globalization

Globalization, while positive in a number of ways, promotes conformity to a certain way of life, of governance, and of doing things in general. Thus, with the collapse of communism in the 1990s, the concept of a New World Order emerged, which according to El-Shibiny (2005) is essentially the progression of Western capitalism as an unchallenged economic, political, and military power: "As part of the strategy to establish a New World Order, a process began which aimed to promote a free global economic market along with global culture, global communication, global democracy, global human rights and global integration" (2005: 16).

El-Shibiny argues that world religions, such as Buddhism, Confucianism, Judaism, Christianity, and Islam, have emerged in history as universal civilizations calling for the welfare of human beings and promoting ethical and social values such as tolerance, human rights, love, and so forth. These religions and their teachings have influenced humanity for more than two millennia, becoming in time universal with global followers. El-Shibiny cautions, however, that in order for a universal culture to develop, those who promote it must be cognizant of the wisdom and values that have emerged through the history of previous civilizations.

Like other developing countries, the Arab world is generally concerned that globalization might obliterate the national, political, societal, and cultural sovereignty of nation states. Yet, when one analyzes Arab opinions on this issue, it becomes clear that they are far from uniform. Some believe that globalization is an imperialist deception designed by the West to intervene in internal affairs of nations, and therefore should be prevented. Others are skeptical and call for caution, while others call for total submission to the wave of change, and still others call for the reconciliation of globalization within the framework of Arab interests, culture, and traditions (El-Shibiny 2005).

For women in Oman, globalization seems to present opportunities as well as challenges. Therefore, to assess the effects of globalization on women, and the opinions of different women on globalization, an original study was conducted. Data were collected using semi-structured interviews of 25 educated women in Muscat, Ibra, and Rustaq. Here, *educated women* are loosely defined as those who have completed at least 12 years of school. The interview results were content-analyzed to identify trends related to different aspects of empowerment and change.

The study confirmed that women see both opportunities and challenges in globalization. The opportunities identified included easy access to information, greater access to goods and services, exposure to different cultures and ideas through the Internet, satellite stations, and other media, freedom to express opinions, easy communication (via e-mail, chat rooms, mobile telephones, teleconferencing, and so forth), and access to long-distance learning opportunities. Regarding challenges, women's responses focused mainly on the fear of the spread of Western materialism, introduction to an alien youth culture, interference in the socialization of children, and media promotion of values that contradict Islamic teachings.

These findings suggest that women are in favor of taking advantage of the opportunities presented by globalization and information technology but are also conscious of the ills that often come with these advances. One response in particular summed up the overall sentiment: "What we need is a balance between the positive aspects of globalization without descending into the negative aspects of Westernization."

The interviews also revealed striking insights into issues that are often assumed by Westerners to keep Middle Eastern women from achieving empowerment and playing an active role in the development of their societies. Following is a summary of statements made by Omani women on such issues, including polygamy, Hijab, discrimination, divorce, position in the family, freedom, and extended family.

On polygamy:
"Islam has allowed it, so we can't say that the husband cannot marry a second wife. However, I have a choice to decide whether I want to accept this arrangement or not."

"Unless the husband can balance and be fair to the wives, he has no right to take a second wife."[10]

"Islam has allowed it but not encouraged it. The conditions that the man has to fulfil are very difficult but men do not often follow these conditions."

"Under certain circumstances, I may allow it."

On Hijab:
"It is a personal choice. I decided to wear it because I believe that a good Muslim woman has to be modest. Nobody forced me."

"Hijab is not oppressive. It is liberating. I feel freer when I am covered."

"Hijab does not prohibit me from doing anything that I want to do."

On discrimination against women:
"We don't feel discriminated in anyway, as far as the government is concerned. However, within the family parents tend to give boys a more privileged treatment."

"It is for me to decide what right I want to possess."

"I possess all rights within the family, at work, and in society. I have to only make personal decisions regarding which rights I want to exercise."

On divorce (considered a contentious issue that reflects gender discrimination between spouses, the women interviewed had different opinions):

"I think it's best that Islam gave men the last word in divorce, because women are emotionally unable to handle stress. If it was left up to us, we would have divorced our husbands long ago."

"Divorce is increasing, especially with the young generation. I suppose it is because they are contributors to family income and not dependant on men."

On position in the family (Middle Eastern societies are generally paternalistic, and male members of households often have a dominant role. This question was intended to assess whether improved education for women has impacted the role distribution within the family):

"The woman takes most of the responsibility of children and their welfare. The father provides income and he is mainly responsible for discipline. He has the final decision."

"I like to feel that my husband is in charge. I don't think there is competition because our roles are different."

"I think that the woman loses a lot when she wants to control everything."

On freedom:

"I feel free to do what I want. I can express my opinion and take my own decisions. What is important is that I do not abuse the freedom given to me by my family."

"Freedom to me is to do what Islam has instructed to me to do. The government has given us freedom but we have to make our own choices."

"We have to know our limits as defined in our religion and culture."

On extended family (preference for extended or nuclear family):

"Extended families are supportive especially in the early years of marriage. It is always useful to have your family around you. They help resolve problems."

"I like my family to be nearby, but I do not like them to live with me."

"A working woman needs the extended family to keep an eye on the children even if she has domestic help."

In summary, these responses clearly indicate that despite marked improvements in education, earning-power, available opportunities, and freedom of choice, Omani women continue to strive to maintain their identity, enhance their culture and traditions, and confirm their social roles and responsibilities. Thus, the more or less traditional stances that Omani women continue to support do not appear to inhibit them from contributing extensively to the development of their societies.

In this respect, Omani women seem to be redefining empowerment and change. They have embraced advancement and taken full advantage of new opportunities and realities, but have done so at their own pace, on their own terms, and within the framework of their own religion and culture. They also clearly understand that empowerment does not lie in their ability to become Westernized but rather in their ability to use their collective wisdom to maintain the delicate balance that will establish, restore, and nurture the dignity of their womanhood and at the same time ensure their continued contribution to the development and wellbeing of their societies.

Conclusion

Omani women, like other Middle Eastern women, continue to be portrayed by Westerners as silent shadows or helpless victims of suppressive customs and traditions (Chatty 2000; Al-Hegelan 1980). However, the present chapter provided comprehensive statistical evidence coupled with interview-based qualitative data that strongly refute this concept. A very different picture has emerged, one that challenges the typical stereotype of ignorance, submission, and suppression. Based on the existing data on the four main indicators of empowerment, namely, education, health, employment, and participation in society, one cannot but conclude that women are not only empowered but they also operate within a supportive and nurturing environment that makes it possible for them to make choices that reflect their identity.

Omani women have asserted their role as equal partners in the development of their societies. However, the decision to focus government spending on human resource development irrespective of gender, the issuance of positive gender-sensitive civil service and labor laws, and the equal opportunity policy that has been implemented in workplaces have all contributed to the empowerment of Omani women.

Armed with an education, economic independence, and an enabling and supportive environment, Omani women are breaking new ground and entering the workforce with the skills and technical know-how necessary to compete for available jobs. They are increasingly participating in the labor market, and competently taking over jobs that used to be held by foreign workers, thus making an important contribution to the adjustment of the demographic imbalance that is typical of Gulf states.

With more young women pursuing higher education and training, technical and professional jobs traditionally filled by men are now becoming accessible to women. Thus, women are now able to contribute more to decision making and social change.

The stable, additional income provided by working female members of families has significantly improved the economic wellbeing of those families. This has in turn improved the health and hygiene of the entire family (Ministry of Health 2006), which is clearly reflected in the improved health indicators, healthier lifestyles, and an enhanced standard of living that is discernible in families around the country.

Education has also enabled the Omani woman to recognize her role and responsibility towards her community. She now has a strong voice in the community through active advocacy and by supporting community-based functions, promoting the advancement of women, and getting involved in child-development activities.

One can confidently say that Omani women have earned their respect in their societies. And they command respect not only due to their important contributions but also because of the maturity and dedication with which they take up their roles and responsibilities. They seem to have defined their own parameters and to have recognized that their advancement relies on their ability to understand the sensitive balance between their culture and traditions on the one hand and the demands of a globalizing world on the other.

Notes

1 She is a strong voice in issues related to the advancement of women in general and Gulf and Qatari women in particular.
2 Sayings and deeds attributed to Prophet Muhammad (SAW).
3 Islamic jurisprudence.
4 The dominant religious sect in Oman is Ibadhiya followed by Sunni and then Shia.
5 Oman is now implementing its seventh five-year development plan.
6 Sultan Qaboos University (SQU) was the first university established in Oman and is the only public university in the country.
7 In the 1996/1997 academic year, the government introduced a lower criterion for the admission of boys.
8 It is an elected body similar to what may countries call the lower house.
9 Oman now boasts 51 women's associations and a number of community development centers that develop leadership and other skills of women in villages and smaller population centers throughout the country.
10 Balance refers to the husband's ability to treat his wives equally.

14 Perpetuating authority

Ishelhin women's rituals and the transmission
of Islamic knowledge in southwestern
Morocco

Margaret J. Rausch

Fatima, your father has taken away our sanity,
And our health. We are lost in the wilderness from the pain of longing. [1]

Earlier scholars of Islamic history, blinded by the colonial legacy, failed to
recognize the vibrancy and polyvocality of Islam as a religious, legal, and cultural
tradition. They viewed the tradition as stagnant and intolerant of intellectual
creativity and reflection, and they completely overlooked Muslim women's
participation in its formation, transmission, and preservation. [2] Moreover, the
perception that the Islamic tradition is inherently oppressive toward women, and
that veiling is an outward sign of that oppression, is a product of the colonial
era. [3] Relinquishing one's Muslim identity, or at least confining any articulation of
that identity to the private sphere, came to signify one's acknowledgment of what
was perceived as the exclusively backward and patriarchal worldview inherent in
Islamic religion, law, and culture. The ways Muslim women in particular were
"remade," or participated in their own "remaking," in accordance with Western
models as part of the colonial project has recently been highlighted. [4] The extent
and significance of Muslim women's religious participation has only recently
come to light. The innovative ways women practitioners adapt their religious
activities in ways that promote their liberation from male-dominated hierarchical
structures has constituted an important scholarly focus. These activities have
been commonly perceived as forums where practitioners can escape from
these structures and process their daily encounters with them. [5] More recently,
scholars have begun to characterize Islamist women's activities as significant
sites of female agency, a concept once reserved by feminists for women who
openly or obliquely undertake forms of resistance to patriarchal ideologies and
structures (Badran 2002; Mahmood 2005; Sadiqi 2003). In a parallel fashion,
the growing number of Muslim women today advocating the preservation of the
Islamic religious, legal, and cultural tradition by articulating revisions to former
approaches to the two central sources of Islamic doctrine and practice, the Qur'an
and *ahadith*, or official compilations of reports on the Prophet Muhammad's
exemplary words and deeds, have recently been characterized as pioneers, and
labeled Islamic feminists. [6]

Arguing that this recent rise in the audibility of Muslim women's voices is a sign of continuity rather than novelty, I briefly highlight some of Muslim women's historical contributions to the vibrancy and polyvocality of the Islamic tradition. I assert that Muslim women have served historically as "agents of change," by actively participating in the formation, preservation, and revision of the Islamic tradition in their local contexts through their creative input in the spheres of religious scholarship, education, and ritual. This chapter illustrates this historical agency by investigating the ways Ishelhin women actively participated in the proliferation of Islamic knowledge among the Tashelhit-speaking inhabitants of the Sous region of southwestern Morocco.[7] They incorporated elements of Islamic doctrine and practice into existing rituals of pre-Islamic origin, further expanding and enriching this local Islamic tradition.[8] Furthermore, serving as scholars, teachers, poetesses, and ritual leaders in a regional Sufi educational initiative, Ishelhin women creatively intertwined Islamic doctrine, practice, and values with remnants of centuries-old religio-cultural beliefs and practices regarding women, their communal roles, and their religious expression to produce a local tradition of Islamic educational and ritual practices. Today's remnant rituals serve as sites for the ongoing renegotiation of local Islamic identity and gender roles and status.

Women and the transmission of Islamic knowledge

The transmission of Islamic knowledge, according to much of the scholarly literature, especially pre-1990s, was deemed an exclusively male, repetitive, and unreflective endeavor. Recent scholarship has begun to resurrect the multi-level, creative, and "polyvocal" character of this transmission process (Berkey 2007; Chamberlain 1994; Eickelman 1992; Messick 1993; Nasr 1992). While a vast majority of scholarly studies of the transmission of Islamic knowledge continues to focus on the central male participants, the *'ulama*, or Muslim scholarly elite, explorations of the interaction, linkages, and mutual exchange between this scholarly elite and the masses, and of the impact of each of these two groups on the lives and worldviews of the other, are on the rise. Recognition of the Sufi affiliation of members of the *'ulama* is increasing, as is the acknowledgment of the significance of this affiliation. The role of Sufis in the transmission of Islamic knowledge is particularly notable outside the heartland territories of the Muslim world (Dudoignon 2004; Elboudrari 1993; Reese 2004). Educational initiatives undertaken by Sufis in these former frontier regions were widespread and essential for proliferating Islamic knowledge among the non-Muslim inhabitants in the early periods following the advent of Islam to these regions. A common means for ensuring this proliferation was popular Sufi poetry in local languages (Schimmel 1982,1985). This popular religious poetry, and its employment in the spread of Islamic doctrine, practice, history, and lore, has begun to gain wider recognition. Women's participation, however, continues to be overlooked altogether, or characterized as insignificant.[9] Only recently have scholarly studies begun to tangentially explore women's participation on a variety of levels, and to acknowledge its significance (Berkey 1992, 2001, 2003; Chamberlain 1994).

Already during the lifetime of the Prophet Muhammad at Medina, women served as crucial repositories of Qur'anic verses and *ahadith*. Along with transmitting these central sources of sacred knowledge among the members of the earliest Muslim community, they analyzed and discussed their meaning. They collaborated with the Prophet Muhammad in negotiating significant roles for women within the community through their inquiries, comments, and proposals regarding these sources. Muslim women's role as *ahadith* transmitters continued beyond this crucial formative phase into the medieval period. Male scholars attended their *halqas*, or teaching circles held in mosques, and collected *ijazas*, or certificates of successful completion of training, from these prominent women scholars. Highly trained women from scholarly families, but also self-taught women from a variety of socio-economic backgrounds, ventured into even more public spaces, such as open-air religious pilgrimage festivals, to instruct mixed-gendered audiences from a variety of backgrounds. Their instruction, centering on *ahadith* and the tales of the prophets, was enhanced by oral commentaries of their own authorship (Berkey 2003). Some women studied *fiqh*, or Islamic jurisprudence, when it emerged as the queen of the Islamic sciences (Berkey 1992; Roded 1994). Of the relatively small number of women who completed training in *usul al-fiqh*, legal methodology, some went on to issue official legal decision, either in conjunction with male colleagues or independently (Roded 1994). Women more commonly studied *furu' al-fiqh*, guidelines for worship and interpersonal transactions, which they taught to other women from scholarly families, as well as to illiterate women. In women's *ribats* and *zawiyas*, or Sufi centers, over which these highly educated women presided, they directed and taught in educational programs of their own design and led their women students and followers in *dhikr*, or Sufi remembrance ritual (Berkey 1992; Cornell 1998; Ibn Ibrahim 1983).

Women's most significant contribution to the transmission of Islamic knowledge was precisely in their function as links between the scholarly circles and the general population. Educational campaigns initiated by Sufi scholars in an effort to ensure the proliferation of Islamic knowledge among local illiterate inhabitants, Muslim and non-Muslim, in their regions spawned the development of several forms of women's participation. Institutionalized roles, such as that of *otins*, or Uzbek and Tajik women who served as religious experts, teachers, and ritual leaders, emerged within one such Sufi educational campaign in Central Asia (Fathi 1997; Kamp 2006; Kleinmichel 2003; Kraemer 2002). Institutional structures, such as the network of women's mosques in China, provided another means for their participation (Jaschok and Jingjun 2000). Sufi poetry in local languages, often composed specifically for this purpose, served as didactic tools for the instruction offered by women (Kleinmichel 2003; Kraemer 2002). Sometimes women undertook campaigns independently using available Sufi poetry in their local language. The nineteenth-century Tatar women's campaign to convert local women in the Middle Volga region to Islam constitutes one example

(Kefeli 2001). In other contexts, women created their own didactic poetry for this purpose, such as in northern Nigeria where the renowned Qadiri woman scholar Nana Asma'u composed a body of didactic poems in Hausa and Fulfulde for the women's instruction in her region (Boyd and Mack 2000). This Sufi didactic poetry, composed for popular audiences, was often more explicit in its imagery and style than classical Sufi poetry. It served as a means of "translating" Islamic and Sufi doctrine, practice, history, and lore into local modes of expression, linguistically and culturally. A common mode for the transmission of this poetry was communal ritualized chanting, giving birth to rituals, many of which are still performed today.

Ritual constitutes a significant site for Muslim women to participate in the creation of local "translations" of the Islamic tradition, an area of their participation that remains relatively unexplored. The number and variety of Muslim women's rituals across the globe today give evidence to the extent of their "translation" work. These women's rituals can be divided into two broad categories. The first category encompasses rituals that were created in the early stages after the arrival of Islam to the local contexts where these rituals are performed today. These rituals served as an integral part of Sufi initiatives to spread Islamic knowledge in newly Islamized territories. These initiatives were particularly common in non-Arabic-speaking settings, and Sufi poetry in local vernaculars served as the ritual texts. Thus, these women's rituals were instrumental in endeavors to "translate" Islamic knowledge into local modes of thought and expression. Through these rituals, and their poetic texts, the women practitioners intertwined elements of Islamic doctrine, practice, history, and lore with local beliefs, practices, and modes of expression. These women performed the significant task of molding these elements to create local Islamic traditions.

An example of this type of ritual is the widely performed *mawlid*, or *mevlud*, meaning birth, which celebrates the birth of the Prophet Muhammad. Muslims throughout the world commemorate the Prophet's birth in various ways during the week in the Islamic calendar when the Prophet Muhammad's birthday actually falls. By contrast, in some contexts, such as Turkey (Tapper and Tapper 1987), the Balkans (Sorabji 1994), and Central Asia (Kleinmichel 2003; Kraemer 2002), *mevlud* was and still is celebrated in gender-segregated communal rituals, which are held periodically throughout the year. In these locations, *mevlud* consists of the chanting of long poems in local languages that relate important events from the Prophet Muhammad's life. Though similar, some aspects of *mevlud* are regionally specific. In parts of Central Asia for example, *otins*, mentioned above, preside over the *mevlud*, performing it in the homes of local women who invite them in conjunction with the celebration of rites of passage of family members (Kleinmichel 2003; Kraemer 2002). Like a variety of other women's communal rituals found elsewhere, *mevlud* served as a site for the "translation," of the Islamic tradition into local modes of expression. The rituals created for the transmission of the didactic poems composed by Nana Asma'u, mentioned above, constitute another regionally specific example (Boyd and Mack 2000). As these examples illustrate, Muslim women participated significantly as producers and propagators of local Islamic traditions, contributing to the production and propagation process through their communal rituals, and in some cases their own poetic compositions.

The second category consists of women's rituals that existed prior to the advent of Islam. Local women practitioners revised these rituals over time by incorporating Islamic beliefs and practices. One example is a ritual performed by Farsi speakers, of which two Islamized versions exist today. *Sofreh*, or tablecloth, is the name given to this ritual in Iran today (Torab 2005), and *mushkulkushod*, or problem solving (Kleinmichel 2003; Kraemer 2002), designates the version held in Uzbekistan and Tajikistan. Both appear to have originated from the same votive ritual. Performed by a woman intermediary, both versions center on a ritual meal and on the spiritual mediumship of two female patrons. These patrons were responsible for transmitting requests made by supplicants to a higher being, and to God in the Islamized versions in both contexts today. While these patrons are believed to have originally been goddesses or spirits, they are held to be *jinn*, or spiritual beings acknowledged by Islam, in today's Iranian version (Torab 2005), and the pious maternal aunts of the founder of the Naqshbandi Sufi Order, Baha' ud-Din Naqshband (1389), in the Central Asian context today (Kleinmichel 2003; Kraemer 2002). These rituals, like many other exclusively women's rituals still performed throughout the world, were Islamized by their women practitioners. The rich and complex intermingling of former practices with elements of Islamic doctrine, practice, history, and lore found in these rituals constitutes an important contribution of Muslim women as historical "agents of change" in their local contexts.[10]

Both of these types of rituals, which can be found among Ishelhin women in southwestern Morocco's Sous region, constitute the primary focus of the remainder of this chapter. The following section outlines some of the basic elements of the region's pre-Islamic religio-cultural heritage, the traces of which are still evident in daily life practices, including two remnant rituals that were Islamized over time by local women, and exemplify rituals of the second type. The subsequent sections provide background on the regional Sufi educational initiative and Ishelhin women's contributions to it, as well as on elements of the indigenous poetic tradition that were incorporated into the initiative's didactic poetry. Citing couplets from the poetry chanted in Ishelhin women's rituals, which developed in the initiative, the final sections illustrate some of the ways in which the rituals, which belong the first type, bear traces of both sources of influence, the regional religio-cultural heritage and Islamic doctrine and practice. Subject to ongoing alteration, these rituals constitute spaces where the practitioners perpetuate their role in the revision of their local Islamic tradition.

Ishelhin women's religious expression: wombs, looms, and poems

Two communal women's rituals conducted today, which exemplify the second type, constitute Islamized remnants of beliefs and practices that existed among the Imazighen inhabitants of North Africa prior to the advent of Islam. Precise details about these religious beliefs and practices are scarce. However, elements of them are observable in the daily lives and religious rituals of Ishelhin, or the primary Imazighen inhabitants of southwestern Morocco's Sous region. Drawing on fieldwork findings and two contemporary sources (El Mountassir 2004; Becker 2006), this section describes these elements, and the two communal rituals situated within them.

Fertility was a central theme in the earlier religious beliefs and practices of the Ishelhin and other Imazighen. Its centrality is still evident in the material culture, religious rituals, and literary expression of Ishelhin women. Originating with an emphasis on the female body and its capacity to produce, bear, and nurse children, fertility, by extension, was understood to encompass the productive capacity of the land. Mountains, rocks, rivers, and springs were locations and sources of spiritual power. Women were considered repositories and guardians of life and sustenance deriving from their bodies and from the land. Crafts and poetry were integral to the cultural articulation of this theme in daily life, as well as in rituals. Rituals served to preserve the fecundity of both the female body and the land, and the sustenance produced by them.

Ishelhin women's lives revolved around the production, preservation, and perpetuation of life and sustenance through their practical tasks and religious ritual expression. In addition to bearing and nursing their children, Ishelhin women were responsible for food production at all levels, including agricultural and animal husbandry tasks, as well as the organization, furnishing, and maintenance of the home. They produced household items and articles of attire through weaving, jewelry making, and pottery production. The products of these crafts bore symbolic representations of the theme of fertility through the colors and shapes integrated into their decorative elements (Becker 2006). Their daily life activities, which centered on the performance of these crucial communal roles, were replete with ritualized acts symbolically articulating these women's roles. Likewise, rituals were enacted using items produced and used in daily life.

Beliefs and ritualized acts connected to looms and weaving were central to the articulation of the theme of fertility. On the one hand, the role of the loom in the production of a piece of cloth was symbolically equated with the role of the womb in the production of offspring. On the other hand, the various phases in the weaving of a piece of cloth paralleled stages in the life of a human being. The initial attachment of the vertical loom thread signified birth, and the cutting of the warp threads death. This symbolic signification of weaving and the loom linked women's reproductive and creative powers, and their roles in the articulation and propagation of local identity and the preservation of the family and tribe (Becker 2006). With the advent of Islam, Ishelhin women in many parts of the region modified aspects of the beliefs undergirding these practices to adapt them to their understanding of Islamic beliefs and values. One example is a ritualized act for ensuring the virginity of unmarried girls, which is highly valued in Islam. By passing through a small opening in the threads before a piece of cloth is removed, the virginity of the unmarried girl will be protected until she is ready to marry. In preparation for her marriage, the unmarried girl passes through the loom threads once more to release her from this state of protection. This ritualized act reinforces the perceived connection between the womb and the loom.

The chanting of poetry was and still is integral to the performance of ritualized acts in daily life. It is a common feature of the execution of domestic tasks, especially when carried out in groups. Composed and retained in oral form by the women, poetry was also a central element of two women's communal rituals of distant historical origin still performed in parts of the Sous region today. These two rituals, belonging to the second type, bear the imprint of the earlier religio-cultural heritage articulated through the material culture, texts, and practices found in them.

The first ritual, known locally as *belghunja*, referring to the large wooden soup ladle which is central to the ritual, is a women's group ritual performed spontaneously a couple of times a year. Its original purpose was to ensure adequate rainfall, and therefore the fecundity of the land. Women practitioners in some locations today emphasize the ritual's role in guaranteeing the fecundity of the female members of their community. A large wooden soup ladle, wrapped in multiple layers of colored cloth and adorned with jewelry to look like a bride according to local wedding tradition, is paraded through the streets. The women participants chant poetic couplets in unison, punctuating the rhythm of their chanting by clapping their hands or beating on hand drums. According to the couplets chanted, the symbolic bride serves as an intermediary presenting the community's request for rainfall to God. The procession ends at the site of a nearby river or spring into which the symbolic bride is immersed headfirst.[11] The ritual derives from the system of religious beliefs and practices originating prior to the advent of Islam. Formerly, the request for rainfall was central, and this request was addressed to a local fertility deity. Today, the fecundity of female community members is central, and God is the one to grant this fecundity. The women practitioners revised this centuries-old ritual to fit it into the broader framework of today's life conditions, and, more importantly, of the ritual practices constituting their local Islamic tradition.

The second ritual, referred to locally as *agharda*, meaning mouse, is a parallel women's communal ritual performed once a year in the early spring. Originally, it was intended to protect the grain formerly stored in large communal storage spaces from rodents or other pests.[12] Before the existence of these granaries, the ritual is believed to have served to guarantee a successful growing season, by protecting the crops in the field from pests. Today, with these granaries no longer in use, its purpose, according to local women practitioners, is to ensure that all the members of the community will have sufficient food to eat throughout the coming year. Chanting poetic ritual texts in unison, the women beat on hand drums or clap as they walk to the edge of the residential area. Standing just outside the town wall, they gather stones from the ground and throw them forcefully in front of them, symbolically chasing away mice, rats, birds, or any other pests that might damage grain growing in the field or stored in granaries. Again, the ritual texts have been modified to address God instead of a former deity, making possible the ritual's inclusion into the broader regional religio-cultural tradition defined as Islamic.

Ishelhin women constituted sources of knowledge of the central religio-cultural beliefs regarding the production and preservation of life and sustenance, as well as of the techniques for the practical application of these beliefs in daily life activities and in ritual. They articulated these beliefs through various modes of creative expression. These modes took a tangible form in articles of attire and furnishings in their homes. The women gave expression to these beliefs through the decorative elements found in the products of their weaving, jewelry making, and pottery work. Intangible articulations are found in images in the poetry they composed and performed in daily life and ritual. They were recognized for their expertise in these significant areas of religio-cultural knowledge, and were also respected for their role as teachers. They preserved the knowledge and expertise for future generations by passing it on to their daughters.

It was these roles as experts and educators that gained women recognition for their participation in the process of creating a local Islamic tradition. Ishelhin women enhanced and supplemented their former beliefs and practices by intertwining them with Islamic doctrine, practice, history, and lore. The product is a rich and complex religio-cultural tradition, which they perceive as belonging to their local Islamic tradition.

Ishelhin women and the localization of Islam: scholars, teachers, and poetesses

The acknowledgment of women's longstanding central roles as religious experts, transmitters of religious knowledge, poetesses, and ritual leaders also found articulation during the formation of a first type of ritual, which originated after the advent of Islam to the region. This ritual form was created by Ishelhin women from scholarly families in the context of the educational campaign initiated by male scholars belonging to local branches of the Darqawi, Nasiri ,and Tijani Sufi orders between the sixteenth and eighteenth centuries.[13] The goal of the campaign was to transmit Islamic knowledge to the general Tashelhit-speaking population of the Sous region. This ritual is still central to women's religious ritual expression in the local Islamic tradition in many locations in the Sous region today. In spite of its relatively recent origin, this ritual bears the imprint of the centuries-old religio-cultural heritage of the region.

Ishelhin women from scholarly families were trained in Tashelhit religious didactic poetry composed by Ishelhin Sufi scholars in the context of this historical Sufi educational initiative. Like their male counterparts, these women memorized these didactic poetic texts, which encompassed *fiqh* manuals, *ahadith* compilations, and *nasihas*, or exhortatory treatises on a variety of topics regarding Islamic belief and practice. These didactic poetic texts provided these men and women, who were to serve as teachers in the initiative, with the necessary background in Islamic doctrine and practice. These men and women teachers used parts of these texts as instructional material in their lessons. Furthermore, they internalized another genre of religious didactic poems composed for memorization by the general population, which was to receive their instruction. Simpler in style, these long, popular Tashelhit religious didactic poems provided general knowledge on Islamic doctrine, practice, history, and lore. Some of these poems, which exist only in oral form today, were composed by later women teachers.

The first generation of women teachers received their training from male relatives who also served as scholars and teachers in the Sufi educational campaign. These women eventually trained other scholarly women, establishing a tradition for transmitting the instructional materials among women teachers from one generation to the next. The women devised their own programs of educational sessions for the transmission of Islamic knowledge to the rest of the female population in their local contexts. These sessions included lessons in the *fiqh*, *ahadith*, and *nasiha* materials, the chanting of the long, popular Tashelhit religious didactic poems, and the ritualized chanting of individual couplets from these poems.

This once elaborate system of religious education is in recession today due to a number of factors including the development of the national public education system. In many locations, the educational practices were detached from the male-dominated Sufi orders. They were moved from their two original locations in the large residences owned by scholarly families and *zawiyas*, or Sufi centers, to local sanctuaries dedicated to local pious men and women. The chain of transmission of knowledge among the generations of women teachers is gradually disappearing, and the educational component of the sessions has been discontinued in many locations. The sessions were transformed into a form of communal worship ritual consisting of the chanting of the long, popular didactic poems and couplets excerpted from them. These rituals are still commonly held by autonomous groups of women throughout the region. Headed by a ritual leader, the variety characterizing them is increasing as the rituals undergo revision to meet the changing needs and expectations of today's women participants.

In spite of its recent origin and ongoing revision, this ritual form still bears the imprint of the local religio-cultural heritage, as well as traces of the process of "translating" Islamic knowledge into local modes of expression that was integral to its creation. The men and women authors of the long, popular didactic poetic texts contributed significantly to this process, as did the generations of women who participated in the creation and revision of the ritual form. Serving as teachers, religious experts, ritual leaders, and poetesses, these women perpetuated the long tradition of women's religio-cultural roles as religious experts, poetesses, and transmitters of knowledge and expertise that had been central to the local religio-cultural heritage since the pre-Islamic period.

Amarg: oral poetry and longing

Traces of the local pre-Islamic religio-cultural heritage found in this communal ritual tradition are particularly evident in its ritual poetic texts. The content and form of the ritual texts reflect the influence of poetic practices and themes that have a much earlier origin. This section draws on some of the poetic texts chanted in today's rituals to examine the traces still found in today's rituals.

Integral to Ishelhin women's roles as producers and guardians of religio-cultural knowledge described above was their role as poetesses. Oral poetry was one means of articulating this knowledge. The Tashelhit word *amarg* means both poetry and love. Poetry is understood among Tashelhit speaker as poetic texts composed and performed in oral form. In the local understanding, this word for love refers to a sense of longing for something that is absent, unattainable, or lost. Among the centuries-old genres of Tashelhit oral poetry is one specific to women known as *tizrarin*, meaning couplets. The term *tizrarin* is used locally to refer to poetry chanted by women during the two women's rituals of *belghunja* and *agharda* described above, during the *ahwash*, or wedding celebration, as well as during the group execution of domestic or agricultural tasks (El Mountassir 2004). Consisting of series of couplets, this poetic genre, like other local genres, frequently centers on the theme of longing.

The thematic content and form of the poetic texts chanted in today's women's rituals conform to the parameters of this poetic genre. The long, popular Tashelhit religious didactic poems composed initially for the educational sessions consist of multiple series of couplets, which are broken up into segments by refrains. In addition, today's rituals include the chanting of individual Tashelhit couplets extracted from the poems, which the women repeat multiple times, in a similar fashion to the local wedding musical performance tradition, but also to the Sufi *dhikr*, or remembrance ritual, with which they share their ultimate intent. Thus, the form, rhyme, and rhythm of these poetic texts and their ritual performance bear the imprint of a centuries-old tradition and genre of women's poetic expression.

The content of the long, popular Tashelhit religious didactic poems chanted in the rituals, though Islamic, resonates with some themes commonly found in the centuries-old Ishelhin women's poetic tradition including the central one of longing. The poetic texts provide information on Islamic doctrine, practice, history, and lore. Sometimes in the form of stories, other times providing explanations of a variety of Islamic doctrinal and practical topics, they give evidence to their origin as instructional material. Nonetheless, today's rituals are ultimately considered occasions for remembering God, as expressed in the following self-referential couplet:

The abundant food in the mountains attracts the moose.
The gathering in honor of God is what we seek, O My Friends[14] (of God).[15]

Integrally connected to this intent is the central theme of honoring the Prophet Muhammad by remembering events in his life and his roles in the broader community of Muslims. The refrains repeated intermittently throughout the chanting of all of these poems regardless of the main topic underscore the significance of these roles and events by referring to the Prophet's titles related to them, as in the following refrain:

> Blessings be upon you, O Prophet and Master of Buraq,
> O Intercessor, O Messenger of God, we long to join you.[16]

Besides his role as Prophet, the first line mentions his title Master of Buraq. This title makes reference to the Prophet's nightly journey when he rode on the back of the white steed named Buraq to the Seventh Heaven accompanied by the Angel Gabriel. The second line recognizes the Prophet's important role as intercessor on the Day of Judgment providing assistance to humans in the attainment of salvation. The second line ends with the theme of longing, which is often connected to the love and respect for the Prophet articulated in the ritual poetry.

Remembrance of the Prophet brings relief from the pain and suffering connected to the love and longing that is felt for him. The pain and suffering of longing for him are experienced physically and mentally, as expressed in the following couplet:

> Fatima, your father has taken away our sanity,
> And our health. We are lost in the wilderness from the pain of longing.[17]

In this couplet, the complaints of discomfort are addressed to the Prophet's daughter Fatima, with whom he had a close relationship. Likewise, the following couplet, which articulates the intense love and longing as a potential source of physical distress and of feelings of confusion and disorientation, is addressed to Fatima:

> Fatima, victorious is he who has seen your father and remains well.
> I fear getting lost in the forest of longing for him.[18]

Equal to the intensity of the discomfort is that of the joy found in contemplating, meditating on, and remembering the Prophet, as articulated in the following couplet:

> He is dear to me, the Prophet Muhammad
> When I remember him, it makes my heart rejoice.[19]

The second line underscores remembrance of the Prophet as a source of relief, a source of joy.

Amarg became the medium for Ishelhin women's "translation" of Islamic doctrine, practice, history, and lore into a local mode of religio-cultural expression.

It provided the form and the central theme of longing that pervades the rituals today as in the past. It offered the means for rendering the new Islamic content accessible and meaningful, linguistically, religio-culturally, and emotionally, facilitating the integration of these rituals into the broader framework of religio-cultural expression in the region.

Female power: sacred and profane

Another important theme in the ritual poetic texts chanted by Ishelhin women in their communal rituals, historically and currently, is that of female power. The articulations of this theme resonate both with the pre-Islamic beliefs and practices of the region and with aspects of Islamic doctrine and practice. Deceased pious men and women, to whom sanctuaries have been dedicated throughout the Sous region and elsewhere in Morocco, as well as in other Muslim contexts, can also provide relief from the pain caused by longing for the Prophet, as well as other sources of pain and suffering:

O Lady 'A'isha Tahir, O Pious One,
Open the springs for the friends (of God) to drink.[20]

According to this couplet, the relief from suffering that results from visiting the sanctuaries of pious men and women, such as that of Lady 'A'isha Tahir, derives from drinking spring water. Drinking spring water, understood figuratively here, provides spiritual refreshment and *baraka*, or spiritual power. As the couplet implies, the male and female patrons of the sanctuaries control the flow of this spiritual refreshment, and of *baraka*. The role of water as the source of relief provided by the exemplary pious men and women resonates with the centrality of water as the source of life, sustenance, and wellbeing, and with the religious ritual roles of women in perpetuating its flow, ensuring rainfall and the fecundity of the land, in the local religio-cultural heritage. The sanctuary that Lalla 'A'isha Tahir shares with her father in southwestern Moroccan town of Tiznit is one of four sanctuaries where the women's rituals are held in that town. Exemplary pious women, who are honored by sanctuaries throughout Morocco, though fewer in number, are considered equal to pious men in their status and ability to provide relief to those in need. The recognition of this woman as possessing the power to heal, and venerating her through the visitation of her sanctuary, resonate with the role of the fertility goddess of the local pre-Islamic tradition.

Likewise, motherhood figures prominently in the poetic ritual texts, both as a physical source of life and sustenance, of knowledge and of power. The following verses are found in a section of a well-known long, popular Tashelhit religious didactic poem entitled *Bahr ad-Dumu'*, or the Ocean of Tears.[21] The section of the poem entitled "All the Good Given by God to Humanity in This World" places the processes of gestation, birth, and breast-feeding, as well as the organs of the female body involved in these processes, among the wonders of creation which should be admired, valued, and appreciated:

> With closed eyes and mouth, you received nourishment through the umbilical cord,
> Until God made you emerge from the tightness into the expanse of the world.
> He put milk in your mother's two breasts for you…
> Your father and mother were happy when you were born.
> He filled them with the tenderness and desire needed to raise you.
> He made them love you, even when you were 'dirty.'

Interestingly, it states that God instills mothers, as well as fathers, with love for their children, and with the desire to care for and raise them in spite of the burden and hardships that these tasks entail. The section continues with several verses glorifying the boundlessness of motherly love, and the recognition and respect due mothers from their children. By including women's unique physical and emotional capacities as mothers among the wonders of God's creation, the poem intertwines the emphasis on fertility and motherhood in both the local pre-Islamic and Islamic traditions.

Similarly, another poem assigns status and power to a woman in her role as mother. This poem describes the Prophet's intercession in the case of a man, who, upon his death, is unable to recite the *shahada*, the profession of faith, which is necessary for entrance into Paradise. The Prophet sends the man's friends to bring his mother for questioning:[22]

> Indeed, the friends went to the old woman.
> They told her that the Prophet Muhammad, the Messenger
> Requested that she come to him. 'If you cannot,' they said,
> 'He said that he would come to you.'

The old woman agrees to go to the Prophet. Upon her arrival, he asks her about her son's wrongdoings during his lifetime. She explains that his behavior was reprehensible in only one way. As he attained adulthood, he sometimes neglected his duty to show her love and respect.

> This, O Prophet, Muhammad, O Messenger, the heart cannot accept:
> Was it not, O Prophet, my right (as mother) to be recognized by him?
> I bore him for nine months, my stomach swollen.
> I breastfed him on my lap for two years.[23]

The Prophet acknowledges this wrongdoing and begins to prepare for the man's punishment. Realizing the fate of her son, she takes pity on him and forgives him, enabling him to avoid the punishment. In these verses, the old woman is shown great respect, and she wields considerable power, in several ways. Not only does the Prophet offer to come to her, if she is unable to come to him, but he agrees with her that it is her right as mother to receive the utmost love and respect from her son even after his attainment of adulthood. Moreover, the woman is the source of knowledge about the man's behavior during his lifetime, and the power to influence her son's fate is placed in her hands. The image of motherhood in this poetic text reflects an intermingling of local historical values regarding fertility and women's central communal roles as producers and guardians of life and sustenance, as well as sources of communal knowledge, in this case of personal history, with the value placed on motherhood, and all the roles it entails, in Islam.

Amarg became the medium for Ishelhin women's "translation" of Islamic doctrine, practice, history, and lore into a local mode of religio-cultural expression. It provided the form and some of the thematic content for the poetic texts that are central to today's Ishelhin women's rituals. It rendered the new Islamic content accessible and meaningful, linguistically, religio-culturally, and emotionally, facilitating the integration of these rituals into the broader framework of religio-cultural expression in the region.

Conclusion

Ishelhin women, like other Muslim women throughout history, have contributed significantly to the preservation of the vibrancy and polyvocality of the Islamic religious, legal ,and cultural tradition across the globe. They "Islamize" beliefs and practices originating before the advent of Islam to their region, and participate in the local Sufi educational initiative as poetesses, teachers, and ritual leaders. Forging a link between the scholarly Islamic tradition in their local contexts and their religious, cultural, and linguistic heritage, passing knowledge to female members of the general population, they serve as "translators" of Islamic doctrine, practice, history, and lore into their local vernacular, both linguistically and religio-culturally. Their "translation" work has brought about the creation of a local tradition of women's communal rituals. Functioning as "agents of change," they have contributed significantly to transformations in their local contexts. The contemporary prevalence of Muslim women's communal rituals, and the absence of men's, underscores the historical extent of this function and its gender specificity.

The growing body of scholarship on the revision of existing rituals, as well as the creation of new ones (Andezian 1997; Raudvere 2003; Torab 2006), gives evidence to the continuation of this function and provides details on its parameters in specific contexts. This scholarship has brought to light the extent to which these rituals have become sites where the women practitioners can process and negotiate new transitional moments and contemporary issues and discourses, as well as formulate their own responses to and interpretations of these issues and discourses. Through these responses and interpretations, they are retaining or reinhabiting their roles as "agents of change" in their local contexts. The direct impact of the "change" that they are promoting may be most evident at the local level, but their perpetuation of these communal rituals, and their adjustment to address new needs and expectations, constitutes resistance to the penetration of other perspectives, restricting the success of movements, organizations, and institutions promoting these perspectives.

Notes

1 This couplet, one of many chanted in today's Ishelhin women's rituals, will be explained below.
2 A prominent example of a scholar who misunderstood Islamic education and neglected women's roles in it is Marshall G. S. Hodgson (1974).
3 Scholars highlighting this connection include Carl W. Ernst (2003).
4 Both dimensions of the process of "remaking" women are dealt with in the volume bearing this title edited by Lila Abu-Lughod (1998).
5 Examples include Sossie Andezian's (1997) study of a ritual created by Algerian women to process their exclusion from positions of leadership in and access to the main rituals of the Issawi Sufi Order, Mary Hegland's (1998, 2003) work on Pakistani women who build their self-esteem through participation in women's communal Shi'i rituals, and Willy Jansen's (1987) research on religious ritual and professional activities among marginalized women in Algeria.
6 Examples of prominent Islamic feminists include Amina Wadud and Shirin Ebadi.
7 The term Ishelhin is a transliteration of the local self-designation for the primary inhabitants of the Sous region of southwestern Morocco. It is the plural adjective and adjectival noun for speakers of Tashelhit, one of three Moroccan Berber dialects. Ashelhi, the masculine singular, Ishelhin, the plural, and Tashelhit, the feminine singular will be used in this chapter. To refer to Berbers more broadly, Amazigh, Imazighen, and Tamazight will be used instead of the term Berber, which is of foreign origin, non-specific, and wrought with negative connotations. The English word Berber derives from the Arabic term '*barbara*' signifying "those who babble or speak in a loud, chaotic manner," which was adopted from the Roman term '*barbarus*' designating "uncultured vagabonds living on the outskirts of the empire." The Roman term originated from the Greek term '*barbaros*' meaning "mumblers or speakers of an incomprehensible language." All of these terms portray Berbers and their language in a negative light.
8 The data presented in this chapter were collected during research carried out in multiple phases. The field research was made possible by an American Council of Learned Societies Fellowship (September 2002–May 2003) and a University of Kansas New Faculty General Research Fund Grant (June–July 2002), as well as a University of Kansas International Faculty Research Travel Grant (December 2004– January 2005) and Kansas African Studies Center Faculty Research Travel Grant (December 2001–January 2002). Support for the transcription and translation of the ritual texts was provided by the American Institute of Maghrib Studies (May–June 2003 and December 2003–January 2004). Support for publications was provided by two internal University of Kansas General Research Fund Grants (July 2003 and July 2005).
9 The only study of these Sufi religious educational initiatives in the Sous region of southwestern Morocco neglects the participation of Ishelhin women, claiming that it was non-existent, or at best insignificant (Boogert 1997).
10 Exclusively men's Sufi, Shi'i and *mevlud* communal rituals, which are all frequently paralleled by women's in the same context, but the extent and variety of opportunities for communal ritual observance available to women across the globe today do not exist for men.

11 See Becker (2006) for further details, including some of the couplets chanted by the women.

12 These details were collected from women ritual participants during fieldwork in the town of Tiznit in 2004 after the performance of the ritual.

13 The beginning point for these practices is not documented. See Rausch (2006, 2008), Boogert (1997) and as-Susi (1971) for more details on these educational practices, as well as the Tashelhit didactic poetic texts composed for use in them.

14 The Arabic word *'ahbab'* can be translated as friends or loved ones. It commonly refers to Sufis in the advanced stages of the quest for Divine Union. Here it is employed for those who attend the women's rituals.

15 The Tashelhit original reads: *hantifirdi hudrar udadn katiwimt, tamunt firbbi ukan ansigil alahbab.* The first verse refers to those who are preoccupied with material things, those who focus solely on their daily subsistence. The second verse makes reference to those for whom spiritual pursuits are more important, those who seek nourishment in spirituality. The gathering in honor of God refers to communal rituals dedicated to the remembrance of or meditation on God. This phrase could signify the *dhikr*, or Sufi remembrance ritual. In this couplet, however, it is self-referential, indicating the women's rituals, underscored by the use of "we" in the second verse, with "My Friends" referring both to "Friends of God," or Sufis, and to fellow women participants.

16 The Tashelhit original reads: *salat wa sallam 'alayk anabi buburaq, ayashafi' ar-rasul lillah nirja adidikanmuni.*

17 The Tashelhit original reads: *fatima babam ur anh ifi l-'aqli, ula lun nga ukan akhalawi s-umargi.*

18 The Tashelhit original reads: *fatima babam isirwa walli tizran, ksudh aijlu kfin awint ataganti.*

19 The Tashelhit original reads: *ya'iza dari an-nabi Muhammad, ihatadarah sfarh lkhatr.*

20 The Tashelhit original reads: *aywa lalla 'aisha dahr atashaikhti, arzmi l'ayun adsun lmuhibbin.*

21 This poem, composed by the famous Sufi scholar Muhammad U-'Ali Awzal in the early eighteenth century, is still well known throughout the Sous region. See Boogert (1997) for more details on this poem and its author.

22 The *shahada* is the first pillar of Islam, the profession of belief in the oneness of God and in Muhammad as His Messenger.

23 This poem, like the one from which the preceding excerpts were drawn, are of male authorship. However, some of the poetic texts chanted in Ishelhin women's rituals are reported to be of female authorship. For an example of a poem in this tradition composed by a woman see Rausch (2008).

15 Moroccan women contrabandists

Interferences in public space

Touria Khannous

Introduction

Women, through their involvement in contraband, are changing the space of Moroccan cities, particularly the Fes medina. In the traditional concept of the city, public space was the domain of men.[1] A woman entered it only if covered, veiled, and escorted by a man—for the place of women was in the home.[2] French colonialism and post-colonial secularization and globalization affected not only the economy, but also urban social patterns. This chapter seeks to clarify the realities facing women who partake in contraband activities.[3] Notably, it discusses how women, as individuals but also as members of collectives, actively develop strategies to participate in the contraband economy in Morocco. It aims to show further how contraband, as a manifestation of transnational capital, is changing Moroccan women's identity. Of equal importance, we must consider how women's dealings in contraband impact on the globalized reality of old Fes, whose many shops and markets attest to postmodern fragmentation. Fes represents less and less a local territorial culture, as more foreign goods and images flood through its gates, affecting the everyday lives of its inhabitants. As foreign products infiltrate and permeate Moroccan culture, an important question is: What effect will these women's new commercial endeavors have on local traditions, and how will they redefine the old medina?

The feminization of contraband

When we talk about the feminization of contraband, we usually mean that women in Morocco engage just as vigorously as men in contraband activities. Contraband is one of the many strategies used nowadays by low-income Moroccan women to secure resources and to provide for their dependents. It is necessitated by new obligations thrust upon Moroccan women and made possible by the demands of globalization and the "new economy." Although contrabanding for women remains more difficult than for many men because it drains away women's time and energy from obligations that men escape, women often have certain emotional and linguistic skills that translate into market language when necessary.[4]

The strengths and resourcefulness of Moroccan women (and of non-Western women generally) should not be underestimated. In her book *Doing Daily Battle: Interviews with Moroccan Women*, Fatima Mernissi recounts the story of a woman who migrated from the Middle Atlas Mountains to find a job in Rabat, where she later encountered severe difficulties in a commune in the suburbs. Mernissi then warns us that "it is necessary to avoid generalizing, to avoid projecting on poor women our own preoccupations and problems, and above all, to do our work as intellectuals. By this I mean: to develop our listening capacity, to be sure that we hear everything, even those things that don't fit into our theories and pretty constructs" (Mernissi 1989: 176). Mernissi's cautionary note is reminiscent of Chandra Mohanty's call to Western feminists to avoid stereotyping Third World women as passive and powerless victims, whose only means of liberation is Western feminism: "It is in this process of discursive homogenization and systematization of the oppression of women in the third world that power is exercised in much of recent Western feminist discourse, and this power needs to be defined and named" (Mohanty 1991: 54). Mohanty criticizes Western feminists' portrayal of Third World women as lacking in agency and suggests that women's subordination must be addressed within their own cultural context.

African feminists have also stressed that in order for African forms of feminism to be effective agents of change, they must incorporate women at the grassroots —that is, women of low socio-economic status, particularly the non-literate rural women and the urban poor. African feminist Obioma Nnaemeka insists that she has been inspired by the strength of the women she knows in her village of Agulua, "women who would plant their feet firmly on the ground and with arms akimbo look anyone (men included) in the eye and speak their mind without batting an eyelid" (Nnaemeka 1998: 2). Nigerian writer Flora Nwapa notes that she was inspired by the strong women of Igboland where she grew up. These were women who "were solid and superior women who held their own in society. They were not only wives and mothers but also successful traders who took care of their children and their husbands as well. They were very much aware of their leadership roles in their families" (Nnaemeka 1998: 13).

In traditional Western feminism, women have often been theorized as powerless victims exchanged between men. In "Women on the Market" Luce Irigaray notes that

> all the systems of exchange that organize patriarchal societies and all the modalities of production that are recognized, valued and rewarded in these societies are men's business. The production of women, signs and commodities is always referred back to men, and they always pass from one man to another, from one group of men to another. The workforce is thus always assumed to be masculine, and "products" are objects to be used, objects of transaction among men alone.
>
> (Irigaray 1985: 171)

Gendered constructs such as "breadwinner" and "housewife" have been central to modern Western definitions of masculinity, femininity, and capitalism. Even though many women do work outside the home for wages, the association of women with domestic roles, such as housewife, has become institutionalized. Women's identities thus are determined by men, who also exert economic domination over them. With the advent of global capital, Mernissi's and Mohanty's cautionary notes regarding the Third World woman are very relevant here. In order to highlight women's consciousness and agency, we need to recognize that women's identities are fluid rather than fixed, since women have been shown to be able to negotiate the boundaries of identity politics in some social contexts through their contribution in the economic and social spheres of their societies.

Within the Moroccan context, while we tend to think of women as marginalized figures, they are far from being peripheral to the unfolding of modern Moroccan history. Women have emerged from socio-cultural traditions, roles, and patterns prescribed for centuries by men, and increasingly carved out places for themselves in Moroccan society. Sadiqi and Ennaji offer examples of the situation of Moroccan women in the early post-independence era:

> Although upper and middle social classes in the fifties and sixties encouraged the education of girls, they considered the work of women, and hence their money, as a dishonor to the family. For these, women's education aimed at producing good housekeepers and child rearers, not money-earners. The public space was seen as a "dangerous" space where women might meet with men who were not part of the family. This explained the fact that work outside the home was considered inadequate or inappropriate for women.
>
> (Sadiqi and Ennaji 2006: 5)

But with the advent of globalization, women can now be seen serving food in restaurants, or dealing with customers in shops, a sight hardly imaginable decades ago: "Women's work outside the home and migration (either from rural to urban areas or from Morocco to Europe) has created deep social mutations that resulted in more interactions between the public and private spaces and a re-establishment of men and women in a common space given their collective participation in social dynamics" (Sadiqi and Ennaji 2006: 11).

Contraband, as an informal sector, has widened the scope of available employment for women. Moroccan women's participation in the labor force through contraband has increased in recent years. Not only are these women engaging in contraband by placing themselves within the economic, cultural, and political context of Morocco, they are also at its center. Earlier representations of Moroccan women relegated them to the margins of history, outside postcolonial forms of capitalism. Passing contraband, they now prove to be vital links between women and capitalist enfranchisement, with profound economic impact. Individually, these women contribute to household support. In the aggregate, engaged in survivalist activities, these women mediate between their communities and globalization, becoming transnational economic agents and a collective force to be reckoned with.

Although the social effects of globalization on nation-states have remained for the most part construed in terms of masculinity, reconsideration of women's roles and strategies is overdue. As groups of women provide for themselves and their households, the question arises, How do they become female equivalents of (or come to rival and displace) male breadwinners? Contraband is a demonized and criminalized activity according to the male-dominated state; yet, women continue to sell products just for subsistence. They break the law to put food on the table. These resourceful women have a work ethic, because such businesses on the side (like traveling and selling clothes and other products people need) enable them to sustain their families. In their book *Empire*, an illuminating analysis of globalization, Michael Hardt and Antonio Negri identify the imminent power of the poor person who is "in a certain respect an eternal postmodern figure: the figure of a transversal, omnipresent, different, mobile subject" (Hardt and Negri 2001: 174). It is important to emphasize that it is not just the rich who participate in the contraband trade. Most are poor women from the lower classes. As Elizabeth Fernea points out, high divorce rates in Morocco, as well as recent waves of immigration to Europe, have produced many women heads of households: "Absent fathers. Absent sons. This meant women-headed households and a real shift in the patterns of authority in the traditional Moroccan family" (Fernea 1998: 116). Not only divorce but also old age or incapacity of husbands has nudged women into the marketplace even as contrabanding provides opportunities for their independence. While the emancipation of women within global forces has conferred new powers, it has also imposed new burdens.

The women interviewed by one of my students all shared the same problem of having to support their husbands.[5] One woman who smuggles goods from Nador to Fes confesses that she does contraband because her husband is old and he therefore cannot work:

> I started smuggling goods more than 15 years back. I bring whatever I see suitable: clothes, shoes, food, cosmetics, etc. I have seven children, and if I don't work I will have to beg in the streets. Nobody helps, you know? Nobody at all.... This job is trouble, and they don't know that. One earns a few dirhams a week, and I usually borrow money when I have extra dues.... First I had to work in houses, but it was not the perfect job for me; then I met a lady in a "Hammam" who told me about smuggling. She encouraged me and said I should give it a try. I sold my earrings, got 1000 dirhams and then started doing contraband.
>
> (Interview 17)

In Morocco, harsh as it may seem to say so, it is thus in part the default or defection of men that has impelled poor, uneducated women into the public sphere to fill a niche in the market that involves contraband activities.

Women in the public sphere

Sadiqi and Ennaji argue that in traditional Moroccan society, "the public space is a men's space which dictates the social norms, while the private space is women's space. The two spaces are strictly dichotomized and interact in a dynamic way in the sense that one cannot exist without the other. It is true that women can be in some public spaces—for example, on the street, but they cannot stay there as men are encouraged to" (2006: 3). As Sadiqi (2006) argues, public and private spaces were formerly segregated and complementary. This is no longer the case today, where women seem to have a permitted or at least tolerated public space. More and more divorced, widowed, as well as married poor women are participating to a greater extent in Moroccan public space. Feminists such as Mernissi and Sadiqi emphasize the urbanization and mobility of the female workforce; they describe the daily presence of urban and rural Moroccan women in public space as they struggle to forge a future for themselves and their families.

The democratic ideal of the public space as a place where anyone has the right to participate without exclusion because of economic, social, political, or legal factors is a view that is increasingly becoming evident in Morocco, as citizenship is extended to men and women alike. The public sphere, as Jürgen Habermas indicates, is the realm where citizens can freely discuss issues of common concern. It is "the domain of our social life in which such a thing as public opinion can be formed" (Habermas 1996: 55). While Habermas's concept of the public sphere is a useful one for the purpose of this study, it has been criticized by philosophers and social scientists who see it as emphasizing a unitary, bourgeois public sphere that has effaced differences in culture and identity. Such critics have countered the dominant model of the bourgeois public sphere with the concept of a proletarian public sphere. American feminist Nancy Frazer, for instance, points out that it is only through these subaltern, counter-public spheres that inequalities come to light, and groups that are marginalized on the basis of class or gender are able to attain a voice. She adds that an "egalitarian, multicultural society only makes sense if we presuppose a plurality of public arenas in which groups with diverse values and rhetorics participate. By definition, such a society must contain a multiplicity of publics" (Frazer 1992: 126).

Poor, uneducated women in Morocco increasingly contribute to the public sphere by their involvement in contrabanding, which offers opportunities because of its simplicity. One woman from Nador describes the way she spends her day doing contraband. This is what she had to say during the interview:

> I work every day, and I make the same trip from Melilla to Nador daily. I go to the frontiers in the early morning at around 5 a.m., and I pick up four to six products such as shampoos, perfumes, toothpastes, etc. (I take up to five brands of each product), and then I come back to Nador around 7:00 a.m. By 9:00 a.m., I would have sold all my merchandise, and then I go home to look after my family.
>
> (Interview 8)

For such a woman, the economy offers a niche which has no prerequisites to entering.

Women's increasing participation in contraband in recent years, triggered by an ever-deepening crisis in Moroccan society and economy, changes the very nature of the market. In her book *Gender on the Market*, Deborah Kapchan asserts that in this altered market, over the past twenty years, women vendors are increasingly selling women's products to women in the marketplace. Kapchan argues that women-sellers "actually define the fashionable commodity for the developing middle class by introducing new and foreign items to the market" (Kapchan 1996: 56). Additionally, she notes that these women "by stepping into the public sector because of economic necessity, they exemplify self-sufficient women who are nonetheless marginalized because poverty has forced them into the public eye—and public ear as well" (1996: 56). These changes in women's economic activities signal these women's creation of their own public culture: "Women's physical presence in the marketplace grounds them in a new domain of discourse, while their speech indexes their emergent status in the public realm" (1996: 141).

Changing the space of the Fes medina

Women contrabandists were not the first to initiate change in the public realm, for few episodes are as dramatic as the transformation of the Fes medina in the annals of French colonialism. Khalid Bekkaoui illustrates very well such reimagining of the medina spaces as colonial ones in his essay "Fes Medina: Creation, Conquest and Contraband." Drawing upon old photographs and postcards, Bekkaoui points out that "As a visual symbol of the subjugation of the city, the colonizer decided to erect a new gate on the outer wall of the medina, next to the sultan's garden in *Fas Jdid*. Its massive size was deliberately conceived to rival the city's original gates; its architectural design invoked the Parisian Arc de Triomphe, with two visible crosses decorating each side of the gate. The gate was christened: Bab Boujloud, Porte des Français."[6] General Lyautey, Bekkaoui notes, later made the medina his primary residence in an attempt to convince the French and foreign tourists to come and settle in the old medina.

The French empire has globalized the old medina, for the French Bab Boujloud gate has now exposed the medina to new commercial activities, tourists, and traders, and thus opened it to a new global culture. The French revision of the medina space as a colonial one was an attempt to usurp sovereignty, a usurpation which demanded the physical change of the medina. Moreover the religious and colonial mappings of the old medina came into conflict when discord became endemic between the mosque and the French state, and indeed between the local secular elite and religious imams. Transformation of the old medina was carried out not only by the French but also by the secular local elite. The Fes medina was the birthplace of the secular nationalist movement and the Istiglal party, whose male leaders' decision to dismantle harem spaces and to open schooling to women was in part influenced by the French educational system.

Nowadays, it is the average local Moroccan woman who is claiming the space of the old medina, which she has entered by necessity and by the desire to reap the economic benefits of globalization. Women have always been in the market and at the forefront of the workforce; this is not a modern phenomenon. What has changed in Morocco, and in general all over the developing world with the processes of globalization and modernization, is that there has been a shift of the locale of their economic enterprises from the rural setting to the city. Since the late 1960s, the rural populations, including peasant women, have migrated and brought their small businesses to overcrowded cities that are already struggling with poverty and unemployment. It is also worth noting that the Fes medina is different from the rural areas where women have traditionally participated in the marketplace. The city of Fes has changed in recent years, losing its bourgeoisie to rural populations. Most wealthy families relocated to Casablanca and its once huge Jewish community migrated to Europe and to Israel at the end of the 1960s. In addition to the influx of rural people moving in, several other factors have affected the Fes medina. In the postcolonial era, Fes has had a hard time defining a market for itself. In the historic past, it was known as the imperial city, but now its important indigenous merchants have left. The city benefits little from tourism. It does not have a significant number of businesses and investment in economic sectors that generate money for the local populace. People must, therefore, employ themselves. With unemployment currently as high as 30 percent in some urban areas, the people of Fes have to rely on their own resources. Unemployment and poverty generate numerous street vendors and much more contraband activity than in other Moroccan cities, for people need low-cost commodities; and whenever there is demand, there is supply.

This shift to the city has also defined the kinds of products women are selling. The onslaught of new music, images, sounds, computers, and cell phones brought by them has secularized the Fes medina at an unprecedented scale. Women bring their wares, which range from food items to electronic devices, including, even at times, cigarettes and alcohol, and buyers await them in the Fes medina. Women selling contraband in the market or in stores they own comprise at least half of the marketplace population. The Fes medina has different business areas with a significant centralization of shops dealing in contraband goods sought by a specific clientele. Such shops and markets, spread out all over the city, are slowly taking over and transforming the space of the old medina.

Thus women are changing the city's everyday life and thereby exposing tensions and contradictions in Morocco's process of modernization. Tensions derive from dichotomies between more prosperous urban areas and the impoverished rural areas; from widening economic and social gaps between classes; and from the clearly evident gender inequalities. The everyday is thus of critical importance because it encompasses not only the city's leisure activities, entertainment, and cultural life, but also the most elemental, minutest routines such as eating, drinking, sleeping, etc. As contraband changes people's consumption patterns and lifestyle, new identities are formed and require adaptations.

Women contraband-vendors emerging into public culture define fashion by introducing commodities. These products range from foreign clothes, to electronics and mobile accessories, and they overshadow the traditional artifacts of old bazaars and famed ancient souks such as Al Attarin, Al Charratin, and Al Saffarin. Furthermore, contraband shrinks trading in local products which have historically given the Fes medina its traditional flavor. Fieldwork carried out by one of my students in the Fes medina underlines the way trading in the Fassi traditional carpet has been seriously affected. Contraband provides the Fes medina with carpets that are cheaper than the traditional ones. A still unanswered question is: To what extent is the collapse of traditional products like the Fassi traditional carpet indicative of cultural change in Morocco and of new consumerism trends? Circulation of foreign products fosters cosmopolitan consumers, which is apt to make the old space of the Fes medina look like other parts of the modern world. More dismaying still, to the locals, the mere presence of illicit contraband products like alcohol has "contaminated" what had been sacred space.

Beyond basic commodities like clothes, food, and furniture, contraband products represent cultural competition. The circulation of imported commodities such as films, tapes, and music videos that women transfer via contraband has shaped a new popular culture. Pop music, soap operas, and sporting events are now more accessible to the locals due to contraband. Moreover, local people have the global market coming to them in the form of foreign buyers interested not only in real estate (the traditional riads), but also in smuggled goods.

Women's adaptations to resist power

Central to the everyday life, and being the site from which many women engage with the world, the contraband market may also imply the need for rethinking the legal codes. In the market, illegal activity is evident and thriving. Yet contraband violates national and international trade agreements and copyright law. The contraband trade needs to be held accountable sometimes for piracy of foreign products, as well as for negatively affecting legitimate local goods. Test cases emerge. For instance, the American company Warner Brothers went to the market of Derb Ghalaf in Casablanca, with the intention of suing the merchants for pirating their films. The company finally realized that they could not sue these stores because their technology could not infiltrate the markets of Morocco. They also realized that the shops were local and poor; so filing a suit against them would damage a helpful local economy. Likewise, the individual stores and traders in the historic Fes medina form a tight and locally grounded community, an entity which would be impossible to infiltrate. They deal with modern commodities such as laptops and other electronic devices in a traditional way, accessible only to locals. Thus they remain untouched by the big corporations whose businesses they subvert. Such local trading communities are empowering to women who have been marginalized by poverty and lack of access to public services such as health care, education, etc. Attacking these communities would do more harm than good.

Meanwhile, contraband trade means risks for vulnerable women. When they engage in this trade, they are not protected by the state that criminalizes the activity. Such risks and impediments as police harassment, lack of infrastructure, crime, and unfair competition are shared among all these women despite their belonging to different age groups. Consider, for example, a sentiment expressed by an interviewed 44-year-old woman: "the most frequent sources of trouble are the authorities who stop the bus several times, and there's always the risk that they confiscate our goods. The policemen ask us to either give them bribes or they will keep our merchandise; thus the bus owners negotiate the sum of money to be given in advance, and they pay it from our own money" (Interview 14). It is women who are disproportionately stopped, interviewed, and searched for contraband by Moroccan Customs Service agents.

The profiling of women travelers can also be linked to historical and contemporary cultural images that criminalize women who travel on their own without male accompaniment. Since his coronation in 1999, King Mohammed VI has changed the laws regarding women who travel alone. In the new family code (Moudawana), women are guaranteed certain protections under the law. The 2003 reforms of the Moudawana have brought invaluable gains for Moroccan women, who have sprung from the margins of a patriarchal order to the center of a heated debate that heralds a new and democratic Moroccan society. However, women traveling alone are still often viewed with suspicion. Moroccan women who cross from Spain back over into Morocco are perceived by border guards as being out of "their place," and hence likely to be engaged in illicit activities. More women than men smuggle goods through customs, especially cigarettes and alcohol, since women can easily hide these items under their veils or djellabas. However, women are also more likely than men to bear the brunt of insults and harassment by the police, because they are viewed as vulnerable.

Interviews with these women reveal how gender shapes interaction with the police. Women typically report more police aggression and violence and express concern about police sexual misconduct:

> Once on one of my usual trips, and while pregnant in my seventh month, I rode the bus on one of those very hot days of summer. The cops entered into the bus, took the smuggled goods, and started asking me questions in a vulgar manner; when I resisted, one of them pulled me harshly and forced me to leave my seat; I was about to fall, and I begged them in vain. I am fed up with the humiliating insults of the police and the vulgar people on the road.
>
> (Interview 15–16)

These women prefer to deal in commodities rather than commodifying the body in prostitution. Searches, confiscations, and bribery are the cost of doing business.

Despite these deterrents, women are adept at a certain cunning that enables them to work the economic system to their advantage. These adaptations occur not in spite of the Moroccan authorities' control, but because of it. One woman admits that "in the past, when we were not required to have travel papers and passports, I used to cross the frontiers to Melilla, and I suffered from the same problem with the Moroccan police; the Spanish authorities used to turn the blind eye to me, but I had problems with the Moroccan ones, who used to take away my merchandise" (Interview 14–15).[7] To evade police scrutiny, some women adopt veiling. Wearing large djellabas or donning haiks or niqabs permits these women a freer mobility and thus greater access to contraband opportunities. Media reports indicate a rising number of women caught smuggling items hidden under their niqab, the black veil covering all but the eyes.

The situation of such Moroccan women is reminiscent of Algerian women who likewise used the veil to smuggle weapons during their country's fight for independence. Frantz Fanon in his analysis of women's involvement in the war speaks about the "instrumentalization of the veil." Contrary to common representations of the veil as a fixed signifier, Fanon shows that the veil is a changing signifier, which can be an empowering means for women in resisting domination. He describes veiled women carrying guns and bombs beneath their veils and passing them to male fighters. He also describes young Algerian women being able to pass through the controlled borders that separate the European city from the Kasbah (Fanon 1965: 40). In crossing borders, Moroccan women contrabandists are not, however, fighting for independence like the Algerian women; they are rather changing the world economy, and proving true what Hardt and Negri proclaim in their book on globalization when they state: "As the world market today is realized even more completely, it tends to deconstruct the boundaries of the nation-state. In a previous period nation states were the primary actors in the modern imperialist organization of global production and exchange; to the world market they appear increasingly as mere obstacles" (2001: 168–169).

Conclusion

In sum, while Moroccan women have gained more freedom and rights since the 2003 reforms of the Moudawana, they still face challenges that only men confronted in the past: supporting a family and finding work. Globalization and evolving mores have brought greater acceptance of women in the workplace. This acceptance, however, comes at a price. Ironically, those very markets that are now used as vehicles for expressing defiance in the face of patriarchal codes and for the social promotion of disadvantaged women are also sites of acts of violence against them. It remains a fact, nevertheless, that contraband, as a manifestation of transnational capital, is changing Moroccan women's identity and hinting at new directions for social change.

The 2006 interviews with Moroccan women contrabandists conducted by my student at the University of Fes reveal an extensive use of male discourse. Interviewees used the name of God multiple times and made mention of Islam to justify their vending and claim legitimacy even though contraband is by definition illegal. The following quotation from an interview with a woman who smuggles goods from Nador to Fes demonstrates that faith in God resolves many of the personal issues she has with participating in the contraband trade: "All I can do is resign to my fate. I don't love this job; my trips are the last thing I could praise. In fact, I thank God for having a well-paying, though humiliating, job. At least my children don't have to work or wait for charity from other people; I can provide them with what they need for school, food, and housing. Thanks to God indeed" (Interview 20–21).

Participating in contraband, these women appropriate traditionally male roles and realms. Additionally, and ironically, by justifying themselves on religious grounds, and by invoking God in their speech, they seek to legitimize their acts in a male-dominated space, where patriarchal religion remains powerful. A possible inference is that these women trust Islam as an egalitarian religion, and imply that women have mattered in the basic Text.

Notes

1 Contraband goods are by definition prohibited by law, and hence the term draws attention to why the goods are illegal and what prompts a law against dealing in them; by whom it was drafted; whose interests it protects; who it renders disadvantaged or vulnerable. There is a difference between dealing in banned substances (hence the "ban" of "contraband"), and dealing in commodities that support basic human life, like water, food, clothing, and shelter— entitlements that laws regulate and ban. In using the term contraband, this chapter is therefore indirectly calling attention to questions of justice as well as of lawfulness. Moroccan women practice contraband counter to state laws, and in breaking civil law, these women in a sense do embody resistance.
2 Fatima Mernissi has pointed out that Moroccan women were members of the Muslim space, but it was interior for them. Cf. to Fatima Mernissi. *Dreams of Trespass: Tales of a Harem Girlhood*. Reading, MA: Addison-Wesley, 1994.
3 I delivered a version of this chapter during a seminar entitled "The Contraband Modern in the Fes Medina" that was organized by the Ferguson Center for Asian and African Studies at Open University in September 2006.
4 In her book *Gender on the Market: Moroccan Women and the Revoicing of Tradition*, Deborah Kapchan examines how Moroccan women in the marketplace manipulate certain linguistic strategies to their advantage. Such language patterns, she argues, allow them to lay claim to male-dominated oratory as well as to the new feminine forms of exchange. D. Kapchan. *Gender on the Market: Moroccan Women and the Revoicing of Tradition*. Philadelphia: University of Pennsylvania Press, 1996, p. 66.
5 Excerpts from the interviews conducted by student Hind Salhi from Sidi Mohammed University in Fes will be cited in this chapter.
6 Khalid Bekkaoui delivered a version of this paper during "The Contraband Modern in the Fes Medina" seminar that was organized by the Ferguson Center for Asian and African Studies at Open University in September 2006. The paper is also available online.
7 Melilla and Sebta are two Moroccan cities which are occupied by the Spanish. The two cities are located on the Mediterranean coast and are populated by Spanish and Muslims (mostly Berbers).

16 The Orient within

Women "in-between" under Francoism

Aurora G. Morcillo

"I believe that being from Granada gives me a fellow feeling for those who are being persecuted. For the Gypsy, the Negro, the Jew ... the Morisco, who all granadinos carry inside of them."

Federico García Lorca, 1931

The history of Spain has been a gendered one. Since Roman times and throughout the Middle Ages the Iberian peninsula has remained in the margins of Christian European consciousness, "always the site of difference, always 'queer' Iberia" (Hutcheson and Blackmore 1999: 1). To the early modern period we might ascribe the creation of a mythic Spanish monolithic Catholic identity forged during the *Reconquista* and fully accomplished in 1492 with the expulsion of Muslims and Jews—the *other* religious groups that coexisted together with Christians for eight centuries. The cultural monolith established in 1492 by Isabella of Castile and Ferdinand of Aragon avowed Catholicism as the guiding force behind Spanish national identity. Such cultural monolith was re-enacted in the Civil War (1936–1939) to be restored and propped up after 1939 under Francisco Franco's dictatorship. Certainly, this prolonged understanding of Spanish identity led scholars inside and out of the country to see Spain as a European anomaly or a subaltern appendix at best.

Historians of the modern period followed the same line of thought when highlighting how the industrial and subsequent bourgeois revolutions had failed in Spain. Adrian Shubert and José Alvarez Junco remind us how "historians' shortcomings have been reinforced by trends emanating from the broader centuries-long Western culture in which Spain has been both demonized and 'orientalized'" (Alvarez Junco and Shubert 2000: 1). In this chapter I propose a gendered reading of the orientalization of Spain—an orientalization that Francoism reinvented during the Cold War with the regime's international rehabilitation. The second half of the chapter addresses the issue of Spanish women as agents of change in the context of this orientalized Spain and more specifically in the transitional period from autarky to consumerism in the 1950s. The 1950s are a period that represents, in Homi Bhabha's terms, an "in-between moment" when there is a redefinition of the regime's foundations and of gender relations and domesticity. This chapter intends to challenge the representation of women as victims under Francoism and proposes to utilize oral history to unveil the multiple acts of resistance of anonymous women in their everyday lives under the dictatorship.

By orientalization, I am referring here to the process of exotization of Spain in the Western cultural imaginary manufactured by Spanish and foreign writers alike. The exotization of Spain was possible because it was based on a long cultural tradition that had placed Spain in the margins of European imagination based on its Islamic and Jewish historical roots. Spain remained the "Other" due to a hybrid historical experience—eight hundred years of coexistence and warfare among "the people of the Book" but mainly between "moros y cristianos." Spain's location in the margins of European consciousness gave Spanish Catholicism a peculiar branding of its own. Such Catholicism led African American writer Richard Wright to refer to the country under Franco's rule as a sacred state not Christian but rather "pagan." Following the Pact of Madrid in 1953, an economic and military agreement with the United States, Spain entered modernity through the back door. The regime proclaimed itself the "sentinel of the west" in its fight against communism utilizing National Catholicism as the adhesive ideology. The 1960s economic plans favored the transition from autarky to consumerism. An avalanche of tourists visited Spain. Manuel Fraga Iribarne was appointed minister of information and tourism established in 1962. The slogan coined to attract visitors was "Spain is different." By setting themselves as the sentinel of the West and the guardians of eternal Christian values, with National Catholicism Francoist Orientalist/subaltern discourse was updated. Francoist propaganda reinvented republican dissidence—the reds—along with old long-learned oppositions—that of the infidel (Morales Lezcano 1990: 104).

The study of Spain's place in the European imaginary, promises to shed some light on the question of Europeanism/Westernness. As Gerard Delanty proposes "what is to be questioned is the idea of a European identity as a totalizing project" (Delanty 1995). Delanty examines how Europe is a cultural construction and cannot be regarded as a self-evident entity; rather Europe is a contested concept borne out of the conflict among the different European powers. So what we call Europe, Delanty reminds us, is a "historically fabricated reality" and "European identity did not exist prior to its definition and codification" (ibid.: 3).

Spain represents a key piece in this conflict to understand how Europeanism turned into a metaphor for modernity, whiteness, and Christian values. Enrique Dussel points out that it was in the fifteenth century with the colonial expansion of Portugal and Spain that we can talk of a first step towards modernity. Europe established itself as the "center" of the world—as the embodiment of universal values and truths (Dussel 2000: 470). The Enlightenment further developed the notion of "Eurocentrism." Hegel defined Europe as the beginning and end of history. Hegel identified a "number of Europes" but establishes that only the northern European nations possessed the modernizing force. According to Hegel there were even two Norths: the east (Poland and Russia), considered relatively negligible because of its relation with Asia; and the northwestern part, which he regarded as the motor of modernity. For Hegel, southern Europe, more specifically "the land of the South of the Pyrenees," namely Spain, lacked cohesion:

> Here one meets the lands of Morocco, Fas (not Fez), Algeria, Tunis, Tripoli. One can say that this part does not properly belong to Africa, but more to Spain, with which it forms a common basin ... when one is in Spain one is already in Africa. This part of the world ... forms a niche which is limited to sharing the destiny of the great ones, a destiny which is decided in other parts. It is not called upon to acquire its own proper figure.[1]

Spain remains Africa in the works of Spanish writers as well. José Cadalso wrote in 1773–1774 his *Cartas Marruecas*.[2] Published in the daily *Correo de Madrid* in 1784 they comprised 90 letters between three fictional characters that Cadalso describes as *Cartas escritas por un moro llamado Gazel Ben-Aly, a Ben-Beley, amigo suyo, sobre los usos y costumbres de los españoles antiguos y modernos, con algunas respuestas de Ben-Beley, y otras cartas relativas a éstas.*

Letter XI remarks on the similar custom between Morocco and Spain of locking women in a separate space:

> The news we had so far in Morocco of the social life of Spaniards we consider very good, because it is very similar to our own, and being natural in a man to evaluate following this rule the merits of other men. The women kept under many locks, the conversations among the men very private, their demeanor very serious [...] these particular customs are not so much the result of their climate, religion or government, as some may prefer, but rather the testimony of our past rule. It is in those customs where we see the survival of our supremacy, even more than in the presence of the buildings still standing in Cordoba, Granada, Toledo and elsewhere.[3]

Cadalso represents just one example of what some scholars call "Spanish Orientalism." In *Africanismo y Orientalismo Español*, a collection of articles on the subject edited by Victor Morales Lezcano in 1990, Spanish scholars addressed Edward Said's concept of "Orientalism" from within Spanish intellectual debates in the nineteenth and twentieth centuries. For to nineteenth-century Spaniards, who had read *Cartas Marruecas* what was "Oriental" was North African, and more specifically Moroccan. However during the nineteenth century neither Spain nor Portugal produced any studies that fit "Orientalism" in the way that the British and the French did. That is looking outside their geographical borders. Scholars and intellectuals contributed to the study of Muslim Spain and Spanish Islam utilizing as their guiding principle 1492 and the Christian "reconquest" of the Iberian peninsula.

Spain remained *orientalized*[4] in the European psyche throughout the nineteenth and into the twentieth century. In the first half of the nineteenth century, especially after the Napoleonic invasion (1808–1814), a plethora of American, British, and French memoirs and travelers' depictions of Spain (notably the American

Washington Irving's *Tales of the Alhambra*, along with works by Lord Byron, Victor Hugo, Theophile Gautier) were published creating an *imagined and enchanted community*.[5] Those Romantic accounts continued to depict a premodern untamed society much in the same way as the relation between the sexes had been played out for centuries.

Like a woman, Spain attracted the European virile-modern-rational ethos uttered by these authors. Like a woman, the travelers fancied Spain irrational and wildly passionate, mysterious and childish. Like a woman, Spain was different, the "Other," desirable yet not to be imitated. The best-known example of the "natural" Spanish woman was afforded in 1845 by Frenchman Prosper Mérimée with his novella *Carmen,* which became widely popularized by his fellow countryman George Bizet's operatic version in 1875 and prolonged the female stereotype into the twentieth-century European psyche. Mérimée's description of Carmen exudes the irresistible sexual power of the Spanish Gypsy woman. It implicitly predicts the fate of the novel's male character bound to succumb to her—the embodiment of his sexual fantasy.

> Her skin, though perfectly smooth, was almost of a copper hue. Her eyes were set obliquely in her head, but they were magnificent and large. Her lips, a little full, but beautifully shaped, revealed a set of teeth as white as newly skinned almonds. Her hair—a trifle coarse, perhaps—was black, with blue lights on it like a raven's wing, long and glossy. Not to weary my readers with too prolix a description, I will merely add, that to every blemish she united some advantage, which was perhaps all the more evident by contrast. *There was something strange and wild about her beauty. Her face astonished you, at first sight, but nobody could forget it. Her eyes, especially, had an expression of mingled sensuality and fierceness, which I had never seen in any other human glance.* "Gypsy's eye, wolf's eye!" is a Spanish saying, which denotes close observation. If my readers have no time to go to the "Jardin des Plantes" to study the wolf's expression, they will do well to watch the ordinary cat when it is lying in wait for a sparrow.
>
> (Mérimée 1845; emphasis added)

A constitutive element of the orientalization of Spanishness throughout the romantic period and beyond is precisely the reflexive mechanism of citation and endless repetition of inherited images. Thus in 1826 Alfred Vigny writes in *Cinq Mars*, "Un Espagnol est un homme de l'Orient, c'est un Turc catholique."

Some of the trends towards a Spanish Orientalism in the late 1800s were the institutionalization of Arabic in the Spanish universities in 1887, followed by the formation of *Al Andalus: La Revista de Las Escuelas de Estudios Arabes de Madrid y Granada*—a philological journal which began in 1933—directed by two Spanish Orientalists: Miguel Asín Palacios and Emilio García Gómez.

Carl Jubran shows "how the Orientalist project set forth by the Hispano-Arabists in the late nineteenth century supports and amplifies the development of an internal racial hierarchy linked to the Castilian centered historiography produced by the

Spanish modernist intelligentsia and later reproduced (and I will say perfected by the Francoist regime) Francisco Franco" (Jubran 2002). Jubran's work illustrates how the Spanish intelligentsia contributes to the "Orientalist" scholarship that Said unveiled. However, the purpose of the Spanish Orientalism was to utilize this oppositional discourse based on the concept of "otherness within" to Europeanize Spain.

Spanish Orientalism is utilized by both traditional and progressive intellectuals. Liberals saw in Spain a particular brand of constitutionalism and religious tolerance while the conservatives elaborated a version rooted in the Council of Trent's Catholicism, monarchy, and Castilian centrism.

The role of the Orient in Spanish identity was best personified in the debate between two Spanish historians on opposite sides of the discussion. Americo Castro's *España en su historia* (1948) celebrated Spain's hybridity while Claudio Sánchez-Albornoz's *España un enigma histórico* (1957), in response to Castro, voiced the non-Semitic components of Spanish culture. Castro saw the Muslim invasions in 711 as a birth of Spanish hybridity while Sánchez-Albornoz saw this year as the cause of Spanish entrapment in centuries of cultural and economic backwardness with respect to Europe.

Spain entered modernity through the back door. The Francoist dictatorship achieved international rehabilitation in the summer of 1953 after the signing of the Pact of Madrid, a military and economic agreement with the United States, and the Concordat in September 1953 with the Vatican. The economic take-off meant the transition from autarky to consumerism in the 1950s and 1960s, with an avalanche of tourists visiting the country. The regime banked on the familiar orientalizing discourse of the Romantics to enter the international political scene in the mid-twentieth century. The newly established Ministry of Tourism under Manuel Fraga Iribarne attracted visitors with the slogan "Spain is different."

National Catholicism remained the ideological substratum lending cohesion and legitimacy to a military dictatorship under the personal power of Francisco Franco. Ultra-Catholic values dictated the law of the land, making Spain a backward remnant in the European context. Certainly, the marginality of Spain was more than cultural or religious. Since the fall of the last colonies in 1898, Spanish intellectuals had striven to find a new sense of self among the new imperial powers. No longer a hegemonic European power, Spain was seen under Western eyes as belonging to a lesser developed stock. Spain hence was orientalized because it was possible for the European-Atlantic tradition to view it in that light due to Spain's Jewish and Muslim heritage. The examination of Spanish international rehabilitation in the 1950s and 1960s offers us the opportunity to test Said's assertion that it is "wrong to conclude the Orient is just an idea or a creation with no corresponding reality," and furthermore the Spanish case exemplifies how "the relationship between the Occident and the Orient is a relationship of power, of domination, of various degrees of complex hegemony. The two geographical entities thus support and to an extent reflect each other;" and this is so because Spain is at the same time Europe and the Orient. Spain is where the end of one reality and the beginning of the "Other" coexist; always Queer Iberia.

In an article published in 1956 entitled "Spain, Spanish Morocco and Arab Policy," John D. Harbron remarked "Spain is unique among Western European nations who have colonial and strategic interests in the Islamic area, in that her past is interwoven with that of the Arab world" (Harbron 1956: 135). The author points out the fact that Spanish colonial rule is viewed more benignly by Muslim subjects than the dominance of other European powers such as France or Britain in the region. North Africa became a matter of foreign prestige for Spain after the 1898 war against the United States. In 1952 Franco's only daughter, interestingly called Carmen, led a visit of goodwill to the region; this visit, according to Harbron, "became the spearhead of Spanish drive to close the gap between modern Spanish and the modern Middle Eastern republics." The author sees clearly the value of Spain as mediator, as agent of the West and asserts "[Spain's] experience with the Moslem problems is a direct result of the *Arab blood which flows in Spanish veins and of a common history*" (Harbron 1956: 136; emphasis added). Harbron explains how the Spanish language is "liberally supplied with Arabic words" and mentions Andalusia as the best example. The southern region of Spain, home of Al-Andalus, the "'Thousand-and-one Nights' atmosphere of Spanish-Umyyad caliphate." However, Harbron recognized that the Muslim culture developed in Spain "posed a superior position culturally" (Harbron 1956: 137), just because of its location in European soil. The resulting hybridity (in Bhabha's sense) was welcomed by the West in the context of the Cold War.

Harbron declares that Spain's main success in the early 1950s was "selling herself as a nation *of Christian culture* which understands the Arab struggles for nationhood" (Harbron 1956: 142). Following King Abdulla I of Jordan's visit to Franco in 1949, the Spanish foreign policy program began in 1952 with a visit to the Middle East by a delegation led by Carmen Franco, daughter of the dictator, and Marquesa de Villaverde, Martín Artajo, Minister of Foreign Affairs, and 17 leading diplomats and members of the press. This delegation visited Lebanon, Jordan, Iraq, Egypt, and Saudi Arabia. There were symbolic speeches and editorials in the Spanish press. There was also the creation of Muslim studies in Spain supported with funds from Egypt, Lebanon, and Iraq.

The Francoist discourse was one of pro-Arab Catholic Hispanic nationalism. It was charged with contradicting ideas. The Francoist colonialist discourse presented an image in North Africa that scholar Hishaam D. Aidi calls "the older brother" who imparted "soft domination" (Aidi 2006: 73). Aidi points out how the regime deployed the idea that Arab and Hispanic identity are connected.

Following on the tradition of Western travelers, African American writer Richard Wright visited Spain in 1954 and recorded his impressions in his book *Pagan Spain*, first published in 1957. A reading of this work allows us to examine what I will call Spain's "orientalization from within" during the 1950s and 1960s. What makes the reading of *Pagan Spain* valuable is the fact that it is not just a travel book but rather an introspective narrative that takes the author to question his own Westernness:

I protested to myself for wanting to dump the entire life of a European nation into the lap of the irrational. It just could not be, I argued with myself, that a nook of Europe had completely escaped the secularizing processes that were now rampant even in Asia and Africa. But, in the end, I had had no choice.

(Wright 2002: 230)

Wright, although a marginal individual victim of racism in his native country, the United States, becomes the expert Edward Said warned us about in his study of Orientalism: the "Orientalist," "poet," or scholar authority. His "objective appraisal" of the non-Westerner prevails over any self-representation of the natives—Spaniards living under Francoism. Although highly critical of the racism suffered by his people in the U.S. deep South, Richard Wright turns into the authoritative Westerner examining Spain. He mentions Americo Castro's *The Structure of Spanish History* and Salvador de Madariaga's *Spain* as monuments of scholarship that might hint to the "truth" but he felt these works did not go "deeply and boldly enough into the real heart of the question of the *Spanish animal*" (ibid.; emphasis added).

Since 1946 Richard Wright had lived in Paris where he met other intellectuals who encouraged him to visit Spain. "Dick, you ought to go to Spain," Gertrude Stein said to him, "You'll see what the Western world is made of." Certainly Wright's visit to Spain made him more conscious of his "Westernness;" more than a cultural element, for Wright being Western was problematized by his being African American. Being a black intellectual and by the early 1950s no longer a member of the Communist Party, Wright was highly critical of Western colonialism and imperialism while at the same time he espoused the Western values of freedom, equality, and the pursuit of happiness. These sentiments suffered a profound revision in his outlook of both his own Westernness and the hypothesis that Spain was out of the occidental orbit. Wright had resisted traveling to Franco's Spain. "An uneasy question kept floating in my mind," he writes. "How did one live after the death of the hope for freedom? Suddenly resolved, I swung my car southward, toward those humped and rugged peaks of the Pyrenees which, some authorities claim, mark the termination of Europe and the beginning of Africa" (Wright 2002: 4). What he found after traveling through the country was that although "Spain was geographically a part of Europe, it had had just enough western aspects of life to make me feel a little at home. *But it was not the West.* Well, what then was it?" (Wright 2002: 228; emphasis added). Spain was a "holy nation" he concluded, "a sacred state…. *All was religion in Spain.*"

I have argued elsewhere that National Catholicism was crucial to define Francosim's hold on political and social consensus. It served its purpose also in the context of the Cold War to reenter the international scene.

Richard Wright saw a Spain highly polarized along gender lines. "Spanish men have built a state," he remarks, "but they have never built a society, and the only society that there is in Spain is in the hearts and minds and habits of and love and devotion of its women" (Wright 2002: xviii). Rather than a simple travel log *Pagan*

Spain is a collection of reflections on the country he found engulfed in misery after the Spanish Civil War. For Wright women were the backbone of society. "I marveled," he wrote, "at how strong and self-possessed the women of Spain were in comparison to the men" (ibid.).

> The Spanish male learns early to divide all women into two general categories: one group of women are those with husbands, children, and a home; or they are young women whose hymen rings are technically intact. These are the good women and you bow low to them and tenderly kiss their hands, murmuring compliments the while. The other group of women has been placed on earth by God, just as He placed rabbits, foxes, lions, etc., to be hunted and had.

Far from eroticizing Spanish women into the Carmen myth like previous Romantic travelers had done, Wright recognized the silent resistance exercised by the women of Spain. He saw how religion and politics collided. Hunger and sex, misery and sin had to be navigated constantly to avoid social disapproval and the regime's political repression.[6]

The most important shift in social mores taking place after the Francoist Victorian 1939 was the criminalization of other sexual behaviors. The regime was truly ambivalent about the practice of prostitution. On the one hand it saw prostitution as a necessary evil—a healthy outlet for natural male desires. This image of the sexually potent man fit with the regime's promotion of itself as a virile, masculine ideology. The thinking went that if these strong men did not have the prostitute's body as a barrier, they would surely defile the pure and chaste bodies of their fiancées—true Catholic women and the future mothers of the New Spain. Officially sanctioned, this moral double standard (allowing prostitution but demonizing the prostitute) developed into a dysfunctional sexuality disguised under the appearance of Christian purity and normalcy.[7]

The Francoist regime reformed the Penal code in 1944 and enacted a series of laws dealing with "sexual indecency" immediately after the Civil War. By the law of January 24 1941, abortion was declared illegal. Subsequently the law of March 12 1942 prosecuted adultery, infanticide, and abandonment of the conjugal home and family obligations.[8] Virginity became the most valued trademark for the "good" woman. As Wright described it:

> Being a virgin, evidently, was a kind of profession in itself. It seemed that she stayed home with her mother and was never allowed out except in the company of the immediate members of the family, a situation that constituted proof of her virginity. I understood now why she had been so wonderstruck by me; she had not had an opportunity to meet many men, and I was, moreover, a different sort of man: brown.... Her being a virgin was all in the world she knew, felt, and thought about. Hence, each man that she saw she regarded as a possible agent of defloration, an agent which, no doubt, she longed to meet and embrace. Her living the role of a virgin has steeped her personality

with an aura of sex and she unconsciously attracted men to her body with
more definiteness than even a professional prostitute. Her entire outlook was
one of waiting to be despoiled, longing for the day when she could shed her
burdensome and useless role, when she could live a free and normal life like
the older women about her.

(Wright 2002: 100)

Catholicism imbued political discourse with only one purpose: to regenerate the
whorish body politic of the Second Republic. The National Catholic state's zeal to
protect Christian family values led to a twofold policy. Initially the state practiced
a policy of controlled leniency towards prostitution that lasted until 1956. Later,
by the decree of March 3 1956, the Francoist regime declared prostitution illegal
and joined the international community in the fight against it. To purify the
nation's body, the regime established the *Patronato de Protección de la Mujer*
(Foundation for the Protection of Women) in 1941. The Foundation's task was
further strengthened by the Convention on the Political Rights of Women law
of December 20 1952 and the decree abolishing prostitution in 1956. Seeped
in Catholic values this agency carried out the state's task of surveillance and
rehabilitation of the prostitute's body and soul.

Wright witnessed the polarized womanhood personae resulting from National
Catholic discourse. The virgin/whore binomial was only possible in the context
of a theocratic society. The religious hyper-saturation was key to Wright and
explained the non-Western nature of Spain in the 1950s. The good Spanish woman
was under lock and veiled, her nemesis was "Carmen" the fallen woman.[9] For
Wright, uncovering the condition of women under Francoism was an exercise in
unveiling the Orient within Europe.

The Carmen myth according to Jose Colmeiro "reflects a simultaneous
repulsion and attraction toward the other." Colmeiro also points out how the
notion of "Carmen as the ultimate essence of Spanishness is troubling referring
to the exotic French fabrication known as the 'espagnolade.'"[10] In the process
both Carmen and her lesser sisters are instrumentalized and further orientalized
by the Western feminist illusion of sameness in universal sisterhood. The 1950s
represented a transitional space in the Francoist regime's identity, what Homi
Bhabha calls "an in-between space."

These "in-between spaces" provide a terrain for elaborating strategies of
selfhood—singular and communal—that initiate new signs of identity and
innovative signs of collaboration, and contestation, in the act of defining the
idea of society itself.

(Bhabha 2006: 2)

The regime redefined itself on the international and domestic fronts with the
explosion of tourism and the emigration of Spanish male workers. These events
opened the small crack in the door for dissent. Consumerism and tourism's service

industry relied on the increasing work of women. With increasing economic power women began to exert influence on the political side of life.

The hybridity of Spanish Orientalism became useful in this in-between moment. The myth of Carmen becomes the missing link between the Judeo-Christian Western feminist and her counterpart Muslim orientalized victim. Carmen acts as an in-between identity, malleable at both ends: utilized as broker of Western feminism and welcome rescuer for the infantilized third world woman.

Central to the National Catholic discourse was the construction of what I call "true Catholic Womanhood."[11] *Españolas:* How to define Spanish women? How to look back to Spain's female historical flux? *La madre patria* conveys a hermaphrodite-like essence of the nation's notion. *Mater* and *Pater* involved in the unfolding of time. Past/present/future slashed from each other by death, by ghosts, invisible yet present. Was there a bourgeois revolution for women? And whether there was one or not, what difference does it make in the Spanish historical context? Why needs all of Europe fit the mold of the chosen few northern countries? To approach historical unfolding from such an *androcentric* Western perspective promises a bleak and depressing chronicle—a chronicle of victimization, colonization, and marginality, a myopic historical account at best. Furthermore, bestowing the bourgeois revolution (an intrinsically male-centered political process that only benefited a particular male ruling class anyway) as the *sine qua non* step to modernity falls in many nations outside the norm.

There has been much writing about women "becoming visible" in historical narratives. The unveiling exercise done by women's historians for the last three decades of the twentieth century led in the beginning to a so-called "compensatory history" based on the doctrine of separate spheres first identified by Anglo-Saxon feminist historians as apt to identify women's past. Certainly, this hide-and-seek drill departed from the traditional chronicle of noble women, who had been part of mainstream history writing, being, as they were, part of the public record and hence part of the elite by birth or marriage.

The haunting matter in a feminist reading of history at the turn of the twenty-first century is the application of *gender* as a category of analysis. Gender understood as the socio-semantic construction of feminine and masculine roles. Modern Western understandings both conventional and subliminal of our "selves" have been informed by biological determinism endorsed by scientists and the medical profession at the turn of the twentieth century. The objectivity presumed in scientific discourse turned rational religious prescriptions about the different social roles and value for men and women. Mind and body gatekeepers agreed in shaping male and female bodies into manly men and womanly women.

The Francoist regime's official discourse drowned three generations of Spaniards's dissenting cry in a Lorquian grieving sea. Spain in the 1950s was welcomed back into the Western brotherhood of nations as a staunch ally in the fight against Soviet Communism. Forgotten and forgiven for its Axis sympathies and its continuing fascist policies, Spain was seen by many outside as the Orient within European borders—the country as a preserve for traditional Catholicism (as mysterious to Protestant Europe as Islam) and cultural values. The real story, the story from inside, was something altogether different. Life for working-class women was an everyday struggle against the repression of male-dominated doctrines of Church and State, and a search for new meaning in the slowly modernizing world that would eventually overtake Spain in the later part of the twentieth century.

The work of French scholar Michel de Certeau analyzes and revises Foucault's concept of social practices in *Discipline and Punish* and Bordieu's concept *of habitus* as his preliminaries to the procedures of everyday creativity (or practices).[12] This theoretical framework is useful to shift from victimization to agency. Furthermore, de Certeau distinguishes two uses of the practices: strategy and tactics. Michel de Certeau proposes that everyday practice is the "investigation of ways in which users operate," or "ways of operating," or doing things.[13] He points out that everyday practice should not be concealed "as merely the obscure background of social activity," but it is necessary to "penetrate this obscurity" and to "articulate" everyday life.

In order to undo the orientalizing depiction of women I propose the use of oral history. Examining the life narratives of women coming of age in the 1950s and 1960s under Franco promises to shed some light on the issue of agency within totalitarian regimes. Sex, love, work, children, families, and religion dominate these women's discourse. What comes out is a bittersweet brew made from unrealized dreams and hard times mixed with the pride of forging a different world for their daughters. Oral history allows us to unveil the many acts of self-empowerment anonymous women exerted under cover and in silence.

To shift from victimization to a chronicle of women as agents of change, what I am proposing here is to look at the minutiae and identify the practice of survival as the self-affirmation of a generation of women who refused to pass down to their daughters a legacy of self-erasure. The tool is oral history and the analysis will call for a questioning of our conventional way of thinking about time. Freedom is realized not in the lifespan of those who lived under the dictator but rather was slowly cultivated in the conscience of their young. The end result is bittersweet, for these old women have the real awareness of having been able to transgress by proxy in the flesh of their children.

In today's Spain, a six-months' pregnant woman reviewed the military troops, her troops, as she has taken the post of Minister of Defense. For every one of her, there were at least 20 and probably more of the women I interviewed knocking down the stone walls of antiquity that had for so long kept Spanish women cloistered. The twist is that it was this isolation and segregation that gave them room to grow and subvert the status quo.

Notes

1 Hegel, *The Philosophy of History* was based primarily on lectures presented by Hegel in the winter of 1830–1831.
2 In 1721 Montesquieu published the *Persian Letters*. Cadalso follows the same format of epistolary narrative.

3 "Las noticias que hemos tenido hasta ahora en Marruecos de la sociedad o vida social de los españoles nos parecía muy buena, por ser muy semejante aquélla a la nuestra, y ser natural en un hombre graduar por esta regla el mérito de los otros. Las mujeres guardadas bajo muchas llaves, las conversaciones de los hombres entre sí muy reservadas, el porte muy serio, las concurrencias pocas, y ésas sujetas a una etiqueta forzosa, y otras costumbres de este tenor no eran tanto efecto de su clima, religión y gobierno, según quieren algunos, como monumentos de nuestro antiguo dominio. En ellas se ven permanecer reliquias de nuestro señorío, aun más que en los edificios que subsisten en Córdoba, Granada, Toledo y otras partes" (Cadalso 2000).

4 I utilize Edward Said's definition of Orientalism here: Orientalism is a "*distribution* of geopolitical awareness into aesthetic, scholarly, economic, sociological, historical, and philological texts; it is an *elaboration* not only of a basic geographical distinction ... but also of a whole series of 'interests' ... it *is* ... a certain *will* or *intention* to understand, in some cases to control, manipulate, even to incorporate what is a manifestly 'different' ... world; it is, above all, a discourse that is by no means in direct, corresponding relationship with political power in the raw, but rather is produced and exists in an uneven exchange with various kinds of power" (Said 2003: 12).

5 On the birth of national identity, see Serrano 1999 and Alvarez Junco 2001.

6 On the regime's policy on prostitution, see Morcillo 2007.

7 On Francoist public morality, see Morcillo 2007.

8 According to the Foundation for the Protection of Women, the number of suicides in Spain rose from 1,787 in 1934 to 3,091 in 1941, while crimes for murder and assault declined from 18,952 to 15,186. There were however significantly more crimes for theft, which increased from 50,232 in 1934 to 67,977 in 1941, a clear indicator of the extreme misery of post-war conditions (Junta Nacional Secretaría Técnica 1943, *Informe sobre la moralidad pública*, p. 56).

9 See Yegenoglu 1998 and Mernisi 1987.

10 In a recent poll in the European Union, Carmen was the character most identified with Spain and 20 percent of those polled considered Spain an "oriental nation" (Colmeiro 2002).

11 See Morcillo 2000.

12 http://www.eng.fju.edu.tw/Literary_Criticism/cultural_studies/decerteau.htm#2

13 http://www.eng.fju.edu.tw/Literary_Criticism/cultural_studies/decerteau.htm#2 Michel de Certeau, *Making Do*, p. 474.

Bibliography

Abdi, A.A. (1999) 'Frantz Fanon and Post-Colonial Realities: A Temporal Perspective', *Wasafiri* 30: 51–54.

Abou Zeid, N.H. (1992) *Al Khitab al-Dini. Ro'ya Nakdia*, Beyrouth: Dar el-Montakhab al-Araby.

Abou Zeid, N.H. (2000) *Dawaer al-Khouf. Kiraa fi Khitab al-Mar'a*, Beyrouth: Al Markaz al-Thakafy al-Araby.

Abouzeid, L. (1983) *Year of the Elephant: A Moroccan Woman's Journey Toward Independence*, trans. Barbara Parmenter (1989), Austin, TX: Center for Middle Eastern Studies.

Abouzeid, L. (1993) 'An Interview with Leila Abouzeid', *Ad-Dad: A Journal of Arabic Literature*, 2: 7–8.

Abu-Lughod, L. (1998) *Remaking Women: Feminism and Modernity in the Middle East*, Princeton, NJ: Princeton University Press.

Abun-Nasr, J.M. (1975) *A History of the Maghreb*, 2nd ed., Cambridge: Cambridge University Press.

Acar, F. (1995) 'Women and Islam in Turkey', in S. Tekeli (ed.) *Women in Modern Turkish Society*, London: Zed Books.

Accad, E. (1990) *Sexuality and War: Literary Masks of the Middle-East*, New York: New York University Press.

Addi, L. (Nov. 23 1995) 'Le Régime Algérien et ses Oppositions', *El Watan*.

Agarwal, B. (1997) 'Bargaining and Gender-Relations: Within and Beyond the Household', *Feminist Economics* 2(1): 1–50.

Aggoun, L. and Rivoire, J-B. (2004) *Françalgérie, crimes et mensonges d'États. Histoire secrète, de la guerre d'indépendance à la "troisième guerre" d'Algérie*, Paris: La Découverte.

Ahmed, L. (1992) *Women and Gender in Islam: Historical Roots of a Modern Debate*, New Haven, CT: Yale University Press.

Aidi, H.D. (2006) 'The Interference of Al-Andalus. Spain, Islam, and the West', *Social Text* 87/24(2): 67–88.

Ait Hammou, L. (December 2004) 'Women's Struggle against Muslim Fundamentalism in Algeria: Strategies or a Lesson for Survival?', in Ayesha Imam et al. (eds) *Warning Signs of Fundamentalisms*, London: WLUML Publications, pp. 117–124.

Al-Ahnaf, M., Botiveau, B., and Frégosi, F. (1991) *L'Algérie par ses Islamistes*, Paris: Karthala.

Al Ashmawy, M.S. (2002) *Hakikat Al-Hijab Wa Hogueyet Al-Hadith*, Cairo: Rose-Al-Youssef Publishing.

Al Balushi, K. (2000) *Omani Women from History.* www.nct-muscat.net/archive/ index.phe/t-6384 (in Arabic).

Al Barwani, T. (2000) Social Development Imperatives of Omani Women. Paper presented at Omani Cultural week, Brussels, Belgium.

Al Barwani, T. (2003) Towards the Empowerment of Women in the Sultanate of Oman. Paper presented at a special meeting of Ministers of Women's Affairs, Washington, DC.

Al-Hegelan, N. (1980) 'Women in the Arab World', *Arab Perspectives* 1(7).

Al Missned, Sheikha M. bint N. (2007) The Woman Issue in Context: Deframing the Discourse on Middle Eastern Women. Paper presented at the James Baker III Institute for Public Policy, Rice University, Houston, TX.

Almond, G.A. and Powell, G.B. (1966) *Comparative Politics: A Developmental Approach*, Boston: Little, Brown.

Al-Sayyid, M.K. (1993) "A 'Civil Society' in Egypt?", *Middle East Journal* 47(2) (Spring): 228–242.

Alvarez Junco, J. (2001) *Mater Dolorosa*, Madrid: Taurus.

Alvarez Junco, J. and Shubert, A. (eds) (2000) *Spanish History since 1808,* New York: Arnold.

Amin, A.H. (1987) *Dalil al-Moemen al-Hazin*, Cairo: Madbouli.

Amir, D. and Benjamin, O. (1992) "The Abortion Committees: Educating and Controlling Women", *Journal of Women and Criminal Justice* 3: 5–25.

Amir, D., Fogiel-Bijoui, S., Giora, R., and Shadmi, A. (eds) (1997) 'Feminist Theory and Research: Israeli Institutions and Society', *Israel Social Science Research* 12(1): 1–144.

Andezian, S. (1997) 'The Role of Sufi Women in an Algerian Pilgrimage Ritual', in E. Rosander and D. Westerlund (eds) *African Islam and Islam in Africa: Encounters between Sufis and Islamists,* Athens: Ohio University Press.

An-Naim, A. (2002) *Islamic Family Law in a Changing World*, London: Zed Books.

Arab Human Development Report, 2006: http://www.directtextbook.com/search.php? isbn=0804755302&dtkts=Arab_Human_Development&classes=gbc

Arat, Y. (1995) 'Feminism and Islam: Considerations on the Journal *Kadin ve Aile'*, in S. Tekeli (ed.) *Women in Modern Turkish Society*, London and New Jersey: Zed Books.

Arat, Y. (2000) 'Gender and Citizenship in Turkey', in Suad Joseph (ed.) *Gender and Citizenship in the Middle East*, New York: Syracuse University Press, pp. 275–286.

Ashcroft, B., Griffiths, G. and Tiffin, H. (1989) *The Empire Writes Back: Theory and Practice in Post-colonial Literatures*, London: Routledge.

as-Susi, M.M. (1971) *al-Ma`sul*, 20 Volumes, Casablanca: Matba`at al- Najah.

Awad, H. 'The German Experiment in Giving a Quota to Women in the Elected Councils.'

Aydin, S. and Çakir, R. (2007) 'Political Islam in Turkey', *Centre for European Policy Studies*. CEPS Working Documents, No. 265.

Ayubi, N. (1991) *Political Islam: Religion and Politics in the Arab World*, London and New York: Routledge.

Azmon, Y. and Izraeli, D. (eds) (1991) *Women in Israel*, London: Transaction Publishers.

Badran, M. (1991) 'Competing Agenda: Feminists, Islam and the State in the Nineteenth and Twentieth Century Egypt', in Deniz Kandiyoti (ed.) *Women, Islam, and the State*, London: Macmillan.

Badran, M. (2002) 'Islamic Feminism: What's in a Name', *Al-Ahram Weekly Online*, Issue 569: 17–23.

Baraka, I. (1993) 'Hidjab,' in *Encyclopedia of Islam*, vol. 3. Leiden: Brill.

Baraka, I. (2002) *Al Hijab: Ro'ya Assreya*, Cairo: Rose-Al-Youssef Publishing.

Baykan, A. (1990) 'Women between Fundamentalism and Modernity', in B.S. Turner (ed.) *Theories of Modernity and Postmodernity,* London: Sage.

Beaver, S.E. (1975) *Demographic Transition Theory Re-interpreted,* London: Lexington Books.

Becker, C. (2006) *Amazing Arts in Morocco: Women Shaping Berber Identity,* Austin: University of Texas Press.

Beijing Report (1995) *A Decade of Progress: The Israeli Report to the Fourth World Conference on Women, Jerusalem:* Government Printing Office.

Bekkaoui, K. (2006) 'The Contraband Modern in the Fes Medina', Online. Available HTTP: (accessed 5 September 2008).

Benallegue, N. (1983) 'Algerian Women in the Struggle for Independence and Reconstruction', *International Social Science Journal* 35(4): 703–717.

Bennouna, M. (1999) *Les Algériennes Victimes société néopatriarcale,* Algiers: Marinoor.

Berkey, J.P. (1992) *The Transmission of Knowledge in Medieval Cairo: A Social History of Islamic Education,* Princeton, NJ: Princeton University Press.

Berkey, J.P. (2001) *Popular Preaching and Religious Authority in the Medieval Islamic Near East,* Seattle: University of Washington Press.

Berkey, J.P. (2003) *The Formation of Islam. Religion and Society in the Near East, 600–1800,* Cambridge: Cambridge University Press.

Berkey, J.P. (2007) 'Madrasas Medieval and Modern: Politics, Education and the Problem of Muslim Identity', in R.W. Hefner and M.Q. Zaman (eds) *Schooling Islam: The Culture and Politics of Modern Muslim Education,* Princeton, NJ: Princeton University Press.

Bernstein, D. (ed.) (1992) *Pioneers and Homemakers: Jewish Women in Pre- State Israel,* Albany: SUNY University Press.

Bessis, S. (1999) 'Le Féminisme Institutionnel en Tunisie [Institutional Feminism in Tunisia]', *Clio* Vol. 9. Online. Available HTTP: <http://clio.revues.org/document286.html> (last visited November 29, 2007) (on file with the *Washington and Lee Law Review*).

Beydoun, A.S. (2002) *Nisa Jam'eyyat: Libnaneyat bayna Insaf el-that wa Khedmat al-Ghayr* (Women and Societies: Lebanese Women between Self Assertive and Caring for the Others), Beirut: Dar el-Nahar.

Bhabha, H. (2006) *The Location of Culture,* London and New York: Routledge.

Bill, J. and Leiden, C. (1974) *The Middle East: Politics and Power,* Boston: Allyn and Bacon.

Binder, L. (1986) 'The Natural History of Development Theory', *Comparative Studies in Society and History* 28(1) (January).

Bishara, A. (1996) *Mossahama Fi Nakd Al Mujtam'a Al Madani* (A Contribution to the Critique of Civil Society), Ramallah, West Bank: Muwatin—Palestinian Institute for the Study of Democracy.

Boogert, N. van den (1997) *The Berber Literary Tradition of the Sous,* Leiden: Nederlands Instituut voor het Nabije Oosten.

Bouchama, M. (2006) The Traditional Fassi Carpet: A Case Study. Unpublished thesis, Moroccan Cultural Studies Center, Sidi Mohammed Ben Abdellah University, Online. Available HTTP: <http://www.open.ac.uk/Arts/ferguson-centre/fesmedina/papers/kaushik-bhaumik-paper.htm> (accessed 5 September 2008).

Bourquia, R. (1997) 'Les Femmes: un objet de recherche', in *Etudes Féminines notes: méthodologiques,* Rabat, Faculté des Lettres et des Sciences Humaines.

Boyd, J. and Mack, B. (2000) *One Woman's Jihad,* Bloomington: Indiana University Press.

Brand, L.A. (1998) *Women, the State, and Political Liberalization: Middle Eastern and North African Experiences*, New York: Columbia University Press.

Cadalso, J. (2000) *Cartas Marruecas, Carta XI Edición digital a partir del manuscrito de la Real Academia de la Historia, Sala 9, Segundo Armario de Códices, 122ff. 1–165 y cotejada con las ediciones críticas de Joaquín Arce,* Madrid: Cátedra, 1983, 7a ed. y Emilio Martínez Mata, Barcelona, Crítica, 2000.

Casanova, Jose (1994) *Public Religions in the Modern World*, Chicago: University of Chicago Press.

Centre of Arab Women for Training and Research (2001) *Arab Women's Development Report: Globalization and Gender – Economic Participation of Arab Women*, Tunis: Centre of Arab Women for Training and Research.

Chafik, M. (1982) 'Pour l'Elaboration du Berbère Classique à Partir du Berbère Courant', In *Actes de la 1ère Rencontre in Actes de l'Université d'Eté d'Agadir*: 191–197.

Chamais, A. (1987) *Obstacles Hindering Muslim Women from Obtaining a Divorce*, Cairo, Egypt: UNISEF.

Chamari, A.C. (1991) *La Femme et la Loi en Tunisie*, Casablanca, Morocco: United Nations University and Editions le Fennec.

Chamberlain, M. (1994) *Knowledge and Social Practice in Medieval Damascus, 1190–1350*, New York: Cambridge University Press.

Charrad, M.M. (1994) 'Repudiation versus Divorce: Responses to State Policy in Tunisia', in E.N. Chow and C.W. Berheide (eds) *Women, the Family and Policy: A Global Perspective*, Albany: State University of New York Press, pp. 51–69.

Charrad, M.M. (1998) 'Cultural Diversity Within Islam: Veils and Laws in Tunisia', in H.L. Bodman and N. Tohidi (eds) *Women in Muslim Societies: Diversity Within Unity*, Boulder, CO: Lynne Rienner, pp. 63–79.

Charrad, M.M. (2000) 'Becoming a Citizen: Lineage Versus Individual in Morocco and Tunisia', in S. Joseph (ed.) *Gender and Citizenship in the Middle East*, Syracuse, NY: Syracuse University Press, pp. 70–87.

Charrad, M.M. (2001) *States and Women's Rights: The Making of Postcolonial Tunisia, Algeria and Morocco*, Berkeley, CA: University of California Press.

Charrad, M.M. (2007) 'Contexts, Concepts and Contentions: Gender Legislation in the Middle East', *Hawwa: Journal of Women in the Middle East and the Islamic World* 5(1): 55–72.

Chaterjee, P. (1993) *Nationalist Thought and the Colonial World: A Derivative Discourse*, Minneapolis: University of Minnesota Press.

Chatty, D. (2000) 'Women Working in Oman: Individual Choice and Cultural Constraints', *International Journal of Middle East Studies*, 32: 241–254.

Chatty, D. and Rabo, A. (1997) *Organizing Women, Formal and Informal Women's Groups in the Middle East*, Oxford: Berg.

Coates, J. (1993) *Women, Men and Language: A Sociolinguistic Account of Sex Differences in Language*, 2nd edn, London: Longman.

Colmeiro, J. (2002) 'Exorcising Exoticism: Carmen and the Construction of Oriental Spain', *Comparative Literature*, provided by ProQuest.

Cooke, M. (2001) *Women Claim Islam. Creating Islamic Feminism Through Literature*, New York, London: Routledge.

Cornell, V.J. (1998) *Realm of the Saint. Power and Authority in Moroccan Sufism*, Austin: University of Texas Press.

Curtin, P.D. (1969) 'Oral Traditions and African History', *Journal of the African Folklore Institute* 6(2/3): 137–155.

d'Evaluation des Progrès Réalisés dans la Mise en Œuvre du Programme d'Action de Beijing en Afrique (Beijing +10): Rapport des ONG du Maroc. Online. Available HTTP: <www.wildaf-ao.org> (accessed on 21 August 2008).

Daoud, M. (2001) 'The Linguistic Situation in Tunisia', *Current Issues in Language Planning* 2(1): 1–52.

Daoud, Z. (1996) *Féminisme et Politique au Maghreb: Sept décennies de lute*, Casablanca: Editions Eddif.

Das, V. (1996) Sexual Violence, Discursive Formations and the State. Paper presented at the conference on Violence Against Women: Victims and Ideologies, Colombo, Sri Lanka, March.

De Certeau, M. (1988) *The Practice of Everyday Life*, Berkeley: University of California Press.

Delanty, G. (1995) *Inventing Europe. Idea, Identity, Reality*, New York: St Martin's Press.

Delcroix, C. (1986) *Espoirs et Réalité de la Femme Arabe (Algérie, Egypte)*, Paris: l'Harmattan.

Department of Statistics, 2004: http://dor.wa.gov/Docs/Pubs/News/2005/NR_2004_Stats_ Online.pdf

Djebar, A. (1957) *La Soif*, Paris: éditions Julliard; and also (1970), Alger: SNED.

Djebar, A. (1980) *Femmes d'Alger dans leur appartement*, trans. Marjolijn de Jager (1992) *Women of Algiers in Their Apartment*, Charlottesville: University Press of Virginia.

Djebar, A. (1987) *Ombre Sultane*, trans. Dorothy S. Blair (1987) *A Sister to Scheherazade*, London: Quartet.

Djebar, A. (1995) *Vaste est la prison*, Paris: Albin Michel.

Doraid, Moez (2000) Human Development and Poverty in the Arab States. Report by the United Nations Development Program.

'Dress code for women according to Qur'an.' Online. <http://theseheadcoverings.google pages.com/islamicheadcoverings> and Available HTTP: <http://www.submission.org/ dress.html - khimar> (accessed 14 February 2008).

Dudoignon, S.A. (ed.) (2004) *Devout Societies vs. Impious States? Transmitting Islamic Learning in Russia, Central Asia and China, through the Twentieth Century*, Berlin: Klaus Schwarz Verlag.

Durakbasa, A. (1988) 'Cumhuriyet Döneminde Kemalist Kadin Kimliginin Olusumu' (Formation of the Kemalist Woman's Identity in the Republican Era), *Tarih ve Toplum*, 51.

Dussel, E. (2000) 'Europe, Modernity, and Eurocentrism', *Nepantla: Views from South* 1(3), Duke University Press.

Eckert, P. (1989) 'The Whole Woman: Sex and Gender Differences in Variation', *Language Variation and Change* 1: 245–268.

Eckert, P. and McConnell-Ginet, S. (1992) 'Think Practically and Look Locally: Language and Gender as Community-based Practice', *Annual Review of Anthropology* 21: 461–490.

Eckert, P. and McConnell-Ginet, S. (1999) 'New Generalizations and Explanations in Language and Gender Research', *Language in Society* 28: 185–201.

Egyptian Constitution of 1956, Cairo, United Arab Republic, Al Matbaa al Amirya.

Egyptian Constitution of 1971, Cairo, Egypt: Al Matbaa al Amirya.

Eickelman, D. (1992) 'The Art of Memory: Islamic Education and Its Social Reproduction', in Juan R.I. Cole (ed.) *Comparing Muslim Societies: Knowledge and the State in a World Civilization*, Ann Arbor: University of Michigan Press.

Eickleman, D.F. and Pasha, K. (1991) 'Muslim Societies and Politics: Soviet and US Approaches – A Conference Report', *Middle East Journal* 45(45) (Autumn): 630–647.

Eickelman, D.F. and Piscatori, J. (1996) *Muslim Politics*, Princeton, NJ: Princeton University Press.

Elboudrari, H. (ed.) (1993) *Modes de Transmission de la Culture Religieuse en Islam*, Cairo: IFAO.

El Mountassir, A. (2004) *Amarg: Chants et Poesie Amazigh (Sud-Ouest du Maroc)*, Paris: L'Harmattan.

Elhoussi, M. (2005) 'Le français en Tunisie aujourd'hui et demain', *Actes du Colloque de Bari 4–5 mai 2005*, Presses de l'université de Paris—Sorbonne: Hikma.

El-Shibiny, M. (2005) *The Threat of Globalization to Arab Islamic Culture. The Dynamics of World Peace*, Pittsburgh, PA: Dorrance.

Encyclopaedia of Islam (1993). Leiden: Brill Academic.

Ennaji, M. (2004a) 'Civil Society, Gender, and Social Cohesion', in Moha Ennaji (ed.) *Société Civile, Genre et Développement*, Fès: Fès-Saiss Publications, pp. 81–89.

Ennaji, M. (2004b) 'Moroccan Women and Development', in Sadiqi, Fatima (ed.) *Femmes Méditerranéennes*, Fès: Fès-Saiss Publications, pp. 39–46.

Ennaji, M. (2005) *Multilingualism, Cultural Identity, and Education in Morocco*, Boston: Springer.

Ennaji, M. (2006) 'Social Policy in Morocco: History, Politics and Social Development', in Massoud Karshenas and Valentine Moghadam (eds) *Social Policy in the Middle East*, UNRISD, London: Palgrave, pp. 109–134.

Ennaji, M. (2008) 'Steps to the Integration of Moroccan Women in Development', *British Journal of Middle Eastern Studies* 35(33): 339–348.

Ennaji, M. and Sadiqi, F. (2008) *Migration and Gender in Morocco: The Effects of Women Left Behind*, Trenton, NJ: Red Sea Press.

Ernst, C.W. (2003) *Following Muhammad: Rethinking Islam in the Contemporary World*, Chapel Hill: University of North Carolina Press.

Esposito, J.L. (1988) *Islam: The Straight Path*, New York: Oxford University Press.

Esposito, J.L. and Voll, J.O. (1996) *Islam and Democracy*, New York: Oxford University Press.

Fanon, F. (1965) *A Dying Colonialism*, trans. H. Chevalier, New York: Grove Weidenfeld.

Fanon, F. (2001) *L'An V de la révolution algérienne*, Paris: La Découverte.

Fasold, R. (1990) *The Sociolinguistics of Language*. Oxford: Blackwell.

Fathi, H. (1997) 'Otines: The Unknown Women Clerics of Central Asian Islam', *Central Asian Survey* 16(1): 27–43.

Feminist declaration on 8th March 1989 in Algiers (1989) WAF Articles, Journal no. 1: 15–16.

Ferguson, Ch. A. (1959) 'Diglossia', *Word*. Journal of the Linguistic Circle of New York, 15(2): 325–340.

Fernea, E. (1988) 'State of the Art: Research on Middle Eastern Women', *Journal of Comparative Studies*.

Fernea, E. (1998) *In Search of Islamic Feminism: One Woman's Global Journey*, New York: Doubleday.

Findley, C. (1992) 'Knowledge and Education', in C.E. Black and L.C. Brown (eds) *Modernization in the Middle East: The Ottoman Empire and Its Afro-Asian Successors*, Princeton, NJ: Darwin Press, pp. 121–149.

Fishman, P. (1980) 'Conversational Insecurity', in H. Giles *et al.* (eds) *Language: Social Psychological Perspectives*, Oxford: Pergamon, pp. 127–132.

Foda, F. (1988) *Al-Hakika al Gha'iba*, Cairo: Masr Al Gadidah Publishing.
Foda, F. (1990) *Nakoun Aw la Nakoun*, Cairo: Masr Al Gadidah Publishing.
Frazer, N. (1989) *Feminist Talk and Talking about Feminism*, Oxford: Oxford University Press.
Frazer, N. (1992) 'Rethinking the Public Sphere: A Contribution to the Critique of Actually Existing Democracy', in C. Calhoun (ed.) *Habermas and the Public Sphere*, Cambridge, MA: MIT Press.
Gacemi, B. (1997) 'Hopes and Lost Illusions', *Le Monde diplomatique*.
Garçon, J. (4 July 1989) 'Fin du Monopole Politique du FLN', *Libération*.
Geertz, C. (1971) *Islam Observed: Religious Development in Morocco and Indonesia,* Chicago: Chicago University Press.
Ghaussy, S. (1994) 'A Stepmother Tongue: Feminine Writing', in Assia Djebar *Fantasia: An Algerian Cavalcade, World Literature Today*, 68(3): 457–462.
Gheytanchi, E. (2001) 'Civil Society in Iran: Politics of Motherhood and the Public Sphere', *International Sociology* 16(4): 557–576.
Godlas, A. (1996) "A Commentary on 'What is Tasawwuf?': An Anonymous Persian Poem", *Sufi Illuminations* 1 (August): 31–62.
Goetz, A.M. (ed.) (1997) *Getting Institutions Right for Women in Development*, London: Zed Books.
Goetz, A.M. (2003) 'Women's Political Effectiveness: A Conceptual Framework', in M.A. Goetz and S. Haseem (eds) *No Shortcuts to Power: African Women in Politics and Policy Making*, New York: Zed Books.
Golan, G. (1997) 'Gender and Militarization', *Women's Studies International Forum* 5–6: 581–586.
Golan, G. and Herman, T. (2005) 'Parliamentary Representation of Women—The Israeli Case', in M. Tremblay (ed.) *Parliamentary Representation of Women—A Comparative International Study* (in French), Montreal: Remue-menage Press, pp. 251–274.
Göle, N. (1992) *Modern Mahrem: Medeniyet ve Örtünme (The Forbidden Modern: Civilization and Veiling)*, Istanbul: Metis Publication.
Göle, N. (1996) *The Forbidden Modern: Civilization and Veiling*, Ann Arbor: University of Michigan Press.
Gologlu, M. (1972) *Türkiye Cumhuriyeti 1923 (Republic of Turkey 1923)*, Ankara: Basnur Publication.
Gordon, D.C. (1968) *Women of Algeria*, Cambridge, MA: Harvard University Press.
Grace, D. (2004) *The Woman in the Muslin Mask: Veiling and Identity in Postcolonial Literature*, London: Pluto Press.
Guenena, N. and Wassef, N. (1999) *Unfulfilled Promises*, Cairo: AUC.
Guezali, S. (1996) 'Citoyenneté contre barabaries', *Le Monde diplomatique*, Mars: 17.
Günes-Ayata, A. (2001) 'The Politics of Implementing Women's Rights in Turkey', in J. H. Bayes and N. Tohidi (eds) *Globalization, Gender, and Religion: The Politics of Women's Rights in Catholic and Muslim Contexts*, New York: Palgrave.
Habermas, J. (1996) 'The Public Sphere', in P. Marris and S. Thornham (eds) *Media Studies: A Reader*, Edinburgh: Edinburgh University Press.
Haenni, P. (1993) *Le théatre d'ombre de l'action féminine. Femmes, Etat et société civile au Maroc*, Paris.
Haeri, N. (1996) *The Sociolinguistic Market of Cairo: Gender, Class and Education*, Monograph No. 13, London: Kegan Paul International.
Halimi, G. (1962) *Djamila Boupacha: The Story of the Torture of a Young Algerian Girl which Shocked Liberal French Opinion*, London: Cox and Wyman.

Halimi, G. (1992) *La Cause des Femmes*, Paris: Gallimard.

Halpern, M. (1963) *The Politics of Social Change in the Middle East and North Africa*, Princeton, NJ: Princeton University Press.

Harbi, M. (1994) 'L'Algérie prise au piège de son histoire', *Le Monde Diplomatique*.

Harbron, J.D. (1956) 'Spain, Spanish Morocco and Arab Policy', *African Affairs* 55(219): 135–143.

Hardt, M. and Negri, A. (2001) *Empire*, Cambridge, MA: Harvard University Press, Online. Available HTTP: <http://www.angelfire.com/cantina/negri/HAREMI_ unprintable.pdf> (accessed 10 May 2008).

Harlow, B. (1986) 'Introduction', in M. Alloula *The Colonial Harem*, Minneapolis: University of Minnesota Press.

Harrison, E. (1997) 'Fish, Feminists and FAO: Translating "Gender" through Different Institutions in the Development Process', in A.M. Goetz (ed.) *Getting Institutions Right for Women in Development*, London: Zed Books.

Hatem, M. 'Towards a Critique of Modernization: Narrative in Middle East Women Studies', *Arab Studies Quarterly* 15(2): 117–122.

Haykal, M.H. (1997) *The Life of Muhammad*, Plainfield, IN: American Trust Publications.

Hegland, M.E. (1998) 'Flagellation and Fundamentalism: (Trans) forming Meaning, Identity, and Gender through Pakistani Women's Rituals of Mourning', *American Ethnologist* 25: 240–266.

Hegland, M.E. (2003) 'Shi'a Women's Rituals in Northwest Pakistan: The Shortcomings and Significance of Resistance', *Anthropological Quarterly* 76(3): 411–442.

Hélie-Lucas, M. (2004) 'What is your Tribe? Women's Struggle and the Construction of Muslimness', WLULM: Dossier 26, October: 25–35.

Helm, Y.A. (ed.) (2000) *Malika Mokeddem: envers et contre tout*, Paris: L'Harmattan.

Herzog, H. (2002) *Gendering Politics: Women in Israel*, Ann Arbor: University of Michigan Press.

Higgot, R.A. (1983) *Political Development Theory: The Contemporary Debate*, London: Croom Helm.

Hodgson, M.G.S. (1974) *The Venture of Islam: Conscience and History in a World Civilization*, Chicago: University of Chicago Press.

Holmes, J. (1995) *Women, Men and Politeness,* London: Longman.

Holmes, J. (1998) Response to Koenraad Kuiper, *Journal of Sociolinguistics* 2: 104–106.

Holmes, J. and Marra, M. (2004) 'Relational Practice in the Workplace: Women's Talk or Gendered Discourse?', *Language in Society* 33: 377–398.

Hoodfar, H. (2000) 'Iranian Women at the Intersection of Citizenship and the Family Code: The Perils of Islamic Criteria,' in Suad Joseph (ed.) *Gender and Citizenship in the Middle East*, Syracuse, NY: Syracuse University Press.

Hopwood, D. (1993) *Egypt Politics and Society, 1945-1990*, New York: Routledge.

Houdebine-Gravaud, A-M. (2003) 'Trente ans de recherche sur la différence sexuelle, ou le langage des femmes et la sexuation dans la langue, les discours, les images', *Langage et société*, No. 106 (December).

Hudson, M. (1980) 'Islam and Political Development', in John L. Esposito (ed.) *Islam and Development: Religion and Socio-Political Change*, Syracuse, NY: Syracuse University Press, pp. 1–24.

Hughes, S.E. (1992) 'Expletives of Lower Working-class Women', *Language in Society* 21: 291–303.

Human Development Report, 2004: http://hdr.undp.org/en/media/hdr04_complete.pdf

Hussein, A. (1985) 'Recent Amendments to Egypt's Personal Status Laws', in E.W. Fernea (ed.) *Women and the Family in the Middle East: New Voices of Change*, Austin: University of Texas Press.

Hutcheson, G.S. and Blackmore, J. (eds) (1999) *Queer Iberia: Sexualities, Cultures, and Crossings From the Middle Ages to the Renaissance*, Durham, NC: Duke University Press.

Ibn Ibrahim, A. (1983) *Al-i'lamat bi-man halla marrakush wa-aghmat*, ed. by 'Abd-l Wahhab ibn Mansur, 10 vols, Rabat: al-Matba'a al-Malakiyya.

Ibn Khaldun, A. (1967) *The Muqaddimah, An Introduction to History*, trans. Franz Rosenthal, Bollingen Series XLIII, 3 vols, Princeton, NJ: Princeton University Press.

Ibrahim, I. (1987) 'Religion and Politics under Nasser and Sadat', in B.F. Stowasser (ed.) *The Islamic Impulse*, London: Croom Helm, pp. 121–134.

Ibrahim, S. (ed.) (1993) *Al-mujtama' Al-madani wal Tahawol al Ddimoqrati fil Watan al-Arabi* (Civil Society and Democratic Transformation in the Arab World), Annual Report, Cairo: Markaz Ibn Khaldoun.

Ibrahim, Saad Eddin, and Hopkins, Nicolas (eds) (1996) *Arab Society: Class, Gender, Power and Development*, Cairo: AUC Press.

Ilkkaracan, I. and Ilkkaracan, P. (1998) 'Kuldan Yurttasa: Kadinlar Neresinde?', in A. Ünsal (ed.) *75 Yilda Tebaa'dan Yurttas'a Dogru (From Subject to Citizen in Seventy-Five Years)*, Istanbul: Türkiye Ekono mik ve Toplumsal Tarih Vakfi, Is Bankasi Yayinlari.

Ilyasoglu, A. (1994) *Örtülü Kimlik: Islamci Kadin Kimliginin Olusum Ögeleri (Veiled Identity: Formation Elements of the Islamist Women's Identity)*, Istanbul: Metis Publication.

Insel, A. (2003) 'The AKP and Normalizing Democracy in Turkey', *South Atlantic Quarterly* 102(2/3): 293–308.

Interview with Gamal al-Banna (2008) 'Ashhar el egtehadat: al higab li- Gamal al Banna" in "88 imaan fi maaraket al-tagdid', *Al Masry Al Youm*, No. 1651 (20 December).

Ireland, S. (2001) 'Voices of Resistance', in M. Mortimer (ed.) *Maghrebian Mosaic: A Literature in Transition*, Boulder, CO: Lynne Rienner.

Irigaray, L. (1985) *Women on the Market*, in *This Sex Which is not One*, trans. C. Porter, Ithaca: Cornell University Press, pp. 170–197.

Izraeli, D. (1992) 'The Women Workers' Movement: First Wave Feminism in Pre-State Israel', in D. Bernstein (ed.) *Pioneers and Homemakers: Jewish Women in Pre-State Israel*, New York: SUNY University Press, pp. 183–209.

Izraeli, D. (ed.) (1987) Special Issue 'Women in Israel', *Israel Social Science Research* 5(1-2): 1–183.

Jackson, C. and Pearson, R. (1998) *Feminist Visions of Development: Gender Analysis and Policy*, London: Routledge.

Jad, I. (1990) 'From Salons to the Popular Committees: Palestinian Women, 1919–1989', in J.R. Nassar and R. Heacock (eds) *Intifada: Palestine at the Crossroads*, New York: Praeger.

Jad, I. (2004) "The 'NGOization' of the Arab Women's Movement", in A. Cornwall, E. Harrison, and A. Whitehead (eds) *Repositioning Feminisms in Development*, *IDS Bulletin* 35(4), Brighton: Sussex University Press.

Jad, I., Johnson, P., and Giacaman, R. (2000) 'Gender and Citizenship under the Palestinian Authority', in S. Joseph (ed.) *Gender and Citizenship in the Middle East*, Syracuse, NY: Syracuse University Press.

Jansen, W. (1987) *Women without Men: Gender and Marginality in an Algerian Town*, Leiden: E.J. Brill.

Jaschok, M. and Jingjun, S. (2000) *History of Women's Mosques in Chinese Islam*, Richmond, VA: Curzon.

Jespersen, O. (1922) *Language: Its Nature, Development and Origin*, London: Allen & Unwin.

Jubran, C. (2002) Spanish Internal-Orientalism, Cultural Hybridity and the Production of National Identity: 1887–1940, Ph.D. dissertation, University of California, San Diego. In ProQuest Digital Dissertations [database on-line]; available from http://www.proquest.com.ezproxy.fiu.edu/ (publication number AAT 3071037).

Junta Nacional Secretaría Técnica. (1943) *Informe sobre la moralidad pública en España*, Madrid: Patronato de Proteccion de la Mujer.

Kaar, M. (1996) 'Women and Personal Status Law in Iran: An Interview with Mehrangiz Kaar', *Middle East Report*, no. 198 (January–February): 36–38.

Kamp, M. (2006) *The New Woman in Uzbekistan: Islam, Modernity, and Unveiling under Communism*, Seattle: University of Washington Press.

Kandil, A. (1995) *Civil Society in the Arab World*, Washington, DC: Civicus.

Kandiyoti, D. (1987) 'Emancipated but Unliberated? Reflections on the Turkish Case', *Feminist Studies* 13(2): 317–338.

Kandiyoti, D. (1991) 'Women, Islam and the State', *Middle East Report*, 173: 9–14.

Kapchan, D. (1996). *Gender on the Market: Moroccan Women and the Revoicing of Tradition*, Philadelphia: University of Pennsylvania Press.

Karam, A. (1998) *Women, Islamism and the State: Contemporary Feminism in Egypt*, London: Macmillan.

Keddie, N. and Baron, B. (eds) (1991) *Women in Middle Eastern History*, New Haven, CT: Yale University Press.

Kefeli, A. (2001) 'The Role of Tatar and Kriashen Women in the Transmission of Islamic Knowledge, 1800-1870', in R.P. Geraci and M. Khodarkovshky (eds) *Of Religion and Empire. Missions, Conversion and Tolerance in Tsarist Russia*, Ithaca: Cornell University Press.

Khatibi, A. (1983) *Maghreb Pluriel*, Paris : Denoël.

Khatibi, A. (1998) *L'Alteranance et les Partis Politiques*, Casablanca: Eddif.

Khodja, S. (1991) *A comme Algériennes*, Alger: ENAL.

Khodja, S. (2002) *Nous les Algériennes. La Grande Solitude*, Alger: Casbah Editions.

Kleinmichel, S. (2003) 'Halpa in Choresm (Harazm) und Atin Ayi im Ferghanatal', Zur Geschichte des Lesens in Usbekistan im 20. Jahrhundert', *ANOR* 4(1) and (2).

Knauss, P.R. (1987) *The Persistence of Patriarchy: Class, Gender, and Ideology in Twentieth Century Algeria*, New York: Praeger.

Kraemer, A. (2002) *Geistliche Autoritaet und islamische Gesellschaft im Wandel: Studien ueber Frauenaelteste (otin und xalfa) im unabhaengigen Uzbekistan*, Berlin: Klaus Schwarz Verlag.

Kremnitzer, M. (1978) *Recommendations of the Commission on the Status of Women*, Jerusalem: Israel Women's Network.

Kremnitzer, M. (1997) 'Cultures of Womanhood in Israel', *Women's Studies International Forum* 20(5/6): 573–704.

Kremnitzer, M. (2002) 'The High Court of Justice and the Shaping of Public Policy: Equality and Gender', in D. Nachmias and G. Menahem (eds) *Public Policy in Israel*, London: Frank Cass, pp. 100–132.

Kümbetoglu, B. (2002) 'Kadinlara Iliskin Projeler (Projects Related to Women)', in A. Bora and A. Günal (eds) *90'larda Türkiye'de Feminizm* (Feminism in Turkey in the 1990s), Istanbul: Iletisim Publication.

Labidi, L. (2007) 'The Nature of Transnational Alliances in Women's Associations in the Maghreb: The Case of AFTURD and ATFD', *Journal of Middle East Women's Studies* 3(1).

Lacheraf, M. (1969) *L'Algérie: Nation et Société*, (1978) Alger: SNED.

Lacheraf, M. (1982) *Algérie et Tiers-Monde*, Alger: Enal.

Lakoff, R. (1975) *Language and Women's Place*, New York: Harper and Row.

Laroui, A. (1977) *Les Origines Sociales et Culturelle du Nationalisme Marocain, 1830-1912*, Paris: Maspéro.

Lazreg, M. (2000) 'Citizenship and Gender in Algeria', in S. Joseph (ed.) *Gender and Citizenship in the Middle East*, Syracuse, NY: Syracuse University Press, pp. 58–69.

Lila, A.G. (2000) *Personal Status Laws in Egypt*, National Center of Social and Criminal Studies.

Loewe, M. (2000) Social Security in Egypt: An Analysis and Agenda for Policy Reform. Background paper for the Seventh Annual Conference of the ERF, Amman (26–29 October).

Lutfi Al Sayed Marsot, A. (1990) *A Short History of Modern Egypt*, Cambridge: Cambridge University Press.

Mack, B. (2004) *Muslim Women Sing: Hausa Popular Song*, Bloomington: Indiana University Press.

Mahl (1995) 'Women on the Edge of Time', *New Internationalist* 270, Women. Online. Available HTTP: <http://www.newint.org/issue270/270edge.html> (accessed: 21 December 2005).

Mahmood, S. (2005) *Politics of Piety: The Islamic Revival and the Feminist Subject*, Princeton, NJ: Princeton University Press.

Mama, A. (1995) 'Feminism or Femocracy? State Feminism and Democratization in Nigeria', *Africa Development /Afrique et Développement* 20: 37–58.

Mama, A. (1997) 'Sheroes and Villains: Conceptualizing Colonial and Contemporary Violence Against Women in Africa', in M.J. Alexander and C.T. Mohanty (eds) *Feminist Genealogies, Colonial Legacies, Democratic Futures*, New York: Routledge.

Mehrpour, H. (1995) 'A Brief Review of Women's Economic Rights in Iranian Legal Systems', *Farzaneh* 2(7) (Fall/Winter): 49–64.

Mérimée, P. (1845) *Carmen*, trans. Lady Mary Loyd, January, 2001 [Etext #2465]. The Project Gutenberg Etext of Carmen, by Prosper Mérimée.

Mernissi, F. (1975) *Beyond the Veil*, Cambridge, MA: Schenkman.

Mernisi, F. (1987) *Beyond the Veil: Male–Female Dynamics in a Modern Muslim Society*, rev. ed., Bloomington, IN: Indiana University Press.

Mernissi, F. (1987) 'The Discourse on Arab-Muslim Women', in *Approches: Portraits de Femmes*, Casablanca: Editions Le Fennec.

Mernissi, F. (1989) *Doing Daily Battle: Interviews with Moroccan Women*, New Brunswick, NJ: Rutgers University Press.

Mernissi, F. (1990) *Sultanes oubliées. Femmes Chefs d'Etat en Islam*, Paris. Albin Michel.

Mernissi, F. (1991) *The Veil and the Male Elite: A Feminist Interpretation of Women's Rights in Islam*, Reading, MA: Addison-Wesley.

Mernissi, F. (1993) *Doing Daily Battle*, London: Women's Press.

Mernissi, F. (1994) *Dreams of Trespass: Tales of a Harem Girlhood*, Reading, MA: Addison-Wesley.

Messaoudi, K. and Schemla, E. (1998) *Unbowed: An Algerian Woman Confronts Islamic Fundamentalism*, trans. Anne C. Vila, Philadelphia, PA: University of Pennsylvania Press.

Messick, B. (1993) *The Calligraphic State. Textual Domination and History in a Muslim Society*, Berkeley: University of California Press.

Miller, R. (2007) 'Rights, Reproduction, Sexuality, and Citizenship in the Ottoman Empire and Turkey', *Signs: Journal of Women in Culture and Society* 32: 347–373.

Minces, J. (1978) *The House of Obedience: Women in Arab Society*, London Zed Books.

Ministry of Education (2003) *Statistical Yearbook: 2002*, Muscat, Oman.

Ministry of Education (2004) *Statistical Yearbook: 2003*, Muscat, Oman.

Ministry of Education (2006a) *Statistical Yearbook: 2005*, Muscat, Oman.

Ministry of Education (2006b) *From Access to Success*, Muscat, Oman.

Ministry of Education and UNICEF (2000) *EFA Assessment Report 2000*, Muscat, Oman.

Ministry of Health (2000) *Statistical Yearbook: 1999*, Muscat, Oman.

Ministry of Health (2006) *Statistical Yearbook: 2005*, Muscat, Oman.

Ministry of Information (1995) *The Royal Speeches of H.M. Sultan Qaboos bin Said: 1970-1995*, Muscat, Oman.

Ministry of National Economy (2003) *Oman Human Development Report*, Muscat, Oman.

Ministry of National Economy (2004) *Sultanate of Oman Millennium Development Goals and Targets, Achievements and Challenges*, Muscat, Oman.

Ministry of National Economy, Technical Office of the National Population Committee (2006) *Woman and Man in the Sultanate of Oman in Figures*, Muscat, Oman.

Ministry of Social Development (2003) *A Study of the Status of Omani Women*, Muscat, Oman (in Arabic).

Ministry of Social Development (2007) *Analysis of Basic Data for Social Indicators*, Muscat, Oman (in Arabic).

Mir-Hosseini, Z. (1996) 'Women and Politics in Post-Khomeini Iran: Divorce, Veiling, and Emerging Feminist Voices', in Haleh Afshar (ed.), *Women and Politics in the Third World*, London and New York: Routledge, pp. 142–169.

Moghadam, V. (1994) *Gender and National Identity: Women in Politics in Muslim Societies*, London and New Jersey: Zed Books.

Moghadam, V. (1998) *Women, Work and Economic Reform in the Middle East and North Africa*, Boulder, CO: Lynne Rienner.

Moghadam, V. (2005) *Globalizing Women: Transnational Feminist Networks*, Baltimore, MD: Johns Hopkins University Press.

Moghadam, V.M. (2005) 'Tunisia', in S. Nazir and L. Tomppert (eds) *Women's Rights in the Middle East and North Africa: Citizenship and Justice*, New York: Freedom House and Lanham, MD: Rowman & Littlefield.

Moghadam, V. (2006) 'Maternalist Policies versus Women's Economic Citizenship? Gendered Social Policy in Iran', in Shahra Razavi and Shireen Hassim (eds) *Gender and Social Policy in a Global Context*, Geneva and NY: UNRISD and Palgrave Macmillan.

Moghadam, V. and Roudi-Fahimi, Farzaneh (2005) *Reforming Family Laws to Promote Progress in the Middle East and North Africa*, Cairo: Population Reference Bureau.

Moghadam, V. and Roudi-Fahimi, Farzaneh (2005) *Empowering Women, Developing Society: Female Education in the Middle East and North Africa*, Washington, DC: Population Reference Bureau.

Mohanty, C.T. (1991) 'Under Western Eyes: Feminist Scholarship and Colonial Discourses', in C.T. Mohanty, A. Russo, and L. Torres (eds) *Third World Women and the Politics of Feminism*. Bloomington: Indiana University Press.

Mokeddem, M. (1993) *L'Interdite*, Paris: Grasset.

Mokeddem, M. (1997) *Les hommes qui marchent*, Paris: Grasset.

Mokeddem, M. (2005) *Mes hommes*, Alger: Sedia.

Molyneux, M. (1998) 'Analyzing Women's Movements', in C. Jackson and R. Pearson (eds) *Feminist Visions of Development: Gender Analysis and Policy*, London: Routledge.

Molyneux, M. (2001) *Women's Movements in International Perspective: Latin America and Beyond*, Basingstoke: Palgrave.

Morales Lezcano, Victor (ed.) (1990) *Africanismo y Orientalismo Español, In Awraq: Estudios Sobre El Mundo Arabe E Islámico Contemporáneo*, Madrid. Agencia Española de Cooperacion Internacional, Universidad Nacional de Educación a Distancia.

Morcillo, A.G. (2000) *True Catholic Womanhood. Gender Ideology in Franco's Spain*, DeKalb: Northern Illinois University Press.

Morcillo, A.G. (2007) 'Walls of Flesh. Spanish Post-war Reconstruction and Public Morality', *Bulletin of Spanish Studies* 84(6) (September): 737–758.

Moroccan Weekly Magazine, *Tel Quel*, 28 February 2009.

Morris, P. (1994) *Literature and Feminism: An Introduction*, Oxford: Blackwell.

Mortade, A. (1971) *La Renaissance de la Littérature Arabe Contemporaine en Algérie*, Alger: SNED.

M'rabet, F. (1969) *La Femme Algérienne, suivi de Les Algériennes*, Paris: Maspero.

Murphy, C. (2002) *Passion for Islam: Shaping the Modern Middle East. The Egyptian Experience*, New York: Scribner.

Naccache, G. (1989) 'Langue et Société en Tunisie', *Cahiers Tunisiens*, 3 (May/June): 16–21.

Nadwi, M.A. (2007) *Al Muhaddithat: The Women Scholars in Islam*, London: Interface Publications.

Nasr, S.H. (1992) 'Oral Transmission and the Book in Islamic Education: The Spoken and the Written Word', *Journal of Islamic Studies* 3(1): 1–14.

Nasta, S. (ed.) (1991) 'Introduction', *Motherlands: Black Women's Writing from Africa, the Caribbean and South Asia*, London: Women's Press.

Naveh, H. (2003) *Gender and Israeli Society: Women's Time*, London: Vallentine Mitchell.

Nazir, S. 'Challenging Inequality', in S. Nazir and L. Tomppert (eds) (2005) *Women's Rights in the Middle East and North Africa: Citizenship and Justice*, New York: Freedom House and Lanham, MD: Rowman & Littlefield.

Nazir, S. and Tomppert, L. (eds) (2005) *Women's Rights in the Middle East and North Africa: Citizenship and Justice*, New York: Freedom House and Lanham, MD: Rowman & Littlefield.

Nisbet, A. (ed.) (1980) 'Function of the Female Character in Maghrebian Literature', *1979 Maghrebian Studies Conference, University of New South Wales*, Sydney: New South Wales University Press (961MAG), pp. 30–36.

Nnaemeka, O. (ed.) (1998) *Sisterhood: Feminisms & Power*, Trenton, NJ: Africa World Press.

Norton, A.R. (1993) 'The Future of Civil Society in the Middle East', *Middle East Journal* 47(2): 205–216.

Norton, A.R. (ed.) (1995) *Civil Society in the Middle East*, Vol. I and II, Leiden: E.J. Brill.

Okla, A. (7 January 2007) 'Regulations in Dress Code' and (6 February 2007) 'Three Rules for Dress Code in Islam for Women.' Online. Available HTTP: <http://www.prayerwear.info/spip.php?auteur5> (accessed 14 February 2008).

Ola, A.Z. (2000) 'The Egyptian Experiment in Quota System for Women in the Elected Councils', in Salwa Sharawi Gumaa (ed.) *Tamsil al mar'a fi almagalis al Muntakhaba* (Women Representation in the Elected Council), Cairo: Public Administration and Consultation Center Press.

Ong, W.J. (1982) *Orality and Literacy: The Technologizing of the Word*, London: Methuen.

Orlando, V. (1999) *Nomadic Voices of Exile: Feminine Identity in Francophone Literature of the Maghreb*, Athens: Ohio University Press.

Özyürek, E. (2000) 'The Headscarf Problem in the Parliament', in A.G. Altinay (ed.) *Vatan, Millet, Kadinlar* (Motherland, Nation, Women), Istanbul: Iletisim Publication.

Peteet, J. (1991) *Gender in Crisis: Women and the Palestinian Resistance Movement*, New York: Columbia University Press.

Phillips, W. (1966) *The Unknown Oman*, London: Longman.

Poya, M. (1999) *Women, Work, and Islam*. London: Zed.

Pringle, R. and Watson, S. (1992) '"Women's Interests" and the Poststructuralist State' in M. Barrett and A. Phillips (eds) *Destabilising Theory: Contemporary Feminist Debates*, Cambridge: Polity Press.

Radtke, H.L. and Stam, H.J. (eds) (1994) 'Introduction', in *Power/Gender: Social Relations in Theory and Practice*, London: Sage.

Raudvere, C. (2003) *The Book and the Roses. Sufi Women, Visibility, and Zikir in Contemporary Istanbul*, Istanbul: Swedish Research Institute.

Rausch, M. (2006) 'Ishelhin Women Transmitters of Islamic Knowledge and Culture in Southwestern Morocco', *Journal of North African Studies* 11(2): 173–192.

Rausch, M. (2008) 'The Flower of All Creatures: The Prophet Muhammad and Heavenly and Earthly Women', in F. Sadiqi et al. (eds) *Women Writing Africa: The Northern Region*, New York: Feminist Press.

Reese, S.S. (2004) *The Transmission of Learning in Islamic Africa*, Leiden: E.J. Brill.

République Tunisienne (Republic of Tunisia) (1997) *Code du Statut Personnel* (Code of Personal Status), Tunis: Imprimerie Officielle. First promulgated on 13 August 1956 and periodically updated.

République Tunisienne (Republic of Tunisia) (1998) *Code de la Nationalité Tunisienne* (Code of Tunisian Citizenship), Tunis: Imprimerie Officielle. First promulgated in 1957 and revised several times since then.

Reyniers, F. (1930) *Taougrat, ou les Berbères Racontés par Eux-Mêmes*, Paris: Geuthner Macon.

Rhiwi, L. (2000) 'Mouvement des femmes Au Maroc', in *Rapport Du Social*, Rabat: OKAD.

Roded, R. (1994) *Women in Islamic Biographical Collections: From Ibn Sa'd to Who's Who*, Boulder, CO: Lynne Rienner.

Rowlands, J. (1998) 'A Word of the Times, but What Does it Mean? Discourse and Practice of Development', in H. Afshar (ed.) *Women and Empowerment, Illustration from the Third World*, London: Macmillan Press.

Saadawi, Nawal (1982) *The Hidden Face of Eve: Women in the Arab World*, Buckingham, UK: Brit Books.

Sadiqi, F. (1995) 'The Language of Women in the City of Fès, Morocco', *International Journal of the Sociology of Language* 112: 63–79.

Sadiqi, F. (1997) *Grammaire du Berbère*, Paris: L'Harmattan.

Sadiqi, F. (2003) *Women, Gender and Language in Morocco*, Leiden and Boston: Brill Academic.

The Holy Qur'an, Khalifa translation. Online. Available HTTP: <http://www.submission. org/quran/webqt>

The Holy Qur'an, Yusuf Ali translation. Online. Available HTTP:<http://www.submission. org/quran/webqt>

Thompson, P.J. (1994) 'Beyond Gender', in L. Stone (ed.) *The Education Feminist Reader*, New York and London: Routledge.

Timisi, N. and Gevrek, M.A. (2002) '1980'ler Türkiye'sinde Feminist Hareket: Ankara Çevresi' (Feminist Movement in the 1990s Turkey: Ankara), in A. Bora and A. Günal (eds) *90'larda Türkiye'de Feminizm* (Feminism in Turkey in the 1990s), Istanbul: Iletisim Publication.

Tolson, J. (2001) 'Struggle for Islam', October 15. Online: usnews.com. Available HTTP: <http://www.amislam.com/tolson.htm> (accessed February 10 2007).

Torab, A. (2005) 'Vows, Mediumship and Gender: Women's Votive Meals in Iran', in I.M. Okkenhaug and I. Flaskerud (eds) *Gender, Religion and Culture. Two Hundred Years of History*, Oxford: Berg.

Torab, A. (2006) *Performing Islam. Gender and Ritual in Iran*, Leiden: E.J. Brill.

Trabelsi, Ch. (1991) 'De quelques aspects du langage des femmes de Tunis', in Moha Ennaji (ed.) *Sociolinguistics of the Maghreb, International Journal of the Sociology of Language*, 87: 87–98.

Trudgill, P. (2000) *Sociolinguistics: An Introduction to Language and Society*, 4th edn, London: Penguin.

UNDP, Arab Fund for Economic and Social Development (2002) *Arab Human Development Report 2002*, New York: United Nations.

UNICEF/Government of Oman (2005) *Situation Analysis of Children and Women in the Sultanate of Oman*, Muscat, Oman.

United Nations Population Task Force (n.d.) *Guidelines on Women's Empowerment*, New York: United Nations Population Information Network.

United States Library of Congress (2006) Webcast: *Tunisia—Celebrating Fifty Years of Women's Emancipation*. Available HTTP: <http://www.loc.gov/today/cyberlc/ feature_wdesc. php?rec=4007> (last visited February 5, 2008).

Vatikiotis, P.J. (1991) *The History of Modern Egypt*, Baltimore, MD: Johns Hopkins University Press.

Walby, S. (1991) *Theorising Patriarchy*, London: Blackwell.

Weiner, M. and Huntington, P. (1987) *Understanding Political Development: An Analytic Study*, New York: Harper Collins.

Welchman, L. (2001) 'Capacity, Consent and Under-Age Marriage in Muslim Family Law', *International Survey of Family Law, 2001 Edition*, Cambridge: Cambridge University Press.

Wing, A. and Kassim, H. (2007) 'The Future of Palestinian Women's Rights: Lessons from a Half Century of Tunisian Progress', *Washington and Lee Law Review*, Vol. 64.

Wisker, G. (2000) *Post-Colonial and African American Women's Writing: A Critical Introduction*, Basingstoke: Macmillan.

'Women Dress Code in Islam.' Online. Available HTTP: <http://www.submission.org/ dress4.htm> (accessed 4 December 2001).

Wong, S. (1988) *Emigrant Entrepreneurs: Shanghai Industrialists in Hong Kong*, Hong Kong: Oxford University Press.

Woodhull, W. (1993) *Transfiguration of the Maghreb*, Minneapolis, London: University of Minnesota Press.

Wright, R. (2002) *Pagan Spain*. Banner Books: University Press of Mississippi.

Y.B. (1998) 'Algérie: le Nouveau Roman', *Le Nouvel Observateur*.

Yacine, T. (1987) *L'Izli ou l'amour chanté en Kabylie*, Paris: Publication du Centre d'Etudes et de Recherche Amazigh (CERAM) No. 3.

Yamani, M. (ed.) (1996) *Feminism and Islam: Legal and Literary Perspectives*, Reading: Ithaca Press.

Yeatman, A. (1990) *Bureaucrats, Technocrats, Femocrats: Essays on the Contemporary Australian State*, Sydney: Allen and Unwin.

Yegenoglu, M. (1998) *Colonial Fantasies. Towards a Feminist Reading of Orientalism,* Cambridge: Cambridge University Press.

Yishai, Y. (1997) *Between the Banner and the Flag*, New York: SUNY University Press.

Yuval-Davis, N. (1997) 'Citizenship and Difference', in *Gender and Nation*, London: Sage.

Yuval-Davis, N. (1997) *Gender and Nation*, London: Sage.

Zahia, Z.S. (2008) 'Representations of the "Femmes d'Alger" in French Colonial Media', *Middle East Journal of Culture and Communications* 1(1): 80–93.

Zargooshi, J. (2002) 'Characteristics of Gonorrhoea in Kermanshah, Iran', *Sexually Transmitted Infection: A peer review journal for health professionals and researchers in all areas of sexual health* [STI is the official journal of the British Association of Sexual Health and HIV] 78(6) (December): 460–461. Online. Available HTTP: <http://sti.bmjjournals.com/cgi/content/full/78/6/460> (accessed 20 October 2004).

Zimmerman, D.H. and West, C. (1975) 'Sex Roles, Interruptions and Silences in Conversations', in B. Thorne and N. Henley (eds) *Language and Sex: Difference and Dominance*, Rowley, MA: Newbury House.

Zin al-Din, N. (1988) *Al-Sufur wa'l-Hijab*, Cyprus: al-Mada Publishing.

Zoubir, Y.H. (1993) 'The Painful Transition from Authoritarianism in Algeria', *Arab Studies Quarterly* 15(3): 83–110.

Zoughlami, N. (1989) 'Quel Féminisme dans les Groupes-Femmes des Années 80 en Tunisie? [What Kind of Feminism in Women's Associations during the 1980s in Tunisia?]', *Annuaire de l'Afrique du Nord*, Vol. 26.

Zuhur, S. (1992) *Revealing, Reveiling: Islamic Gender Ideology*, Albany: State University of New York Press.

Zuhur, S. (2003) 'Women and Empowerment in the Arab World', *Arab Studies Quarterly*, 25 (Fall): 17.

Index

Page numbers in *italics* denotes a table

CPSIA information can be obtained at www.ICGtesting.com
Printed in the USA
LVOW12s0325010814

396980LV00002B/3/P